In praise of the

Multimedia Law and Business Handbook

"A much-needed and very clear-headed review of this complicated new world which we are creating."
—*Ed Bernstein, CEO, Palladium Interactive*

"I recommend this book to every multimedia and on-line developer and publisher. It's an easy-to-understand guide through the legal thicket in this new industry."
—*Sueann R. Ambron, President, US WEST Online*

"Mark Radcliffe and Dianne Brinson set the standard in providing sound, practical, and clearly written guidance for navigating the legal thickets of multimedia. This revised and expanded version of their classic handbook includes important new material on the Internet, business practices, and educational uses. Developers should have this book on their desks, ready to consult before they consult an attorney."
—*Brian Kahin, General Counsel, Interactive Multimedia Association*

"I highly recommend this book to software developers and industry neophytes. Much of the information contained in the book is collected from people who've been in the industry and learned the ropes."
—*Halle Eavelyn, President, Hyperbole Studios*

"This book contains the kind of information that all developers need to know."
—*James F. Griffith, President, International Interactive Communications Society (IICS)*

INTERACTIVE MULTIMEDIA ASSOCIATION

Organized in 1987, the IMA is the oldest, largest, and most active trade association devoted to multimedia. Its mission is to promote the success of its member companies by working collaboratively to foster the growth of robust multimedia markets in ways that individual organizations cannot. IMA initiatives and activities serve to:

➤ Bring buyers and sellers of multimedia products together.

➤ Simplify technology for the end user, thereby assuring buyer confidence and excitement.

➤ Provide information and context on legislative and market developments affecting its member companies.

IMA member information is available from Evan Shubin, Business Development Manager, (410) 626-1380; the IMA FAXBack System, (410) 268-2100 (from a faxhandset); via email at info@ima.org or via the IMA Home Page on the World Wide Web, http://www.ima.org.

Multimedia Law
and
Business Handbook

J. Dianne Brinson

Mark F. Radcliffe

Multimedia Law
and
Business Handbook

J. Dianne Brinson

Mark F. Radcliffe

Credits:
Robert Howard, cover design
The Roberts Group, editing, book design, and production
Linda Rich and Darlene de Monfreid, Chapter 9
Larry Kay, Chapter 10
Joanna Tamer, Chapter 22

Some of the material in this book was previously published in the book *Multimedia Law Handbook,* by the same authors (Ladera Press 1994).

This publication is designed to provide accurate and authoritative information in regard to the subject matter covered. It is sold with the understanding that the publisher is not engaged in rendering legal, accounting, or other professional service. If legal advice or other expert assistance is required, the services of a competent professional person should be sought.

All products or services mentioned are trademarks or service marks of their respective owners.

Printed in the U.S.A.

Library of Congress Catalog Card Number: 96-075898

Publisher's Cataloging in Publication
(prepared by Quality Books Inc.)

Brinson, J. Dianne
    Multimedia law and business handbook / J. Dianne Brinson and Mark F. Radcliffe.
    p. cm.
    ISBN 0-9639173-2-3

    1. Multimedia systems—Law and legislation—United States.   2. Multimedia systems industry—Law and legislation—United States. 3 Multimedia systems industry—Management.   I. Radcliffe, Mark F.   II. Title.

KF309.5.M8B75 1996   343.7309'99
                                        QBI96-20247

Contents

Acknowledgments   *xi*

Introduction   *xiii*

How to Use This Book   *xv*

Part 1: Building Blocks

1   **The U.S. Legal System**   *3*
Federal Statutes, State Statutes, The Courts, Finding the Law, Arbitration, Government Offices and Agencies

2   **Copyright Law**   *11*
Introduction, Types of Works Protected by Copyright, Standards, Procedure for Getting Protection, The Exclusive Rights, Infringement, Duration of the Rights, Limitations on the Exclusive Rights, International Protection

3   **Patent, Trademark, and Trade Secret Law**   *19*
Patent Law, Trademark Law, Trade Secret Law, International Protection

4   **Ownership of Copyrights**   *29*
Understanding the Copyright Act, Initial Ownership, The Work Made for Hire Rule, Joint Authorship and Ownership, Community Property, Assignments, Licenses, Termination Right, Owning a Copy of a Work, Patents, Trademarks, and Trade Secrets

5 **Contracts Law**   *39*
What Is a Contract?, Written Contracts, Who Can Enter Into a Contract?, Offer and Acceptance, Consideration, Typical Contract Provisions, Tips for Contracts

Part 2: Production Relationships

6 Development Agreements   *51*
Proposals and Bids, The Contract, Joint Development Agreements

7 Employees   *63*
Works Made by Employees, Who Is an Employee?, Using the Employment Agreement, Giving Ownership to an Employee, Joint Ownership, Rights of Former Employers

8 Contractors and Consultants   *71*
Who Is an Independent Contractor?, Copyright Ownership, Implied Licenses, Contracts with Independent Contractors, Employment Law Risks

9 Creating a Multimedia Title for a Publisher   *81*
How Publishers Pick Titles, Developer Compensation, Compensation Factors, Non-royalty Compensation, The Funding Process, The Schedule, Preparing the Budget, Working with a Publisher

10 Writing for Multimedia   *93*
Scope Issues, Compensation Issues, Ownership Issues, Confidentiality Issues, Care and Feeding

Part 3: Other Production Issues

11 Using Preexisting Works   *107*
When You Need a License, Myths, When You Don't Need a License, Public Domain Works, Using Works That You Own

12 Clearing Rights and Obtaining Licenses   *121*
The Licensing Process, Determining Who Owns the Copyright, Determining What Rights You Need, Obtaining a License, Rights Clearance Agencies, Stock Houses and Libraries, Copyright Assignment, The Visual Artists Rights Act

13 Licensing Content: Industry by Industry   *141*
General Advice, Licensing Text, Licensing Photographs and Still Images, Licensing Film and Television Clips, Licensing Video, Logos and Characters, Licensing Software, Checklist for Licensing Text, Photographs, and Still Images, Checklist for Licensing Motion Picture, Television, and Video Clips

14 Using Music   *159*
Copyrights in Music, Option #1: Creating Original Music, Option #2: Using Preexisting Music, Option #3: Public Domain Music, Option #4: Using Music from Music Libraries, Checklists for Clearing Music

15 The Laws of Publicity, Privacy, and Libel   *177*
The Rights of Publicity and Privacy, Libel, Permits

16 Union Issues   *185*
Signing Collective Bargaining Agreements, Unions and Multimedia, Reuse Provisions, Other Legal Issues

Part 4: Post-Production Issues

17 Choosing a Name for Your Product   *197*
Choosing a Strong Trademark, Clearing a Trademark, Titles, Scope of Trademark Rights, Dilution, International Trademark Protection, Using Third-Party Trademarks

18 Protecting Your Intellectual Property Rights   *209*
Copyright Protection, How to Fill Out Form PA, Copyright Notice and Warnings, International Copyright Protection, Patent Protection, Trademark Protection, Trade Secret Protection

19 Sales Law   *221*
The Uniform Commercial Code, Important Provisions of Article Two

20 Distribution Agreements   *233*
Roles, Scope of the Agreement, Assigning the Rights, Licensing the Rights, Key Issues in License Agreements, Payment, Warranties, Credits, Remedies

21 Publishers' Concerns   *253*
Scope of Rights, Due Diligence, Payment, Right to Sue Third-Party Infringers

22 The Business of Multimedia   *263*
Price Pressures and New Channel Opportunities Demand New Product Planning, Christmas in July: A New Consumer-driven Title Marketing Calendar

Part 5: On-line and Educational Issues

23 On-line Issues   *273*
Law and Cyberspace, Myths, The "White Paper", Fair Use, Implied Licenses, Taking Material from the Net, Developing Your Own Web Site, Domain Names, Operator Liability, Distributing Your Multimedia Products Over the Net

24 Educational and Distance Learning Issues   *299*
Myths, Exceptions for Educators, Teacher Photocopying, Fair Use, Materials Created by Teachers and Faculty Members, Distance Learning, Distribution Agreements, Using Copyrighted Materials for Fund-raisers

Appendices

Appendix A   *325*
The Copyright Act of 1976, Selected Provisions

Appendix B   *341*
Form Contracts

Appendix C   *435*
Rights Clearance Agencies, Search Firms, and Licensing Agents

Appendix D *439*
Stock Houses and Other Content Sources

Appendix E *443*
Multimedia Organizations

Appendix F *445*
Unions, Guilds, and Trade Associations

Appendix G *447*
Copyright Forms

Glossary *455*

Index *461*

Acknowledgments

We would like to extend our profound thanks to all of the individuals who generously provided their assistance in writing this book. In many ways, this book was a collaborative project. It depended on the willingness of many people to provide us with information and keep us informed of the almost daily changes in this area. We wish to thank particularly the partners of Gray Cary Ware & Freidenrich and its Multimedia Law Group, who generously agreed to permit us to use a number of the firm's form contracts in Appendix B. Thanks also to Renée Chernus and Jeremy R. Salesin for providing forms.

This book includes our opinions. They should not be interpreted as those of Gray Cary Ware & Freidenrich or its clients. We have done our best to accurately reflect the practices in this rapidly evolving industry, but any errors are solely our responsibility.

We would like to thank the following individuals for their assistance:

Sueann Ambron, USWest Online
Ed Bernstein, Palladium Interactive
Vincent Castellucci, The Harry Fox Agency, Inc.
Dominique Claessens, Image Smith, Inc.
Sue Collins, American Federation of Musicians
Gary Culpepper, Law Offices of Gary Culpepper
Richard Curtis, Richard Curtis Associates
Bob Derber, Maxis
John Evershed, Mondo Media
Darlene de Monfreid

Halle Eavelyn, Hyperbole Studios
Susan Gerakaris, Writers Guild
Ted Grabowski, Mindscape
James W. Griffith, President, International Interactive Communications
    Society (IICS)
Ellen Guon, Illusion Machines Incorporated
Craig Harding
Steve Horowitz, Palladium Interactive
Bob Kohn, Borland International, Inc.
David M. Lane, Byron Preiss Multimedia Company, Inc.
Rockley Miller, Multimedia Monitor
Deirdre O'Malley, Mondo Media
Jonathan M. Pajion, 2-Lane Media
Jeannine Parker
Michael Prohaska, Screen Actors Guild
Linda Rich
Greg Roach, Hyperbole
Jim Roberts, Image Smith, Inc.
Ian Rose, Mindscape
Kay Schaber, Writers Guild
Sandra J. Shepard, Mindscape
Craig Sheumaker
Lionel Sobel, Loyola Law School
Joanna Tamer
Allen Thygessen, Gold Disk, Inc.
Bryan Unger, Directors Guild of America
Barbara Zimmerman, BZ Rights & Permissions, Inc.

Introduction

The purpose of this book is to give multimedia developers and publishers a basic understanding of the legal issues involved in developing and distributing multimedia works. Reading this book will not make you a lawyer (the authors don't want more competition in their field), but it will enable you to ask appropriate questions and take steps to protect your interests.

We published the first edition of this book in early 1994. In the past two years, the multimedia industry has grown. Yet the legal issues in developing and publishing multimedia products have become even more complex, as the Internet and other on-line environments create new legal problems.

The law also has changed dramatically. For example, Congress has added a new limited public performance right for sound recordings, and the number of works available for use without licensing has decreased dramatically due to a provision in the GATT treaty. Changes in the law are reflected in this new book.

We also have added new chapters dealing with on-line legal issues and educational and distance learning issues. You'll find several new form agreements, including a multimedia development and publishing agreement, a distribution agreement, a location release, and a Web site development and maintenance agreement.

Finally, we have added three new chapters on the business aspects of multimedia—one on writing for multimedia, one on title development, and one on pricing strategies and product planning.

How to Use This Book

The approach taken in this book is what lawyers call "preventive law"—working from a base of knowledge of the applicable law to create strategies and procedures that will help you avoid future lawsuits and legal complications. We have included a number of examples, descriptions of real cases, and checklists to help you understand the issues.

The creation and distribution of an interactive multimedia work is a complex process. It involves a number of legal issues:

➤ Contracting with employees, independent contractors, and consultants for the creation of your multimedia work.

➤ Avoiding infringement of others' intellectual property rights.

➤ Obtaining licenses to use content owned by others.

➤ Complying with union rules.

➤ Contracting for sale or distribution of your multimedia work.

➤ Protecting the intellectual property rights in your multimedia work.

These legal issues are frequently as important to a multimedia developer as the technological and creative issues involved in multimedia projects. A multimedia developer who fails to obtain the necessary rights to use material owned by others can incur liability for hundreds of thousands or even millions of dollars in damages. For example, Delrina used the "flying toasters" made famous by its competitor Berkeley Systems, Inc. in a screen saver product. A court found Delrina guilty of copyright infringement. Even though the Delrina "flying toaster" screen saver was one of twenty on Delrina's product, the court ordered Delrina to pay Berkeley Systems more than $200,000 in damages, to recall all copies of the infringing product from retailers, and to destroy the product.

Part 1 of this book ("Building Blocks," Chapters 1–5) will give you an understanding of the U.S. legal system and legal terminology, and of the fundamentals of copyright, patent, trademark, and trade secret law. A chapter on contracts law also is included.

Part 2 of the book ("Production Relationships," Chapters 6–10) gives you guidelines for setting up development agreements with clients, and for ensuring that you get ownership of material created for your multimedia works by employees and independent contractors. This section also includes a chapter on creating a multimedia title for a developer, written by Linda Rich and Darlene de Monfreid, and one on writing for multimedia, written by Larry Kay.

In Part 3 ("Other Production Issues," Chapters 11–16), you'll learn how to determine when you need permission to use preexisting content in your multimedia works and how to get licenses to use works owned by others. Ownership and licensing practices in the industries that are your most likely sources for preexisting content are described in Chapter 13. The laws of publicity, privacy, and libel are covered in this section, as are union issues.

Part 4 ("Post-Production Issues," Chapters 17–22) is devoted to legal issues that come up after your multimedia work is finished. Topics include how to choose a name for your product, how to protect your own intellectual property rights, sales law, and distribution agreements. Special concerns of multimedia publishers also are addressed in this section. Chapter 22, written by Joanna Tamer, covers pricing strategies and product planning and scheduling.

Part 5 covers on-line legal issues and legal issues for educational use and distance learning.

In the Appendices, we have included sample contracts to assist you in understanding the issues (the contracts are also on the disk attached to the inside back cover). Other appendices contain provisions from the Copyright Act; information on rights clearance agencies, content providers, unions and trade organizations, and multimedia organizations; and copyright office forms.

Part 1

Building Blocks

1 The U.S. Legal System

In the United States, laws are made at the federal and state levels. Laws adopted by legislative bodies—Congress and state legislatures—are called "statutes."

The federal and state courts enforce statutes. They also create law.

This chapter describes some of the basic concepts of our legal system, and the roles played by legislatures and courts.

Federal Statutes

The U.S. Constitution gives Congress the power to enact federal laws or statutes on certain subjects.

The Copyright Act is one example of a statute adopted by Congress. Congress's power to enact the Copyright Act stems from Article I, Section 8, of the Constitution, which authorizes Congress to establish laws giving "authors and inventors the exclusive right to their respective writings and discoveries" to encourage progress in the arts and sciences.

The Copyright Act is discussed in Chapter 2.

According to the Constitution, all powers not expressly delegated to Congress are reserved to the states. The "commerce clause" of the Constitution (which concerns interstate commerce) generally is viewed as giving Congress broad power to regulate matters affecting interstate commerce— trademarks used in interstate commerce, for example.

Federal lawmaking begins when a member of the Senate or the House of Representatives introduces a bill. Most bills are referred to standing committees (for example, the House Committee on the Judiciary) and to subcommittees for study. Bills are later brought before the Senate or House for debate and vote. Differences between the Senate and House versions of a bill are resolved in joint conference committees.

After the House and Senate have approved a uniform version of the bill, the bill is sent to the President. If the President signs the bill, it becomes law. If the President vetoes the bill, it becomes law only if the Senate and House override the veto. This requires the consent of two-thirds of the members of the Senate and House.

State Statutes

State legislatures can pass laws on matters for which they share jurisdiction with Congress. Trademark law is an example of a shared jurisdiction. In other matters, the federal government has taken exclusive jurisdiction. Copyright is an example: The Copyright Act prohibits the states from granting copyright-like protection.

States also can pass laws on matters in which the Constitution does not grant jurisdiction to the federal government.

State lawmaking occurs through a process that is similar to the federal process.

The Courts

The courts enforce statutes and interpret them. They also invalidate unconstitutional statutes, and make law in areas not covered by statutes. Here are some examples of the four main roles played by our courts:

➤ **Enforcement.** The Copyright Act gives a copyright owner the exclusive right to reproduce the owner's work. A copyright infringement suit is an example of court enforcement of a statute.

➤ **Interpretation.** According to the Copyright Act, the copyright in a work created by an employee within the scope of his or her employment is owned by the employer. The Copyright Act does not define the term "employee." The Supreme Court case that defines the term is an example of court interpretation of a statute.

➤ **Invalidation.** The courts invalidate unconstitutional laws. Unconstitutional laws are laws that conflict with provisions of the Constitution. The Constitution is the supreme law of the United States. Many "constitutionality" cases involve claims that a law violates the Constitution's Bill of Rights (the first ten amendments). In *Roe v. Wade,* the Supreme Court invalidated a state statute restricting women's access to abortion. According to the Court, the statute violated a pregnant woman's constitutional right of privacy.

➤ **Making Law.** The courts create the law for "common law" subject areas. Common law covers areas not covered by statutes. In many states, for example, individuals' rights of privacy and publicity (discussed in

"The Rights of Publicity and Privacy," Chapter 15) are protected under common law rather than under statutory laws.

Types of Courts

There are several types of courts. The federal and state court systems consist of two levels of courts: trial courts and appellate courts. Cases are tried in trial courts. Appellate courts review the decisions of the trial courts.

The federal court system is divided into 13 judicial circuits. Eleven of the circuits are numbered. Each of the numbered circuits contains more than one state. The Ninth Circuit, for example, covers California, Oregon, Washington, Idaho, Nevada, Arizona, Alaska, and Hawaii. The Twelfth and Thirteenth circuits are the District of Columbia Circuit and the Federal Circuit. The Federal Circuit handles appeals in patent cases and Claims Court cases.

Each federal circuit has one appellate court. These courts are known as Courts of Appeals or Circuit Courts. The Supreme Court reviews the decisions of the Courts of Appeals.

Each federal circuit is divided into judicial districts. A district can be as small as one city or as large as an entire state. The trial courts are known as the United States District Courts.

Jurisdiction

The federal courts have jurisdiction over cases involving federal statutes (the Copyright Act, for example) and other "federal questions." They also have jurisdiction over cases in which the party filing the suit and the party being sued reside in different states. This type of federal jurisdiction is known as "diversity" jurisdiction.

Other types of cases must be brought in state court.

Civil and Criminal Cases

A criminal case is brought by the federal government or a state to prosecute a defendant (the party sued) for violations of the government's criminal laws. Murder and burglary are examples of violations of criminal laws. If the defendant in a criminal case is found guilty by the jury, he or she is sentenced by the court to serve a jail sentence or pay a fine as punishment for the crime.

A civil case is a case brought by one party (the "plaintiff") against another party (the "defendant") to resolve a legal dispute involving rights based on statutory law or common law.

A copyright infringement case is an example of a civil case involving statutory law. A suit seeking damages for a writer's breach of a contract (in which the writer promised to create a script for a movie but failed to do so) is an example of a civil case involving common law rights.

While certain violations of the Copyright Act and the Lanham Act (the federal trademark statute) are criminal violations, multimedia developers and publishers will be concerned primarily with civil cases.

Civil Lawsuits

There are several stages in civil lawsuits, from initiation to trial and then on to stages of appeal. We'll discuss these stages in this section.

Initiation

A civil lawsuit is initiated when the plaintiff files a "complaint" against the defendant alleging that the defendant has wronged the plaintiff in some way recognized by the law. In most civil lawsuits, the plaintiff asks the court to award the plaintiff "damages" (a remedy for the defendant's wrongdoing—usually money) or to order the defendant to do something.

The defendant responds to the allegations in the complaint by filing an "answer" (a document in which the defendant admits or denies the complaint's allegations and states defenses). The defendant also can file a "counterclaim" against the plaintiff (allegations that the plaintiff has wronged the defendant).

Trial

If the parties do not "settle" the case (reach their own agreement on how to resolve the dispute), the case eventually goes to trial. In most types of civil cases, the Constitution gives the parties a right to a jury trial. The role of the jury is to decide questions of fact. However, in some complex cases, the parties choose to dispense with the jury and have the case decided by the trial judge.

Appeal

If the losing party in a civil lawsuit is not satisfied with the decision of the trial court, the losing party can appeal the case to the appropriate appellate court.

In the federal court system, the appeal generally must be filed with the Court of Appeals for the judicial circuit in which the trial was held. A case tried in the United States District Court for the Northern District of California, for example, must be appealed to the Court of Appeals for the Ninth Circuit.

An appellate court's job in reviewing a trial court's decision is to look for "mistakes of law" made by the trial court. Appellate courts do not "second guess" factual issues decided by trial courts. In our legal system, factual issues are supposed to be resolved by the jury, not by the appellate court. So long as there is adequate factual evidence to support the verdict, an appellate court will not reverse a trial court's decision or "remand" the case (send it back to the trial court for retrial) unless the appellate court finds that the trial court made a "mistake of law."

Filing an appeal is probably a waste of money unless a losing party can reasonably hope to convince the appellate judges that there is insufficient evidence to support the trial court's decision, or that the trial court misapplied the law.

 Plaintiff's lawsuit alleges that Defendant infringed the copyright on Plaintiff's song by copying the melody of the song. The jury found that Defendant did not infringe Plaintiff's copyright. If the jury reached its decision after being told by the judge that a song's melody is not protected by copyright (a mistake in the applicable law, copyright law), Plaintiff has a good basis for appeal. However, if the jury reached its decision after listening to Defendant's song and concluding that the melody of Defendant's song is not similar to the melody of Plaintiff's song, Plaintiff does not have a strong basis for appeal. (Whether or not the songs have similar melodies is a factual determination.)

Appellate courts generally issue written opinions explaining how they reached their conclusions on whether to affirm (uphold), reverse, or remand a case. These opinions are important parts of the development of the law because our legal system is based on "precedent" (reliance on previously decided cases).

The role of precedent is discussed in "Precedent," later in this chapter.

Supreme Court Review

There are two ways to get a case reviewed by the U.S. Supreme Court: by appeal and by certiorari. The losers in certain types of cases—for example, cases involving claims that state statutes are unconstitutional—have a right to appeal to the Supreme Court.

For most cases, though, there is no right of appeal to the Supreme Court. However, a party who has lost a case at the federal Court of Appeals level can file a petition for certiorari with the Supreme Court. A petition for certiorari is a document explaining why the Supreme Court should review a case. If the Supreme Court grants certiorari, the appeal proceeds. If the Court denies it, the Court of Appeals' decision stands.

Thousands of petitions for certiorari are filed each year, and most are denied. The Supreme Court is likely to grant certiorari on a case only if the case involves a matter of national interest or the Court believes that it must decide the case to resolve conflicts among the Circuit Courts and create uniformity in federal law.

Precedent

An appellate court's decision on an issue is binding on lower courts in the appellate court's jurisdiction. Thus, an appellate court's decisions are "precedents" that the lower courts in the appellate court's jurisdiction must follow (apply).

In *Effects Associates, Inc. v. Cohen,* 908 F.2d 555 (9th Cir. 1990), the United States Court of Appeals for the Ninth Circuit held that the grant of a nonexclusive copyright license can be implied from the copyright owner's conduct. This decision is binding on the federal district courts located in the Ninth Circuit. Those courts are not free to decide that a nonexclusive copyright license cannot be implied from conduct.

A lower court's decision is not binding on a higher court. In fact, appellate courts frequently reverse decisions made by trial courts to correct the trial courts' "mistakes of law."

Because the United States Supreme Court is the "highest court in the land," the Supreme Court's decisions are binding on all courts in the United States.

In *Community for Creative Non-Violence v. Reid,* 490 U.S. 730 (1989), the Supreme Court decided how to apply the Copyright Act's "work made for hire" rule to works created by independent contractors. That decision is binding on all courts in the United States.

A court's decision may "be persuasive" outside its region. For a decision to "be persuasive" means that other courts, while not compelled to follow it, choose to follow it. For example, if the Court of Appeals for the Eleventh Circuit has never decided whether a nonexclusive copyright license can be implied from the copyright owner's conduct but the Ninth Circuit has, the Eleventh Circuit may reach the same conclusion as the Ninth Circuit when it decides that issue because it believes that the Ninth Circuit's decision was correct.

Earlier court decisions generally are "followed" by the deciding court in all later cases involving the same issue. For example, if the Ninth Circuit decides a case that involves the same legal issues that were involved in a previous case, it is likely to decide those issues as it did in the previous case.

The reliance that our courts put on previously decided cases in deciding new cases is known as *stare decisis.* That is Latin for "let the decision stand." The doctrine of *stare decisis* does not prevent a court from "overruling" its own previously decided cases. However, *stare decisis* discourages rapid and radical changes in the law. As Supreme Court Justice William O. Douglas once wrote in the *Columbia Law Review,* "stare decisis provides some moorings so that men may trade and arrange their affairs with confidence.... It is the strong tie which the future has to the past."

The doctrine of *stare decisis* is the reason that an attorney performs legal research hoping to find cases supporting the attorney's position on a legal issue.

Finding the Law

Because law is made by the courts on a precedent basis following the doctrine of *stare decisis* and because law also is made by Congress and the state legislatures, knowing the law on a given topic generally requires a review of both statutory law and case law.

Statutes

Federal and state statutory laws can be found by consulting published "codifications" of laws in law libraries maintained by law schools, law firms, courts, and bar associations. To find a federal law such as the Copyright Act, for example, you would look in the United States Code, which is divided into "titles." Federal and state statutory laws can also be obtained on-line from Westlaw or Lexis, two computerized legal research services.

Recently adopted laws may not be included in the published codifications of statutes. While the publishers of these codifications add new material regularly (in "pocket parts" inserted at the back of appropriate volumes), even the pocket parts may not include laws adopted in the most recent session of the legislature.

Court Decisions

Court decisions (also known as "case law") can be found in publications called "reporters." For example, decisions of the United States Supreme Court are published in the *United States Reports,* the *Supreme Court Reporter,* and the *Lawyers Edition* (three different "reporters" from three different publishers).

These decisions also are available from computerized services such as Westlaw and Lexis, which provide on-line research assistance for locating cases on desired topics. "Digests" that divide decided cases into topics also are helpful for locating relevant cases. Other research resources help lawyers determine whether cases in which they are interested have been reversed by a higher court or overruled (modified by a later decision of the same court).

This book contains "citations" for a number of cases relating to matters discussed in this book. The citations use standardized abbreviations for the names of "reporters." For example, 490 U.S. 730 refers to volume 490, page 730 in the *United States Reports.* Law library staff members generally can "decode" citations for you and help you find the reporters you need, if you have the citation.

Various publishing companies publish "annotated" statutory codes, which bring statutes and relevant court decisions together in one source. West Publishing Company, for example, publishes the *United States Code Annotated* (*USCA*), which lists the court decisions enforcing or interpreting each provision of the United States Code.

Arbitration

The parties to a dispute sometimes choose to resolve a dispute through arbitration rather than through court litigation. In arbitration, a dispute is resolved by a neutral arbitrator rather than by a judge or jury.

Arbitration is generally quicker and cheaper than court litigation. Specially qualified arbitrators often are used to resolve technical disputes.

Both parties must agree to submit their dispute to arbitration. Many contracts require that disputes be resolved through arbitration rather than through litigation.

In the United States, many arbitration cases are handled by arbitrators approved by the American Arbitration Association, which has offices in a number of cities. Arbitration is similar to a trial in that both parties present their cases to the arbitrator, who renders a decision. Appeals of arbitrators' decisions generally are possible only if the arbitration was conducted improperly.

Government Offices and Agencies

Government offices and agencies play an important role in our legal system. The Copyright Office and the U.S. Patent and Trademark Office are the key federal government offices for multimedia developers and publishers. The Copyright Office is discussed in "Copyright Protection," Chapter 18. The U.S. Patent and Trademark Office is discussed in "Patent Law" and "Trademark Law," Chapter 3.

2 Copyright Law

There are four major intellectual property laws in the United States that are important for multimedia developers and publishers:

➤ Copyright law

➤ Patent law

➤ Trademark law

➤ Trade secret law

In this chapter, we discuss copyright law, the most important of the intellectual property laws for developers and publishers of multimedia works. Patent law, trademark law, and trade secret law are discussed in Chapter 3.

Ownership of copyrights and other intellectual property is discussed in Chapter 4. On-line copyright issues are discussed in Chapter 23. In Chapter 18, we discuss ways in which you can use the four intellectual property laws to protect your multimedia works.

Other laws that create rights somewhat like intellectual property law rights—privacy, publicity, and dilution laws—are discussed in Chapters 15 and 17.

Introduction

Copyright law in the U.S. is based on the Copyright Act of 1976, a federal statute that went into effect on January 1, 1978. We'll refer to this statute throughout the book as the Copyright Act. Excerpts from the Copyright Act appear in Appendix A.

States cannot enact their own laws to protect the same rights as the rights provided by the Copyright Act. For example, a state cannot pass a law to extend copyright protection on works in the state beyond the term of protection given by the Copyright Act. State "copyright" laws exist, but they are limited to works that cannot be protected under federal copyright law. (Requirements for federal protection are discussed in "Standards," later in this chapter.)

Copyright law is important for multimedia developers and publishers for two reasons:

Steps to maximize your protection are discussed in "Copyright Protection," Chapter 18.

➤ Original multimedia works are protected by copyright. The Copyright Act's exclusive rights provision gives developers and publishers the right to control unauthorized exploitation of their works.

➤ Multimedia works are created by combining "content"—music, text, graphics, illustrations, photographs, software—that is protected under copyright law. Developers and publishers must avoid infringing copyrights owned by others, as explained in Chapter 11.

Types of Works Protected by Copyright

Copyright law protects "works of authorship." The Copyright Act states that works of authorship include the following types of works:

➤ **Literary works**. Novels, nonfiction prose, poetry, newspaper articles and newspapers, magazine articles and magazines, computer software, software documentation and manuals, training manuals, manuals, catalogs, brochures, ads (text), and compilations such as business directories.

➤ **Musical works**. Songs, advertising jingles, and instrumentals.

➤ **Dramatic works**. Plays, operas, and skits.

➤ **Pantomimes and choreographic works**. Ballets, modern dance, jazz dance, and mime works.

➤ **Pictorial, graphic, and sculptural works**. Photographs, posters, maps, paintings, drawings, graphic art, display ads, cartoon strips and cartoon characters, stuffed animals, statues, paintings, and works of fine art.

➤ **Motion pictures and other audiovisual works**. Movies, documentaries, travelogues, training films and videos, television shows, television ads, and interactive multimedia works.

➤ **Sound recordings**. Recordings of music, sounds, or words.

➤ **Architectural works**. Building designs, whether in the form of architectural plans, drawings, or the constructed building itself.

Standards

To receive copyright protection, a work must be "original" and must be "fixed" in a tangible medium of expression. Certain types of works are not copyrightable.

Originality

The originality requirement is not stringent: A work is original in the copyright sense if it owes its origin to the author and was not copied from some preexisting work. A work can be original without being novel or unique.

 Betsy's book, *How to Lose Weight,* is original in the copyright sense so long as Betsy did not create her book by copying existing material—even if it's the millionth book to be written on the subject of weight loss.

Only minimal creativity is required to meet the originality requirement. No artistic merit or beauty is required.

A work can incorporate preexisting material and still be original. When preexisting material is incorporated into a new work, the copyright on the new work covers only the original material contributed by the author.

 Developer's multimedia work incorporates a number of photographs that were made by Photographer (who gave Developer permission to use the photographs in the multimedia work). The multimedia work as a whole owes its origin to Developer, but the photographs do not. The copyright on the multimedia work does not cover the photographs, just the material created by Developer.

Facts owe their origin to no one and so are not original. A compilation of facts (a work formed by collecting and assembling data) is protected by copyright only to the extent of the author's originality in the selection, coordination, and arrangement of the facts.

 Ralph created a neighborhood phone directory for his neighborhood by going door-to-door and getting his neighbors' names and phone numbers. The directory's facts (names and phone numbers) are not original. Ralph's selection of facts was not original (he "selected" every household in the neighborhood). His coordination and arrangement of facts (alphabetical order by last name) is routine rather than original. The directory is not protected by copyright.

Fixation

According to Section 101 of the Copyright Act, a work is "fixed" when it is made "sufficiently permanent or stable to permit it to be perceived, reproduced, or otherwise communicated for a period of more than transitory duration." It makes no difference what the form, manner, or medium. An author can "fix" words, for example, by writing them down, typing them on an old-fashioned typewriter, dictating them into a tape recorder, or entering them into a computer. A live television broadcast is "fixed" if it is recorded simultaneously with the transmission.

Uncopyrightable Works

Works prepared by federal government officers and employees as part of their official duties are not protected by copyright. Consequently, federal statutes (the Copyright Act, for example) and regulations are not protected by copyright. This rule does not apply to works created by state government officers and employees.

The design of a useful article is protected by copyright only if, and to the extent that, the design "incorporates pictorial, graphic, or sculptural features that can be identified separately from, and are capable of existing independently of, the utilitarian aspects of the article." For example, while a "normal" belt buckle is not protected, a three-dimensional belt-buckle design with a dolphin shape qualifies for limited protection.

See "Public Domain Works" in Chapter 11.

Uncopyrightable works and works for which copyright protection has ended are referred to as "public domain" works.

Procedure for Getting Protection

Copyright protection arises automatically when an original work of authorship is fixed in a tangible medium of expression. Registration with the Copyright Office is optional (but you have to register before you file an infringement suit).

The use of copyright notice is optional for works distributed after March 1, 1989. Copyright notice can take any of these three forms:

➤ "©" followed by a date and name.

➤ "Copyright" followed by a date and name.

➤ "Copr." followed by a date and name.

The benefits of registering a copyright and using copyright notice and how to register are discussed in Chapter 18. The role of notice for works distributed prior to March 1, 1989, is discussed in "Public Domain Works," Chapter 11.

The Exclusive Rights

A copyright owner has five exclusive rights in the copyrighted work:

➤ **Reproduction Right**. The reproduction right is the right to copy, duplicate, transcribe, or imitate the work in fixed form.

➤ **Modification Right**. The modification right (also known as the derivative works right) is the right to modify the work to create a new work. A new work that is based on a preexisting work is known as a "derivative work."

➤ **Distribution Right**. The distribution right is the right to distribute copies of the work to the public by sale, rental, lease, or lending.

➤ **Public Performance Right**. The public performance right is the right to recite, play, dance, act, or show the work at a public place or to transmit it to the public. In the case of a motion picture or other audiovisual work, showing the work's images in sequence is considered "performance."

➤ **Public Display Right**. The public display right is the right to show a copy of the work directly or by means of a film, slide, or television image at a public place or to transmit it to the public. In the case of a motion picture or other audiovisual work, showing the work's images out of sequence is considered "display."

Exclusive rights are discussed in more detail in "Myths," Chapter 11, and in the "Determining What Rights You Need," Chapter 12.

Infringement

Anyone who violates any of the exclusive rights of a copyright owner is an infringer.

Developer scanned Photographer's copyrighted photograph, altered the image by using digital editing software, and included the altered version of the photograph in a multimedia work that Developer sold to consumers. If Developer used Photographer's photograph without permission, Developer infringed Photographer's copyright by violating the reproduction right (scanning the photograph), the modification right (altering the photograph), and the distribution right (selling the altered photograph as part of the multimedia work).

A copyright owner can recover actual or, in some cases, statutory damages from an infringer. The federal district courts have the power to issue injunctions (orders) to prevent or restrain copyright infringement and to order the impoundment and destruction of infringing copies.

See Copyright Protection, Chapter 18.

There are two essential elements to an infringement case: (a) that the defendant copied from the plaintiff's copyrighted work; and (b) that the copying was improper appropriation. Copying generally is established by showing that the defendant had access to the plaintiff's work and that the defendant's work is substantially similar to the plaintiff's.

Duration of the Rights

For works created on and after January 1, 1978, the copyright term for works created by individuals is the life of the author plus 50 years.

See "The Work Made for Hire Rule," Chapter 4.

The copyright term for "works made for hire" is 75 years from the date of first "publication" (distribution of copies to the general public) or 100 years from the date of creation, whichever expires first. Works made for hire are works created by employees for employers and certain types of specially commissioned works.

The duration of copyright for pre-1978 works is discussed in "Public Domain Works," Chapter 11.

Limitations on the Exclusive Rights

See "When You Don't Need a License," Chapter 11.

The copyright owner's exclusive rights are subject to a number of exceptions and limitations that give others the right to make limited use of a copyrighted work. Major exceptions and limitations are outlined in this section.

Ideas

Copyright protects only against the unauthorized taking of a protected work's "expression." It does not extend to the work's ideas, procedures, processes, systems, methods of operation, concepts, principles, or discoveries.

Facts

A work's facts are not protected by copyright, even if the author spent large amounts of time, effort, and money discovering those facts. Copyright protects originality, not effort or "sweat of the brow."

Independent Creation

A copyright owner has no recourse against another person who, working independently, creates an exact duplicate of the copyrighted work. The independent creation of a similar work or even an exact duplicate does not violate any of the copyright owner's exclusive rights.

Fair Use

The "fair use" of a copyrighted work, including use for purposes such as criticism, comment, news reporting, teaching, scholarship, or research, is not an infringement of copyright. Copyright owners are, by law, deemed to consent to fair use of their works by others.

The Copyright Act does not define fair use. Instead, whether a use is fair use is determined by balancing these factors (discussed in "When You Don't Need a Lincense," Chapter 11):

➤ The purpose and character of the use.

➤ The nature of the copyrighted work.

➤ The amount and substantiality of the portion used in relation to the copyrighted work as a whole.

➤ The effect of the use on the potential market for, or value of, the copyrighted work.

International Protection

U.S. authors automatically receive copyright protection in all countries that are parties to the Berne Convention for the Protection of Literary and Artistic Works, or parties to the Universal Copyright Convention (UCC). Most countries belong to at least one of these conventions. Members of the two international copyright conventions have agreed to give nationals of member countries the same level of copyright protection they give their own nationals.

 Publisher has discovered that bootleg copies of one of its multimedia works are being sold in England. Because the United Kingdom is a member of the Berne Convention and the UCC, Publisher's work is automatically protected by copyright in England. When Publisher files a copyright infringement action in England against the bootlegger, Publisher will be given the same rights that an English copyright owner would be given.

Works first published in a Berne Convention or UCC country as well as works of foreign authors who are nationals of Berne Convention and UCC countries automatically receive copyright protection in the United States. Unpublished works are subject to copyright protection in the U.S. without regard to the nationality or domicile of the author.

3 Patent, Trademark, and Trade Secret Law

While copyright law is the most important intellectual property law for protecting rights in multimedia works, you need to know enough about patent, trademark, and trade secret law to avoid infringing intellectual property rights owned by others and to protect your multimedia works. These three intellectual property laws are discussed in this chapter.

In Chapter 18, we discuss ways in which you can use these three laws and copyright law to protect your multimedia works. Ownership of intellectual property is discussed in Chapter 4. Choosing product names is covered in Chapter 17.

Patent Law

Patent law in the U.S. is based on a federal statute, the Patent Act. States are prohibited from granting protection similar to that provided by the Patent Act.

Types of Works Protected

Patent law protects inventions and processes ("utility" patents) and ornamental designs ("design" patents).

Inventions and processes protected by utility patents can be electrical, mechanical, or chemical in nature. Examples of works protected by utility patents are a microwave oven, genetically engineered bacteria for cleaning up oil spills, a computerized method of running cash management accounts, and a method for curing rubber.

Examples of works protected by design patents are a design for the sole of a running shoe, a design for sterling silver tableware, and a design for a water fountain.

Standards

There are strict requirements for the grant of utility patents and design patents. We'll discuss the requirements in this section.

Utility Patents

To qualify for a utility patent, an invention must be new, useful, and "nonobvious."

To meet the novelty requirement, the invention must not have been known or used by others in this country before the applicant invented it, and it also must not have been patented or described in a printed publication in the U.S. or a foreign country before the applicant invented it. The policy behind the novelty requirement is that a patent is issued in exchange for the inventor's disclosure to the public of the details of his invention. If the inventor's work is not novel, the inventor is not adding to the public knowledge, so the inventor should not be granted a patent.

Meeting the useful requirement is easy for most inventions. An invention is useful if it can be applied to some beneficial use in society.

To meet the nonobvious requirement, the invention must be sufficiently different from existing technology and knowledge so that, at the time the invention was made, the invention as a whole would not have been obvious to a person having ordinary skill in that field. The policy behind this requirement is that patents should only be granted for real advances, not for mere technical tinkering or modifications of existing inventions.

Protests Derail Patent

Compton's was granted a patent on a method for accessing information on CD-ROMs, but there was so much protest from the multimedia industry that the Patent and Trademark Office reviewed the patent application and determined the patent had been improperly granted. A revised application with narrower claims was rejected by the Patent and Trademark Office recently.

It is difficult to obtain a utility patent. Even if the invention or process meets the requirements of novelty, utility, and nonobviousness, a patent will not be granted if the invention was patented or described in a printed publication in the U.S. or a foreign country more than one year before the application date, or if the invention was in public use or on sale in the U.S. for more than one year before the application date.

If you think your multimedia work involves technology that might be patentable, you should contact a patent attorney before you display or distribute your work. In the multimedia field, an example of an invention that might be patentable is a software engine for multimedia works. An example of a process that might be patentable is an instructional method for using interactive video technology in classrooms. (Optical Data Corporation was granted two patents covering such a process.)

Unrealized mental conceptions are not patentable. Methods of transacting business and printed matter without physical structure are not patentable. Discoveries of scientific principles, laws of nature, and natural phenomena are not patentable (although applications of such discoveries are). The discovery of a new use for an old product is not patentable.

Design Patents

To qualify for a design patent, a design must be new, original, and ornamental. Design patents may be an option for protecting some elements of multimedia works (user interfaces, for example, which also can be protected through copyright law). However, design patents are considered rather weak intellectual property protection, and owners of design patents rarely sue to enforce their patents against infringers.

Procedure for Getting Protection

Patent protection is obtained by demonstrating in an application filed with the U.S. Patent and Trademark Office that the invention meets the stringent standards required for the granting of a patent. The patent application process is expensive and time-consuming (it generally takes at least two years). Although you can file a patent application yourself, the application process is complex. You should consider using an experienced patent attorney or patent agent (a nonlawyer who has passed the special patent bar exam given by the U.S. Patent and Trademark Office).

If you want to be able to claim "patent pending" status without undertaking the expense and paperwork involved in a regular patent application, consider filing a "provisional patent application" (PPA). A PPA remains in effect for one year. The PPA filing date can be used to prove that the invention described in the PPA document predates other inventions in the field.

Exclusive Rights

A patent owner has the right to exclude others from making, using, or selling the patented invention or design in the United States during the term of the patent. Anyone who makes, uses, or sells a patented invention or design within the United States during the term of the patent without permission from the patent owner is an infringer—even if he or she did not copy the patented invention or design or even know about it.

Developer's staff members, working on their own, developed a software program for manipulating images in Developer's multimedia works. Although Developer's staff didn't know it, Inventor has a patent on that method of image manipulation. Developer's use of the software program infringes Inventor's patent.

Duration

As of June 8, 1995, utility patents are granted for a period of 20 years from the date the application was filed. For patents in force prior to June 8, 1995, and patents granted on applications pending before that date, the patent term is the greater of 17 years from the date of issue (the term under prior law) or 20 years from the date of filing. Design patents are granted for a period of 14 years. Once the patent on an invention or design has expired, anyone is free to make, use, or sell the invention or design.

Limitations on the Exclusive Rights

There are two major limitations on the patent owner's exclusive rights. They are discussed in this section.

Functionally Equivalent Products

A patent owner can exclude others from making, using, or selling products or using processes that do substantially the same work as the patented invention in substantially the same manner. However, a patent does not protect the patent owner from competition from functionally equivalent products or processes that work in different ways.

 Microco owns a patent covering a laser printer. While Microco can prevent others from making, using, or selling laser printers that work in substantially the same manner as Microco's printer, it cannot prevent others from making, using, or selling laser printers that operate in a different manner.

Invalidation

The validity of an issued patent is subject to challenge in an infringement proceeding. Defendants in infringement suits usually raise the defense of patent invalidity, asserting that the invention covered by the patent was not novel or nonobvious. It is not unusual for a patent infringement suit to result in a determination that the U.S. Patent and Trademark Office made a mistake in granting the patent.

Trademark Law

Trademarks and service marks are words, names, symbols, or devices used by manufacturers of goods and providers of services to identify their goods and services, and to distinguish their goods and services from goods manu-factured and sold by others.

 The trademark WordPerfect is used by the WordPerfect Corporation to identify that company's word processing software and distinguish that software from other vendors' word processing software.

For ease of expression, we will use "trademark" in this book to refer to both trademarks (used on goods) and service marks (used for services).

For trademarks used in commerce, federal trademark protection is available under the federal trademark statute, the Lanham Act. Many states have trademark registration statutes that resemble the Lanham Act, and all states protect unregistered trademarks under the common (nonstatutory) law of trademarks.

Types of Works Protected

Examples of words used as trademarks are Kodak for cameras and Burger King for restaurant services. Examples of slogans used as trademarks are "Fly the Friendly Skies of United" for airline services and "Get a Piece of the Rock" for insurance services. Examples of characters used as trade-marks are the Pillsbury Dough Boy for baked goods and Aunt Jemima for breakfast foods.

Sounds can be used as trademarks, such as the jingle used by National Public Radio. Product shapes and configurations, such as the distinctively shaped bottle used for Coca-Cola, also can serve as trademarks.

Standards

Trademark protection is available for words, names, symbols, or devices that are capable of distinguishing the owner's goods or services from the goods or services of others. A trademark that merely describes a class of goods rather than distinguishing the trademark owner's goods from goods provided by others is not protectible.

 The word "corn flakes" is not protectible as a trademark for cereal because that term describes a type of cereal that is sold by a number of cereal manufacturers rather than distinguishing one cereal manufacturer's goods.

A trademark that so resembles a trademark already in use in the U.S. as to be likely to cause confusion or mistake is not protectible. Geographi-cally descriptive marks—"Idaho" for potatoes grown in Idaho—are not protectible trademarks for products that originate in the geographical area (all Idaho potato growers should be able to use "Idaho" to market their potatoes).

Procedure for Getting Protection

The most effective trademark protection is obtained by filing a trademark registration application in the Patent and Trademark Office. Federal law also protects unregistered trademarks, but such protection is limited to the geographic area in which the mark is actually being used.

Federal Protection

Federal registration is limited to trademarks used in interstate commerce (or intended for use in interstate commerce). Before November 1989, a trademark application could be filed only after the trademark's owner actually had used the trademark in commerce. Under current law, a person who has a "bona fide" intention to use a trademark in commerce may apply to register the trademark.

For federally registered marks, the use of notice of federal registration is optional. A federal registrant may give notice that his or her trademark is registered by displaying with the trademark the words "Registered in U.S. Patent and Trademark Office" or the symbol "®".

State Protection

State trademark protection under common law is obtained simply by adopting a trademark and using it in connection with goods or services. This protection is limited to the geographic area in which the trademark is actually being used.

State statutory protection is obtained by filing an application with the state trademark office. Those relying on state trademark law for protection cannot use the federal trademark registration symbol, but they can use the symbol "™" (or for a service mark, "SM").

Exclusive Rights

Trademark law in general, whether federal or state, protects a trademark owner's commercial identity (goodwill, reputation, and investment in advertising) by giving the trademark owner the exclusive right to use the trademark on the type of goods or services for which the owner is using the trademark. Any person who uses a trademark in connection with goods or services in a way that is likely to cause confusion is an infringer. Trademark owners can obtain injunctions against the confusing use of their trademarks by others, and they can collect damages for infringement.

Tips on how to avoid trademark infringement in naming your multimedia products are given in Chapter 17.

 Small Multimedia Co. is selling a line of interactive training works under the trademark Personal Tutor. If Giant Multimedia Co. starts selling interactive training works under the trademark Personal Tutor, purchasers may think that Giant's works come from the same source as Small Multimedia's works. Giant is infringing Small's trademark.

One of the most important benefits of federal registration of a trademark is the nationwide nature of the rights obtained. For the registrant, federal registration in effect reserves the right to start using the mark in new areas of the U.S.

 Small Multimedia Co., a California corporation, obtained a federal trademark registration on the trademark *Abra* for video games. Small Multimedia did not begin using the trademark on video games in New York until two years after it obtained its federal registration. In the meantime, Giant Multimedia Co. had started using *Abra* on video games in New York. Because Small Multimedia's federal registration gives Small a right to use *Abra* that is superior to Giant Multimedia's right to use *Abra*, Small Multimedia can stop Giant Multimedia from using *Abra* on video games in New York—even though Giant Multimedia started using *Abra* on video games in New York before Small Multimedia did.

For other advantages of federal registration, see "Trademark Protection," Chapter 18.

A trademark owner's rights under state trademark law (and the rights of an unregistered trademark owner under federal law) generally are limited to the geographical area in which the owner has used the trademark.

 (For this example, we changed just one fact from the previous example.) Small Multimedia Co. did not get a federal trademark registration. Now Giant Multimedia Co.'s right to use *Abra* on video games in New York is superior to Small Multimedia's right to use *Abra* on video games in New York, because Giant Multimedia was the first to actually use the trademark on video games in New York.

Duration
A certificate of federal trademark registration remains in effect for 10 years, provided that an affidavit of continued use is filed in the sixth year. A federal registration may be renewed for any number of successive 10-year terms so long as the mark is still in use in commerce. The duration of state registrations varies from state to state. Common law rights endure so long as use of the trademark continues.

Limitations on the Exclusive Rights
Trademark law does not give protection against use of the trademark that is unlikely to cause confusion, mistake, or deception among consumers, but dilution laws may provide such protection.

See "Dilution," Chapter 17

Western Software has a federal registration for the use of Flash on multimedia development tool software. If Giant Multimedia Co. starts using Flash on desktop publishing software, Giant Multimedia may be infringing Western Software's trademarks, because consumers may think the desktop publishing software and the multimedia development tool software come from the same source. If Giant Multimedia starts using Flash on fire extinguishers, though, Giant is probably not infringing Western Software's trademark. Consumers are unlikely to think that the Flash software and the Flash fire extinguishers come from the same source.

Trade Secret Law

A trade secret is information of any sort that is valuable to its owner, that is not generally known, and that has been kept secret by the owner. Trade secrets are protected only under state law. The Uniform Trade Secrets Act, in effect in a number of states, defines trade secrets as "information, including a formula, pattern, compilation, program, device, method, technique, or process that derives independent economic value from not being generally known and not being readily ascertainable and is subject to reasonable efforts to maintain secrecy."

Types of Works Protected

The following types of technical and business information are examples of material that can be protected by trade secret law:

➤ Customer lists.

➤ Designs.

➤ Instructional methods.

➤ Manufacturing processes and product formulas.

➤ Document-tracking processes.

Inventions and processes that are not patentable can be protected under trade secret law. Patent applicants generally rely on trade secret law to protect their inventions while patent applications are pending.

Standards

Six factors generally are used to determine whether material is a trade secret:

➤ The extent to which the information is known outside the claimant's business.

➤ The extent to which the information is known by the claimant's employees.

➤ The extent of measures taken by the claimant to guard the secrecy of the information.

➤ The value of the information to the claimant and the claimant's competitors.

➤ The amount of effort or money expended by the claimant in developing the information.

➤ The ease with which the information could be acquired by others.

Information has value if it gives rise to actual or potential commercial advantage for the owner of the information. Although a trade secret need not be unique in the patent law sense, information that generally is known is not protected under trade secret law.

Procedure for Getting Protection

Trade secret protection attaches automatically when information of value to the owner is kept secret by the owner.

Exclusive Rights

A trade secret owner has the right to keep others from misappropriating and using the trade secret. Sometimes the misappropriation is a result of industrial espionage. Many trade secret cases involve people who have taken their former employers' trade secrets for use in new businesses or for new employers.

Trade secret protection endures so long as the requirements for protection—generally, value to the owner and secrecy—continue to be met. The protection is lost if the owner fails to take reasonable steps to keep the information secret.

 After Sam discovered a new method for manipulating images in multimedia works, he demonstrated his new method to a number of other developers at a multimedia conference. Sam lost his trade secret protection for the image manipulation method, because he failed to keep his method secret.

Limitations on the Exclusive Rights

Trade secret owners have recourse only against misappropriation. Discovery of protected information through independent research or reverse engineering (taking a product apart to see how it works) is not misappropriation.

International Protection

To obtain patent, trademark, and trade secret protection in another country, you must comply with that country's requirements for obtaining protection. For these intellectual property rights, there are no international conventions that provide automatic protection for U.S. rights owners.

4 Ownership of Copyrights

This chapter covers the Copyright Act's ownership rules, and, in less detail, the ownership rules for patents, trademarks, and trade secrets. Ownership rules discussed here apply only in the United States (other countries have their own rules of intellectual property ownership).

Ownership issues that arise in specific types of relationships are covered in Chapters 6, 7, 8, 9, 20, and 21.

Understanding the Copyright Act

If you are a multimedia developer or publisher, you should become familiar with the Copyright Act's ownership rules. Multimedia works and many of their components—music, graphics, text, software, and video, film, and television show clips—are protected by copyright. If you fail to deal with ownership issues while creating a multimedia work, you may not have clear title to the work and all its components. If there is uncertainty concerning your title to the work, it may complicate distribution of the work.

 April hired Don, a free-lance software designer, on a contract basis to develop the software for April's multimedia work. April and Don did not discuss who would own the copyright in the software. According to the Copyright Act's "default" rule for works created on commission by independent contractors, Don owns the copyright in the software.

The Copyright Act's default rules on ownership apply if the parties—employer and employee, employer and independent contractor, developer and client, or developer and publisher—do not reach their own agreement on ownership. Those rules are discussed in "Initial Ownership" and "The Work Made for Hire Rule" in this chapter.

Initial Ownership

Ownership of copyright initially belongs to the author or authors of the work.

 Sarah, a photographer, took a photograph of the Lincoln Memorial. Sarah is the author of the photograph and the initial owner of the copyright in the photograph.

The "author" is generally the individual who created the work, but there is an exception for "works made for hire."

The Work Made for Hire Rule

The "author" of a work made for hire is the employer or hiring party for whom the work was prepared. This default ownership rule is known as the work made for hire rule. Unless the parties have agreed otherwise in a signed written document, the employer or hiring party owns the copyright of a work made for hire.

There are actually two branches to the work made for hire rule: one covering works made by employees, and one covering specially commissioned works. We discuss these in this section.

Works Made by Employees

A work created by an employee within the scope of his or her employment is a work made for hire. The employer for whom the work is made is the "author" of the work for copyright purposes and is the owner of the work's copyright (unless the employee and employer have agreed otherwise).

 As part of his job, John, an employee of Big Co.'s training division, created a training film using Big's facilities. Even though John created the film, Big Co. is the author for copyright purposes. Big owns the copyright in the film (unless John and Big have agreed in a signed contract that John owns the copyright).

The work made for hire rule does not give employers ownership of works made by employees outside the scope of their employment.

 Darryl, an engineer at Productions, Inc., wrote the script for Productions' newest multimedia work on his own initiative on weekends. Because Darryl did not write the script within the scope of his employment, the work made for hire rule does not apply. If Productions wants ownership of the copyright in the script, it must get an "assignment" (discussed in "Assignments," later in this chapter) from Darryl.

Specially Commissioned Works

The second category of works made for hire is limited to eight types of specially ordered or commissioned works. These are works commissioned for use as:

➤ A contribution to a collective work.

➤ Part of a motion picture or other audiovisual work.

➤ A translation.

➤ A supplementary work.

➤ A compilation.

➤ An instructional text.

➤ A test or answer material for a test.

➤ An atlas.

For these types of works, if the hiring party and independent contractor creating the work agree in writing to designate the work as a work made for hire, the work is a work made for hire. If the parties do not have an agreement to treat the independent contractor's work as a work made for hire, it's not a work made for hire.

 April got Don, an independent software developer, to design the software for April's multimedia work. April and Don did not agree in writing to consider the software a work made for hire. The software is not a work made for hire. Don owns the copyright in the software.

Even if the hiring party and independent contractor agree in writing to consider the independent contractor's work a work made for hire, the work is not a work made for hire unless it falls into one of the eight special categories listed above.

 Sarah commissioned John, a free-lance painter, to do an oil painting of Sarah's home. Although Sarah and John agreed in writing that the painting would be considered a work made for hire, the written agreement does not make the painting a work made for hire because the painting is not in one of the eight categories of works that can be specially commissioned works made for hire.

The rules governing ownership of copyrights in works created before January 1, 1978 (the effective date of the Copyright Act of 1976) were different from the rules described in this chapter. The 1909 Copyright Act did not distinguish between employees and independent contractors (works created by both independent contractors and employees automatically were owned by the employer or hiring party unless the parties agreed otherwise). In a 1989 case, *Community for Creative Non-Violence v. Reid,*

490 U.S. 730, the U.S. Supreme Court made it clear that the current Copyright Act does distinguish between employees and independent contractors.

The issue in *Reid* was who owned the copyright in a sculpture created by the artist Reid for the Community for Creative Non-Violence (CCNV). The Court concluded that the work made for hire rule did not apply for two reasons: Reid was not an employee of CCNV, and the sculpture was not one of the eight types of works that could be designated a work made for hire by written agreement of the parties.

Foreign Copyright Law

The work made for hire rule discussed in this chapter and in other chapters of this book applies to copyrights in the United States. Other countries have different rules on copyright ownership. Although many countries have rules similar to the first branch of the Copyright Act's rule (works made by employees), the second branch (specially commissioned works) is not covered by most countries' work made for hire rules.

See "Copyright Ownership," Chapter 8.

To obtain international copyright ownership for works that fall within the second branch of the Copyright Act's work made for hire rule, parties that commission works should obtain "assignments" of copyrights (see "Assignments," later in this chapter) from independent contractors.

Joint Authorship and Ownership

According to the Copyright Act, the authors of a joint work jointly own the copyright in the work they create. A joint work is defined in Section 101 of the Copyright Act as "a work prepared by two or more authors with the intention that their contributions be merged into inseparable or interdependent parts of a unitary whole."

 Ann and Bruce worked together to create a multimedia work, with Ann developing the software and user interface and Bruce developing the content. The work is a joint work, and Ann and Bruce jointly own the copyright.

You do not become the author of a joint work merely by contributing ideas or supervision to a work. You do so by contributing material that meets the standards for copyright protection.

See "Standards," Chapter 2.

 Susan suggested that John write a book on how to beat the stock market, and John did so. Susan is not a joint author of John's book.

If you want joint authorship status for a work to which you will be contributing only uncopyrightable elements (concepts and facts, for example), you may be able to strike a deal with the person who actually will create the copyrighted material: Agree to disclose your elements in exchange for an assignment of part ownership of the copyright. (See "Assignments," later in this chapter.)

When the copyright in a work is jointly owned, each joint owner can use or license the work in the United States without the consent of the other owner, provided that the use does not destroy the value of the work and the parties do not have an agreement requiring the consent of each owner for use or licensing. A joint owner who licenses a work must share any royalties he or she receives with the other owners.

> ### A Joint Authorship Dispute
> Actress Clairce Taylor hired a playwright, Alice Childress, to write a play about a legendary Black comedienne. Taylor turned research material over to Childress, suggested several scenes for the play, and discussed the play with Childress while Childress was writing it. Taylor was found not to be a joint author, because she contributed only uncopyrightable material and because Childress did not view Taylor as a co-author. *Childress v. Taylor*, 945 F.2d 500 (2d Cir. 1991).

The issue of joint ownership has arisen in a dispute about the ownership of the copyright in the *Spaceship Warlock* product. In a lawsuit filed in San Francisco, Joe Sparks, who worked on *Spaceship Warlock*, claimed he was joint owner of the copyright in the product. However, Michael Saenz of Reactor, Inc. claimed that Sparks was an employee of Reactor. If Sparks was an employee and his work on the project was within the scope of his employment, Reactor would be the owner of the copyright in *Spaceship Warlock*. If Sparks was not an employee, he could be a joint owner of the copyright, entitled to 50 percent of the profits from the sale of this product. The lawsuit was recently settled.

Many foreign countries (Germany and France, for example) require that all joint owners consent to the grant of a license. Generally, joint ownership is not recommended because of the complications it adds to licensing worldwide rights. In addition, it is unclear what effect the filing of bankruptcy by one joint owner would have on co-owners.

Community Property

In nine states (Arizona, California, Idaho, Louisiana, Nevada, New Mexico, Texas, Washington, and Wisconsin), any property acquired during a marriage is jointly owned by the husband and wife. Several years ago, a court in California held that the copyrights in several books created by a man during his marriage were jointly owned by the man and his wife. *In re Worth*, 195 Cal. App. 3d 768, 4 U.S.P.Q. 1730 (Ct. of App. 1987). The court's reasoning—that the copyrights were community property because they were the result of one spouse's expenditure of time, effort, and skill during the marriage—could apply to patents, trademarks, and trade secrets as well.

Assignments

These rights are discussed in "The Exclusive Rights," Chapter 2.

A transfer of copyright ownership is known as an assignment. When a copyright is assigned, the assignee (individual or company to whom it is assigned) becomes the owner of the exclusive rights of copyright in the protected work.

 Tom, an individual working on his own, created multimedia software and then assigned the copyright in the software to Developer. After the assignment, Developer has the exclusive right to reproduce and publicly distribute the software. If Tom starts selling the software, he will be infringing the Developer's rights as copyright owner.

The ownership of copyright may be transferred in whole or in part. Examples of partial transfers are an assignment of the copyright for a term of 10 years (time limitation) and an assignment limited to California (geographic limitation). In addition, the individual exclusive rights (reproduction, modification, and so forth) can be transferred.

Assignments are common in many industries—for example, music composers often assign copyrights in their compositions to music publishers.

An assignment is not valid unless it is in writing and is signed by the owner of the rights conveyed or the owner's authorized agent.

Constructive notice is discussed in more detail in "Obtaining a License," Chapter 12.

An assignment can be recorded in the Copyright Office to give others "constructive notice" of the assignment. Constructive notice is a legal term that means you are presumed to know a fact (because it is a matter of public record) even if you have no actual knowledge of the fact.

Recording an assignment in the Copyright Office to give constructive notice protects the assignee from future conflicting transfers. An assignment that is recorded properly within one month after its signing prevails over a later assignment. If the assignment is signed outside the U.S., the assignee has two months to record it.

 Songwriter assigned the copyright in her song to Music Publishing Co. in Boston on August 1, 1993. On August 15 of the same year, Songwriter assigned the copyright in the same song to Media Enterprises. So long as Music Publishing Co. recorded its assignment properly in the Copyright Office by September 1, Music Publishing Co. owns the copyright because its assignment prevails over Songwriter's later assignment to Media Enterprises.

The benefits of recording an assignment are discussed in more detail in "Determining Who Owns the Copyright," Chapter 12.

A properly recorded assignment even prevails over an earlier assignment that was not recorded if the later assignment meets two criteria:

➤ The later assignment was taken in good faith and without notice of the earlier assignment.

➤ The assignee paid money or something of value for the assignment or made a promise to pay royalties.

 Author assigned the copyright in his novel to Publishing, Inc. on November 1, 1993. Publishing, Inc. did not record the assignment. On January 15, 1994, Author assigned the copyright in the same novel to Media, Inc. for $10,000. Media, Inc. recorded its assignment in the Copyright Office. So long as Media, Inc. acted in good faith and did not know or have reason to know about Author's 1993 assignment to Publishing, Inc., Media, Inc. owns the copyright. The assignment to Media, Inc. prevails over Author's earlier assignment to Publishing, Inc.

Licenses

A license is a copyright owner's grant of permission to use a copyrighted work in a way that would otherwise be copyright infringement. A copyright owner who grants a license is known as a licensor. A party receiving a license is known as a licensee.

Implied in every license is a promise by the licensor to refrain from suing the licensee for infringement based on activities within the scope of the license.

A copyright license can be exclusive or nonexclusive. An exclusive license is a license that does not overlap another grant of rights.

 Author granted Publisher the exclusive right to sell Author's novel in the United States. She granted Movie Developer the exclusive right to create and distribute a movie version of the novel. Both Publisher and Developer have exclusive licenses. There is no overlap between the two licenses.

Licensing is discussed in detail in Chapter 12.

Under copyright law, an exclusive license is considered a transfer of copyright ownership. An exclusive license, like an assignment, is not valid unless it is in writing and signed by the owner of the rights conveyed. A nonexclusive license is valid even if it is not in writing.

An exclusive license, like an assignment, can be recorded in the Copyright Office to give constructive notice. Recording the exclusive license protects the license against unrecorded earlier transfers of copyright ownership and against later transfers. (See "Assignments," earlier in this chapter.)

Termination Right

The author of a work other than a work made for hire has the right to terminate any license or assignment granted on or after January 1, 1978, during a five-year period that starts 35 years after the grant was made. If the grant involves the right to distribute the work to the public, the termination period begins 35 years after distribution begins or 40 years after the grant was made, whichever is earlier. For works published before January 1, 1978, the five-year termination period begins 56 years after the work was first published.

The termination right cannot be waived in advance. If the author dies before the termination period begins, the termination right can be exercised by the author's widow or widower, children, and grandchildren.

Owning a Copy of a Work

Copyright law distinguishes the ownership of a copy of a protected work (a print of a photograph, a compact disc, a book, a diskette) from ownership of the intangible copyright rights. The transfer of a copy of a work does not transfer any rights in the copyright. Thus, purchasing a book (a copy of a literary work, in copyright terminology) does not give you permission to make copies of the book and sell those copies. There are two exceptions to this.

If you buy a copy of a work, you have a right to resell, rent, or loan out that copy (but you cannot rent out software or sound recordings without the copyright owner's permission). This exception is known as the "first sale doctrine." Copyright Act Section 109(a). You also have the right to display your copy publicly, "either directly or by the projection of no more than one image at a time, to viewers present at the place where the copy is located." Section 109(c). These two exceptions do not give you any right to exercise the copyright owner's reproduction, modification, or public performance rights.

 Don bought a copy of Publisher's multimedia work. Don can resell his copy of the work. The "first sale doctrine" gives him that right. If he makes copies of the work, though, he will be infringing Publisher's copyright.

Patents, Trademarks, and Trade Secrets

Patent law does not have a work made for hire rule. Patentable inventions created by employees within the scope of their employment are owned by the employee. However, the employee may have a legal obligation to transfer ownership to the employer under patent law's "hired to invent" doctrine. This doctrine provides that when an employee is hired to perform research or solve a specific problem, the employer is entitled to get an assignment of a patent received by the employee on the results of the research.

Generally, as a condition of employment, employers require employees to agree to assign their interests in patentable inventions to the employer. The Patent Act implicitly recognizes the validity of such agreements, providing that a patent may be granted to the assignee of the inventor.

A trademark is owned by the first party to use it in connection with goods or services or the first to apply to register it. A trademark can be owned by an individual, company, or any other legal entity.

An employer or hiring party generally owns trade secrets developed by employees and by independent contractors who are hired to invent.

Ownership of patents, trade secrets, and trademarks, like the ownership of copyrights, can be assigned. As with copyrights, owners of these types of intellectual property frequently grant licenses authorizing others to do things that would otherwise violate the owner's exclusive rights.

Trademark rights are discussed extensively in Chapter 17.

5 Contracts Law

Multimedia developers enter into business relationships with both individuals and businesses to help them create and distribute multimedia works. Most of these relationships result in "contracts" with legal consequences. Most contracts don't have to be in writing to be enforceable.

The purpose of this chapter—one of the "building block" chapters—is to provide an overview of the basic principles of contracts law.

In later chapters, we discuss special types of contracts: Development agreements are discussed in Chapter 6, contracts with employees are discussed in Chapter 7, contracts with independent contractors are discussed in Chapter 8, and distribution agreements are discussed in Chapters 20 and 21. The special legal rules that apply to contracts for the sale of goods are discussed in Chapter 19.

What Is a Contract?

A contract is a legally enforceable agreement between two or more parties. The core of most contracts is a set of mutual promises (in legal terminology, "consideration"). The promises made by the parties define the rights and obligations of the parties.

Contracts are enforceable in the courts. If one party meets its contractual obligations and the other party doesn't ("breaches the contract"), the nonbreaching party is entitled to receive relief through the courts.

Developer promised to pay Graphic Designer $5,000 for creating certain promotional materials for Developer's multimedia work. Graphic Designer created the materials and delivered them to Developer, as required in the contract. Developer admits that the materials meet the contract specifications. If Developer does not pay Graphic Designer, Graphic Designer can go to court and get a judgment against Developer for breach of contract.

Generally, the nonbreaching party's remedy for breach of contract is money damages that will put the nonbreaching party in the position it would have enjoyed if the contract had been performed. Under special circumstances, a court will order the breaching party to perform its contractual obligations.

Because contracts are enforceable, parties who enter into contracts can rely on contracts in structuring their business relationships.

 Developer entered into a contract with Composer, promising to pay Composer $4,000 for composing a brief composition for Developer's multimedia work. Shortly after Composer started work on the piece for Developer—before Developer paid Composer any money—Composer got an offer from a movie studio to compose all the music for a movie and abandoned Developer's project. Developer had to pay another composer $6,000 to do the work that Composer had contracted to do. Developer can sue Composer and obtain a judgment against Composer for $2000 (the amount that will result in Developer's obtaining the music for a net cost of $4,000, the contract price).

In this country and most others, businesses have significant flexibility in setting the terms of their contracts. Contracts are, in a sense, private law created by the agreement of the parties. The rights and obligations of the parties are determined by the contract's terms, subject to limits imposed by relevant statutes.

 Developer promised to pay Composer $5,000 to create music for Developer's multimedia training work. Composer created the music and delivered it to Developer, as required in the contract. Developer did not pay Composer, so Composer sued Developer for breach of contract. Developer's defense was "Composer did what she promised to do, but I never should have agreed to pay her $5000 for that work. $2000 is a fair price." The court will enforce Developer's promise to pay Composer $5,000.

Written Contracts

A deal done on a handshake—"You do X for me, and I'll pay you Y"—is a contract, because it is a legally enforceable agreement involving an exchange of promises. Most contracts are enforceable whether they are oral or written. Nonetheless, you should always have written contracts for all your business relationships.

There are several reasons why written contracts are better than oral contracts:

➤ The process of writing down the contract's terms and signing the contract forces both parties to think about—and be precise about—the obligations they are undertaking. With an oral contract, it is too easy for both parties to say "yes" and then have second thoughts.

➤ When the terms of a contract are written down, the parties are likely to create a more complete and thorough agreement than they would by oral agreement. A hastily made oral agreement is likely to have gaps that will have to be resolved later—when the relationship may have deteriorated.

➤ With an oral contract, the parties may have different recollections of what they agreed on (just as two witnesses to a car accident will disagree over what happened). A written agreement eliminates disputes over who promised what.

➤ Some types of contracts must be in writing to be enforced. The Copyright Act requires a copyright assignment or exclusive license to be in writing. State law requirements vary from state to state, but in most states, a contract for the sale of goods for $500 or more must be in writing.

See "Assignments and Licenses," Chapter 4, and "Important Provisions of Article Two," Chapter 19.

➤ If you have to go to court to enforce a contract or get damages, a written contract will mean less dispute about the contract's terms.

Who Can Enter Into a Contract?

Minors and the mentally incompetent lack the legal capacity to enter into contracts. All others generally are assumed to have full power to bind themselves by entering into contracts. In most states, the legal age for entering into contracts is 18. The test for mental capacity is whether the party understood the nature and consequences of the transaction in question.

Corporations have the power to enter into contracts. They make contracts through the acts of their agents, officers, and employees. Whether a particular employee has the power to bind the corporation to a contract is determined by an area of law called agency law or corporate law. If you question whether an individual with whom you are dealing has authority to enter into a contract with you, insist that the contract be reviewed and signed by the corporation's president.

A corporation has a separate legal existence from its founders, officers, and employees. Generally, the individuals associated with a corporation are not themselves responsible for the corporation's debts or liabilities, including liability for breach of contract.

Offer and Acceptance

A contract is formed when one party (the "offeror") makes an offer which is accepted by the other party (the "offeree"). An offer—a proposal to form a contract—can be as simple as the words, "I'll wash your car for you for $5." An acceptance—the offeree's assent to the terms of the offer—can be as simple as, "You've got a deal." Sometimes acceptance can be shown by conduct rather than by words.

When an offer has been made, no contract is formed until the offeree accepts the offer. When you make an offer, never assume that the offeree will accept the offer. Contractual liability is based on consent.

 Developer offered to pay Photographer $500 to use Photographer's photo in Developer's multimedia work. Photographer said, "Let me think about it." Developer, assuming that Photographer would accept the offer, went ahead and used the photo. Photographer then rejected Developer's offer. Developer has infringed Photographer's copyright by reproducing the photograph for use in the multimedia work. Developer must now either remove the photo from the multimedia work before distributing the work (or showing the work to others) or reach an agreement with Photographer.

When you are an offeree, do not assume that an offer will remain open indefinitely. In general, an offeror is free to revoke the offer at any time before acceptance by the offeree. Once the offeror terminates the offer, the offeree no longer has the legal power to accept the offer and form a contract.

 Animator offered his services to Developer, who said, "I'll get back to you." Developer then contracted with Client to quickly produce a multimedia work involving animation (making the assumption that Animator was still available to do the animation work). Before Developer could tell Animator that he accepted Animator's offer, Animator sent Developer a fax that said, "Leaving for Mexico. I'll call when I get back." Developer and Animator did not have a contract. Developer should not have assumed, in entering into the contract with Client, that Animator was still available.

When you are the offeree, do not start contract performance before notifying the offeror of your acceptance. Prior to your acceptance, there is no contract. An offer can be accepted by starting performance if the offer itself invites such acceptance, but this type of offer is rare.

Big Co. offered to pay Developer $5,000 to create a corporate presentation multimedia work for Big Co. Before Developer's president notified Big Co. that Developer accepted the offer, Big Co. sent Developer a fax that said, "We've changed our minds. Due to budget cuts at Big Co., we can't afford to do the multimedia project." In the meantime, Developer's staff had begun preliminary work on the project. Developer and Big Co. did not have a contract, so Developer has no legal recourse against Big Co. for loss of the deal or for the costs of the preliminary work.

Until an offer is accepted, the offeror is free—unless it has promised to hold the offer open—to revoke the offer.

 On June 1, Big Co. offered to hire Developer to create an interactive training work for Big Co. On June 4 (before acceptance by Developer), Big Co. notified Developer that it was giving the contract to Developer's competitor. Big Co. terminated the offer to Developer. Developer has no legal recourse against Big Co.

If you need time to make up your mind before accepting an offer, get the offeror to give you a written promise to hold the offer open for a few days. That will give you time to decide whether to accept.

Don't reject an offer and then try to accept it. Once an offeree rejects an offer, the offer dies and the offeree's legal power to accept the offer and form a contract terminates.

 Publisher offered to buy all rights in Developer's multimedia work for $100,000. Developer, hoping for a better offer, said no. Then Developer realized that Publisher's offer was the best Developer could do. Developer called Publisher and said, "I accept your offer." Because the offer was no longer open, Developer cannot form a contract by trying to accept the offer.

Except for the simplest deals, it generally takes more than one round of negotiations to form a contract. Often, the offeree responds to the initial offer with a counteroffer. A counteroffer is an offer made by an offeree on the same subject matter as the original offer, but proposing a different bargain than the original offer. A counteroffer, like an outright rejection, terminates the offeree's legal power of acceptance.

 Publisher offered to buy all rights in Developer's multimedia work for $100,000. Developer responded by saying, "I'll give you the right to distribute the work in the U.S. for $100,000." Developer's response to the offer was a counteroffer. Developer no longer has the legal power to form a contract based on Publisher's offer to purchase all rights in the work.

Consideration

Consideration, in legal terminology, is what one party to a contract will get from the other party in return for performing contract obligations.

 Developer promised to pay Artist $500 if Artist would let Developer use one of Artist's drawings in Developer's multimedia work. The consideration for Developer's promise to pay Artist $500 is Artist's promise to let Developer use the drawing. The consideration for Artist's promise to let Developer use the drawing is Developer's promise to pay Artist $500.

According to traditional legal doctrine, if one party makes a promise and the other party offers nothing in exchange for that promise, the promise is unenforceable. Such a promise is known as a "gratuitous promise." Gratuitous promises are said to be "unenforceable for lack of consideration."

 John told Sam, "When I buy a new car, I'll give you my truck." John bought a new car but did not give Sam the truck. According to traditional legal doctrine, John's promise to give Sam the truck is an unenforceable gratuitous promise. Sam gave nothing to John in exchange for John's promise to give Sam the truck.

In some states, a gratuitous promise can be enforced if the party to whom the promise was made relied on the promise. Other states no longer require consideration for certain types of promises.

Lack of consideration is rarely a problem for promises made in the context of business relationships. In most business contracts, there is consideration for both parties ("mutual consideration," in legal terminology).

The lack of consideration problem can arise in the context of amendments to contracts. Also, in some states, a promise to hold an offer open (see "Offer and Acceptance," earlier in this chapter) is unenforceable unless the offeree gives the offeror consideration (pays the offeror money) to keep the offer open.

A special application of the problem of lack of consideration in contracts with employees is discussed in "Using the Employment Agreement," Chapter 7.

Typical Contract Provisions

Many contracts include special types of provisions. We'll discuss these common types of provisions in the following sections.

Duties and Obligations

The duties and obligations section of a contract is a detailed description of the duties and obligations of the parties and the deadlines for performance.

If one party's obligation is to create a multimedia work, software, or content for a multimedia work, detailed specifications should be stated.

Warranties

A warranty is a legal promise that certain facts are true. Typical warranties in contracts concern such matters as ownership of the contract's subject matter (for example, real estate) and the right to sell or assign the subject matter. In multimedia industry contracts, warranties of ownership of intellectual property rights and noninfringement of third parties' intellectual property rights are common. These warranties are discussed in "The Contract," Chapter 6, in "Contracts with Independent Contractors," Chapter 8, in "Obtaining a License," Chapter 12, in "Warranties," Chapter 20, and in "Due Diligence," Chapter 21.

For contracts involving the sale of goods, certain warranties are implied under state law unless they are specifically disclaimed by the parties.

> Warranties and remedy clauses in contracts for the sale of goods are discussed in "Important Provisions of Article Two," Chapter 19.

Termination Clauses

These clauses ensure that either or both parties have the right to terminate the contract under certain circumstances. Generally, termination clauses describe breach of contract events that trigger the right to terminate the contract (for example, nonpayment of royalties). Termination clauses also describe the methods of giving notice of exercise of the termination right, and whether the breaching party must be given an opportunity to cure the breach before the other party can terminate the contract.

Remedy Clauses

These clauses state what rights the nonbreaching party has if the other party breaches the contract. In contracts for the sale of goods, remedy clauses are usually designed to limit the seller's liability for damages.

Arbitration Clauses

An arbitration clause states that disputes arising under the contract must be settled through arbitration rather than through court litigation. Such clauses generally include the name of the organization that will conduct the arbitration (the American Arbitration Association, for example), the city in which the arbitration will be held, and the method for selecting arbitrators.

> Arbitration is discussed in "Arbitration," Chapter 1.

Merger Clauses

Merger clauses state that the written document contains the entire understanding of the parties. The purpose of merger clauses is to ensure that evidence outside the written document will not be admissible in court to contradict or supplement the terms of the written agreement.

Tips for Contracts

The contract formation process varies widely, from contracts formed quickly in face-to-face meetings to contracts formed after teams of attorneys have spent months in negotiations. Contracts covering specific multimedia industry relationships are covered elsewhere in this book: Development agreements are covered in Chapter 6; contracts with employees, Chapter 7; contracts with independent contractors, Chapter 8; and distribution agreements, Chapters 20 and 21.

Here are some general tips for all types of contracts:

➤ **Write it down.** All contracts should take the form of a written document signed by both parties. You do not have to hire an attorney to create a written contract. If you reach an agreement over the phone or in a meeting, write the agreement up as soon as possible and have the other party sign the written memorandum. If you are making a written offer, you may want to make your offer in the form of a letter, with a space at the end for the offeree to indicate acceptance by signing.

➤ **Make sure you are comfortable with your obligations.** If a term— for example, a deadline—makes you uneasy, make a counteroffer that substitutes a term with which you are more comfortable. Do not assume that the other party will excuse you from strict compliance and do not rely on the other party's oral assurances that it will not insist on strict compliance.

➤ **Remember Murphy's Law.** Before you sign a contract, consider what could go wrong or what could make performance of your obligations difficult or expensive. If the actual performance is more difficult or expensive than you anticipated, that is not a valid excuse for not performing. Enter into a contract only if you believe that you can meet your obligations.

➤ **Don't leave anything out**. Accurately cover all aspects of your understanding with the other party. If the other party wrote the agreement based on an oral understanding reached earlier, make certain that the written terms match the terms of your oral agreement. Don't leave points out of the written document, even if the other party says, "We don't need to put that in writing."

➤ **Cover all options.** Cover all options, consequences, and possibilities. You should not fail to address an issue because it is "sensitive."

Deal with the sensitive issue during the negotiations. Make sure that your contract includes a merger clause (see "Typical Contract Provisions," earlier in this chapter) to avoid disputes about whether proposals made during negotiations but not included in the final written agreement are part of your contract.

➤ **Don't use unclear language or try to sound like a lawyer.** If you don't understand exactly what the other party is expecting you to do, don't try to camouflage the lack of understanding by using vague language. Vague language leads to misunderstandings, disputes, and lawsuits. Use simple language that accurately expresses your agreement with the other party. Don't try to sound like a lawyer, and don't complicate things unnecessarily.

➤ **Define any ambiguous terms.** There's a classic contracts case in which one party contracted to sell chickens to the other party. The seller thought "chicken" meant chicken of any age, including old and tough chickens. The buyer assumed "chicken" meant tender young chickens suitable for frying. The seller shipped old chickens, and the buyer screamed "breach." To avoid such misunderstandings, define any terms that may be ambiguous.

➤ **Be careful using "terms of art."** Terms of art are words with specific meaning in the law. "Assignment," for example, has a number of meanings in the English language. In intellectual property law, "assignment" means a transfer of ownership of intellectual property. Use "assignment" in your contracts when you mean transfer of ownership of intellectual property. Don't use the word in its other meanings or you will create confusion. A number of terms of art are defined throughout this book and in the Glossary.

See "Assignments," Chapter 4.

➤ **Use terms consistently.** When you write contracts, you are creating your own "law." Legal writing is not creative writing. Don't use "royalty" in one paragraph, "license fee" in a second paragraph, and "use fee" in a third paragraph to refer to the same concept. Pick one term and stay with it throughout the contract.

Part 2

Production Relationships

6 Development Agreements

This chapter covers the special legal issues that a developer should consider when asked by a client to create a multimedia work for the client's use (a multimedia training program for a corporation, for example). Development agreements between a developer and a publisher are discussed in Chapter 9 (although many of the issues discussed in this chapter also apply). Joint development projects are covered at the end of the chapter.

Proposals and Bids

Don't spend a lot of time and effort on a proposal for a potential client without first qualifying the client. Make sure that the client is seriously considering the project and has the ability to pay for the work.

Make certain that the person with whom you are dealing has the authority to approve the project. If that person does not have the authority, find out as soon as possible whether the person with authority is really interested in doing the project.

Don't start work on the project until the client has signed a written contract. Your proposal to a client is an offer. Until your client accepts the offer, there is no contract.

See "Offer and Acceptance," Chapter 5.

Some companies send requests for proposals (RFPs) to several multimedia developers. Responding to an RFP takes considerable time and effort. If you respond with a bid but do not get the contract, you will have no legal basis for getting reimbursement for your costs from the company that sent out the RFP.

Any proposal that you send to a potential client is protected by copyright. However, copyright protection does not cover the ideas used in the bid. If the recipient of a proposal photocopies all or part of your proposal, that's copyright infringement. If the recipient hires another multimedia developer to create a multimedia work based on the ideas used in your proposal, that's not copyright infringement. You may be able to get some protection for a proposal containing novel ideas by getting your potential client to sign a nondisclosure agreement (Form 1 in Appendix B).

Make your proposals in writing. Oral proposals are rarely complete (it is difficult in a phone conversation or face-to-face meeting to remember everything that you need to tell the client). If you make an oral proposal and it is accepted, you still should have the client sign a written contract. If the written contract contains terms that you did not mention in your oral proposal, the client may think that you are trying to change the deal.

Some multimedia developers have a standard proposal format that they use with all clients. This saves time and eliminates the possibility that a key provision will be left out of a particular proposal.

If your bid is accepted, you will be bound by the price and terms of your bid. If you discover that you made a mistake in calculating the bid price—you forgot to add in the cost of hiring a music composer, for example—you probably will still have to do the work at the bid price and absorb the added cost yourself (and that will lower your profit). It is difficult to cancel contracts made through the bid process.

See "Limitations on the Exclusive Rights," Chapter 2.

See "Written Contracts," Chapter 5.

The Contract

An agreement between a developer and a client should always take the form of a written contract signed by both parties. If your written proposal to a client is complete, you and your client can form a contract by having the client sign the proposal to indicate acceptance. You may want to finish your proposals with acceptance instructions, such as, "If you wish to accept this proposal and form a contract on the terms stated in this proposal, please sign below and return this proposal to me." It's permissible for you and your client to make handwritten changes to the proposal or mark provisions out, but both parties should initial any changes or deletions to avoid disputes later.

The balance of this section discusses the issues you should cover in your contract to create a multimedia work for a client.

Deliverables

In both the formal proposal and the contract, be as specific as possible about what you are to create for the client. Vagueness in the proposal and in the contract can camouflage misunderstanding that will come to light when you deliver the finished work to the client.

The inclusion of a detailed statement of deliverables will help you and your client make certain that you agree on the nature, content, quality, and uses of the work you are promising to create. Some deliverables that are frequently found in development agreements are:

➤ Design document (detailed description of the product to be made by the developer).

➤ Technical design document (delivery platforms, choice of programming language, authoring environment, graphic resolution, and so forth).

➤ Elements (script, storyboards, graphics/design, audio, video, "talent").

➤ Prototype.

➤ Beta version.

➤ Packaging.

➤ "Gold disk" (final CD-ROM version).

The design document and technical design document have two purposes: First, the process of creating and reviewing these documents helps clear up potential misunderstandings between the developer and the client about the scope of the developer's responsibilities. Second, if there is a dispute later about whether the developer has fully performed its contractual obligations, these documents will establish the scope of those obligations.

Content

You should discuss the range of content options with the client before you enter into a contract. If the client is expecting you to use expensive content—an excerpt of Michael Jackson singing "Bad," for example—the contract should state that requirement (and you should raise your price or get the client to reimburse you for the costly license fees). Be careful not to commit yourself to obtaining rights in specific works, because those works may not be available for licensing. If the client requests specific works, make sure that you have the right to substitute different works if the requested works are not available.

The licensing process is discussed in Chapter 12.

Licensing costs for obtaining permission to use content owned by third parties can be substantial. It may be possible to obtain suitable material relatively inexpensively from stock houses and libraries. A resource list appears in Appendix D. Consider making licensing fees the client's responsibility.

Deadlines and Delivery Schedule

See Stock Houses and Libraries, Chapter 12.

The contract should state when you must deliver the finished project to the client. In setting deadlines, remember that it probably will take more time than you expect to clear the rights to any third-party content that is used and to make certain that the components fit together.

Make certain that the deadlines are realistic. Serious delay on your part can be grounds for termination by the client—especially if the contract states that "time is of the essence" for performance of contract obligations. If the client is entitled to terminate the contract because of your failure to deliver the project on time, you may have to absorb the costs that went into the project before the termination. Normally, the client will have no obligation to reimburse you for those costs.

Clearing rights is discussed extensively in Chapter 12.

The contract should include deadlines for the client's decisions and approvals. Such deadlines will protect you, if the project is finished late because of client delay. In addition, the contract should include an acceptance clause that requires the client to "sign off" on the whole project by a certain date. (See "Acceptance Clause" below.)

Payment

The contract should state the amount and form of your payment—whether it is on a time-and-costs basis, a fixed-price basis, royalty, or other basis—and when payment is due. Some contracts provide for installment payments (for example, one-third upon execution, one-third at the delivery of the gold disk, and one-third when the final product is accepted by the client).

Acceptance Clause

For your protection, the proposal and contract should provide a procedure for objections to any deliverables. It's a good idea to require that objections be made in writing. You should have the right, if an objection is made, to attempt to cure the problem during a stated period of time after the objection. There also should be a deadline for objections to the finished project. You need to know that after a certain period of time passes, it will be too late for the client to say, "I won't accept this. Do it again."

Ownership of Copyright

One of the most important issues to address in the contract is who will own the copyright. By addressing this issue in the written agreement, you will eliminate future legal disputes over ownership. We'll discuss the two ownership options in "Client Ownership" and "Developer Ownership."

Client Ownership

Your client does not obtain ownership of the copyright by paying for its development. For copyright purposes, when you create a multimedia work for a client, you work as an independent contractor, not as the client's employee. A work created by an independent contractor for a client generally is owned by the independent contractor unless the client obtains an assignment of the copyright.

A work can be automatically owned by the client only in very limited circumstances: if the agreement describes the work as a "work made for hire" and if the work is one of eight special types of works listed in the Copyright Act's definition of specially commissioned works made for hire. These rules apply only in the United States.

Assigning the Copyright. If the client is to own the rights in the multimedia work, the contract should provide for an assignment of these rights to the client. You should be prepared to sign a separate "short form" copyright assignment (Form 2 in Appendix B) for filing with the Copyright Office. Your client may want you to grant it a power of attorney authorizing the client to execute and file assignment documents. If you are married, live in a community property state, and work as an individual, your client may ask that you get your spouse to sign a statement acknowledging that he or she does not claim any ownership interest in the work's copyright. This sort of statement is known as a "quitclaim." A quitclaim form is included in Appendix B (Form 3).

Legal Effect of Assignments. If you agree to assign the copyright in the multimedia work to the client, you will not be able to sell copies of that work to other clients. Unless you retain the modification right or have the client grant you a license to modify the work to create new works, you will not be able to modify the work for sale to other clients. Once you assign the copyright, the client will have the exclusive rights to reproduce the work, distribute it, publicly perform it, publicly display it, and modify it for use in derivative works. However, you still will be able to reuse ideas that you used in the work.

Retaining Ownership of Components. If you are creating a multimedia work to fill a client's special needs, you may not object to giving the client ownership of the copyright. However, you may want to retain ownership of components—for example, a software engine—that you created for the work, or at least reserve the right to use the components in future projects. Unless you retain ownership of the components or get a license from your client to reuse them, your use of the components in future projects will infringe the client's copyright.

See "Who Is an Independent Contractor" and "Copyright Ownership," Chapter 8.

See "The Work Made for Hire Rule," Chapter 4.

See "Assignments" and "Community Property" in Chapter 4.

See The "Exclusive Rights," Chapter 2, and "Licenses," Chapter 4.

See
Assignments,
Chapter 4.

 Developer created an interactive training program for Big Co. that used a software engine for manipulating game images. Developer assigned the copyright in the work to Big Co. If Developer uses the software engine in a new multimedia project without getting a license from Big Co., Developer will be infringing Big Co.'s copyright.

Third-Party Components. Assigning the copyright to the client does not give the client ownership of components owned by third parties. You cannot assign rights that you do not own.

 The interactive training program that Developer created for Big Co. contained an excerpt of a song written by Joe Composer. Since Developer did not own the copyright in Joe's song, Developer's assignment of its copyright in the program to Big Co. did not give Big Co. ownership of the copyright in Joe's song.

Demo Rights and Credits. If the copyright is to be owned by the client, you may want to include a clause in the contract authorizing you to retain a copy of the work to show to future clients and to show at trade shows. Such demonstrations are "public performances" of the work. You also may want to specify how your credit should appear in the client's copies of the multimedia work.

Developer Ownership

The term "public
performance" is
defined in "The
Exclusive Rights,"
Chapter 2.

If you are to retain the copyright in the multimedia work, the contract should state that you retain copyright ownership. If the contract says nothing about ownership of the copyright, you, as an independent contractor, automatically will own the copyright in the work. However, including a statement to that effect in your contract will help you avoid misunderstandings with clients who think that ordering and paying for a work gets them ownership of the copyright.

See "Copyright
Ownership,"
Chapter 8.

If the client contributes "copyrightable" material to the work, the client may be a joint author and thus a joint owner of the copyright. Stating in the contract that you will own the copyright in the entire work may help you avoid joint ownership claims by clients.

Reimbursement of License Fees and Costs

See "Standards,"
Chapter 2, and
"Joint Authorship
and Ownership,"
Chapter 4.

The contract should state whether any license fees, union reuse fees, and other costs you incur in creating the multimedia work will be reimbursed by the client.

Warranties and Indemnities

The client probably will insist that the contract include representations and warranties from you. Typical warranties in development agreements are as follows:

➤ You have the right to enter into the agreement.

➤ You have title to the multimedia work and all intellectual property rights in the work.

➤ You have the right to grant the client the assignment of copyright or to license the work.

➤ The work does not infringe third parties' intellectual property rights.

See "Obtaining a License," Chapter 12, and "Reuse Provisions," Chapter 16.

Warranty clauses typically include an indemnity provision in which the developer promises to indemnify and hold the client harmless for the breach of any of the warranties (in other words, pay for all costs arising out of the breach of the warranties).

Reason for Warranties

Clients have good reason for asking for warranties and indemnities. If you infringe any third-party intellectual property rights in making a multimedia work, your client will become an infringer by using the work (even though innocent of intent to infringe).

 Developer created a kiosk-type multimedia work called Cheese Expert for client, owner of a gourmet grocery. Cheese Expert contains pictures of Minnie Mouse and Mickey Mouse. Developer did not obtain permission from Disney to use Minnie and Mickey. Client's "public performance" of Cheese Expert in the grocery store infringes Disney's copyright and trademark rights.

Levels of Warranties

There are three levels of intellectual property warranties:

➤ **The "absolute" warranty.** "The work does not infringe any third-party intellectual property rights."

➤ **The "know or should know" warranty.** "To the best of my knowledge, the work does not infringe any third-party intellectual property rights."

➤ **The "actual knowledge" warranty.** "To my actual knowledge, the work does not infringe any third-party intellectual property rights."

As a developer, you should try to negotiate for the "know or should know" warranty or "actual knowledge" warranty rather than the unlimited "absolute" warranty. Although you should do everything possible to ensure that your multimedia work does not infringe third parties' intellectual property rights, you can never be certain that a work composed of many components does not infringe others' copyrights. For example:

➤ The employee who created the software code for your work may have reused code that is owned by a former employer.

➤ An independent contractor that you hired to create a component may have copied someone else's work.

➤ A composer who granted you a license to use his music throughout the world may turn out to not be the owner of the copyright in the music in all countries.

You should try to get "absolute" warranties from all your independent contractors and licensors.

See "Rights of Former Employers," Chapter 7.

Duration of Warranties

The contract should state whether the warranties continue during the term of the contract or are limited to the date on which the final product is delivered to the client.

Patent Warranties

Consider whether you want to warrant that your work does not infringe any patents. Patent applications in the United States are secret, so there is no way you can find out what patents might be granted during the term of your agreement. If you give a warranty that your work does not infringe any patents, you may be liable for infringing a later-issued patent that you did not know about. You may want to limit your exposure. One way to do that is to warrant only that, to the best of your knowledge, the multimedia work does not infringe any patents in effect on the date the finished product is delivered to the client.

See "Contracts With Independent Contractors," Chapter 8, and "Obtaining Licenses," Chapter 12.

Other Important Provisions

The contract also should contain several other provisions.

Modifications

The contract should state whether the client is permitted to change the design document or technical design document once work has begun. It should state whether the client has any right to require you to make changes to the multimedia work after it is delivered, and if the client must pay for modifications.

If you are retaining ownership of the copyright, the contract should state whether the client has the right to modify the work to correct errors. If the client does not have that right, modification by the client may infringe your modification right. If the contract provides that the client will own the copyright, the client as owner of the modification right automatically will have the right to make changes.

The contract should state who is responsible for correcting performance errors in the multimedia work. Many development contracts provide that the developer will make changes to correct performance errors for free during a "warranty period" and will provide maintenance for an annual fee after the warranty period ends.

Merger Clause

The contract should include a merger clause to help eliminate claims that the "real deal" is something other than what is stated in the contract (for example, an earlier proposal that was modified during negotiations).

Termination Clause

The parties may wish to provide that the contract can be terminated for cause (which should be defined) or even at will.

The termination provision should state how notice of breach that justifies termination should be given. The provision should include a "cure period" during which the breaching party has a right to cure the breach and avoid termination of the contract.

Nondisclosure Agreement

If the client will be giving you access to proprietary or confidential information or trade secrets, you may be asked to include a nondisclosure agreement in the contract. If you will be disclosing trade secrets and other proprietary information to your client as well, get the client to sign your nondisclosure agreement (see Apendix B, Form 1).

The nondisclosure agreement should state what information is to be considered confidential information, and how confidential information must be treated (for example, whether the receiving party can disclose the information to all employees or only to certain employees or to consultants). It also should state the duration of the obligation to keep the information confidential.

Generally, confidential information is defined in one of these two ways:

➤ Information marked confidential by its owner.

➤ Information that the receiving party knows or should know is confidential.

If you use the first definition, you need to include a method for identifying confidential information disclosed orally or by exhibition. In general, the following types of information are generally specifically excluded from the definition of confidential information:

See "The Exclusive Rights," Chapter 2.

See "Typical Contract Provisions," Chapter 5.

➤ Information that is in the public domain at the time it is disclosed to the receiving party.

➤ Information that later enters the public domain (but not through the fault of the receiving party).

➤ Information that is required to be disclosed by a court or government.

➤ Information that is received from a third party without restrictions on disclosure.

Information which is independently developed by the receiving party (in addition to being received as a disclosure from the other party) is sometimes excluded from the definition as well. Some agreements require the party claiming that information is not confidential under this exception to bear the burden of proving that it independently developed the information.

Disclaimer of Implied Warranties

When goods are sold, according to the law of every state except Louisiana, certain warranties are implied as part of the transaction unless they are disclaimed. Because a contract for the development of a multimedia work could be considered a contract for the sale of goods, implied warranties may apply to a development agreement unless they are disclaimed.

Remedies

You may want to limit the remedies available to the client should you breach the contract.

"Battle of the Forms"

Disclaimer of the implied warranties and limitation of remedies are covered in "Important Provisions of Article Two," Chapter 19.

In the business world, contracts are often created based on an exchange of forms. The offeror sends a proposal to the offeree, and the offeree accepts by sending back a purchase order form. While the purchase order normally contains a number of terms that match the proposal's terms (price and delivery date, for example), it generally will include additional or contradictory terms as well.

The legal rules for determining what terms are included in a contract created this way are complex (attorneys call the process the "battle of the forms"). To avoid the "battle of the forms," don't create a contract with a client by exchanging documents containing inconsistent terms. Make every effort to get the client to sign your proposal or negotiate a separate contract. If the client must use a purchase order, read it carefully, including its fine print, as soon as you receive it. If the purchase order form contains terms that are unacceptable to you, notify the client of your objection as soon as possible.

Joint Development Agreements

Individuals or companies that plan to work together on multimedia projects should enter into written joint development agreements documenting the terms of the relationship.

A joint development agreement should state who will do what, when each party's performance is due, and how much time each party will devote to the project (particularly if the parties have other jobs or other projects).

In the United States, the Copyright Act provides that joint authors of a work have equal undivided interests in the work's copyright. However, the parties to a joint development agreement can provide that royalties and profits from a work will be divided in a manner other than fifty-fifty— and one party can assign its interest in the copyright to the other.

According to U.S. copyright law, each single joint owner can, without getting the consent of the other owners, grant nonexclusive licenses to third parties to use the work in "nondestructive" ways. Nondestructive use is a use that does not diminish the value of the work. A joint owner who grants a license must share any royalties received with the other owners. Joint owners can provide by contract that the consent of all owners is required for granting licenses.

The rules for joint ownership of copyright vary from country to country. In many countries in Europe (Germany and France, for example), the consent of all joint owners of a copyright is necessary to obtain an enforceable license. This rule applies even if the work was created in the United States by U.S. citizens. This issue is very complex. You should try to avoid joint ownership if the work will be distributed overseas.

One risk that joint development agreements pose is that it is sometimes difficult to draw the line between a joint development agreement and a general partnership. Partners in a general partnership are all liable for the debts of a partnership. To avoid this problem, many joint development agreements state that the parties are not forming a general partnership. The purpose is to protect each developer from liability for general debts of the co-developers (debts arising out of ventures or projects other than the joint development project).

See "Joint Authorship and Ownership," Chapter 4.

7 Employees

If you are a multimedia developer with employees, you should take proper steps to ensure that you own your employees' contributions to your multimedia works. This chapter focuses on practical applications of the Copyright Act's "work made for hire" rule, on the limitations of the rule, and on strategies for overcoming those limitations.

The rights of publicity and privacy are addressed in Chapter 15. Union issues are addressed in Chapter 16. Other employment issues—for example, employment law and labor law issues—are beyond the scope of this book.

Works Made by Employees

According to the Copyright Act's work made for hire rule, an employer is the "author" and copyright owner of a work made for hire unless the parties agree otherwise. A work made for hire is a work created by an employee within the scope of his or her employment. Certain types of specially commissioned works also can be works made for hire, as discussed in "The Work Made for Hire Rule," Chapter 4, and in "Copyright Ownership," Chapter 8.

The work made for hire rule reverses the Copyright Act's general rule on copyright ownership, which states that the individual who creates a work owns the copyright in that work.

See "Initial Ownership," Chapter 4.

The Copyright Act's general ownership rule and the work made for hire rule apply only in the United States. Other countries have their own copyright ownership rules. Most have something similar to the "employee branch" of the Copyright Act's work made for hire rule.

The work made for hire rule applies only to works created by employees within the scope of their employment. It does not apply to works created by employees on their own, nor does it apply to works created by independent contractors for hiring parties.

See "The Work Made for Hire Rule," Chapter 4.

Who Is an Employee?

The Copyright Act does not define the term "employee." The Supreme Court has held that 13 factors must be considered to determine whether a worker is an employee or an independent contractor. No one factor is determinative. The factors are:

➤ Whether the hiring party had a right to control the manner and means by which the product is accomplished.

➤ The level of skill required.

➤ Whether the instruments and tools used were provided by the hiring party or the hired party.

➤ Whether the hired party worked at the hiring party's place of business or the hired party's place of business.

➤ The duration of the relationship between the two parties.

➤ Whether the hiring party had the right to assign additional projects to the hired party.

➤ The extent of the hired party's discretion over when and how long to work.

➤ The method of payment.

➤ Whether the hired party had a role in hiring and paying assistants.

➤ Whether the work was part of the regular business of the hiring party.

➤ Whether the hiring party was in business at all.

➤ Whether employee benefits were provided by the hiring party for the hired party.

➤ How the hiring party treated the hired party for tax purposes.

Whether your employee creates a short tune for your multimedia project or handles the entire project, you, the employer, own the copyright in the employee's work so long as the employee's work is done within the scope of employment. An employee—although the actual author—is not considered the author of a work made for hire for copyright purposes. Of course, you and your employee can agree that the employee will own the copyright, as discussed in "Giving Ownership to an Employee," later in this chapter.

Writer, employed by Developer to write scripts for multimedia works, wrote the script for Developer's new medical training work during normal working hours as part of Writer's job. The script is a work made for hire. The copyright law considers Developer the author of Writer's text. Unless Writer and Developer have agreed otherwise, Developer owns the copyright in the script.

Because you, the employer, are deemed the author and copyright owner of works made for hire, you can use works made for hire without obtaining permission from the employees who created them. Any employee who exercises the copyright owner's exclusive rights in a work made for hire infringes the employer's copyright.

Writer in the previous example quit working for Developer and formed his own multimedia production company. Writer has informed Developer that Developer no longer has Writer's permission to use the script created by Writer. In his first project for the new company, Writer used a modified version of the script Writer had written for Developer's medical training work. Because Developer owns the copyright in the script, Developer does not need Writer's permission to continue to use the script. Writer's modification of the script infringes Developer's modification right (discussed in "The Exclusive Rights," Chapter 2).

The work made for hire rule applies whether the employer is an individual, partnership, or corporation. For corporate employers, the rule applies to works created by officers and managers as well as to works created by rank and file employees.

John, the cofounder and president of ABC Multimedia Co., a California corporation, created the retail kiosk work Cheese Expert within the scope of his employment with ABC. The copyright in Cheese Expert belongs to ABC Multimedia, not to John. Although John may think of ABC as his company, the corporation is a separate legal entity. If John has a falling out with his cofounder and leaves ABC, ownership of the copyright in Cheese Expert remains with ABC.

Using the Employment Agreement

Don't rely solely on the Copyright Act's work made for hire rule as a means of obtaining ownership of works made by your employees. Supplement the work made for hire rule by getting all employees to sign an "Employee Nondisclosure and Assignment Agreement" (Form 6 in Appendix B). In the rest of this chapter, we'll refer to this agreement as the "Employment Agreement."

The Employment Agreement protects you against employee claims that works were created outside the scope of an employee's employment. It gives the employer an assignment of intellectual property rights in:

➤ Works conceived or developed during the period of the employment.

➤ Works that relate at the time of conception or development to the employer's business or research.

➤ Works that were developed on the employer's time or with the use of the employer's equipment, supplies, facilities, or trade secret information.

➤ Works that resulted from work performed for the employer.

Assignments are discussed in "Assignments," Chapter 4.

Limitations on the Work Made for Hire Rule

There are four limitations on the work made for hire rule that make it prudent for you to use the Employment Agreement (with its assignment provision) with all employees as a back-up to the work made for hire rule. They are discussed in this section.

International Ownership

In other countries, ownership of employee-made works will be determined by applying local law rather than U.S. law. Although many countries have rules similar to the work made for hire rule, some do not. The assignment provision of the Employment Agreement (see Article 3 of Form 6 in Appendix B) is designed to give you ownership rights in employee-made works that will be recognized throughout the world.

Works Outside the Scope of Employment

The rule does not give employers ownership of works created by employees outside the scope of their employment. In new fields such as multimedia development, job descriptions are sometimes vague or nonexistent, and employees frequently wear many hats or take on responsibilities beyond those contemplated at hiring time. These factors could provide a basis for an employee's claim that you, the employer, do not own the copyright in a particular work because the work was created outside the scope of the employee's employment.

> **Employee or Independent Contractor? A Real Dispute**
>
> Three New York artists who had created a sculpture in a warehouse on Long Island claimed they owned the copyright in the sculpture because they had artistic control over the work and used their own materials and tools. The U.S. Court of Appeals for the Second Circuit, however, held that the sculpture was a work made for hire because the employer treated the workers like employees. They received a weekly salary, took paid vacations, and had payroll taxes and Social Security withheld—and the employer assigned them additional projects elsewhere in the building. *Carter v. Helmsley-Spear, Inc.* __F. 3d__ (2d Cir. 1995).

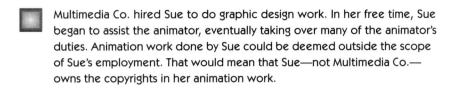 Multimedia Co. hired Sue to do graphic design work. In her free time, Sue began to assist the animator, eventually taking over many of the animator's duties. Animation work done by Sue could be deemed outside the scope of Sue's employment. That would mean that Sue—not Multimedia Co.— owns the copyrights in her animation work.

Employee or Independent Contractor?

The rule applies only to works created by employees, not to works created by independent contractors. It is sometimes difficult to tell, using the factors discussed in "Who is an Employee?," earlier in this chapter, whether a worker is an employee or an independent contractor.

Media Co. hired Mark, an animator, to do the animation work for Media's new work, City Tour. Three factors in Mark's relationship with Media indicate that Mark is an independent contractor: Mark worked at home, Media had no right to assign him more work, and Media did not give him employee benefits. However, three factors indicate that Mark is an employee of Media Co.: Media provided the tools for the job, Media provided detailed instructions for the work, and Media required Mark to work normal working hours. In this situation, it is difficult to tell whether Mark is an independent contractor or Media's employee.

Should one of your employees someday maintain that he or she worked for you as an independent contractor rather than as an employee and that, therefore, you can't rely on the work made for hire rule for ownership of copyrights in works he or she created, you can say, "It doesn't matter whether you were an employee or an independent contractor. You assigned me those copyrights when you signed the Employment Agreement."

Patents, Trademarks, and Trade Secrets

The work made for hire rule does not apply to patents, trademarks, trade secrets, or other forms of intellectual property. The assignment provision of the Employment Agreement (Article 3 of Form 6, Appendix B) gives you, the employer, ownership of these other forms of intellectual property. That means you don't have to worry about these other laws' ownership rules for works created by your employees.

> **Avoid Litigation Over Copyright Ownership**
>
> A *significant* percentage of the copyright cases filed each year are disputes over who owns the copyright in a work created by an employee or an independent contractor. Frequently litigated issues include whether a worker was an employee or independent contractor; whether an employee created a work within the scope of employment or own his own; and whether work created by an independent contractor was specially commissioned work covered by a valid work made for hire agreement. Why pay an attorney to litigate such issues? To avoid litigation, follow the suggestions of this chapter (for employees) and of the next chapter (for independent contractors).

Provisions of the Employment Agreement

The Employment Agreement contains three important provisions.

The Confidentiality Provision

See "Trade Secret Protection," Chapter 18.

The confidentiality provision of the Employment Agreement (Article 2 of Form 6) is a necessary part of your trade secrets protection program. "Confidential information" is defined as any information not generally known in the relevant trade or industry that is either obtained from the employer, or learned or developed by the employee in the scope of the employment.

The Assignment Provision

The assignment provision of the Employment Agreement (Article 3 in Form 6) is broad enough to give you ownership of trade secrets, trademarks, and patent rights arising out of an employee's work for you.

The "power of attorney" aspect of the agreement (Section 7.2) gives you the authority to execute and file copyright assignment documents on behalf of the employee to secure and record your ownership rights in intellectual property created by the employee. The power of attorney does not give you authority to act for the employee in other ways.

If you are located in California, you should be aware of Section 2870 of the California Labor Code. It states that any employment agreement provision that requires an employee to assign to the employer any inventions the employee developed entirely on his or her own time without using the employer's equipment, supplies, facilities, or trade secret information is unenforceable and against public policy. The statute makes an exception for inventions that relate to the employer's business, research, or development, or that result from work performed by the employee for the employer. The Employment Agreement's assignment provision does not give you ownership of inventions that are nonassignable under Section 2870. See the "Limited Exclusion Notification" at the end of Form 6.

List of Employee Inventions

See "Assignments and Licenses," Chapter 4, and "Obtaining a License," Chapter 10.

The Employment Agreement does not give you ownership of intellectual property already owned by an employee when he or she started work for you (see Section 3.2(b) in Form 6). If the employee owns copyrights or other intellectual property at the time the employment begins, they should be listed in Exhibit A to the agreement, "Prior Work Products." If you want to use listed inventions, you will have to negotiate with the employee to obtain a separate license or an assignment.

When Employees Should Sign

Each employee should sign a copy of the Employment Agreement before he or she begins work or on the first day of work. That way, the job will be the consideration that you give the employee in exchange for the employee's signing the Employment Agreement. An Employment Agreement that is signed later may be unenforceable for lack of consideration, although in some states, continued employment may count as consideration for "at will" employees (those without employment contracts).

Delayed Signing

Getting an Employment Agreement signed by an employee after the employee has started work is better than not getting the agreement signed at all. It is a good idea to offer some consideration—money or a promotion—to a late signer in order to avoid a "lack of consideration" defense. The Employment agreement, in that case, should state what consideration you gave the employee in exchange for the employee's signing the Agreement.

Former Employees

If you are concerned that the work done by a former employee was not covered by the work made for hire rule—because it might have been done outside the scope of employment, or because the individual may have been an independent contractor rather than an employee—consider asking the individual for an assignment. (See Form 9 in Appendix B.) If he or she agrees to execute an assignment, provide some consideration for the assignment. Asking for an assignment, of course, will alert the individual to the fact that you think there may be some defect in your title to the work. The former employee may refuse to give you the assignment.

Independent Contractors

Do not use the Employment Agreement with individuals who work as independent contractors. Instead, use the Independent Contractor Agreement (Form 7 in Appendix B), which is discussed in "Copyright Ownership," Chapter 8.

Determining whether an individual is an employee or an independent contractor can be complex (see "Who is an Employee?," earlier in this chapter). You should consider consulting an experienced attorney in close cases. As a practical matter, it probably will be difficult for you to convince a court that an individual whom you did not treat as an employee for tax or employment-benefit purposes should be treated as an employee for copyright ownership purposes.

Consideration and the problem of lack of consideration are discussed in "Consideration," Chapter 5.

Giving Ownership to an Employee

If you want to give a key employee ownership of a work created within the scope of employment, it is easy to do so. You and the employee simply have to sign a written agreement stating that the employee owns all copyright rights in the work. An oral agreement is not sufficient to give an employee ownership of works made for hire.

License provisions are discussed in "Obtaining a License," Chapter 12.

If you sign an agreement giving copyright ownership in a work to an employee, you as the employer will still be considered the "author" of the work for copyright purposes, but the employee will be the copyright owner. If you give an employee copyright ownership, you should consider having the employee grant you an irrevocable, nonexclusive, royalty-free, world-wide license to use the work in existing multimedia projects and to modify the work for use in future multimedia projects.

Joint Ownership

An employee is not a joint owner of a work made for hire unless the employer assigns an ownership interest to the employee. An employee's contributions to a work made for hire do not make the employee a joint author or a joint copyright owner.

 Dan hired Janet to help develop a multimedia work, Restaurant Guide. Janet helped Dan with all aspects of the development of Restaurant Guide. If Janet was Dan's employee and Janet's contributions to Restaurant Guide were made within the scope of Janet's employment, Dan, as the employer, owns the entire copyright in Restaurant Guide.

Rights of Former Employers

Respect the intellectual property rights of your employees' former employers. If one of your employees created a copyrighted work within the scope of employment with a former employer, the former employer owns the copyright (unless the employee and former employer agreed otherwise). Trade secrets developed for a former employer also are normally the property of the former employer.

While employees are free to reuse ideas that they used for a former employer and to draw on their general knowledge and job skills, do not permit your employees to use copyrighted material or trade secrets belonging to former employers without getting licenses.

8 Contractors and Consultants

Many multimedia developers use free-lancers and consultants to create content, develop software and user interfaces, and even to supervise production. Most free-lancers and consultants are considered "independent contractors" for copyright law purposes. According to copyright law, when an independent contractor creates a work for a hiring party, the copyright is owned by the independent contractor unless the hiring party takes steps to secure ownership.

This chapter deals with legal issues arising out of a developer's use of independent contractors, including the steps that a developer should take to get ownership of copyrights in works created by independent contractors such as graphic artists, writers, content specialists, and software designers.

Who Is an Independent Contractor?

The Copyright Act does not define "independent contractor" or "employee." Instead, according to the Supreme Court, whether a worker is an employee or an independent contractor must be determined by weighing 13 factors. (These are the same 13 factors listed in "Who is an Employee?," Chapter 7.)

No one factor is determinative. The factors are as follows:

➤ Whether the hiring party had a right to control the manner and means by which the product is accomplished.

➤ The level of skill required.

➤ Whether the instruments and tools used were provided by the hiring party or the hired party.

➤ Whether the hired party worked at the hiring party's place of business or the hired party's place of business.

➤ The duration of the relationship between the two parties.

➤ Whether the hiring party had the right to assign additional projects to the hired party.

➤ The extent of the hired party's discretion over when and how long to work.

➤ The method of payment.

➤ Whether the hired party had a role in hiring and paying assistants.

➤ Whether the work was part of the regular business of the hiring party.

➤ Whether the hiring party was in business at all.

➤ Whether employee benefits were provided by the hiring party for the hired party.

➤ How the hiring party treated the hired party for tax purposes.

Independent Contractor Ownership: A Real Dispute

Artist Patrick Nagel, working as a free-lance artist, created works of art which appeared in *Playboy*. After Nagel's death, his widow granted reproduction rights to these works to a company unrelated to *Playboy*. *Playboy* sought a declaratory judgment that it was the copyright owner. Some of Nagel's works were found to be owned by Nagel's widow, because the works were not covered by work for hire agreements or assignments. *Playboy Enterprises, Inc. v. Dumas,* 53 F.3d 549 (2d Cir. 1995).

Much of the work that is done on multimedia projects is done by free-lance professionals who work on a project basis. A worker who is hired on a project basis—whether for a lump-sum fee or at an hourly rate—is probably an independent contractor rather than an employee, especially if the worker provides his or her own workplace and tools, and works without day-to-day supervision. Partnerships and corporations also can be hired on an independent contractor basis.

Unless you have good reason to believe (based on the 13-factor test) that a particular worker hired on a project basis is an employee, you should assume that such a worker is an independent contractor. As a practical matter, it probably will be difficult for you to convince a court that an individual whom you did not treat as an employee for tax or employment-benefit purposes should be treated as an employee for copyright ownership purposes.

Copyright Ownership

When a hiring party and an independent contractor fail to address the issue of ownership of copyrights in works created by the independent contractor, the copyrights are owned by the independent contractor. This "default rule" is the opposite of the default rule for works created by employees (discussed in "The Work Made for Hire Rule," Chapter 4, and in "Works Made by Employees," Chapter 7).

You should try to obtain ownership of copyrights in all works created for you by independent contractors. There are two ways to obtain ownership:

> ➤ **Assignment**. For all types of works created for you by independent contractors, you can obtain ownership of copyrights by including an assignment provision in your contract with the independent contractor.

> ➤ **Work made for hire agreement**. For contributions to audiovisual works and seven other types of works (listed in "Work Made for Hire Agreements," later in this chapter), you can obtain ownership of copyrights by including a "work made for hire" agreement in your contract with the independent contractor. This approach makes use of the second branch (specially commissioned works) of the Copyright Act's work made for hire rule.

These two options for obtaining ownership are discussed in the next two subsections, "Assignments" and "Work Made for Hire Agreements." Unless you use one of these two options, the copyrights in works done for you by independent contractors will be owned by the contractors—even though you ordered and paid for the works.

 Developer hired Software Design House on a project basis to create the software for Developer's multimedia work. Developer did not get Software Design House to sign a work made for hire agreement, nor did it get an assignment of the copyright in the software from Software Design House. Software Design House owns the copyright in the software that it created for Developer's multimedia work.

Assignments

If you get an assignment of copyright from an independent contractor who creates material for your multimedia work, you will own the copyright in the contractor's work.

The independent contractors who give you assignments will have the right to terminate the assignments in 35 years. There is nothing you can do about this situation.

For an example of an assignment provision that you can use in contracts with independent contractors, see Section 4.4 of the Independent Contractor Agreement (Form 7 in Appendix B). This assignment provision states that:

See "Assignments" and "Termination Right," Chapter 4.

➤ Inventions resulting from the contractor's work under the Independent Contractor Agreement and copyrightable works developed within the scope of the contractor's work for the hiring party are the exclusive property of the hiring party.

➤ The contractor assigns all intellectual property rights in those inventions and copyrightable works to the hiring party.

This assignment provision includes a power of attorney. Other aspects of the Independent Contractor Agreement are discussed in "Contracts With Independent Contractors," later in this chapter.

If you are in a community property state, you may want to get the spouses of married independent contractors to sign quitclaims.

Power of attorney provisions are discussed in "Using the Employment Agreement," Chapter 7.

See "Community Property," Chapter 4.

Work Made for Hire Agreements

For certain types of works, you can obtain ownership of works created by independent contractors by using a work made for hire agreement (Form 8 in Appendix B). This method of obtaining ownership makes use of the second branch of the Copyright Act's work made for hire rule.

Both you and the independent contractor must sign the work made for hire agreement in order to make the contractor's works into works made for hire.

Limitations

If you are going to use a work made for hire agreement rather than get an assignment, make sure you understand the limitations of work made for hire agreements.

Types of Works

A work made for hire agreement is only effective for eight types of specially commissioned works:

➤ Contributions to collective works.

➤ Part of a motion picture or other audiovisual work (many multimedia works are audiovisual works).

➤ Translations.

➤ Supplementary works (works prepared as adjuncts to other works).

➤ Compilations.

➤ Instructional texts.

➤ Tests or answer material for tests.

➤ Atlases.

These are the same eight types of works listed in "The Work Made for Hire Rule," Chapter 4, in the discussion of the "specially commissioned works" branch of the rule.

While some books of legal forms—particularly older ones—give you the impression that you can make any type of specially commissioned work a work made for hire by getting a work made for hire agreement from the independent contractor, that is not true.

John hired Writer, a free-lancer, to write John's biography. John got Writer to sign an agreement stating that the work was to be considered a work made for hire. The agreement was worthless. Biography is not one of the types of specially commissioned works that can become a work made for hire based on agreement of the parties. Unless John got an assignment from Writer, Writer owns the copyright in the biography.

Existing Works

You can't use a work made for hire agreement to acquire ownership of existing material. To obtain ownership of material you did not commission, you need an assignment.

Writer wrote an original script for an interactive game. Developer wants to buy the script and modify it for use in a new product. To acquire ownership of the copyright, Developer needs to get an assignment from Writer. A work made for hire agreement will not give Developer ownership.

Unsolicited Works

You can't use a work made for hire agreement to obtain ownership rights in works that "came in over the transom"—that is, unsolicited work. You need an assignment.

Foreign Rights

A work made for hire agreement probably won't get you foreign rights in the commissioned works because most countries' rules do not have anything comparable to the "specially commissioned works" branch of the Copyright Act's work made for hire rule. To protect your ownership abroad, you should obtain assignments from independent contractors.

Timing

One federal appellate court has held that a work made for hire agreement for a specially commissioned work is valid only if the agreement is signed before the work is

> ### Existing Works: A Real Dispute
>
> Jerome Siegel conceived the idea of Superman in 1933 and, with a partner, created several weeks' worth of material for a Superman comic strip. In 1938, they submitted the materials to Detective Comics. In a later dispute between Seigel and Detective's successor over ownership of Superman, the court—noting that "Superman and his miraculous powers were completely developed long before the employment relationship was instituted"—held that Superman was not a work for hire. *Siegel v. National Periodical Publications, Inc.*, 508 F.2d 909 (2d Cir. 1974).

created. *Schiller & Schmidt, Inc. v. NordiscoCorp.*, 969 F.2d 410 (7th Cir. 1992). However, another federal appellate court recently held that the agreement can be signed after the work is created, so long as the parties agree orally, explicitly or implicitly, before the work is created, that the work will be a work made for hire. *Playboy Enterprises, Inc. v. Dumas,* 53 F.3d 549 (2d Cir. 1995). Nonetheless, you should make every effort to get your independent contractors to sign work made for hire agreements before they start work on your projects.

If you discover that an independent contractor has started work without signing the work made for hire agreement, you should try to get the contractor to sign an assignment. (See Form 9 in Appendix B.)

If the contractor refuses to give you an assignment, try to get a broad written license from the contractor. If the contractor refuses to grant a written license, you will have to either rely on an implied license (discussed in "Implied Licenses," later in this chapter), or remove the contractor's work from your multimedia project.

You can claim copyright for the multimedia work as a whole even though an independent contractor owns the copyright in a component.

California Labor Code

For details on registering copyrights, see "How to Fill Out Form PA," Chapter 18.

A provision of the California Labor Code states that a person who commissions a work made for hire is the employer of the hired party for purposes of worker's compensation, unemployment insurance, and unemployment disability insurance laws. No one is certain exactly what the provision means. If you are located in California, you may want to acquire ownership of copyrights in works made by independent contractors by assignment rather than using work made for hire agreements.

Implied Licenses

If you order and pay for a work created by an independent contractor and fail to get an assignment or a work made for hire agreement, you may have an implied license to use the contractor's work as intended by you and the contractor. An implied license to use the work is much less valuable than owning the copyright in the work.

See "The Exclusive Rights," Chapter 2.

If you own a work created by a independent contractor, you can exercise all of the copyright owner's exclusive rights in the work—in other words, you can make copies of the work, modify the work, distribute the work, and publicly perform and display the work. If you merely have an implied license to use the work, you can only do those things that are within the scope of the license (and you and the contractor may not agree on the scope of the license).

Developer hired Composer to create music for a multimedia work commissioned by a client. The music is so good that Developer would like to modify it for use in other multimedia works. If Developer owns the copyright in the music, Developer can modify and reuse the music. If Developer just has an implied license to use the music, the implied license probably only authorizes Developer to use the music in the original client's project.

License scope is discussed in "Determining What Rights You Need," Chapter 12.

Contracts with Independent Contractors

You should have written contracts with all of your independent contractors for the reasons stated in "Written Contracts," Chapter 5.

Contract Provisions

The contract with an independent contractor should include, in addition to an assignment or a work made for hire agreement (see "Copyright Ownership," earlier in this chapter), the following provisions:

➤ Deliverables or services, described as specifically as possible.

➤ Deadlines.

➤ Payment and payment schedules.

➤ Responsibility for expenses.

Such provisions are discussed in "The Contract," Chapter 6.

Services of Individuals

If you enter into a contract with a corporation and expect to get the services of particular individuals employed by the corporation, your contract should state that the work can be done only by the named individuals. Otherwise, the corporation will be free to use any of its employees to do the job.

Warranties

You should get warranties and an indemnity from each independent contractor. For sample provisions, see Sections 4.6 and 4.8 of the Independent Contractor Agreement (Form 7 in Appendix B).

Warranty and indemnity provisions are designed to give you legal recourse against a contractor who uses works belonging to others. If a contractor gives you material that infringes a third party's copyright, incorporating that material into your multimedia work will make you liable for infringement of the third party's copyright.

Developer hired Graphic Artist to create original graphics for Developer's multimedia work Downtown Tonight. Graphic Artist copied some designs from a design book and delivered them to Developer to fulfill her contract with Developer. When Developer incorporated the designs into Downtown Tonight, Developer infringed the copyright owner's reproduction and modification rights (see "The Exclusive Rights," Chapter 2).

Warranty provisions are discussed in more detail in "The Contract," Chapter 6.

Of course, these provisions are not worth much if the contractor does not have the resources to pay the damages. You may want to consider obtaining insurance to cover that risk.

The contractor also may ask you for warranties and an indemnity. For example, if you will be giving the contractor material to use in the project, the contractor may want you to warrant that you own the material, or that use of the material in the project will not infringe third party copyrights.

Nondisclosure Provisions

See "Trade Secret Protection," Chapter 18.

The contract should contain a nondisclosure provision. Such provisions are part of a trade secrets protection program. For an example, see Section 4.2 of the Independent Contractor Agreement (Form 7 in Appendix B).

Miscellaneous Issues

If you will be using an independent contractor's voice, image, or face in a multimedia work, your contract should include a release authorizing that use to avoid violations of the laws of publicity and privacy (see Chapter 15).

If you will be hiring independent contractors who belong to entertainment industry unions, read about union issues in Chapter 16.

Standard Agreements

Independent contractors in many fields have professional associations that have developed and distributed standard agreements. The Graphic Artists Guild, for example, has standard contracts for use by graphic designers and illustrators with clients.

If a contractor insists on using a standard form, read the form carefully, particularly the ownership of rights provision, and be prepared to negotiate over deleting unacceptable provisions and adding your own provisions.

Employment Law Risks

If federal or state authorities conclude that an individual that you have treated as an independent contractor is an employee, you could have a number of problems. They could include:

➤ Tax liability for failure to withhold payroll taxes for the individual.

➤ Liability for workers' compensation awards paid to the individual.

➤ Liability for violation of state and federal wage and hours laws.

➤ Liability for violation of wrongful discharge laws.

You should be aware that the distinction between employees and independent contractors has importance in areas of the law other than copyright law. An individual who is an independent contractor for copyright law purposes may not be an independent contractor for employment law purposes.

9 Creating a Multimedia Title for a Publisher

by Linda Rich and Darlene de Monfreid

The authors of this chapter have worked as entertainment industry publishing executives and as developers of original interactive titles. In this chapter on budgeting a multimedia project, they discuss title selection, developer compensation for title development, the funding process, scheduling, and budget preparation. Finally, they offer some advice for working with a publisher to create a title.

How Publishers Pick Titles

Publishers choose multimedia titles for their profit potential. Factors that determine the profit potential of a title include the development budget; likelihood of "on time, on budget" delivery (regardless of how long the contract negotiations take or how tight the budget is); manufacturing and packaging costs; marketing and distribution expenses; and the number of units publishers think they will sell.

Publishers fund titles they think will earn back more money than they cost to develop and publish. As the consumer CD-ROM industry is highly competitive with few titles reaping profits, more publishers only are funding titles they think will be hits. In the autumn of 1995, the CD-ROM titles that topped the entertainment bestseller lists were similar to ones that were the hits of 1994: *Myst, Encarta, Star Trek,* and *The Lion King*

Animated Storybook, to name a few. The publishers of these hits have follow-up titles in production.

Publishers are cautious about trying out new title concepts and taking chances on unproven developers. They are looking for value that is evident on the computer screen—for speedy, addictive play (in the case of a game); for thoughtful, intuitive interface design; for stunning graphics, animations, video, and effects; and for high quality sound design. These are features that will be discussed in product reviews and visible in product demonstrations—in short, these are features that help a title sell and repay the publisher's investment.

Developer Compensation

Developers often want to know, "Where in the title budget is my compensation?" They think that the budget should include payment for the developer's overhead and time. Generally, it does not. Instead, the developer's compensation usually takes the form of royalties, or royalties with a recoupable advance.

Why Royalties?

Multimedia publishers believe they are taking all of the risks in the multimedia business. After all, the publisher advances the money for a title's production expenses, testing, manufacturing, packaging, and marketing. Often the publisher also provides production supervision and technical expertise. All of these expenses must be recovered before the publisher makes a profit on a title. When a title fails to earn back the money the publisher has spent on its production, the publisher loses money. The vast majority of CD-ROM titles have not sold well enough to break even.

Royalties are discussed in "Payment," Chapter 20, and in "Payment," Chapter 21.

A typical developer, of course, believes that the developer's title will be a hit—that is, unless the publisher doesn't promote the title properly or doesn't choose the right distribution channels. Although this viewpoint is understandable, developers with no track record must be realistic. Publishers demand that the developer's production budget for a multimedia title be as low as possible, to build the title as defined in the game design document. To keep the budget low, the budget generally will not include any compensation to the developer for the developer's time spent on the project. The developer's compensation and profits will come after the product is on the market, in the form of royalties. A royalty is a payment of some percentage of the gross or net revenues from the sale of the product.

Advances

Often, the publisher pays the developer an advance to help fund the development of a title. Many publishers will not advance funds to produce a title until the developer has shown the publisher a working prototype—not just a demo. Some publishers will advance funds for the developer to create sample art and game play. A prototype is a technologically functional embodiment of the title; it actually proves that the title will work and play as the developer envisions. A demo is just the sample art, sound, and interface design for a project.

Advances are discussed in "Payment," Chapter 20.

A developer who is able to underwrite the development of the prototype will have an easier time convincing a publisher to go with a title. Unfortunately, a struggling, under-funded developer rarely will be able to afford the time and expense required to take a title concept through the prototype phase. Taking a title from concept to prototype can cost between 10% to 30% of the total development costs. Few starting developers have these resources.

Certainly a publisher will expect to see a demo of the title before making an advance to the developer. Publishers are extremely conservative when it comes to judging whether a demo-stage project is worth funding. This is because a publisher must expend a great deal of time, effort, and expense to take a project from the demo stage to the prototype stage.

Recoupment

Advances are usually "recoupable" from royalties due the developer. Recoupment is the repayment to the publisher, out of royalties due the developer, of the advance paid by the publisher to the developer at the start of the project. If an advance is fully recoupable, the developer will receive no royalty payments until the publisher has recovered the advance.

Recoupment is discussed in "Payment," Chapter 20, and in "Payment," Chapter 21.

Publisher paid Developer a $100,000 advance which is recoupable from a 10% royalty on net revenues from the sale of the product. Net revenues are $500,000 in the first quarter and $600,000 in the second quarter. Publisher will be repaid the advance in full in the second quarter. Developer will receive no royalties until the second quarter, when Publisher must pay Developer $10,000.

Only extremely successful title developers would be allowed no recoupment or partial recoupment of their advance.

Policies on advances, royalty rate, and recoupment vary substantially among publishers. Sometimes a developer can get a higher advance by agreeing to accept a lower royalty rate until the development and production costs are recouped, with an increased royalty after these costs are fully recouped by the publisher. Also, it may make sense for a developer to accept a lower royalty rate in exchange for getting the publisher to commit to a healthy marketing budget for the title.

Compensation Factors

There are a number of factors that a publisher and a developer must consider when negotiating the developer's compensation for producing a title. We'll discuss three factors in this section.

Copyright Ownership

See "Scope of the Agreement," Chapter 20.

Who will own the copyright in the title, the developer or the publisher? If the title is based on the developer's concept and the developer will be assigning the copyright to the publisher, the developer may expect the budget to include compensation to the developer for the assignment. This copyright has value, especially if the title turns out to be a hit—in which case, money can be made from licensing sequel rights, rights to develop the title for other platforms, and rights to create ancillary products.

Content Ownership

Licensing third-party content is discussed in Chapter 12.

If the title is based on the developer's concept and the publisher wants a copyright assignment, the publisher may not be willing to pay the developer much for the copyright if the publisher views most of the value of the title as stemming from content owned by the publisher—for example, a multimedia travel guide that makes extensive use of text and photographs belonging to the publisher. The same may be true if the publisher views most of the value as stemming from third-party content which must be licensed.

Tools

Who owns the software tools and technology that will be used in a title— a game engine, for example? If the developer does, the developer may expect compensation for assigning or licensing that technology to the publisher.

Non-royalty Compensation

Compensation does not always take the form of royalties. For example, a publisher who hires a developer to port an existing title to a new platform may prefer to pay the developer a lump sum rather than royalties for the developer's work. If the developer will not be receiving royalties, the budget must include an amount for developer compensation sufficient to pay for the developer's overhead and efforts.

The Funding Process

When a publisher accepts a title proposal based on a demo, the publisher usually wants to approve a prototype prior to committing to the full project and budget. Generally, the formal contract will not be in place until the publisher has approved the prototype. While the prototype is being developed, a signed letter of intent should be used to protect both the publisher and the developer. A signed letter of intent enables all parties to agree on broad budget criteria, milestones, and schedule expectations and reduces the risk of misunderstandings. Negotiation of the full contract generally takes place while the prototype is being developed.

Publishers generally supply funding for a title in increments, as the developer finishes key stages of the title development process. These key stages are known as "milestones." Some typical early-stage milestones are completion of the design document, interface design, the script, and the program code. Typical late-stage milestones are delivery to the publisher of the tested alpha, beta, and "golden master" (final) versions of the title. The contract usually provides that if the developer fails to meet the requirements set out for one of the milestones, the project can either revert to the publisher or be cancelled.

The Schedule

A publisher always will want any component of the full project accomplished in far less time than the developer thinks is needed to create the component. When the project is chosen based on a demo, the publisher generally will want full script development to occur simultaneously with the development of the prototype.

Publisher scheduling is discussed in "Planning for Distribution," Chapter 22.

We recommend that a developer determine the minimum amount of time required for each component of the project and then double that time, reworking the schedule until it can meet *realistic* publisher expectations. A savvy publisher will maximize demands on the developer, but also will know when to back off and trust the developer's judgment.

Accomplishing a start-to-golden master schedule for a project of any complexity in less than nine months is ambitious. A timeline of 12 to 18 months is more viable. How much time is needed will depend on the complexity of the project, the size of the budget, and the resources available to the developer.

Preparing the Budget

A publisher and a developer must come to an agreement on a title budget through a give-and-take process. The budget preparation process is discussed in this section.

Early Decisions

Several crucial decisions must be made before the final budget is created. Those decisions are discussed in this section.

Platform

During the project's design and script development, the preproduction team must choose the platforms for the title. For example, will the title play on a personal computer or on a set-top box such as the Sony Playstation?

Testing Responsibility

Who will be responsible for full multi-platform matrix and compatibility testing? The developer and the publisher should prepare and agree on written testing criteria, including all equipment and peripherals to be tested.

We recommend that compatibility testing be the responsibility of the publisher. It is probably not economically feasible for the developer to set up a compatibility testing department unless the developer is creating multiple titles simultaneously.

If compatibility testing is to be the responsibility of the developer, the developer should use an independent testing service. A developer may choose to contract with an independent testing service for interim testing during the project's production as well as for the final compatibility testing.

See "Motion Pictures and Television," "Video Footage," and "Photographs," Chapter 13.

Type of Visuals and Audio

The preproduction team must make decisions about the general nature of the title's visual and audio components. Possible elements for the visual component include original live action, licensed video footage, animation, still photographs, and graphic art.

Involve the art director in budgeting for animation, still photographs, other non-video art, and interface graphics. Involve a knowledgeable video producer when estimating the costs that are part of the video shoot (actors, union fees, set creation, direction, equipment rental, and licensing video footage). Consult an experienced licensing professional when budgeting for licensing film and video footage and photographs. For original live action shoots, include the cost of a knowledgeable director.

The "audio" category of the budget includes the production of all sound, including the sound components of video shoots. This budget category includes overall sound design, music, voice talent, sound effects, sound studio, and sound engineers. Hiring an experienced audio producer will prove cost effective and result in a higher quality audio production.

Licensing

Licensing content owned by third parties is tedious and time-consuming. If the developer's personnel will be handling the licensing, do not underestimate the amount of personnel time required for licensing.

If the developer does not include an experienced licensing person, consider hiring a licensing professional (see Appendix C for a list). Some licensing professionals specialize in one type of content. Consider using a different licensing specialist for each type of content being licensed—one for music and another for film footage, for example.

Licensing content is expensive. Often, several licenses will be required for a single item of content. Getting the right to use a few seconds of a recording of a song by a popular recording artist, for example, generally will require licenses from the song's copyright owner (a music publisher, most likely); licenses from the sound recording copyright owner (a record company, most likely); and permission from the recording artist and the American Federation of Musicians.

Talent

If the title will include original live action, decide whether the talent will be union or nonunion talent. This decision will have an impact on the budget. If union talent is to be used, the developer must become a signatory to the union's collective bargaining agreement . Once a director commits to using union talent on a project, union talent generally must be used for all performances throughout the project.

Milestones

If publisher funding is to be supplied in increments, as the developer meets milestone requirements, structure the funding so that an interim payment precedes delivery of each milestone. When the publisher accepts a milestone, the publisher should be required to advance the first payment for the work of the next milestone (within seven to 30 days after acceptance of the milestone).

Budget Categories

In this section, we'll describe the budget categories that generally are used in preparing the budget for a multimedia title. A budget preparation form using these categories is in Appendix B (Form 21). Typical budget categories include:

Content licensing is discussed in Chapter 12.

See "Option #2: Using Preexisting Music," Chapter 14.

Entertainment industry unions are discussed in Chapter 16.

➤ **Project design/design document.** The project's designer is the hands-on creator of the overall project and is responsible for designing the overall interactivity, flow, hierarchy, branching, activities, and games in a title. Getting it right in the design phase saves money and time (savings that are always needed as the golden master delivery date approaches). Be sure the designer works in tandem with the lead programmer and the scriptwriter, and that each is consulted when building the project's budget. The designer works full-time from a project's beginning through the first part of production, then should be available for consultation as needed.

➤ **Interface design/art.** The interface designer creates the look and feel of the title. The interface designer works in consultation with the project designer and with the lead programmer. Take advantage of the interface designer's input while building the project's budget. Include funding for the interface designer to work from the project's start through the production phase. Graphic artists will start when the prototype phase begins.

➤ **Story/script/editing.** A script includes the back story, all character dialogue and actor directions, all narrative (text or spoken), and specifications for all visuals for every scene in the title. When estimating the costs, be certain to include fees for editors and proofreaders. An understanding of how the visuals, sound, and activities are integrated is essential to creating the complete script. A project's writer (or writing team) usually begins as soon as the treatment is accepted. Once the final script is accepted, at least one writer should be available part-time as needed for rewrites and revisions.

➤ **Project management.** Usually, there is a project manager on both the developer and publisher sides. On the developer side, the project manager functions as the line producer on the project. He or she is responsible for the delivery of the golden master to the publisher—on time and on budget. The line producer finalizes all creative, budgetary, and technical decisions (with the guidance of others on the production team). The publisher's project manager works mainly as the point person and facilitator, making sure the developer's needs are met, troubleshooting, putting out fires, extending encouragement (helping the developer meet the on time and on budget commitment). Project managers should be involved from the outset of the project.

➤ **Development tools.** In the course of designing an interactive title, a developer may need to purchase special, dedicated software tools for use in the title's creation. While most publishers will fund the developer's purchase of these tools as part of the budget, publishers may be able to furnish them directly to the developer, eliminating the need to include these items in the project's budget. The developer and the publisher are both responsible for making certain that they have any necessary licenses to use the development tool software in a commercial project.

➤ **Programming.** The technology components of a project are probably the most difficult to estimate in a budget. Developers and publishers should take into account whether a title will be built from original code, with off-the-shelf tools such as *Director,* or with a combination. If the title will be developed for more than one platform, create a separate programming budget for each platform. Consider whether the programmers assigned to the project have experience programming on the chosen platforms. If they do not, build in more time for programming.

➤ **Testing.** Publishers expect the developer to do in-house testing of the title on each of the chosen platforms, even if the publisher is responsible for the final compatibility testing. Budget for the proper equipment to test the title at certain points throughout production. Do not try to use the same equipment for production and testing (doing that is likely to create a bottleneck, slowing down production). Consider renting the testing equipment. System requirements and platforms change often, making this equipment obsolete rather quickly.

➤ **Insurance.** Publishers may expect developers to carry Errors and Omission (E&O) insurance as well as intellectual property and general liability insurance. Unless developers have multiple titles in production and can amortize the insurance premium among several titles, E&O insurance is extremely expensive. It may make more sense to add the developer's title to the publisher's insurance (possibly charging back to the developer the added premium expense). This chargeback can be part of the recoupable project cost without being an out-of-pocket expense to the developer. If the publisher insists on the developer providing insurance, the developer should get the publisher to specify the types of coverage and amount. The cost of this coverage should be added to the overhead portion of the budget. The developer also has the right to know the type of insurance the publisher carries.

➤ **Overhead.** Publishers closely scrutinize overhead charged to a title's budget. In all cases, overhead costs should be kept to a minimum. If the developer has several titles under development (or if the development of this title represents only a part of the developer's business), overhead costs should be prorated based on the resource drain of various titles or other projects during the development period. Expenses that belong in the overhead category include equipment rental, insurance, a percentage of office rent, prorated salaries for administrative employees, storage media and office supply costs, one-offs (CD-ROM master discs, usually recorded by the developer), telephone, messenger and shipping costs, legal fees, and travel costs.

➤ **Developer agent fees.** Publishers are likely to be opposed to paying the developer's agent fees as a part of the title's budget. It is best if a developer can find a way to absorb that cost rather than placing the agent's fee as a line item in the budget.

➤ **Contingency.** Most developers add a 5% to 10% contingency fee as a line item for each section of the budget. While publishers prefer developers to complete a title for their original estimate, some publishers accept contingencies as realistic (production cycles often involve unanticipated changes in the title's design specifications, assets, or delivery schedule). Contingency funds usually are released to the developer only on the written approval of the publisher.

➤ **Kill fees.** The purpose of a kill fee is to protect the developer from unexpected cancellation of the project for any reason other than the fault of the developer. For example, marketplace changes or lack of funds might cause a publisher to cancel a title. Generally, kill fees decrease in size as the amount of money a publisher already has spent on your project (through milestone payments) grows. The form and size of a kill fee is highly negotiable. A kill fee could take the form of reversion of all rights to the title back to the developer—or it could be a percentage of the next milestone payment.

Working with a Publisher

The projects that have the greatest chance of actually getting produced are ones for which both the developer and the publisher think the deal they have struck is fair. The best advice for both developers and publishers is to be dependable and make a fair deal.

Here are things you can do to be a dependable developer:

➤ Determine your costs up front and stick to the budget.

➤ Deliver a great title, on time and on budget.

➤ Don't waste production advances (they are part of your income).

➤ Plan carefully to minimize mistakes (they are expensive).

➤ Be prepared to show your publisher where you are spending money.

➤ Tell your publisher how things are going.

A dependable publisher should do the following things to make the developer's work easier:

➤ Send advances when promised (late payments may delay the project).

➤ Assign a competent in-house producer.

➤ Build a relationship with your developer.

➤ Involve the developer in the marketing and PR processes.

➤ Deliver what you promised in terms of support.

Linda Rich has more than 10 years of experience in the interactive multimedia industry. She has published, developed, and produced award-winning interactive products for Warner New Media, Media Vision Publishing, and The Record Group. In 1995, she formed CHARLIE Entertainment, an interactive multimedia company that develops original interactive games and edutainment programming for PCs and on-line services. Rich is the author of two photography books; her photographs are in the permanent collections of several museums. Her address is 6050 Woodland View Drive, Woodland Hills, CA 91367; telephone (818) 346-6807; fax (818) 346-6665; email richlinda@aol.com.

Darlene de Monfried has managed creative businesses for more than 23 years. For the past five years, she has worked in the interactive entertainment industry. At Media Vision Publishing and Warner New Media, de Monfried negotiated and managed contracts with artists, developers, licensing agencies, and production groups. She also was responsible for budgeting, scheduling, and testing of multimedia projects. Currently she is a business management consultant. Her address is 10947 Bloomfield, #308, Toluca Lake, CA 91602; telephone (818) 985-5456.

10 Writing for Multimedia

by Larry Kay

There are many reasons to include a writer in a multimedia project. Sometimes a writer is brought onboard at the very beginning. Perhaps a multimedia software development company or publisher has an idea for a project, and needs to hire a writer and/or interactive designer. Or maybe it's the writer/designer who has the original concept, treatment, script, or design document and needs a software development company or publisher to actualize the title. Or perhaps a producer, software developer, or publisher has licensed an existing literary work, such as a book or movie property, and now needs a writer/designer to make the project interactive. Or perhaps an educator or trainer has some educational or instructional goals and objectives that could be met via an interactive project.

Sometimes a writer is brought onto a project that's already well underway. Perhaps that educator or trainer has an excellent curriculum and workbook, but the materials need to be re-purposed for an interactive product. Or a company may bring a writer on in mid-project, where an outline has been constructed and a number of assets (such as video, audio, stills, animation, and graphics) have been produced and now a writer must organize all this material. Or maybe the project is a new revision of an already-existing reference title, and a writer is needed to write new articles. Or the project could be one in which the concept is fully developed and written by a designer or design team, but now it's time to write the whole thing. Perhaps it's an already-existing project that just needs a dialogue polish.

Each of the above models sets into motion a different combination of legal issues. This chapter synthesizes these issues into a few key areas: scope, compensation, ownership, and confidentiality.

Scope Issues

Make no mistake about it, a good multimedia project typically requires a truckload of writing, rewriting, and polishing. Every good project evolves, iterates, changes, expands, and contracts through successive drafts as it comes to life. Oftentimes, the trickiest part about engaging the multimedia writer on a project is to determine accurately the scope of the writing. Most good multimedia writers find themselves faced with interactive design decisions in mid-project.

For a producer, who will follow a project all the way through the entire software development cycle from concept to finished product, the least expensive and most effective approach to navigating these inevitable and desirable changes is to discover and make the right changes as early as possible. It becomes far more expensive to make changes once assets have been produced and once software code has been written. Thus, for the producer, the most cost-effective time to make these changes is during the initial design and writing phase. This places a substantial responsibility and burden on the writer's shoulders. For the benefit of the writer, the producer, and the project, the scope of the written work must be determined in advance.

The scope of a writer's contribution to a project can be determined in a number of ways. But even with the best of intentions, none of these ways can absolutely predetermine what the writer will end up writing, what the producer will end up wanting, and what the project will end up needing. But we still need ways by which a writer and a producer can agree in advance about the scope of an assignment. Here are some suggestions on how to do that.

Milestones

Usually the best way to begin to determine scope is to break down the writing assignment into milestones: a set of written deliverables and time deadlines. A dialogue polish might have just one milestone, while an assignment for writing and design of a full project might include several milestones: written concept, synopsis, treatment, creative design document, and technical design document.

Concept

Some written concepts can be presented adequately in a one-sentence TV log line, while others need 10 pages to convey adequately the focus of the project. For example, if the project is a training or educational CD-ROM, the concept typically would include an overview of basic learning goals, the interactive methodology, and the creative elements. By contrast, the concept for an entertainment title could simply be the title of a hit movie and a game genre, such as "*Driving Miss Daisy*: the racing simulator." An edutainment concept proposal using a brand new, original set of characters or creative concept might include an overview of each of the elements, as well as the educational goals and the entertainment paradigm.

Synopsis

The synopsis builds upon the written concept. It begins to organize the material into an interactive paradigm and to dive a little deeper into details. A synopsis might be two pages or 20 pages.

Treatment

In the treatment, the material really begins to take shape. The interface, interactive paradigm, and methodology is designed in some detail. The overall structure is outlined, and emphases are well-understood. Key characters begin to come to life. The educational or training goals become concrete objectives. Sample interactivity is presented in rough form. Some professionals view the treatment as a more detailed synopsis, while others see it as the document where most of the key creative decisions are presented. Thus, at this phase, the length of the treatment can vary greatly depending on the approach taken. A good treatment might be 20 pages or as much as 175 pages.

Design Document

Building upon the treatment, the design document details the specific interactivity for the entire project. It often incorporates some technical information from the designer (who also may be the writer), software engineering, the art department, and physical production. The design document is the blueprint for actualizing the interactive product. Design documents vary the widest, from 20 pages for a very modest project to well beyond 350 pages for a multi-disk extravaganza.

Page Count

A producer might think "the more pages the better." And while that may be true during the brainstorm phase, the inverse is more likely when it comes time to actualize a product based on the written material. When making the writer's agreement, defining page count is useful, but be aware that page count can be misleading. It's often helpful to identify a page count range that both the writer and producer believe is appropriate. Sometimes the written deliverables from a previous project can be used as guidelines for defining the page count of a new project. Be mindful, however, that no two projects are alike.

One way to harm a successful relationship between writer and producer is to present unreasonable expectations on page count, whereupon the writer dutifully delivers the required behemoth document, only to have it go unread or uncommented on until production time where, under the crush of production deadlines, cuts are made haphazardly, and the project quality suffers greatly.

Comment Period

Each time a writer submits a writing assignment, the producer has the obligation to read it and comment on it in a timely fashion. A good agreement usually specifies a comment period for each milestone (usually three to ten working days), plus a time period for one set of revisions based on comments. Good comments take effort. Good comments are a combination of written summary comments, plus mark-up directly on the deliverable, as well as oral discussion between the writer and producer. If a number of people are giving feedback, it is best for the writer to report to a single point person, typically the producer, creative director, or executive. All of this should be defined in the agreement.

Here is an example of a good writer/producer relationship suddenly in danger. An overburdened producer doesn't have time this particular week to give adequate comments on a 50-page treatment; the comment period expires and the milestone is paid without sufficient comment. So, now the writer goes back thinking everything is fine, puts on the harness, and rockets through a 150-page first draft of the design document. This time the producer sets aside two days to really pore over this next draft, and the producer finds a number of revisions that relate to the treatment draft that should have been picked up during the previous milestone review. A reasonable producer working with a reasonable writer will work out some reasonable compromise at the time that this occurs, but it is difficult to account for this kind of a situation with predetermined contract language.

Revisions

The joke goes, "How many writers does it take to change a light bulb?" The bemused but wary writer answers, "Does it have to be changed?" And how many producers does it take to change a light bulb? The ever-eager producer answers, "Does it have to be a light bulb?"

Another vital component in defining scope is to predetermine a reasonable policy on revisions. Any material can always be rewritten again and again and again. When is a writer finished? What is the difference between a polish and a rewrite? When is a revision not a revision, but rather a request for additional writing? The answers to these questions are not easily predetermined. The relationship between writer and producer works best when both parties are reasonable and clear about the revisions policy.

If revisions are agreed to, then a limit of one revision per milestone is reasonable. For revisions to be meaningful, the producer must be able to give sufficient feedback to the writer.

Writers with solid reputations in the industry are paid upon *delivery* of each milestone, rather than on the client's *acceptance* of the deliverable. In this model, all rewrites are defined as additional milestones.

Extending the Scope

Once the writing is complete and production and software development are underway, it is not uncommon to discover new writing needs after the writer has fulfilled the initial contract.

It is often desirable to bring back a writer for a polish during the software development phase. One way to handle this is casually, to re-hire the writer on a daily or weekly rate. But oftentimes a writer will not be available on a casual basis many months later. To guarantee a writer's future availability, the initial agreement could include a provision for a guaranteed retainer paid to the writer.

If the writer is not available at a future date, the producer will need to bring in an additional writer. Since the additional writer is rewriting the first writer, it may become necessary for the producer to procure the right to rewrite the original writer's work.

Compensation Issues

Multimedia writers can be compensated in both monetary and non-monetary terms. Monetary compensation can be calculated as flat fees, word count rates, or time rates. The most important non-monetary compensation is a writer's credits.

How Much Money

When budgeting a multimedia project, a rule of thumb is to allocate 5% to 10% of the entire project budget for writing and interactive design services. For a $500,000 project, that translates into $25,000 to $50,000 for the writer(s)/designer(s). That's quite a large range; there are no standard rates in this young industry.

Flat Fees

Using the 5% to 10% of total budget as a guide, a principal writer/designer can receive a flat fee of from around $5,000 to upwards of $60,000 or more for an assignment that lasts between one and six months. Some writers and producers find it useful for their own calculations to analyze these flat fees as weekly and hourly rates. Doing this arithmetic also helps each party to determine a rate for additional work, if it is required.

Time-Based Rates

There is no standard effective hourly rate for writers. As of this writing, some say that the beginning writer should work up to earning an effective hourly rate of $35 an hour ($280 per day), and that more experienced writers will earn an effective hourly rate of $50 to $75 per hour ($400 to $600 per day). Expert writers earn above that—sometimes well above that. A writer's pay rate also is determined by the budget of the particular project, the market for the product, and ordinary supply and demand dynamics in the negotiation between writer and producer.

Most writers, when charging on an hourly rate basis, figure a minimum number of hours such as a half-day minimum guarantee, or at least a two-hour guarantee. Many writers working on a flat fee basis have a policy of charging an additional hourly rate for extra meetings beyond the scope of the original agreement.

Word Count Rates

For short assignments where scope is clearly understood, it may be most appropriate to pay a writer on a word count basis. This is analogous to freelance magazine writing assignments, and is a model occasionally used on reference titles or titles that have a number of short, well-defined modules that appear as on-screen text or as brief, voice-over narration. There are no standards or even meaningful ranges for word count pay rates, which also are common in the magazine industry. Producers and writers may find it helpful to use comparable magazine word count rates as benchmarks.

Advances

Whether the writer is compensated in flat fees or time-based rates, it is customary to pay a writer an advance. Without an advance, the writer must consider the work as speculative writing. For a brief, one-week assignment that has a clearly defined and limited set of tasks, a writer typically might receive a 50% fee to commence. By contrast, in a large project that extends from concept to final design document and has four milestones (synopsis, treatment, design document first draft, and design document final draft) might require an advance payment of 20% to 35%.

Kill Fees

Sometimes a writer performs quite well but is terminated at the producer's convenience: not because the writer failed to turn in an assignment, but because the producer's or publisher's plans have changed. For this reason, it is customary on lengthy projects to agree to a kill fee. Kill fees range from the writer being paid through the current milestone to some predetermined percentage of the balance of all of the milestones. Some writers, who are in particularly high demand, also can negotiate a pay-or-play provision, which guarantees the writer will be paid for the entire project (unless the writer fails to deliver) even if the producer's plans change for convenience.

Bonuses and Royalties

Bonuses based on sales and royalties are an increasingly valuable part of the writer's deal. But for some classes of product, such as in-house corporate multimedia, there are no sales of the finished multimedia project to generate any additional revenues for anybody. And even if the writer commands a decent royalty payment rate or bonus amount for a title to be sold via retail stores, that doesn't guarantee that the title will sell enough units to make those points worth anything. Ultimately, every royalty or bonus deal is speculative and should be evaluated carefully in conjunction with the portion of the deal that actually guarantees compensation. As the multimedia software market grows, royalties and bonuses will become increasingly valuable.

Royalties are often based on a percentage of the wholesale price and, therefore, payouts to the writer vary as the price varies. Units sold into the domestic retail channel generally have the highest and most easy-to-calculate wholesale price. Anytime the terms "net" or "adjusted gross" are introduced into the formula for calculating rate-based royalties, these terms must be defined and evaluated based on those definitions.

The value of units sold into international markets can vary from territory to territory, as a publisher typically will have other distributors in those countries with which it must share revenues. Units sold into OEM bundles (for example, a bundle of software titles offered as an inducement to buy a new computer or CD-ROM drive) often can be sold for as little as one dollar. It is important for the writer to know as much detail as possible about the projected sales targets and the company's previous track record in order to evaluate the residual offer.

Net and gross revenues as well as bundling are discussed in "Payment," Chapter 20.

Instead of a percentage royalty deal, some companies structure a flat bonus when unit sales of the title reach specific thresholds. Some royalty rates or bonus amounts escalate once the sales of the title reach higher levels.

When a writer licenses an original work to a publisher or developer, then that company typically pays the writer a higher royalty rate, plus a bonus when the project enters production and software development.

Audit rights are becoming increasingly standard, but the cost of an audit to a writer can be expensive. It is not uncommon to see contract language stating that the cost of the audit is borne by the publisher if there is a large discrepancy.

Credits

Credits are a valuable part of the writer's compensation. Credits are currency. Credits are one important way that the writer can self-promote and demonstrate career advancement. Credits can appear on screen, in the product documentation, on the box, and in advertisements, promotions, and public relations.

Screen credits can be placed in a hyperlinked file and, particularly in multimedia entertainment products, also may appear automatically at the beginning or end of the game. One's credit can appear together with other credits on a screen, or more valuably placed on a separate screen or "card." In television and film, credits are determined by the Writers Guild of America. Although some WGA writers work in multimedia, the Guild currently recommends, but does not determine, proper multimedia credits.

Credits in product documentation are considered quite valuable. In fact, more people notice documentation credits than screen credits. The most substantial credit is to have one's name printed on the box, but these credits are rare.

Other Compensation

It is customary to provide the writer/designer with free copies of each stock-keeping unit (SKU) of the title, and allow the writer to purchase promotional copies (not for resale) at cost.

A forward-thinking producer also provides in the budget and agreement funds for expenses, especially during the deadline crunch when phone, fax, email, express mail, travel, and working meals escalate. The producer of even the most well-organized project will find it useful to have an adequate contingency set aside for writing and design services. After all, writing occurs at the beginning of a project when there are the most creative unknowns and when the scope of a project can shift dramatically. The producer's goal is to conserve funds, and an extra dollar spent during the writing and design phase can save ten dollars during production and software development.

Ownership Issues

Copyright Assignment

Traditionally, when a writer is engaged to write an assignment on a property that is owned by another company, that company will retain the copyright to the work. As a rule of thumb, when a writer is a staff writer (IRS W2) under the producer's full-time employ, then a staff employment contract typically will carry some language about writing for hire and copyright assignment. When a writer is brought in as an independent contractor (IRS 1099), then a separate copyright assignment agreement should be executed in addition to the independent contract agreement or deal memo.

When a writer creates an original intellectual or literary property (for example, concept, treatment, script, set of characters), then that writer owns those copyrights until selling them. Multimedia publishers and developers understand the value of an excellent original creation and will often attempt to buy the property with all associated rights (i.e., sequels, exploitation in other media, merchandising). It is strongly advised that the writer engage a knowledgeable, experienced attorney to negotiate these rights.

> Copyright ownership is discussed in Chapters 4, 7, and 8.

Option Agreements

The option agreement is a common practice in film, television, and book publishing, and is just beginning to make its way into the multimedia industry. In an option agreement, the writer/owner of the literary property grants to a company for a specified time period an exclusive opportunity to secure specified rights to the project, in exchange for an option fee, which is a small percentage of the purchase price or license fee. The company has the option, but not the obligation to go forward with the property. The option is a relatively low-cost way for a company to maintain an active interest in a project and keep competition at bay while evaluating whether it really wants to spend the money to actually license the project or buy it outright. If the company decides not to buy or license the project, the company simply lets the option expire and the writer keeps the option fee.

Presently, there is a trend where publishers are trying to buy all rights, or at least all electronic rights, to a given property while writers and creators are trying to maintain as many rights as possible. And to further complicate the scene, the technological landscape continues to change rapidly as the traditional media converge with the interactive media. A creative option agreement may be the best solution for both parties to move forward while potentially protracted decision-making continues.

Confidentiality Issues

When the Publisher or Producer Needs Confidentiality

Protecting confidentiality is often extremely important in a project.

A producer or publisher may require the writer to sign a confidentiality agreement, a nondisclosure agreement (NDA), or a mutual NDA for the duration of the project. A contract usually provides that the writer can discuss the project in general terms. The NDA should have a time limit on it and state that information that is publicly known would not have to be kept secret by the writer. Some producers or publishers allow writers to use a small writing sample from the project to show to a writer's prospective future clients.

One difficulty in maintaining secrecy is that a project can continue for a year or longer during software development and production phase, after the writer has finished the assignment. The writer, eager to advance, needs to be able to tell future prospective clients what he or she has been working on recently.

Nondisclosure agreements are discussed in "The Contract," Chapter 6.

When the Writer Needs Confidentiality

Sometimes it's the writer who presents the NDA to a publisher or developer. When a creator presents a business opportunity to a company, the creator may ask the company to sign an NDA. Some parties (including some writers) will not sign an NDA, because they actually may be working on a similar or competitive idea or project. In fact, some publishers require the writer who is submitting an original project or concept to sign a submission agreement, which states that the publisher may indeed be developing a similar project and that no confidentiality or business obligation is implied.

Most companies are not in business to steal from writers and want to maintain good relations with the writer community. Generally, companies will pay gladly for a valuable project. But it's always best for a writer to know the reputation of company when considering whether to submit an original creative property. And a writer should document all submissions, track rejections, and follow up professionally. Some writers prefer to send out material through a proper agent or attorney, and some companies will accept a writer's creative proposal only through an agent or attorney.

Care and Feeding

So-called "standard" writers' agreements, where all the deal terms are known and there is nothing to be negotiated, are virtually nonexistent in the young multimedia industry. There will be, and should be, negotiation between the writer and producer/publisher. These negotiations are best handled between a writer's agent and/or attorney and the producer's or publisher's business/

legal affairs officer so that the relationship between writer and producer can be focused on creative issues.

Keep in mind that the writer/designer is often brought on at the very beginning of the project, when many questions are unanswered or not even asked. At the beginning of a project, there are typically a number of vague ideas kicking around among a number of people. Part of the writer's job is to interpret, synthesize, and reconcile all these ideas. Sometimes a writer can be caught in the crossfire of competing ideas between, say, a producer and a publisher, or even between two executives at the same company. In the best situations, creative ideas are shared freely during the initial design and writing phase. But when it's time to make creative decisions, projects do better when all parties leave their egos at the door and all abide by the ultimate decisions.

It is also important to keep in mind that most writers are free-lancers, independent contractors, IRS 1099s who must pay their own taxes and who have their own overhead to support. A good producer or publisher is sensitive to this reality by setting in advance a finite number and length of meetings and by using meeting time effectively.

Ultimately, a successful writer/producer relationship is evaluated some-what subjectively, with terms not easily quantifiable or only vaguely definable in a contract—terms such as "quality," "innovative," "communicates clearly," "great structure," "sharp dialogue," "adequate production resources," "productive meetings," "a delight to work with," "team player," and so forth. And like all relationships, it takes two partners actively working in inherently challenging situations with unknowable futures to make a successful one.

Larry Kay is a multimedia writer and game designer. His credits include the award-winning *Freddi Fish and the Case of the Missing Kelp Seeds* for Humongous Entertainment; *Muppet Treasure Island* for Activision; *9* for Tribeca/GTE Interactive; and his original creation, *TOOBERS Surf and Destroy* in association with Toonsmiths and MediaX, published by Grolier Interactive. Kay consults on new media projects for select clients, including: Brøderbund, Disney, Silicon Graphics, and Vortex Media Arts. His address is Toonsmiths®, 15466 Los Gatos Blvd., Suite 109, Los Gatos, CA 95032; email: KayLarry@aol.com.

Part 3

Other Production Issues

11 Using Preexisting Works

Every time you use a copyrighted work owned by a third party, you must determine whether it is necessary to obtain a license from the owner. For most uses, a license should be obtained.

The first two sections of this chapter discuss when you do and don't need a license to use a copyrighted work. The third section covers the use of public domain works. The fourth section covers the use of works that you own. On-line uses of copyrighted works are covered in Chapter 23, and special aspects of educational use in Chapter 24.

When You Need a License

You need a license to use a third party's copyrighted work if your intended use of the work would, without a license, infringe any of the copyright owner's exclusive rights. To use material from a copyrighted work owned by a third party in a multimedia product, you will copy the work and possibly modify it. Therefore, you need a license unless "fair use" or one of the other exceptions to the owner's rights applies. (Exceptions are discussed in "When You Don't Need a License," later in this chapter.)

See "The Exclusive Rights," Chapter 2.

Myths

There are a number of myths concerning the necessity of getting a license. Don't make the mistake of believing them:

Myth #1: "I don't need a license because I'm using only a small amount of the copyrighted work."

It is true that de minimis copying (copying a small amount) is not copyright infringement. Unfortunately, it is rarely possible to tell where de minimis copying ends and copyright infringement begins. There are no "bright line" rules.

Copying a small amount of a copyrighted work is infringement if what is copied is a qualitatively substantial portion of the copied work. In one case, a magazine article that used 300 words from a 200,000-word autobiography written by President Gerald Ford was found to infringe the copyright on the autobiography. Even though the copied material was only a small part of the autobiography, the copied portions were among the most powerful passages in the autobiography. *Harper & Row Publishers, Inc. v. Nation Enterprises,* 471 U.S. 539 (1985).

Copying any part of a copyrighted work is risky. If what you copy is truly a tiny and nonmemorable part of the work, you may get away with it (the work's owner may not be able to tell that your work incorporates an excerpt from the owner's work). However, you run the risk of having to defend your use in expensive litigation. If what you are copying is tiny, but recognizable as coming from the protected work, it is better to get a license (unless fair use or one of the other exceptions discussed in "When You Don't Need a License," later in this chapter, applies). You cannot escape liability for infringement by showing how much of the protected work you did not take.

Myth #2: "I paid for the tape (compact disc, videotape) that I'm going to copy, so I already have the permission I need."

Copyright law distinguishes between ownership of the copyright in a work and ownership of a copy of the work. Purchasing a copy of a work (a tape, compact disc, videotape, book, photographic print) does not give you permission to exercise the exclusive rights of copyright. You can resell and display your copy, but that's all.

See "Owning a Copy of a Work," Chapter 4.

Myth #3: "I didn't know I needed a license. Because my infringement was innocent rather than intentional, I'm not liable for infringement damages."

Lack of intent to infringe is not a defense to infringement—nor is ignorance of the copyright law.

In a recent case involving innocent infringement, a federal appellate court refused to dismiss a case brought against Sara Lee Corporation for unauthorized distribution of books by Sara Lee. Sara Lee Corporation thought it was getting its copies of the book from an authorized distributor. Between the copyright owner and an innocent infringer, the court reasoned, the innocent infringer rather than the copyright owner should suffer. *Pinkham v. Sara Lee Corp.*, 983 F.2d 824 (8th Cir. 1992).

Myth #4: "I don't need a license because my multimedia work will only be used in-house by my client. It will never be shown or marketed to the public."

Technically, you need a license to copy even if you are the only one who will ever use your multimedia work. The Copyright Act does not permit copying for "private use" other than under the "fair use" doctrine.

 Marty's multimedia work, The Country and Western Music Treasury, includes scanned photographs of a number of singers. Even if Marty created the work entirely for his own private use, he has exercised the reproduction right for each photograph. Unless his use is fair use, he should have gotten licenses from the copyright owners. He also should have acquired releases from each singer (see "The Rights of Publicity and Privacy," Chapter 15).

How a work will be shown or used is relevant in determining whether you need permission to exercise the public performance right. Even if you don't need a license for public performance, you need a license to copy a third party's copyrighted work into your multimedia work and to "distribute" to a client a copy of the multimedia work that contains the third party's work.

See "Determining What Rights You Need," Chapter 12.

Myth #5: "I don't need a license because I'm making this multimedia work for a nonprofit group."

Copying for educational or public service use may be fair use but is not necessarily fair use. Type of use is one of the factors that determines whether a use is fair or unfair. Other factors must be considered. (Fair use is discussed in "When You Don't Need a License," later in this chapter.) Even if you are creating a multimedia work for an educational or public service group, you should get a license. Maybe you can get the copyright owners whose works you use to waive the licensing fee to help a good cause.

Myth #6: "I don't need a license because no one will ever have to pay a fee to see my multimedia work."

Whether a fee is charged for public performances of a work is relevant in some situations for determining whether a public performance license is needed (see "Using Copyrighted Materials for Fund-raisers," Chapter 24). It is irrelevant in determining whether a license is needed for copying. Even if it's true that no one will ever pay to see your work, you need a license to copy if you use a third party's copyrighted work (unless fair use or one of the other exceptions in "When You Don't Need a License," later in this chapter, applies).

Myth #7: "My multimedia work will be a wonderful showcase for the copyright owner's song, so I'm sure the owner will not object to my use of the song."

Don't assume that a copyright owner will be happy to have you use his or her work. Even if the owner is willing to let you use the work, the owner probably will want to charge you a license fee.

Myth #8: "The work I want to use doesn't have a copyright notice on it, so it's not copyrighted. I'm free to use it."

For works published on or after March 1, 1989, the use of copyright notice is optional. The fact that a work doesn't have a copyright notice doesn't mean that the work is not protected by copyright. Unless you have good reason to believe a work is in the public domain (see "Public Domain Works," later in this chapter), assume that it is protected by copyright and get a license.

Myth #9: "The developer who created the work I want to use never bothered to file a copyright registration application, so the work is uncopyrighted. I'm free to use it."

Copyright protection arises automatically when an original work of authorship is fixed in a tangible medium of expression. Registration is optional. Checking the Copyright Office's registration files is a good way to find out who owns a registered copyright. It's not a good way to determine whether a work is protected by copyright.

See "Determining Who Owns the Copyright," Chapter 12.

Myth #10: "Since I'm planning to give credit to all authors whose works I copy, I don't need to get licenses."

If you give credit to a work's author, you are not a plagiarist (you are not pretending that you authored the copied work). However, attribution is not a defense to copyright infringement.

Myth #11: "I don't need a license because I'm going to alter the work I copy."

You cannot escape liability for copyright infringement by altering or modifying the work you copy. You can use a copyrighted work's unprotected elements, as discussed in "When You Don't Need a License," later in this chapter, but if you copy and modify protected elements of a copyrighted work, you will be infringing the copyright owner's modification right as well as the copying right. If the work is a "work of visual art," you also may be infringing the owner's rights under the Visual Artists Rights Act.

The Visual Artists Rights Act is discussed in Chapter 12.

Myth #12: "If I paraphrase the author's words rather than use the author's words verbatim, I won't need a license."

Paraphrasing can be copyright infringement. Infringement is not limited to word-for-word copying. If the paraphrased version of a protected work copies the work's protected "expression"—which is more than the words alone—the paraphrased version infringes the copyright on the original work.

Myth #13: "Rather than just scanning in the copyrighted cartoon character I want to use, I'll hire an illustrator to create my own version of the cartoon character. That way, I won't need a license."

Using an illustrator's version of a character is copyright infringement if the illustrator copied the protected character. If you tell the illustrator, "Draw me a character that looks like Garfield," the illustrator's character will be a copy of Garfield (assuming the illustrator is competent). If you can't afford a merchandise license to use a protected character, or the owner will not grant you a license, create your own original characters.

See "Logos and Characters," Chapter 13.

Myth #14: "We've used this song (photo, design, and so on) in our productions in the past, so we don't need to get a license to use the work now."

Don't assume that past use was licensed use. Even if the past use was licensed, the license may not cover your use now because the license may have authorized one-time use only, or may have been limited in duration, or there may have been other restrictions. If use has been licensed in the past, check the license to determine whether it authorizes the use you are planning.

Myth #15: "The author of the work that I want to use lives in England, so the work is not protected by copyright in the United States."

Do not assume that a work lacks copyright protection in the United States because its author is a foreigner. Foreign authors who live in countries that belong to the Berne Convention or the Universal Copyright Convention automatically obtain copyright protection here. Most major countries are members of at least one of these conventions.

See "International Protection," Chapter 2.

When You Don't Need a License

There are several situations in which you can use a copyrighted work without getting a license. We'll discuss them in this section.

Fair Use

You don't need a license to use a copyrighted work if your use is "fair use." Unfortunately, it is difficult to tell whether a particular use of a work is fair or unfair. Determinations are made on a case-by-case basis by considering four factors:

➤ **Purpose and character of use.** The courts are most likely to find fair use where the use is "transformative" and for educational or other non-commercial purposes. The use of a copyrighted work to create a new work is "transformative" if the new work adds some additional element or has a different character or serves a different purpose. Non-transformative use—where the new work merely serves the same objectives as the original work, or supersedes it—is less likely to be fair use.

➤ **Nature of the copyrighted work.** The courts are most likely to find fair use where the copied work is a factual work or a work that has already been distributed. They are least likely to find fair use where the copied work is creative or fictitious, or the work has never before been published.

➤ **Amount and substantiality of portion used.** The courts are most likely to find fair use where what is used is a tiny amount of the protected work. They are least likely to find fair use where much of the protected work is used. If what is used is small in amount but substantial in terms of importance—the heart of the copied work—a finding of fair use is unlikely.

➤ **Effect on the potential market for or value of the protected work.** The courts are most likely to find fair use where the new work is not a substitute for the copyrighted work. They are least likely to find fair use where the new work is a complete substitute for the copyrighted work.

If you are creating a multimedia work for purely noncommercial purposes—for example, for use by the American Red Cross for training—it is possible that you can justify copying small amounts of material as fair use.

Fair use also is discussed in chapters 23 and 24.

If your work is designed for commercial use of any sort—for sale to consumers, for use in retail stores, or even for internal training use in for-profit corporations—it will be hard to succeed on a fair use defense.

If your multimedia work serves traditional "fair use" purposes—criticism, comment, news reporting, teaching, scholarship, and research—you have a better chance of falling within the bounds of fair use than you do if your work is sold to the public for entertainment purposes.

"Reverse Engineering" of Software

In a dispute between Sega and Accolade over Accolade's "reverse engineering" of the control software for Sega's game player, a federal appellate court has held that copying software for such purposes is fair use if it is necessary to understand the ideas and processes used in a copyrighted work. ("Reverse engineering" is taking a product apart to see how it works.) The copying must not exceed what is necessary to understand the unprotected elements of the copied work. *Sega Enterprises, Ltd. v Accolade, Inc., 977* F. 2d 1510 (9th Cir. 1992).

An important element of the *Sega-Accolade* decision was that the Accolade game software did not compete with the copied Sega software. Whether it is permissible to reverse-engineer software to create a competitive product has not yet been decided.

Home Videotaping

Several years ago, in the so-called Betamax case filed against Sony by several motion picture studios, the Supreme Court found that home videotaping of television programs with VCRs was noninfringing fair use. The Court's decision was based on the four-factor analysis discussed in "Fair Use," earlier in this chapter. The Supreme Court emphasized that a study showed that most home VCR users taped television programs for noncommercial, time-shifting purposes (so they could watch the copied programs at a more convenient time). *Sony Corp. v. Universal City Studios, Inc.,* 464 U.S. 417 (1984).

The Betamax case does not say that all videotaping of television programs is fair use. Don't rely on the case to justify videotaping television programs or movies for use in multimedia works.

Other Noninfringing Uses

You don't need a license to copy facts from a protected work, to copy ideas from a protected work, or to parody a protected work.

Copying Facts

The copyright on a work does not extend to the work's facts. This is because copyright protection is limited to original works of authorship, and no one can claim originality or authorship for facts. You are free to copy facts from a copyrighted work.

See "Standards," Chapter 2.

 Susan spent months and thousands of dollars researching President Kennedy's assassination. She discovered a number of never-before-known facts about Lee Harvey Oswald. She reported her discoveries in a book. The copyright on Susan's book does not protect the facts that Susan discovered.

Copying Ideas

Copyright does not protect a work's ideas, processes, or systems. You are free to copy these elements.

 John's copyrighted book explains a new system of bookkeeping created by John. While John's copyright protects his expression in the book (his description of the bookkeeping system), it does not protect the system itself or the ideas that make up the system. Others are free to study John's book, figure out and use the bookkeeping system, and even write their own books describing the system.

Copying Facts

While you are free to copy a work's facts, you must express those facts in your own work in your own way. One writer recently lost on his "historical fact" defense to infringement because the court found that he had taken not just the copyrighted work's facts, but also its "organization, writing style, even punctuation and passed it off as his own." *Robinson v. Random House, Inc.,* 877 F. Supp. 830 (S.D.N.Y. 1995).

Unfortunately, the line between ideas and "expression" is difficult even for experienced attorneys to draw. Only a few generalizations are possible:

➤ A work's theme or purpose—for example, training telemarketers or helping consumers pick wine—is an unprotected idea.

➤ Stock characters and situations are unprotected ideas. Examples of stock characters are the jealous boyfriend, proud grandparents, and starving artist. Examples of stock situations are the conflict between a parent and a teenaged child and the rivalry between two siblings. So-called "distinctively delineated" characters, such as Tarzan, E.T., and Indiana Jones, are protected by copyright and possibly by trademark as well.

➤ A novel's detailed plot is protected expression, even though stock situations within the plot are not protected.

If there is only one way to express an idea (or only a limited number of ways), you can copy the expression as well as the idea. For example, one case permitted the copying of a set of game rules because there were only a limited number of ways to express rules for that type of game. Because this concept, called the "merger" principle, is complex, you should consult an experienced copyright attorney before you rely on it.

Parody

You can copy a protected work for purposes of parodying or satirizing the protected work. Parody is considered fair use if the parody does not replace the copyrighted work in the marketplace, and if no more of the copyrighted work is used than is necessary. In 1994, the Supreme Court heard a case in which a music publisher was suing a rap group for creating a parody of the publisher's song, "Oh, Pretty Woman." The Court held that the rap group's parody of the song could be fair use even though the group's use was for "a blatantly commercial purpose," because parody "can provide social benefit, by shedding light on an earlier work, and in the process, creating a new one." *Campbell v. Acuff-Rose Music, Inc.,* 114 S. Ct. 1164 (1994).

Idea or Expression?

In a recent infringement case involving two interactive football games, the court held that the concept of a predictive football game and the concept of awarding points were unprotected ideas. A particular scoring system, however, was found to be protected expression. *Interactive Network Inc., v. NTN Communications,* 875 F. Supp. 1398 (N.D. Cal. 1995).

See "Logos and Characters," Chapter 13.

Stock Characters and Situations

In the classic case involving use of stock characters and situations, plaintiff claimed defendant's motion picture infringed the copyright on the plaintiff's play. What the play and the motion picture had in common were a quarrel between a Jewish and Irish father, the marriage of their children, the birth of grandchildren, and a reconciliation. The court held that the plaintiff did not have a monopoly on these characters and situations and that the defendant's motion picture did not infringe plaintiff's copyright by using them. *Nichols v. Universal Pictures Corp.,* 45 F. 2d 119 (2d Cir. 1930).

Public Domain Works

You don't need a license to use a public domain work. Public domain works—works not protected by copyright—can be used by anyone. Because these works are not copyrighted, no one can claim the exclusive rights of copyright for such works.

The rules regarding what works are in the public domain vary from country to country. A work in the public domain in the United States may be protected by copyright in Canada or other countries.

There are several ways in which works fall into the public domain in the United States:

> **Notice Problems**
> Most of the Unix operating system is in the public domain because copies were publicly distributed without notice. Recently, the song "How Can I Keep From Singing" was held to be in the public domain because it was published with defective notice (notice was in the name of the magazine in which the song was published rather than in the name of the copyright owner). Sanga Music, Inc., v. EMI Blackwood Music, Inc., 55 F. 3rd. 756 (2d Cir. 1995).

> ➤ **Expiration of the copyright.** A copyright that was in existence before January 1, 1978, and was renewed, has a term of 75 years. All copyright terms run to the end of the calendar year in which they expire. Consequently, in 1996, all works first "published" before January 1, 1921, are in the public domain in the United States.

> ➤ **Failure of the copyright owner to renew the copyright.** Under the 1909 Copyright Act, copyright protection lasted 28 years. A copyright owner could obtain an additional term, known as a "renewal term," by filing an application to renew in the twenty-eighth year. The Copyright Renewal Amendment of 1992 eliminated the requirement of filing a renewal application for works published between 1964 and 1977, inclusive. Renewal is not required for works created after 1977. However, before 1992, a number of works entered the public domain because the copyright owner failed to file a renewal application. For works to which the renewal requirement applies, you can find out whether the owner renewed the copyright by ordering a Copyright Office renewal search. The provisions on renewal are complex, and you should get an experienced attorney or rights clearance agent to help you determine how those rules apply to a particular work.

See "Determining Who Owns the Copyright," Chapter 12, for a discussion of Copyright Office searches.

> ➤ **Failure to use copyright notice on publicly distributed copies of a work (for works published before March 1, 1989).** Under prior law, the distribution of copies without copyright notice or with defective notice resulted in the forfeiture of copyright protection. For works distributed before January 1, 1978, forfeiture was automatic. For works publicly distributed after that date, the copyright law provided ways around the defect created by distribution without notice.

Restored Foreign Copyrights

In the past two years, Congress has passed two pieces of legislation which have the effect of restoring the U.S. copyrights for certain types for foreign works. For works whose copyrights are restored under either of these provisions, the duration of copyright is the same as it would have been had the work never entered the public domain in the U.S. The two provisions are discussed in this section.

NAFTA Legislation

First came the restoration of copyright for 345 movies from Mexico and Canada which had fallen into the public domain here because they were published without notice between 1978 and March 1, 1989. A list of these works appeared in the *Federal Register* in February 1995 (Copyright Office, Copyright Restoration of Certain Motion Pictures, 60 Fed. Regis. 8252). Copyrights for these works were restored effective January 1, 1995. This legislation was part of the North American Free Trade Agreement (NAFTA) with Mexico and Canada.

GATT Legislation

The second piece of copyright restoration legislation restores the U.S. copyrights for certain foreign works which entered the public domain in the U.S. because the copyright owner failed to comply with the formalities once imposed by U.S. copyright law (failure to renew the copyright, lack of proper notice, or failure to comply with domestic manufacturing requirements). This legislation, which is new section 104A of the Copyright Act, also restores the U.S. copyright for certain foreign sound recordings and works first published in a country with which the U.S. did not have a copyright treaty.

Section 104A applies only to foreign works from countries which are members of the Berne Convention or the World Trade Organization, and only if the work is still protected by copyright in the "source country." The effective date for copyright restoration under section 104A is January 1, 1996. The legislation was part of the Agreement on Trade-Related Aspects of Intellectual Property Rights (TRIPs), an annex to the international treaty General Agreement on Tariffs and Trade (GATT). It contains provisions designed to protect the interests of those who used "restored copyright" works prior to the effective date of the legislation.

Copyright Restoration: An Example
Bambi was first published in Germany in 1923. It was registered in the U.S. in 1927. A court recently held that *Bambi* entered the public domain in the U.S. when the author's heirs failed to file a timely renewal in the U.S. *Twin Books Corp. v. Walt Disney Co.*, 877 F. Supp. 496 (N.D. Cal. 1995). Under GATT, the copyright in *Bambi* will be restored.

See "International Protection," Chapter 2.

Finding Public Domain Works

The Copyright Office does not maintain a list of public domain works, nor does it publish annual lists of copyrights that will expire at the end of the year. You have to find these works yourself.

If the copyright notice on a work is dated more than 75 years ago, the work is in the public domain. It will be harder to determine expiration dates for works covered by the current Copyright Act: Except for works made for hire, the duration of copyright is 50 years beyond the life of the author rather than a set number of years.

If you are interested in using a work to which the 1909 Copyright Act's renewal requirement applies, you can order a Copyright Office renewal search to find out whether the copyright was renewed.

> Searches are discussed in "Determining Who Owns the Copyright," Chapter 12.

Unless you know that a work was distributed without copyright notice, you will only learn about it if the issue has been raised in a reported court decision.

The Copyright Office does not keep copies of works whose registrations have expired. Some content providers sell copies of public domain works, such as WPA photographs (see Appendix D). The Library of Congress has copies of some of these works.

Complications

Derivative works (works based on preexisting works) are often created from public domain works. New material in a derivative work is protected by copyright. You cannot copy the new material in a new version of a public domain work unless you obtain a license from the owner of the copyright in the derivative work, but you can use the elements that came from the public domain work.

 The movie *Coast* is based on a public domain novel. If Developer wants to use a clip from the movie in a multimedia work, Developer must get a license from the owner of the copyright in the movie. Developer is free to use an excerpt from the underlying novel.

Sometimes the derivative work is in the public domain because the owner didn't renew the copyright, but the underlying work is still protected by copyright.

The movie *Dream* is based on a novel of the same name. Both the movie and the novel are pre-1978 works to which the 1909 Copyright Act's renewal requirement applied. The owner of the copyright in the novel filed a renewal application at the appropriate time in 1980, but the owner of the motion picture copyright did not renew its copyright. The underlying work, the novel, is protected by copyright. The derivative work, the movie, is not protected.

If the underlying work is protected but the derivative work is not, and you want to use an excerpt of the derivative work, you generally will need permission from the underlying work's copyright owner. This topic is discussed in "Determining Who Owns the Copyright," Chapter 12.

If a public domain work incorporates another work, the incorporated work may still be protected by copyright. If the incorporated work is protected by copyright, you must get a license from the owner of that copyright if you want to use an excerpt of the public domain work that incorporates the protected work.

> **It's a Wonderful Life**
> The copyright on the film *It's a Wonderful Life* expired in 1974 because the copyright owner, Republic Pictures, failed to file a renewal. However, Republic can still control copying and public performance of the film because it bought the copyrights in the underlying story and in the musical score.

 The movie *Mountains* is in the public domain because the renewal requirement applies to the movie and the copyright owner did not renew the copyright. *Mountains* contains a song that is still protected by copyright. If Developer wants to use a clip of *Mountains* that contains the song, Developer needs a license from the owner of the copyright in the song.

Using Works That You Own

You can use works that you own without worrying about obtaining licenses.

Existing Works

If you own the copyrights in all preexisting works that you will be using in your multimedia works, you don't need to obtain licenses.

If you are an employer, you own the copyrights in the United States in works created for you by employees acting within the scope of their employment. You may not own those rights in other countries. However, you do not own even the U.S. rights in works created for you by independent contractors unless you obtained assignments from them or the works had the status of "specially commissioned works made for hire."

If you created a work for a past employer within the scope of your employment, you do not own the copyright in that work. (See "The Work Made

See "The Work Made for Hire Rule," Chapter 4; "Works Made by Employees," Chapter 7; and "Copyright Ownership," Chapter 8.

for Hire Rule," Chapter 4.) You cannot use the work without obtaining a license.

If you created the work as an independent contractor, you own the copyright unless you assigned the copyright to the hiring party or you signed a valid work made for hire agreement.

New Works

You can avoid obtaining licenses to use third-party content if you create your own content. If works will be created by employees or independent contractors, be sure you follow the strategies described in earlier chapters to ensure that you obtain copyright ownership in the United States and throughout the world. (These strategies are described in the "Using the Employment Agreement," Chapter 7, and in "Copyright Ownership," Chapter 8.)

Special rules apply if you plan to modify a "work of visual art" even if you own the work. A work of visual art, for copyright purposes, is a limited edition painting, drawing, print, sculpture, or a photograph produced for exhibition purposes. The rules apply if the work was created by an artist after the effective date of the Visual Artists Rights Act of 1990.

The Visual Artists Rights Act is discussed in Chapter 12.

12 Clearing Rights and Obtaining Licenses

Most of this chapter is devoted to the licensing process and its three steps:

➤ Determining who owns the copyrights in the works you want to use.

➤ Determining what rights you need.

➤ Obtaining licenses from the copyright owners.

At the end of this chapter, we'll discuss how to use a rights clearance agency—a convenient aid for developers who will be licensing a large number of works—and how to use stock houses and media libraries to avoid many of the difficulties involved in licensing. We'll also discuss copyright assignments, an alternative to licensing, and the Visual Artists Rights Act, which imposes restrictions on modifying certain types of works.

The industries that generate the types of works that you are likely to want to license are described in Chapter 13. Music licensing is discussed in Chapter 14.

The Licensing Process

Whether you handle the licensing process yourself or use a rights clearance agency, the process will take time. Make certain that such time is built into your development schedule.

Multimedia is still very new, and many "content" owners may be reluctant to license their works. This is either because they do not understand what multimedia is or because they are concerned that digitization of their works will result in their losing control over their works.

Determining Who Owns the Copyright

The first step in the licensing process is determining who owns the copyright in the work you want to use.

If the work you want to use contains a copyright notice (many works do, although use of copyright notice is now optional), the name on the notice is your starting point. It is the name of the copyright owner at the time your copy of the work was published—but not necessarily the work's creator or the current copyright owner.

Assignments are discussed in "Assignments," Chapter 4.

The copyright owner named in the notice may have assigned the copyright to someone else after your copy was published. You need to trace the work's "chain of title" (just like in real estate) to find the current owner, because your license must come from the current copyright owner.

> John, a free-lance writer, assigned the copyright in his book to Mega Books, Inc. If Developer wants to use excerpts from John's book, Developer must get permission from Mega Books, not from John.

The rest of this section tells you how to check a work's chain of title and how to find the party who has authority to grant you a license to use a work.

Is the Work Registered?

The chain of title for a registered work can be checked by obtaining an "assignment search" of the Copyright Office's files (discussed in "Checking the Chain of Title," later in this section).

There are four ways to find out whether a work's copyright has been registered:

➤ Check the *Catalog of Copyright Entries*, which lists registered works by title. This catalog is published by the Copyright Office. Some libraries have copies of it. The catalog divides works into eight categories (literary works, performing arts, motion pictures and filmstrips, sound recordings, serials and periodicals, visual arts, maps, and renewals). It does not report registrations made in the year before the catalog's publication date.

➤ Order a Copyright Office registration search from the Copyright Office's Reference and Bibliography Section by filling out a copy of a Search Request Form (Form 1 in Appendix G) and sending it to the Copyright Office. Check the "Registration" box at the top and provide as much of the requested information on the work as you can. The Copyright Office will charge you $20 per hour for a search.

➤ Hire a copyright search firm to conduct a Copyright Office registration search for you. A list of search firms appears in Appendix C. Using a search firm will cost more than a Copyright Office search done by the Copyright Office Reference and Bibliography Section staff, but you will get the results faster.

➤ Do a Copyright Office search yourself. If you live in the Washington, D.C. area, you can use microfilm and automated registration records in the Copyright Office. If you live elsewhere, you can do a search on-line using the Dialog database service from Knight-Ridder Information, Inc.

Checking the Chain of Title

How you check a work's chain of title depends on whether the copyright has been registered or not.

Registered Copyrights

If the copyright in the work has been registered with the Copyright Office, you trace the work's chain of title by obtaining a Copyright Office assignment search. The Copyright Act permits assignees to record their assignments with the Copyright Office to give others constructive notice of the assignment, just as purchasers of real estate do in recording their purchases in county records. A Copyright Office assignment search will reveal whether any assignments of the work's copyright have been recorded.

Recording assignments is discussed in "Assignments," Chapter 4.

An assignment search, like a registration search, can be obtained by sending a filled-out Search Request Form (check the "assignment" box) to the Copyright Office's Reference and Bibliography Section, by hiring a copyright search firm, or by checking the Copyright Office's files yourself. These options are described in "Is the Work Registered?," earlier in this section.

If the work was published before January 1, 1978, you may want to request a renewal search as well as an assignment search, to see if the copyright was renewed. If it wasn't, it may be in the pubic domain.

See "Public Domain Works," Chapter 11.

The Catalog of Copyright Entries does not include entries of assignments, so it cannot be used to check the chain of title. However, it does contain information on renewals.

An assignment search will only reveal assignments of registered copyrights that have been recorded in the Copyright Office. It will not reveal recent assignments that have not yet been cataloged. The Copyright Office is frequently six months behind in recording assignments.

Unregistered Copyrights

If the copyright has not been registered, a Copyright Office search will not help you. The only way to check the chain of title for an unregistered work is to contact the copyright owner named in the copyright notice and ask whether the copyright has been assigned.

Secret Assignments

If you obtain a license from the person or company that you think is the current copyright owner (because that's what the Copyright Office's assignment records indicate) and later learn that your assignor actually had assigned the copyright to someone else before giving you a license, your license will still be valid if it meets three criteria:

➤ You didn't know of the unrecorded assignment at the time you entered into the license agreement.

➤ The license is nonexclusive. (An exclusive license is one that does not overlap another grant of rights. See "Licenses," Chapter 4.)

➤ The license is in writing.

According to the Copyright Act, a nonexclusive written license prevails over a conflicting earlier copyright assignment if the license was taken in good faith before the copyright assignment was recorded, and without notice of the copyright assignment.

 According to the Copyright Office's records, songwriter Ben assigned the copyright in Ben's song, "Foggy Day," to Rotten Music in 1988. In January 1993, Rotten assigned the copyright in "Foggy Day" to First State Bank. Bank did not record its assignment. In November 1993, Rotten gave Developer a written nonexclusive license to use Foggy Day in a multimedia encyclopedia. (Rotten didn't tell Developer it had assigned the copyright to Bank, and Developer had no reason to know about the assignment.) Developer's license from Rotten is valid, because it is in writing and nonexclusive and Developer got it in good faith and without notice of Rotten's assignment to Bank. Bank should have protected its interests by recording its assignment. (Recording is discussed in "Assignments," Chapter 4.)

If your license is exclusive, you have to record it in the Copyright Office to obtain protection against a conflicting earlier transfer (see "Obtaining a License," later in this chapter).

Later Assignments

If you get a license from the copyright owner and the copyright owner later assigns the copyright to someone else, the new owner cannot revoke your license if it is nonexclusive and in writing. A nonexclusive, written license prevails over a later assignment.

 On May 1, 1993, Big Music granted Developer a written, nonexclusive license to use the song "Rainy Day." On June 1, 1993, Big Music assigned the copyright in "Rainy Day" to Theme Music. Big Music cannot require Developer to get a new license from Big.

Multiple Assignments

If the copyright has been assigned several times, you need to get your license from the current owner of the copyright—the most recent assignee.

 Composer assigned the copyright in her song to Small Music, which recorded the assignment. Small Music later assigned the copyright to Big Music, which recorded the assignment. If Developer wants to use the song written by Composer, Developer should get a license from Big Music.

Existing Licenses

Both exclusive licenses and nonexclusive licenses can be recorded in the Copyright Office. (Details are discussed in "Obtaining a License," later in this chapter.) Your Copyright Office search report will tell you what kind of existing exclusive licenses there are on a work. Most nonexclusive licensees do not record their licenses.

Unless you want an exclusive license, you don't need to worry about preexisting nonexclusive licenses. An existing nonexclusive licensee has no grounds for complaint if you are granted permission to use the same work on a nonexclusive basis.

Exclusive licenses are a potential problem, though. A copyright owner cannot give you a license that conflicts with an existing exclusive license.

 Developer wants to use excerpts of Publisher's reference book in a multimedia work. Publisher already has granted Massive Multimedia an exclusive license to use the reference book in multimedia works. Publisher cannot give Developer an exclusive or nonexclusive license to use the reference book.

According to U.S. copyright law, an exclusive licensee can grant sublicenses unless the license agreement states otherwise (an exclusive licensee is considered an "owner" of an interest in copyright). In the previous example, Developer should find out whether Massive Multimedia has the right to sublicense. If it does, Developer should ask Massive for a nonexclusive license to use excerpts of the reference book.

Existing exclusive licenses must be reviewed carefully. An exclusive licensee may believe that its license is broad enough to give it the exclusive right to multimedia uses.

 Developer wants to license, for use in a CD-ROM product, clips from a particular film. In 1990, the film's copyright owner granted Video Distributor the exclusive right to distribute the film on videocassettes and any other form of optical recording in any media known or hereafter developed. Video Distributor may take the position that it controls multimedia rights.

In such a situation, the copyright owner and the existing licensee may both demand royalties for your use of the work.

Finding the Owner

If you have obtained a Copyright Office search for the work you want to use, the search report will give you the copyright owner's address.

If the work is unregistered and a Copyright Office search is not possible, the work's copyright notice page may give the copyright owner's address. For books, the publisher may act as the author's licensing agent, even if the publisher does not own the copyright (or at least the publisher may be able to contact the author for you). For motion pictures, the film archives at UCLA, the University of Southern California, and the Academy of Motion Picture Arts and Sciences in Los Angeles may help.

Jointly Owned Works

See "Joint Authorship and Ownership," Chapter 4.

For jointly owned works, a single co-owner can give you a nonexclusive license to use the work in the United States unless the co-owners have a contract requiring the consent of all co-owners. It's safer to contact all co-owners.

Complications

Determining who owns the copyright in the work you want to use can be complicated by a number of factors. We discuss three such factors in this section.

Copyrighted Components

If the work you want to use incorporates several different copyrightable works, you may need more than one license.

Developer wants to use a film clip in a multimedia work that will be shown at trade shows. The film clip contains part of a song. The film's copyright owner does not own the copyright in the song (the film's producer got a nonexclusive license to use the song in the movie). Developer needs to obtain two licenses—one from the owner of the film copyright and one from the owner of the music copyright. The owner of the film copyright cannot authorize Developer to use the music component of the film clip in Developer's work.

If you only want to use a separately owned component of a larger work, you do not need to get a license from the owner of the copyright in the larger work.

 Developer wants to use a photograph that was used in a brochure produced by Graphic Artist. The photograph was created by Photographer, who gave Graphic Artist a nonexclusive license to use it in the brochure. Developer does not need to get a license from Graphic Artist. Developer does need to get a license from Photographer.

Derivative Works

If the work you want to use is a derivative work (a work based on a preexisting work) created and owned by someone other than the owner of the underlying work, you probably will need a license from the owner of the underlying work as well as a license from the owner of the derivative work.

 Developer wants to use a clip from the movie *Rainy Day,* which is based on Jim Brown's novel by the same name. The movie was made by Movieco, which got an exclusive license to make and distribute a movie version of the book. Developer needs licenses from both Movieco and Brown. The license from Movieco will authorize Developer to use the clip of Movieco's film. The license from Jim Brown will authorize Developer to use the book upon which the movie was based.

If the excerpt from the derivative work that you want to use was created entirely by the creator of the derivative work and is not based on the underlying work, you do not need a license to use the underlying work.

 The film clip that Developer wants to use (see the previous example) shows a scene that was in no way derived from Jim Brown's book (it was added by the screenwriter to give "sex appeal" to the movie). Developer does not need to get a license from Brown, just from Movieco.

Split Rights

Copyright rights for certain types of work—books and music, for example— are often split among several parties through the grant of a number of exclusive licenses or assignments of individual copyright rights. If the copyright owner has split the rights geographically, you will have to get licenses from all the exclusive licensees to obtain worldwide rights.

In some industries, rights are split by market segment or medium as well as by geographic territory.

> Author granted Book Publisher an exclusive license to publish Author's novel in book form. Author also granted Book Publisher the exclusive right to license the novel to others for book club and condensed-book publication. Author granted Developer the exclusive right to make a motion picture version of the novel. Author retained all other rights in the novel. The copyright rights in the novel have been split by market segment and medium.

If your Copyright Office search reveals that the rights in a work have been split among several assignees or exclusive licensees, you need to get a license from the assignee or exclusive licensee who owns the particular rights that you need.

> Author granted Book Publisher an exclusive license to publish Author's book in book form, retaining all other rights. If Developer wants to use excerpts of Author's book in Developer's multimedia work, Developer needs to obtain a license from Author (but Developer should carefully review the preexisting license's grant of rights language).

If the rights have been split, it can be difficult to determine which assignee or licensee owns the rights you need.

> Developer wants to use an excerpt from Author's book in a multimedia work. The Copyright Office search shows that Author granted Movieco "all audiovisual rights" in Author's book. Author retained all other rights. Although Developer's multimedia work is an audiovisual work as defined by the Copyright Act (see "Types of Works Protected by Copyright," Chapter 2), it is unclear whether the term "audiovisual rights" as used in Author's grant to Movieco gives Movieco the right to grant licenses for use of the book in multimedia works. To be safe, Developer may have to obtain licenses from both Author and Movieco.

> Developer wants to use an excerpt from Author's book in a multimedia work. Author assigned the copyright in his book to Publisher. Publisher granted exclusive "electronic publishing rights" in the book to Electro Publishing and exclusive "audiovisual rights" to Movieco. It is unclear whether Publisher, Electro Publishing, or Movieco owns the rights that Developer wants to license.

It will be several years before we know whether an exclusive license or assignment using special industry terms—granting a movie developer exclusive audiovisual rights in a book, for example—gives the licensee the right to authorize use in multimedia projects. (In the cases being litigated now, the issue is whether a grant of "motion picture rights" or "television rights" includes the right to distribute a film in videocassette form for home use.) If, after reviewing the Copyright Office search report for a work, you are not sure who owns the rights you need, get help from an experienced copyright attorney or find another work to license.

> **Old License, New Media**
>
> Here's an example of the current crop of "video rights" cases: In the 1940s, Margaret Rey wrote seven books about the adventures of Curious George, a monkey. In the 1970s, she granted an investment firm the fight to produce 104 episodes of *Curious George* for television viewing. In a dispute between Rey and the licensee, a court in 1993 held that the license did not encompass the right to distribute the television shows in videocassette form. *Rey v. Lafferty*, 990 F.2d 1379 (1st Cir. 1993).

Determining What Rights You Need

The second step in the licensing process is determining what rights you need to license from the copyright owner.

Scope of the License

To shield you from an infringement suit, your license must authorize every type of use that you will be making of the licensed work. Consequently, you need to determine how you will be using the work and what rights you need before you seek your license. A license is no protection for uses not authorized in the license.

Developer obtained a license to reproduce Photographer's photograph of the Golden Gate bridge in Developer's multimedia work. Although the license did not authorize Developer to alter the photograph, Developer manipulated the image to eliminate cars and pedestrians and create an uncluttered image of the bridge. If Photographer sued Developer for unauthorized exercise of the modification right, Developer's license would be no defense.

> **Everybody Wants a Cut**
>
> "New Media" uses for existing works can bring copyright claimants out of the woodwork, as Disney found when it released *Fantasia* in videocassette form. *Fantasia* was not a financial success for Disney when it was released in 1940. However, Disney made millions on the 1991 video release. Seeking to share in the money, the orchestra that recorded the sound track filed suit claiming joint ownership, as did the executor for the orchestra's composer.

Using a licensed work in ways not authorized in the license may be material breach of the license agreement. If it is, the licensor can terminate the license. In the previous example, Developer's alteration of the photograph is probably a material breach of Developer's license agreement with Photographer. If Photographer terminates the license, Developer will no longer have even the right granted to Developer in the license (the right to use the original photograph in Developer's multimedia work).

If you want the right to use the licensed work in more than one multimedia project, the license must explicitly give you that right.

 Developer obtained a license to use a five-second clip of Movieco's movie in Developer's work, City Tour. Developer later used the same film clip in another multimedia work, Downtown. Developer's second use of the film clip is copyright infringement.

Disclosure

Before you are quoted a license fee, you will need to disclose to the copyright owner (or the rights clearance agency) all uses you are planning to make of the work, and provide detailed information about your planned use of the work. Copyright owners use this information in determining the license fee.

You may have to explain the nature of multimedia works in general. In negotiating licensing fees, it may be helpful to explain to copyright owners that the market for multimedia works is still small and that your budget is small. Otherwise, the owner may be basing the license fee on unrealistic assumptions about the money to be made in multimedia. If you will be licensing a large number of works, explain that to the copyright owner so that the owner will understand that you cannot afford to pay a large fee for permission to use the owner's work.

> **Get the Rights You Need**
>
> In 1939, employees of Disney created 12 songs for the motion picture *Pinocchio* as works for hire. Disney assigned the copyrights in the songs to a music publisher, which granted Disney back a nonexclusive license to record the songs "in synchronism with any and all of the motion pictures which may be made by you." This language was found by a jury to give Disney the right to use the songs in videocassettes but not in television ads and "trailers." The court ordered Disney to obtain a license before using the songs in ads and trailers. *Bourne Co. v. Walt Disney Co.*, 31 U.S.P.Q. 2d 1858 (S.D.N.Y. 1994).

What Rights?

You may need permission to exercise some or all of the copyright owner's exclusive rights. (These are defined in "The Exclusive Rights," Chapter 2.) This section discusses which of these rights you will need for different types of multimedia works.

Reproduction Right

On-line distribution rights are discussed in Chapter 23.

You need permission to reproduce (that is, copy) the licensed work for use in your multimedia project, whatever the nature of your project. Scanning and digitizing a work is a form of copying.

Modification Right

If you plan to alter or modify the licensed work, you need permission to exercise the modification right.

Distribution Right

Unless your multimedia project is solely for your own personal use, you need permission to distribute the licensed work as contained in your multimedia project. This is true whether you are planning to "distribute" your multimedia work to a single client or to hundreds of customers.

Public Performance Right and Public Display Right

Whether you need permission for public performance and public display depends on how your multimedia work will be used. You don't need such a license if your work will be used only by consumers in their own homes. You do need these rights if the work will be used in one of the following three ways (unless one of the exceptions covered in "Exceptions," later in this section, applies):

➤ If it will be shown at a place open to the public.

➤ If it will be shown at a place where a substantial number of persons outside a normal circle of family and social acquaintances gathers.

➤ If it will be transmitted to the public or to a public place by means of a device or process, whether the audience is in the same place or in separate places.

For example, multimedia works that will be used at information kiosks in places such as convention centers, train stations, and tourist attractions will be publicly performed and displayed, because they will be shown at a place open to the public. Works used for corporate training or presentations will be publicly performed and displayed, because they will be shown at a place where a substantial number of persons outside a normal circle of family and friends gathers. Works that will be transmitted over interactive TV or to hotel rooms will be publicly performed and displayed, because they are transmitted to the public by means of a device.

Video games distributed for home use do not require a public performance and display license, but video games used in arcades do.

Exceptions

A public performance license is not required for the following uses of a copyrighted work:

➤ Classroom performance or display of a work by instructors or pupils of a nonprofit educational institution.

➤ Certain performances by government and religious groups.

➤ Live performance without any purpose of commercial advantage or payment of fees to performers, if there is no admission charge or the proceeds are used exclusively for educational, religious, or charitable purposes.

Details of these very limited exceptions to the public performance right are stated in Section 110 of the Copyright Act, which is discussed in more detail in Chapter 24. Even if the intended use of your multimedia works falls within these exceptions, you still will need a license of the reproduction right to include a copyrighted work in your multimedia work. Section 110's exceptions apply only to the public performance and public display rights.

Obtaining a License

The third step in the licensing process is obtaining a license from the copyright owner. A sample content license is included in Appendix B (Form 12). Guidelines and checklists for licensing different types of content are in Chapters 13 and 14.

Terms

The terms of the license should cover the following seven points:

➤ **Definition of the multimedia product or products in which the licensed work can be used (by title or by description or both).** Pay careful attention to the definition of the multimedia product or products covered by the license. If you want to be able to use the licensed work in future versions of your work or in sequels, include the future versions or sequels in the license's definition of the multimedia product. If your current project involves one medium (CD-ROM, for example) but you might want to shift it to another medium in the future (interactive television, for example), make certain the license does not limit your right to just the current version's medium. Given the rapid advances in technology, you should try to avoid limiting the product definition to a particular format or configuration.

➤ **Whether the license is exclusive or nonexclusive (see "Licenses," Chapter 4, for definitions).** Obtaining a very limited exclusive license to use a "hot" property—for example, an exclusive license to use characters from a popular movie in video games—can be valuable for marketing the work.

➤ **Specific authorized uses, such as reproduction, modification, distribution, public performance, and public display.** Any limitations on the amount of the work that can be copied and used should be stated. For example, if authorization to use a photograph is limited to use of the photograph on a single branch of the multimedia work, the license should state this.

➤ **License fee, whether royalties or one-time fee.**

➤ **Term (duration) of the license.**

➤ **Territory limitations, if any.** You probably want a worldwide license, but the licensor (the U.S. copyright owner with whom you are dealing) may not own the worldwide rights.

➤ **Warranties of ownership and noninfringement.** You should try to get the licensor to warrant three things: That it is the sole and exclusive owner of all rights in the licensed material, that it has the right to grant you the license, and that the licensed material does not infringe any third-party intellectual property rights or other proprietary rights. If you are licensing a film or television show clip or a master recording of music, your license also should include a warranty that any applicable union reuse fees have been paid.

You should try to get the licensor to indemnify you and your distributors for damages arising out of breach of these warranties.

It's possible that you will not be able to obtain these warranties and indemnities, or that the licensor will only give you limited versions. In that case, you must decide if using the work is worth the legal risk involved.

See "Reuse Provisions," Chapter 16.

Warranty and indemnity provisions are discussed in more detail in "The Contract," Chapter 6.

Formalities

There are certain formalities to attend to in getting a license. They are different for exclusive licenses and nonexclusive licenses.

Exclusive Licenses

Exclusive copyright licenses must be signed and be in writing to be valid. It is a good idea to get exclusive copyright licenses notarized. Notarization is legal evidence of the signing of the license.

If you are obtaining an exclusive license, record it in the Copyright Office. If you record it "in the manner required to give constructive notice," your license will take priority over a conflicting assignment or exclusive license, as explained in "Licenses," Chapter 4.

There is no official Copyright Office form for recording assignments or licenses, so you have to create your own document. You can record the license itself, but most people make up a "short form" license (see Form 13 in Appendix B) for recording. The Copyright Office has a cover sheet for submitting the document for recording (Form 2 in Appendix G).

To record "in the manner required to give constructive notice," the document you record must give the title or copyright registration number of the work being licensed. If the copyright in that work has not been registered with the Copyright Office, recording your license will not give constructive notice. If the copyright of the work you are licensing has not

See "How to Fill Out Form PA," Chapter 18.

been registered, insist that the licensor register the copyright by sending a completed registration application to the Copyright Office.

Nonexclusive Licenses

Oral nonexclusive licenses can be enforced—if you can prove their existence. However, you should always get a written license so that you will have proof of the license and its terms. Getting the license in writing will give you protection against conflicting earlier and later transfers, as discussed in "Determining Who Owns the Copyright," earlier in this chapter.

You can, if you wish, record a nonexclusive license in the Copyright Office and get the license notarized. The Copyright Act doesn't say that there is any advantage to doing these things for nonexclusive licenses.

Termination Right

This right is discussed in "Termination Right," Chapter 4.

The Copyright Act gives the author of a work other than a "work made for hire" the right to terminate any license or assignment granted on or after January 1, 1978, during a five-year period that starts 35 years after the grant was made. For works that were first published before 1978, the termination period begins 56 years after the work was first published.

Except for licenses to use works made for hire, all licenses are subject to this termination right. The termination right is likely to be of importance only for a small percentage of multimedia works. For such multimedia works, the effect of the termination right will be mitigated by the termination right's derivative works exception, which states that a derivative work prepared before termination of the license may continue to be used after termination.

 In 1990, Developer got a license to use Author's photograph in Developer's multimedia works, Cityscape and New Town. Developer created Cityscape but did not get around to creating New Town. If Author or Author's heirs terminate Developer's license in 2026, Developer can continue to use the photograph in Cityscape but cannot use the photograph in New Town or in a new version of Cityscape.

Possible Licensor's Title Defect

If your license is for a work first distributed to the public between 1968 and 1977, and if the licensed work was not a work made for hire when created, and if your licensor is someone other than the original copyright owner, your licensor's title to the work has a potential defect. This defect arises from the renewal provisions of the 1909 Copyright Act that were carried forward in "transition" provisions of the 1976 Copyright Act. The Supreme Court has interpreted those provisions as giving the heirs of a copyright owner the right to terminate an assignee's or licensee's right to use the licensed work beyond the original 28-year copyright term.

 In 1993, Publisher granted Developer a license to use an excerpt from a book written by Author, an individual. The book was first published in 1968. Publisher was assigned the copyright and the renewal term rights by Author in 1970. Author died in 1977, long before the renewal period would start (in the 28th year, 1996). Author left a widow and one child. If Author's widow and child apply in 1996 to register a claim to the renewal term, they will be able to terminate Publisher's assignment. That will take away Publisher's right to license the book for the renewal term and the basis for Developer's right to use the book. If Developer wants to use the excerpt of the book beyond 1996—even in a multimedia work that Developer created before 1996 ended—Developer must obtain a new license from Author's widow and child.

See "The Work Made for Hire Rule," Chapter 4.

This defect exists only for works that are not works made for hire as defined under the 1909 Copyright Act. The 1909 Copyright Act applied a broader definition of the term "work made for hire" than the present Copyright Act does. Because the right to cut off licenses and assignments applies only to the author's heirs and not to the author, evaluating the risk means guessing whether the author is likely to die prior to the beginning of the renewal period (the 28th year of the original copyright term).

If you are considering licensing a work that was first distributed between 1968 and 1977 (inclusive), you should be aware of the potential defect in the licensor's title. As each calendar year ends, works published 28 years earlier, by authors still living, become free of this risk. In 1996, the risk exists for works first published between 1968 and 1977 (inclusive). In 1997, the risk exists for works first published between 1969 and 1977.

If you must license a work for which this risk exists, be aware that you may have to obtain a new license from the author's heirs. While you could get a "back-up" license from the author's spouse and children now to protect you from the risk of having your license terminated in the future, this strategy is not foolproof. The spouse and children could predecease the author. Then the right to claim the renewal term would pass to those designated in the author's will (or the author could change spouses before dying).

The "Rear Window" Problem

Copyright attorneys call the title defect referred to here the "*Rear Window* Problem," because the Hitchcock movie of that name was the focus of the Supreme Court case that gave rise to the problem. The movie *Rear Window* was based on a short story by Cornell Woolrich. While Woolrich was alive, he gave a motion picture studio the right to make a movie version of his story. Woolrich also promised to obtain the copyright renewal term for the story and grant renewal term rights to the studio. However, Woolrich died before renewal time came. Woolrich left no spouse or children, so the renewal rights went to his estate. His executor assigned to renewal rights to a Mr. Abend. The Court held that the owner of the movie could continue to use the story in the already-made movie during the renewal term only if Mr. Abend consented. *Stewart v. Abend*, 495 U.S. 207 (1990).

Rights Clearance Agencies

To obtain the licenses that you need, you may want to use a rights clearance agency. These agencies also are known as rights and permissions agencies and copyright clearance agencies. There is a list of such agencies in Appendix C.

A rights clearance agency will find out who owns the rights you need and negotiate licenses for you. (You should still read the first four sections of this chapter and become familiar with licensing issues so that you'll understand the process.) Because these agencies perform rights clearance and licensing as their business, they probably can obtain licenses for you in far less time than it would take you to obtain them yourself.

These agencies are just beginning to handle licensing for multimedia use. They primarily handle rights clearance for movie and television production companies, ad agencies, and corporate video departments. If you use an agency, your agent needs to know exactly how you plan to use the licensed works in your multimedia project. Your intended use of licensed works probably will be different from that of the agent's usual clients.

Most rights clearance agencies charge by the hour. An initial consultation is generally free (but you should ask). You should first determine whether the works you want to use are likely to be available (and for what fee) and whether the agent can suggest alternatives to unavailable or expensive material. Sometimes an agent can give you ideas if you need suggestions for works you might license and use.

See "The Rights of Publicity and Privacy," Chapter 15.

These agencies frequently handle right of publicity releases for photographs of celebrities as well as copyright licensing.

Stock Houses and Libraries

You can obtain film and video clips, photographs, illustrations, music, and sound effects from stock houses and from music and media libraries. A list of stock houses and media libraries appears in Appendix D.

Stock houses and libraries frequently own the copyrights in works that they license (or they provide material that is in the public domain, such as WPA photographs). They will, for a separate fee, do research for you to help you find suitable material (or you can hire your own content specialist).

As with other content licenses, you should make sure that licenses issued to you by stock houses or libraries cover all of the rights needed for your intended uses of the licensed works (see "Determining What Rights You Need," earlier in this chapter).

Copyright Assignment

If you find a work that is owned by a single owner and is suitable for repeated use in multimedia works, a copyright assignment may be preferable to a license. With a copyright assignment, you will be able to modify the work and use it in many multimedia projects (subject to Visual Artists Rights Act and moral rights limitations, discussed in the last section of this chapter). Because an assignment gives you all of the copyright owner's exclusive rights in the work, you won't have to predict in advance what rights you will later need.

See "Assignments," Chapter 4.

If you get an assignment, the assignor will have the right to terminate the assignment in 35 years (or, for works published before January 1, 1978, fifty-six years after the work was first published). However, you still will be able to use the assigned work in multimedia works prepared before termination. (See the discussion of the termination right in "Obtaining a License," earlier in this chapter.)

Termination is discussed in "Termination Right," Chapter 4.

To be valid, a copyright assignment must be in writing and be signed by the copyright owner. You should obtain warranties of title and noninfringement and an indemnity from the assignor. (See the discussion of warranties and indemnities in "Obtaining a License," earlier in this chapter.)

Within one month of getting the copyright assignment, you should record a notarized, short-form assignment (Form 13 in Appendix B) in the Copyright Office "in the manner required to give constructive notice" (see the discussion of this phrase in "Obtaining a License," earlier in this chapter). Use the cover sheet shown in Form 2 in Appendix G. Recording the assignment will protect it against conflicting assignments.

See "Assignments," Chapter 4.

The Visual Artists Rights Act

If you are planning on modifying a third-party work, you should consider whether modification will violate the author's rights under the Visual Artists Rights Act (VARA) or will violate his or her moral rights.

VARA Rights

VARA gives the owner of a "work of visual art" created on or after June 1, 1991, the right to claim authorship of the work and the right to prevent four things:

> ➤ Any intentional distortion, mutilation, or other modification of the work that would be prejudicial to the artist's honor or reputation.

> ➤ Destruction of a work of recognized stature.

> ➤ Use of the artist's name as the author of a work that the author did not create.

➤ Use of the artist's name as the author of a work that has been modified in such a way as to be prejudicial to the artist's honor or reputation.

Artists who created works of visual art before June 1, 1991, also have these rights if the artist did not transfer the copyright in the work before that date.

Definition of Works of Visual Art

According to VARA, works of visual art are limited to the following categories of works (in single copy form or as signed and numbered limited editions of no more than 200 copies):

➤ Paintings.

➤ Drawings.

➤ Prints.

➤ Sculptures.

➤ Photographs produced for exhibition purposes.

Excluded Works

Works made for hire are not works of visual art, nor are the following types of works:

➤ Posters.

➤ Maps, globes, and charts.

➤ Technical drawings.

➤ Diagrams.

➤ Models.

➤ Works of applied art.

➤ Motion pictures and other audiovisual works.

➤ Books, magazines, newspapers, and periodicals.

➤ Databases.

➤ Electronic information services and electronic publications.

➤ Merchandising items.

➤ Advertising material and packaging material.

Duration of Rights

The artist who creates a work that is protected under VARA owns the VARA rights in the work even if he or she has assigned the copyright in the work to someone else. The VARA rights endure for the artist's lifetime. If the work was created prior to June 1991, and is covered by VARA because the artist retained the copyright, the VARA rights endure for the life of the artist plus 50 years.

Waiver

The VARA rights cannot be transferred, but they can be waived through a written document signed by the artist. If you intend to use a work of visual art in your multimedia project in a way that might violate the author's VARA rights, you should obtain a waiver of those rights. This advice applies even if you own the copyright in the work or have obtained a license from the current copyright owner to use the work of visual art.

Moral Rights

VARA was passed shortly after the United States joined the Berne Convention. Signatories to the Berne Convention are obligated to protect authors' rights of attribution and integrity. These are known as "moral rights." Most other countries have long recognized moral rights for many types of copyrightable works, not just for works of visual art. For example, an appellate court in France recently held that colorization of the film *Asphalt Jungle* violated the moral rights of the film's director and screenwriter.

If you will be selling your multimedia work in other countries and are planning on modifying existing copyrightable works, you should find out whether you will be violating the artist's moral rights in the countries in which you will be selling, even if you own the copyrights in the existing works.

Several states—New York and California, for example—have statutes that give limited moral rights to certain types of artistic works. In addition, artists sometimes include moral rights provisions in contracts and assignments with parties who buy their works. Some motion picture directors have contract-based rights to control the alteration of their films.

13 Licensing Content: Industry by Industry

Multimedia developers and publishers use several types of works for "content." Each of the industries from which content is drawn for multimedia has its own licensing issues. Those issues are described in this chapter. Checklists for clearing different types of content are at the end of the chapter.

Music licensing is discussed in Chapter 14. The fundamentals of copyright clearance (applicable to all types of copyrightable works) are discussed in Chapters 11 and 12.

General Advice

The most important lesson in clearing material is to begin early. If you don't, you may find yourself unable to use material simply because you have not allowed enough time to get the licenses, releases, and permissions you need. Consider using an attorney or a rights clearance agency (discussed in Chapter 12) if you are creating a commercial project, particularly one with complex clearance issues.

To be successful in clearing rights, follow these five rules:

➤ **Identify your needs early.** Doing this is critical, because licensing is a slow process. You may find that some of the material you want to use is not available, and you may encounter unexpected delays. For example, in a clearance project undertaken by one of the coauthors of this book, the owner of one of the works had declared bankruptcy several years before the clearance was being done. It took two months just to identify the new owner.

➤ **Budget realistically for the cost of clearance.** Clearing rights can be very expensive, both in license fees and professional fees (for attorneys or clearance agents). For complex projects, the license fees can exceed $100,000, and the professional fees for attorneys and clearance agents can run from $20,000 to $75,000. The costs will depend on the nature of the works you want to use and the rights you want. The shorter the period you have for clearing rights, the more expensive rights clearance will be (because you will have no time to negotiate or to substitute cheaper alternatives).

➤ **Always have an alternative.** Don't plan your project around content owned by a third party unless you are confident that you can obtain the necessary rights. The rights may have been licensed already, or they may not be available at a reasonable price. For example, the owners of the copyright in the official anthem for one state wanted $10,000 to grant permission for use of the anthem in a CD-ROM atlas of the U.S. The fee was simply too much, and the developer did not include the anthem.

➤ **Be prepared for the unexpected**. Be creative in clearing rights. The content owner may be willing to settle for nonmonetary compensation (such as a "credit" on the packaging). In one case, performers were persuaded to accept donations to a designated charity in lieu of the modest amount the developer could have afforded to pay them.

➤ **Be frank.** Be prepared to be frank about the nature of the project and the rights you will need in your first contact. Although you may consider your project to be confidential, you must be prepared to share your plans with the content owner in order to persuade the content owner to grant you a license.

See "Determining What Rights You Need," Chapter 12.

Licensing Text

The primary concern in clearing text is copyright. The first question to ask in clearing text is whether the text is still protected by copyright (see "Public Domain Works," Chapter 11). If you are considering distributing the product outside of the United States (or on the Internet, which is global in nature), you will need to be concerned about foreign copyright laws as well as United States copyright laws. Determining whether a work is in the public domain can be complicated. We recommend that you consult an attorney familiar with U.S. and international copyright law if you think works you want to use are in the public domain.

If the text is based on another work, such as a play or a movie, you may need to get permission from the owner of this other work as well as the copyright owner of the text. (See "Determining Who Owns the Copyright," Chapter 12.) Some materials accompanying the text, such as illustrations and charts, may not be owned by the owner of the copyright in the text. Characters used in the text may be owned by someone else (and used by the text's author under a license). See "Logos and Characters," later in this chapter. Reading the acknowledgments and forwards of books carefully will help you identify separately owned material.

Clearance Steps

If the text you want to use is protected by copyright, you should do the following things to clear it:

➤ **Identify what you want to license.** The license could include the storyline, characters, and setting—or just certain lines of text.

➤ **Identify the rights you need.** If you are simply including part or all of the text in your multimedia product without altering the text (for example, using it in an encyclopedia), you may only need reproduction and distribution rights. However, if the text will be used in a "voice-over" (as spoken works), you may need "spoken-word" rights. If you intend to use the text as the basis for an entirely new work, such as a game based on a book, you will need the modification right. If you are providing the text on-line, you also may need the right to publicly display the text in your work.

See "The Exclusive Rights," Chapter 2, and "What Rights You Need," Chapter 12.

➤ **Determine the geographic scope of the license (territory).** Getting worldwide rights may require you to contact several different licensors (the U.S. licensor may not own worldwide rights). The same is true of rights for foreign translations.

See "Determining Who Owns the Copyright," Chapter 12.

➤ **Determine whether you need sublicensing rights and subsidiary rights.** You need sublicensing rights if you will need to be able to authorize another party to exercise the rights granted to you in the license. Examples of subsidiary rights are the right to use the author's name, image, and biography in your marketing materials and packaging; the right to make sequels or a television show using the licensed text; and the right to use the licensed text in toys, t-shirts, and other merchandise based on the multimedia product.

➤ **Define the "product" in which you will be using the licensed work.** This topic is discussed in "Obtaining a License," Chapter 12. The product definition can be limited by the platforms, operating systems, media, and language.

➤ **Determine whether the text defames or invades the right of privacy or publicity of any actual individuals.** These topics are discussed in Chapter 15. Even "fictional" characters can result in defamation if they are thinly disguised actual individuals. You could seek to obtain a release from the individual, but such a release in these circumstances is not likely to be granted. The most common solution is to obtain strong "representations and warranties" from the licensor that the text does not defame or invade the right of privacy of any third parties. These representations should include an indemnity. The alternative is to review the material yourself with your legal counsel to ensure that you are comfortable with any potential legal risks.

Warranties and indemnities are discussed in "Typical Contract Provisions," Chapter 5, and in "The Contract," Chapter 6.

➤ **Determine whether your use of the material requires any trademark licenses.** Trademarks are discussed in Chapter 3 and in Chapter 17. Characters are protected by both copyright and trademark law. See "Logos and Characters," later in this chapter. The title of a book or an article is generally not protectable by trademark unless it is part of a series or is famous on its own. Generally the use of a trademark in text—for example a "Honda car" or a "Nestle chocolate bar"—is not a violation of trademark rights so long as it does not appear to create an association with the trademark owner. This type of use is called "collateral" (use to identify the product rather than to identify the source of the product).

See "Titles," Chapter 17.

➤ **Determine whether your use of the material violates the author's moral rights.** In many European countries, authors have "moral rights" which remain with the author even after the copyright has been assigned. These rights permit the author to control changes of the work and the use of the author's name in connection with the work. If you will be distributing your multimedia title overseas, you should try to obtain a waiver of these rights.

See "The Visual Artists Rights Act," Chapter 12.

A checklist for text licensing appears at the end of this chapter.

Locating Owners

Identifying rights owners for text can be difficult. Understanding common industry practices will help you figure out where to start.

Books

The book publishing industry has two general categories of books—trade and nontrade.

Trade Books

The term "trade books" means books of general interest (fiction, nonfiction, and poetry). Trade books generally are written by authors who are not employees of publishing companies. The individual author either assigns his or her entire copyright to the publisher or grants the publisher rights that fall short of total assignment—for example, "the right to publish in book form."

In the past, the "all rights" assignment (assignment of the entire copyright) was common, so the publisher was the copyright owner. The current trend is for writers to try to retain rights for licensing to other parties. Whether "new media" rights should remain with the writer or go to the book publisher is currently the subject of spirited debate. Nonetheless, if you want permission to use part of a book, the permissions department of the book's publisher is a good place to start. Even if the publisher doesn't own the copyright, the publisher may be the owner's licensing agent. If not, the permissions department should be able to put you in contact with the copyright owner or the owner's agent.

You should request Copyright Office registration and assignment searches to confirm what the permissions department tells you about ownership of rights.

In book publishing, split rights situations are common, with either the author or the publisher splitting "subsidiary rights" among a number of exclusive licensees. For example, clearing three pages of text for IBM's *Columbus* CD-ROM title required getting permission from seven rights owners (four in the U.S. and three in Europe).

The current trend is to negotiate and grant exclusive licenses by market or media segment. Some common rights categories are the first publication right, the reprint right, the audiocassette right, the audiovisual or motion picture right, and the electronic version right. If the rights are split up, it may be difficult to tell who has the authority to grant you a license.

Copyright Office searches are discussed in "Determining Who Owns the Copyright," Chapter 12.

Nontrade Books

Nontrade books—reference and educational books—usually are written by the publisher's employees and are works made for hire. If you want to use excerpts from a nontrade book, you should contact the publisher. However, if the publisher already has granted exclusive licenses, it may be difficult to determine whether the publisher or one of its licensees has the authority to issue you a license.

 Developer wants to use excerpts from a reference book owned by ED Publishing in his CD-ROM reference work. ED Publishing already has granted "electronic rights" in the book to Electronic Publishing. It is unclear whether ED or Electronic Publishing has the authority to license Developer to use the excerpts.

Newspapers, Magazines, and Journals

If you wish to use factual material from newspapers, magazines, and journals, review it to make sure that you need a license. You do not need a license to use facts. A work's copyright does not cover its facts. The reason is discussed in "When You Don't Need a License," Chapter 11.

Newspapers

Newspaper articles are generally works made for hire written by newspaper employees. However, they may not be employees of the newspaper in which you read the article. Many newspapers are now licensing articles from major newspapers such as *The New York Times* or the *Washington Post*. Special features are often specially commissioned works made for hire. Copyrights in syndicated columns ("Dear Abby," for example) are generally owned by the syndicator.

Magazines

The term "work made for hire" is discussed in "The Work Made for Hire Rule," Chapter 4.

Many magazine articles are written by employees or by free-lancers as specially commissioned works made for hire. Some articles are written by free-lancers who retain their copyrights. The copyright on an issue of a magazine does not cover preexisting material used in the magazine unless the preexisting material has been assigned to the publisher or is a work made for hire.

In the past, many magazines obtained from free-lance authors only one-time publication rights or North American serial rights (that is, the exclusive right to publish the article in newspapers, magazines, and other serials in North America for the copyright term). The free-lance author retained all other rights. Now, an increasing number of magazines require that a free-lance author assign all rights to the magazine.

Journals

Articles in technical and scholarly journals are written primarily by free-lancers. Many are written as specially commissioned works made for hire. Other articles are written by free-lancers and licensed or assigned to the journal.

Other Resources

If you are having trouble locating the author of an article, you may be able to get information from one of the writers' organizations, such as the National Writers Union, the Writers Guild of America, Authors Guild, and the American Society of Journalists and Authors. Three organizations—the Authors Guild, American Society of Journalists and Authors, and the Association of Author's Representatives—have created the Author's Registry which provides contacts for authors and their representatives. Information on how to contact these organizations is in Appendix F.

R. R. Bowker publishes a number of books about the publishing industry that may be helpful in locating authors or their representatives. The most useful of these works for clearance purposes is *Literary Market Place.*

Licensing Photographs and Still Images

The primary concern in clearing photographs and still images is copyright. As with text, the first question to ask in clearing photographs and still images is whether they are still protected by copyright.

A photograph may contain images of other copyrightable works, such as sculpture or paintings, which are separately owned and need to be separately cleared.

Some photographers may be reluctant to grant you a license to use their photographs in your multimedia work. This may be because they are concerned that the digitized version that you create will be redistributed to others and that you and others will alter the image without permission. (Once a photograph has been digitized, it can easily be copied, distributed, and altered).

See "Public Domain Works," Chapter 11.

If you are negotiating with a graphic artist or illustrator for permission to use his or her work, he or she probably will want to know how you plan to use the work. You should be prepared to discuss your potential use in detail, because many graphic designers are concerned about how their works will look when incorporated into larger works. For example, the latest version of the Graphic Arts Guild standard contract states that "any electronic alteration of original art (color shift, mirroring, flopping, combination cut and paste, deletion) is prohibited without the express permission of the artist."

See "Permits," Chapter 15.

Clearance Steps

If the photograph or still image is protected by copyright, you need to identify the rights you will need. If you are simply including part or all of the photograph or still image without alteration, you may only need reproduction and distribution rights. If you intend to alter the photograph, you will need the modification right. If you are using the photograph or still image on-line, you also may need the right to publicly display the photograph in your work.

Review photographs and still images carefully to make sure they do not defame individuals who are shown. A book publisher who inserted an image of a model into a photo of an older man holding a "dirty book" was found liable for defamation.

Using a photograph that shows a recognizable individual or individual's home could violate the individual's rights of privacy and publicity. If the photographer did not obtain a broad release (discussed in "The Rights of Publicity and Privacy," Chapter 15) and it is not possible for you get a release, the most common approach is to obtain strong "representations and warranties," backed by an indemnity, from the licensor that the photograph does not invade any individual's rights of publicity or privacy or defame anyone.

See "Libel," Chapter 15.

If you plan to alter a "work of visual art," you should read "The Visual Artists Rights Act," Chapter 12, and you should get any necessary waivers from the artist who created the work. The act defines a "work of visual art" as a limited-edition painting, drawing, print, sculpture, or photograph produced for exhibition purposes. Works made for hire are excluded from the definition. You also may need waivers of moral rights (also discussed in "The Visual Artists Rights Act," Chapter 12 and in "Licensing Text," earlier in this chapter).

See "Typical Contract Provisions," Chapter 5, and "The Contract," Chapter 6.

You may need permission to use photographs or images of actual goods bearing trademarks. This topic is discussed in "Using Third-Party Trademarks," Chapter 17. Characters shown in photographs and images may be protected by trademark law and copyright law. See "Logos and Characters," later in this chapter.

For the other steps in clearing photographs and images, see "Clearance Steps" in the "Licensing Text" section of this chapter.

Locating Owners

Identifying the owners of photographs and still images can be one of the most difficult clearance tasks. Common industry practices are described in this section.

Photographs

Copyrights in photographs made by employees—a newspaper photographer or an employee of a corporation's communications department, for example—are owned by the employer.

Many photographers work as independent contractors. Copyrights in photographs created by a photographer for a client ("on assignment") are owned by the photographer unless:

➤ The client got an assignment of the copyright (unusual); or

➤ The photograph was made as a specially commissioned work made for hire.

Determining who owns the copyright in a photograph made by a freelance photographer can be difficult. If the photograph was created by a free-lance photographer for a client and the copyright is not registered, the only way to determine who owns the copyright is to ask the photographer or the client. Either or both of these parties may have misconceptions about the rules of copyright ownership or the application of the rules to the particular photograph. For example:

See "Copyright Ownership," Chapter 8.

> ➤ The client may think that because it has a print of the photograph, it owns the copyright and has the right to authorize use of the photograph. This ignores the distinction copyright law makes between ownership of a copy and ownership of copyright rights (discussed in "Owning a Copy of a Work," Chapter 4).

> ➤ The client may think that because it ordered and paid for making the photograph, it owns the copyright. This ignores the ownership rules for works created by independent contractors (discussed in "Copyright Ownership," Chapter 8).

> ➤ The photographer may not remember giving an assignment or signing a work made for hire agreement, or may not understand the legal significance of those agreements.

The problem of determining copyright ownership for photographs is further complicated because photographs are often incorporated in other works—ads, brochures, and magazine articles, for example. Frequently, the only copyright notice in these works is the one for the owner of the copyright in the larger work. To determine who owns the copyright in the photograph, you have to contact the owner of the copyright in the larger work.

If you have a copy of the book or magazine in which the photograph appeared, it may include the name of the photographer. If not, you can call the publication to try and identify him or her. Generally, a search of the Copyright Office will be of limited value because of the difficulty of identifying the photograph. You may be able to locate the photographer by contacting stock agencies or by contacting the Picture Agency Council of America (the trade association of photo stock agencies).

You can avoid ownership questions by using stock photography from stock houses or media libraries, discussed in "Stock Houses and Libraries," Chapter 12. Some of these companies offer image catalogs on CD-ROM and on-line.

Some stock houses have discounted rates for multimedia products. Others charge multimedia producers almost the standard rate for "editorial" use—between $100 and $250 per picture for a run of 10,000 units.

Graphics and Illustrations

Graphics and illustrations created by employees—for example, a magazine cover by an employee of a magazine publisher—are owned by the employer as works made for hire.

If the graphics or illustrations appear in a work created for another party, the other party may own the copyright.

 Ed, an employee of Ad Agency, created an ad for Client. The copyright in the ad belongs to Client if Client got an assignment of the copyright. Otherwise, Ad Agency owns the copyright.

In the United States, much of the graphic design and illustration work is done by independent contractors. Designs and illustrations made by independent contractors may be owned by the hiring parties through assignment or as specially created works made for hire. However, the standard contracts put out by the graphic arts trade associations generally provide that the artist owns the copyright.

Clip Art and Multimedia Tools

See "Copyright Ownership," Chapter 8.

In your multimedia projects, you generally can use clip art and stock content from multimedia development tools without obtaining licenses. However, you should carefully review the written material distributed with these works. In many cases, the material comes with express or implied licenses that restrict use of the collection. Some of these licenses provide only limited permission to use the product—for example, use for noncommercial purposes or use in no more than a stated number of copies. "Public performance" use may not be included.

The packaging for these products can be deceptive. You may have to read the "read me" file to determine what uses are authorized.

Fine Art

See "The Exclusive Rights," Chapter 2, and "Determining What Rights You Need," Chapter 12.

As with photographs, the ownership of copyrights in works of fine art is subject to significant confusion. Owners of a copy of the work—a painting or a sculpture, for example—often think they own the copyright in the work. However, under current law, unless they employed the artist or obtained an assignment of the copyright from the artist, they don't.

If you want to use an image of a work of fine art in your multimedia work and the owner of the copy doesn't own the copyright, you should find the artist and obtain a license from the artist. (This topic is discussed in "Permits," Chapter 15.)

Licensing Film and Television Clips

See "Copyright Ownership," Chapter 8.

Motion pictures and television series, mini-series, and documentaries are protected by copyright law as audiovisual works. To lawfully use a film or television clip, depending on the situation, you may have to obtain licenses or releases from a number of parties:

➤ The owner of the copyright in the underlying work (novel, short story, play) on which the work you want to use is based.

➤ The owner of the copyright in the motion picture, television series, or documentary you want to use.

➤ The performers (and possibly other contributors).

You also will have to pay applicable union reuse fees. If the film clip contains music or choreography, you also may have to obtain separate licenses for those.

The Underlying Work's Copyright

Many movies, television series, and mini-series are derivative works based on original plays, short stories, or novels. If you want to use a clip from a movie that was based on a play, short story, or novel, you should obtain Copyright Office registration and assignment searches to find out who owns the copyright in the underlying work, if it is not in the public domain. Unless the studio acquired all rights in the underlying work, you probably will need a license from the owner of the underlying work.

The Desired Work's Copyright

You should request Copyright Office registration and assignment searches to find out who owns the copyright in the motion picture, television series, mini-series, or documentary. In recent years, many studios have assigned the copyrights in their entire libraries of copyrighted motion pictures, so you cannot assume that the company named in the copyright notice is the current owner of the copyright.

The licensing of motion picture clips—particular a clip from a major motion picture—may be particularly difficult. Studios are sometimes reluctant to license a portion of the work because they are concerned that doing so would cheapen the work as a whole and damage the market for the work. Also, a studio may consider clip licensing more trouble than it's worth, given the complicated multiple permission and release requirements that may apply.

Most prime-time television series and documentaries are not owned by the television networks that broadcast these programs. They are licensed by the networks from independent producers. However, networks sometimes acquire audiovisual rights in series or documentaries. This situation may change as the rules regulating network ownership change.

Copyright Office searches are discussed in "Determining Who Owns the Copyright," Chapter 12.

Performers and Contributors

Find out whether those who worked on the movie, television series, mini-series, or documentary—writer, writer-producer, director, and performers—have an ownership interest in the copyright. Generally they do not, because their contributions are works made for hire.

The Writer

The script is usually a specially commissioned work made for hire owned by the studio. Sometimes, though, an original script created by a writer "on spec" (without a contract) is used. In that situation, the studio usually gets an assignment of the screenplay copyright and registers the assignment in the Copyright Office.

See "Reuse Provisions," Chapter 16.

However, if the script was subject to the Writers' Guild Basic Agreement, the writer may have retained certain rights. Thus, either the producer or the writer may own the rights you need.

The Director

Contracts between motion picture studios and directors generally provide that the director's contribution to a motion picture is a work made for hire that belongs to the studio. However, directors sometimes include in these contracts a clause requiring that the director's consent be obtained if the work is to be altered. Under the Directors Guild Basic Agreement, a director must be consulted if a theatrical motion picture is edited for certain other uses.

Performers

See "The Rights of Publicity and Privacy," Chapter 15.

Contracts between studios and performers generally provide that a performer's contribution is a work made for hire owned by the producer, so you probably don't need to get copyright licenses from performers shown in the clip (although you do need a license from the clip's copyright owner). You probably will need to obtain releases from all performers shown or heard in the clip before using the clip in your multimedia work, if the studio didn't get broad releases from them.

If the performers belong to the Screen Actor's Guild (SAG) or the American Federation of Television and Radio Artists (AFTRA), in most instances union rules require that performers' consent be obtained and that reuse fees be negotiated or paid before a clip containing photography or sound track of the performer is used in another work. A reuse fee is generally charged for such consent.

Union Reuse Fees

Directors, actors, and screenwriters generally belong to unions. The unions have collective bargaining agreements with studios requiring the payment of reuse fees when a film or film excerpt is used in a medium other than the medium for which the film originally was intended. If you use a film clip in a multimedia project, the current owner of the motion picture copyright will have to pay those reuse fees (and will add the fees to the cost of your license). Union reuse fees are discussed in "Reuse Provisions," Chapter 16.

Music or Choreography

If the clip contains music or choreography, you may have to obtain a separate license authorizing you to use it. If the music or choreography was created and recorded as a work made for hire for the studio, the owner of the clip's copyright owns the rights to the music or choreography and can authorize you to use the music. However, if the music or choreography was not created as a work made for hire and is still protected by copyright, the clip's copyright owner usually will not have authority to grant you a license to use the music or choreography as contained in the clip. In that case, obtain Copyright Office registration and assignment searches to determine who owns the music or choreography copyright.

> Copyright Office searches are discussed in "Determining Who Owns the Copyright," Chapter 12.

If the music was recorded from a record company's "master recording," you also may need a separate license from the owner of the "master recording" copyright.

> Music licensing is discussed in "Option #2: Using Preexisting Music," Chapter 14.

Clearance Steps

As with text and photographs, the first step in clearing motion picture and television clips is to find out whether the motion picture, television series, mini-series, or documentary and any incorporated other copyrightable works are protected by copyright. Even if the motion picture is in the public domain, incorporated works such as musical compositions could still be protected—as could the work on which the motion picture was based. You also must consider whether you need releases from performers and contributors and whether you need to pay union reuse fees, as described earlier in this section.

> See "Public Domain Works," Chapter 11.

If you are simply including part or all of the clip without alteration, you may only need reproduction and distribution rights. If you intend to alter the clip, you will need the modification right. To modify the work, you may need a waiver of moral rights, discussed in "The Visual Artists Rights Act," Chapter 12, or permission from the director. If you will be using the clip on-line, you also may need the right to publicly perform it.

Review the clip carefully to determine if there are defamation and right of publicity and privacy concerns for any recognizable individuals shown in the clip. These topics are discussed in Chapter 15. If the studio or producer obtained permits and releases, review those to determine if they will protect you. If the clip shows copyrighted or trademarked products, read "Permits," Chapter 15, and "Using Third-Party Trademarks," Chapter 17.

It probably will be difficult to obtain rights to use stills or characters from a motion picture clip in other products such as toys and t-shirts, because most studios have active merchandising programs. (See "Logos and Characters," later in this chapter.)

The other steps involved in clearing film and television are discussed in the "Clearing the Rights" section of "Licensing Text," earlier in this chapter.

Locating Owners

The credits on a motion picture or television program are your starting point. Unfortunately, older films were not as careful about giving credit, so you need to be particularly careful in relying on credits in such films. Motion picture copyrights are frequently registered with the Copyright Office, so a registration search may be helpful. Contacting the studio or production company may also be helpful. SAG and AFTRA will be able to assist you in locating performers or their agents.

Additional information is available in various film libraries. The largest such library on the West Coast is at the University of California at Los Angeles (UCLA). The UCLA Archive publishes *Collection Profiles and Study Guides* describing its holdings.

See "Determining Who Owns the Copyright," Chapter 12.

Licensing Video

Many of the difficulties in licensing movies can be avoided by using video clips from media libraries. Media libraries are discussed in "Stock Houses and Libraries," Chapter 12. Media libraries generally own the copyrights in their videos. However, they may not have cleared union reuse fees or the publicity rights of the individuals appearing in the video, and they may not be able to grant you all the rights you need for your intended use of the clip.

If you are obtaining video clips from an independent producer or a video library, make certain that the producer obtained the releases required under the law of publicity. If you will be using a video clip that contains copyrighted music or choreography owned by someone other than the producer, get separate licenses to use the music or choreography. Even if you have good reason to believe that a producer has the right to grant you a license to use the music or choreography, your use will infringe the music or choreography copyright if the producer does not have that right. If the clip shows copyrighted objects—sculptures or paintings, for example— you also need a license to use the images of those objects.

Other steps for clearing video footage are discussed in "Clearance Steps," in the "Text Licensing" section of this chapter.

Logos and Characters

If you want to use a title logo or character from a motion picture, television series, fiction series, or cartoon strip in your multimedia work, you need to obtain a "merchandise license" from the owner of the character. So-called "distinctively delineated" characters are protected under both copyright law and trademark law (trademark law protects the owner's right to use the character in connection with goods or services).

See "The Rights of Publicity and Privacy," Chapter 13.

 Developer wants to use a drawing of a famous cartoon character in her multimedia work and on the packaging in which her work will be distributed. The cartoon character is protected by the copyright in the cartoon strip in which the character appears. The name and image of the cartoon character also are protected under trademark law. If Developer uses a drawing of the cartoon character without obtaining a merchandise license, she will be infringing third-party copyright and trademark rights.

A typical merchandise license authorizes the licensee to use the licensed character or title in artwork preapproved by the licensor in connection with the manufacture, sale, and distribution of specified products.

If you are trying to clear characters used in a text work, you should first review the credits page to determine if the character is separately owned. You may want to search the Copyright Office records for the character alone, because characters are separately protectable. Because characters also may be protected by trademark, you may want to perform a search in the U.S. Patent and Trademark Office to determine if the character is registered as a trademark. The trademark registration will include the name and address of the owner of the trademark.

If you are trying to clear cartoon characters, you also should consider consulting the Screen Cartoonists Union, Local 839 of the International Alliance of Theatrical State Employees (IATSE) (see Appendix F).

Licensing Software

Trademark searches are discussed in "Clearing a Trademark," Chapter 17.

If you are using software that is owned by a third party, you should obtain a license from the copyright owner. If your software is developed for you by a software consultant, you should obtain a copyright assignment or license from the consultant. For a sample software component license, see Form 14 in Appendix B.

Checklist for Licensing Text, Photographs, and Still Images

1. Is the material you want to use protected by copyright in the countries in which you wish to use it?

2. Does the material include or show other copyrightable works that require separate clearance, or is it based on another copyrightable work?

3. What elements do you want to license from the copyrighted material?

4. What rights do you need?

5. What geographical areas do you want to cover in your license?

6. Who owns the rights you need in those geographical areas?

7. Do you need sublicensing rights or subsidiary rights?

8. How do you define your product?

9. Does the material include or refer to recognizable individuals or their homes (requiring defamation and privacy/publicity clearance)?

10. Do you need trademark licenses?

11. Do you need waivers of moral rights or Visual Artists Rights Act rights?

Checklist for Licensing Motion Picture, Television, and Video Clips

1. Is the clip protected by copyright in the countries in which you wish to use it?

2. Is the clip based on another work, such as a film based on a book?

3. If the clip contains music, is the music of the soundtrack owned by a different company?

4. If the clip contains music, is the performance of the music in the soundtrack (the sound recording) owned by a different company?

5. Does the clip include dancing? If so, who owns the copyright in the choreography?

6. Does the clip include voice-over? If so, who owns the copyright in the voice-over?

7. Does the clip include animation or other special effects?

8. Does the clip include other copyrightable or trademarked works such as a toy or sculpture which you also will need to clear?

9. What rights do you need?

10. What geographical areas do you want to cover?

11. Who owns the rights you need in those geographical areas?

12. Do you need sublicensing rights or subsidiary rights?

13. How will you define your product?

14. Does the clip include recognizable actors whose rights of publicity need to be cleared?

15. Does the clip include acting by "doubles" or stunt actors whose performance needs to be cleared?

16. What union reuse fees need to be paid? What permissions need to be obtained?

17. Does the clip include recognizable homes or locations which need to be cleared?

18. Does the clip violate the privacy rights of any individual?

19. Are there third-party contract rights which need to be waived (from the writer or director, for example)?

20. Do you need a waiver of moral rights of the producer or director?

14 Using Music

To obtain music for your multimedia works, you can create original music, get permission to use preexisting copyrighted music, find public domain music, or use music from a music library. There are legal issues that must be considered for each of these four options.

Checklists for music licensing are at the end of this chapter.

Copyrights in Music

Original musical compositions are protected by copyright as soon as they are fixed in any tangible medium of expression. As with other intellectual property, the owner of a copyrighted musical composition has the exclusive right to:

➤ Reproduce and distribute the musical composition in sheet music and in phonorecords (defined broadly to include audiotapes and compact discs).

➤ Modify the composition to create derivative works based on the composition.

➤ Publicly display the composition.

➤ Publicly perform the composition.

These are the same rights discussed in "The Exclusive Rights," Chapter 2.

In some respects, music copyright law differs from copyright law in general. Special features of music copyright law are discussed in this section.

Compulsory License Provision

For most types of works, whether to permit third parties to use a copyrighted work is solely up to the copyright owner. However, the Copyright Act has a "compulsory license" provision for music. This provision stipulates that once phonorecords of a musical work have been distributed to the public, any other person may obtain a compulsory license to make and distribute phonorecords of the work to the public for private use (in other words, for home use).

The compulsory licensing provision does not apply to licensing for multimedia works for two reasons:

Compulsory
licenses for
noncommercial
educational
broadcasts are
discussed in
"Distance
Learning,"
Chapter 24.

➤ Multimedia works are not within the Copyright Act's definition of phonorecords ("material objects in which sounds, other than those accompanying a motion picture or other audiovisual work, are fixed by any method now known or later developed").

➤ Multimedia works require "synchronization" licenses—permission to use music in synchronization with an audiovisual work. Synchronization licenses cannot be obtained under the compulsory license provision. (Synchronization licenses are discussed in "Option #2: Using Preexisting Music," later in this chapter.)

Sound Recordings

Once musical compositions are recorded, the resulting sound recording is a separate work. It has a copyright that is separate from the copyrights on the musical compositions used in the recording. The copyright on a sound recording covers the original expression added by the record developer in creating the recording—the way the musical composition is sung on the recording, the way it is played, the musical arrangement, the sound engineer's mixing, and so on. The Copyright Act defines sound recordings as "works that result from the fixation of a series of musical, spoken, or other sounds regardless of the nature of the material objects, such as discs, tapes, or other phonorecords, in which they are embodied." For sound recordings made by U.S. "authors," only those recordings fixed and published on or after February 15, 1972, are protected by copyright. Pre-1972 sound recordings by U.S. authors are not protected by federal copyright law, but they may be protected under state law.

Foreign-made sound recordings, until recently, were treated the same as U.S.-made recordings—i.e., no protection for pre-1972 recordings. However, effective January 1, 1996, pre-1972 foreign sound recordings whose "source country" is a member of the Berne Convention or the World Trade Organization are protected by copyright. (This change in the law is part of the GATT legislation discussed in "Public Domain Works," Chapter 11.)

In the United States, the owner of a sound recording copyright gives notice of copyright by using the℗ symbol. If you carefully examine the packaging that comes with a record, tape, or compact disc, you will see that the packaging contains a sound recording copyright—for example,℗ 1993 Pacific Entertainment." Copyright information for the individual songs usually appears on the liner notes inside the package.

Licensing

What licenses you need to use preexisting music in your multimedia works depends on whether you will be taping a preexisting sound recording or recording your own version of the musical compositions you use.

> **Get a License**
> Virgin Records is suing actress Cindy Crawford for allegedly using the song "Big Wheels in Shanty Town" in an exercise video without paying royalties.

➤ If you will be using musicians to record your own version of a musical composition, you need a license from the owner of the musical composition copyright.

➤ If you will be taping music from a record, tape, or compact disc, you need two copyright licenses—one from the owner of the copyright in the musical composition and one from the owner of the copyright in the sound recording. The owner of the musical composition copyright generally cannot authorize you to copy the version of the song that is fixed in the sound recording. The owner of the sound recording copyright generally cannot authorize you to use the song.

Option #1: Creating Original Music

You may think that creating original music for your multimedia work is not practical, because you don't know any composers and you can't afford to pay for original music. Both of these assumptions are incorrect. Full-service music arranging and composing services with reasonable fees can be found in most major cities (check the Yellow Pages under "Music Arrangers and Composers" and video industry directories).

A full-service arranging and composing facility can provide orchestration and production of the finished piece as well as composition. It also can create a sound recording (known in the music industry as a "master recording") of the original music.

See "Written Contracts," Chapter 5.

Using an Arranging and Composing Service

Like your other production contracts, your agreement with a music arranging and composing service should take the form of a signed written contract. The contract should spell out the rights and duties of each party to the agreement. The contract should cover the following points:

➤ Whether the arranging and composing service is obligated to compose; compose and arrange; or compose, arrange, and produce the master recording.

See "Using Works That You Own," Chapter 11.

➤ Who will own the copyright in the music (and in the master recording, if one is to be made). If you obtain ownership of the copyrights in the music and in the master recording, you can copy the master in the future without worrying about copyright clearance and license fees. To avoid future legal disputes with the arranging and composing service and to provide you with maximum flexibility, the contract should state that you will own all rights, including the copyrights, everywhere in the world and for all time. To ensure that you obtain ownership, your agreement should also contain a copyright assignment or work made for hire provision (as discussed in "Copyright Ownership," Chapter 8).

➤ How much you will pay for the service's work and when payment is due.

See "Unions and Multimedia," Chapter 16.

➤ Who will pay any applicable American Federation of Musicians union fees, if the service is to create the master recording as well as compose and arrange the music.

➤ Whether the agreement is assignable. If you are expecting the work to be done by particular individuals who are employed by the arranging and composing service, the contract should state that the work must be done by those individuals and that the service cannot assign its contract obligations to another party.

Warranties

See "Contracts with Independent Contractors," Chapter 8.

Your contract with the arranging and composing service should include a warranty by the service that the material is original and does not infringe upon third parties' copyrights, trademarks, or other property rights. The contract also should include an indemnity provision.

If the arranging and composing service will be creating the master, it is a good idea to get written consents from musicians and vocalists before the recording session begins. A new anti-bootlegging law prohibits making audio or video recordings of live musical performances without the consent of the performers. While it is possible that performer consent would be implied in a recording studio situation, cautious record producers are obtaining performance consents for recording sessions.

Option #2: Using Preexisting Music

To use preexisting copyrighted music, you must obtain licenses for the chosen musical compositions. To use music you create by copying preexisting recordings, you must obtain master recording licenses from the owners of the sound recordings as well as licenses to use the musical compositions. Most composers in this country assign their copyrights to a music publishing company in exchange for a percentage of all future royalties generated by licensing the composition. If the composer of the musical composition you want to use has assigned the copyright, you need to obtain a license from the current copyright owner, not from the composer.

See "Determining Who Owns the Copyright," Chapter 12.

Myths About Music Copying

The music industry in this country will not permit copyright infringement, and you should not use copyrighted musical compositions or sound recordings without getting licenses—nor should you believe the following myths about music copying:

Myth #1: "Copying a small amount is okay."

Many people think that it is permissible to use three or four bars of a song without getting permission from the copyright owner. This is not true. Copying a small amount of a work is copyright infringement if what is copied is a qualitatively substantial portion of the copied work—part of the chorus of a song, for example.

In one case, the court held that copying a six-note phrase from a work was copyright infringement because the copied phrase, in spite of its brevity, was what caused audiences to listen, applaud, and buy copies of the work. *Baxter v. MCA,* 812 F.2d 412 (9th Cir.), *cert. denied, Williams v. Baxter,* 484 U.S. 954 (1987). In another case, the court held that the sounds "Brrr" and "Hugga Hugga" used in a "rap" song could be sufficiently creative to warrant copyright protection. *Tin Pan Apple v. Miller Brewing Co., Inc.,* 1994 U.S. Dist. LEXIS 2178 (S.D.N.Y. 1994).

Whether copying a small amount of a song is infringement or not can only be decided on a case-by-case basis. Given the costs of copyright litigation and the penalties for infringement, you should obtain a license if you plan to use any portion of a song.

Myth #2: "Digital sampling is okay."

Digital sampling means extracting portions of a prior recording for use in a new recording using a device that can store the copied material in a computer's memory. This process may be copyright infringement of both the sound recording and the copied musical composition.

In 1991, a Federal District Court in New York enjoined all sales of a rap artist's album because the artist had included a digital sample of three words and accompanying music taken from a recording of a Gilbert O'Sullivan song. *Grand Upright Music Ltd. v. Warner Bros. Records, Inc.,* 780 F. Supp. 182 (S.D.N.Y. 1991). While some digital sampling may be noninfringing—using a two-note phrase or a single grunt from a background singer, for example—it is difficult to know where to draw the line between infringing and noninfringing sampling. (De minimus copying—copying a small amount—is discussed in "Myths," Chapter 11.)

Fair use is discussed in "When You Don't Need a License," Chapter 11.

Fair use is unlikely to be a defense to digital sampling for commercial production of multimedia works. Avoid sampling or obtain a license, or sample from copyright-free music (discussed in "Option #4: Using Music from Music Libraries," later in this chapter).

Myth #3: "It's okay to copy a song's melody so long as I don't copy the lyrics."

Using the melody of a copyrighted song without the lyrics is infringement if you don't obtain a license. The copyright on a song covers both the lyrics and the melody. The fact that you have not copied the entire copyrighted work (lyrics plus melody) does not excuse the copying of the protected melody.

Myth #4: "It's okay to copy a song's melody if I use new words with the melody."

When you add new words to a song, you are "reproducing" the melody and creating a "derivative work" based on the original song, violating the copyright owner's reproduction and modification rights. (These rights are discussed in "The Exclusive Rights," Chapter 2.) To lawfully use the melody of a copyrighted song with new lyrics, you need a license to modify the work.

Myth #5: "I bought this record, so it's okay for me to copy it."

The purchase of a copy of a protected work does not give the purchaser permission to exercise the copyright owner's exclusive rights with respect to the work. In copyright law, ownership of a copy of a protected work or of a phonorecord is separate from ownership of the copyright rights. (This topic is discussed in "Owning a Copy of a Work," Chapter 4.)

> ### A Sampling Controversy
> Recording artist Vanilla Ice's 1990 single, "Ice Ice Baby," contained a melody line—clearly recognizable—from a song by David Bowie and Queen. When "Ice Ice Baby" became a hit, the music publisher that owned the Bowie-Queen song sued Vanilla Ice and his record company for a share of the royalties—as did the record company that owned the sound recording copyright for the sampled recording.

Myth #6: "It's okay to secretly tape a live musical performance and use the taped music in my multimedia product."

A 1994 federal anti-bootlegging law prohibits making audio or video recordings of live musical performances without the consent of the performers. The law also prohibits the reproduction and distribution of unauthorized recordings of live musical performances. In addition, the taping and use of the taped music would infringe the copyrights on any copyrighted musical compositions being performed.

Methods of Obtaining Licenses

The performing rights organizations—American Society of Composers, Authors, & Publishers (ASCAP), Broadcast Music Incorporated (BMI), and SESAC—cannot grant you the permission you need to use copyrighted music in a multimedia work (although they can help you locate copyright holders). While most songwriters belong to one of these organizations, ASCAP and BMI grant public performance licenses only. To use music in a multimedia work, you need a "synchronization" license (discussed in "What Rights You Need," later in this chapter).

> The performing rights organizations are discussed in "Public Performance Licenses,", later in this chapter.

There are two types of agencies that can help you get music licenses: the Harry Fox Agency, which represents a number of music publishers, and rights clearance agencies.

The Harry Fox Agency

While some music publishers handle their own music licensing, many publishers have authorized the Harry Fox Agency (established by the National Music Publishers Association) as their licensing agent. The agency's phone number is (212) 370-5330.

This agency has been granting multimedia licenses for several years, both for works designed for in-house use and for works designed for the consumer market. There is no charge for using the agency's services. Of course, the copyright owner will charge you a license fee for using the composition. The agency's fee is paid by the music publisher on whose behalf the agency acts.

Rights Clearance Agencies

You can use a rights clearance agency (also known as a rights and permission agency) to obtain the music licenses you need. A rights clearance agency will find out who owns the copyrights and whether licenses are available for your intended use. These agencies also will negotiate license fees and obtain licenses for you. Rights clearance agencies are discussed in "Rights Clearance Agencies," Chapter 12. A list of these agencies is in Appendix C.

Using a rights clearance agency is a good idea if you are planning on using excerpts of many musical compositions in your work (you may go crazy if you don't use one). If you are using excerpts of only a few, decide whether the clearance fee charged by a clearance agency is worth the trouble you will save yourself.

Music supervisors are available to help you choose musical compositions and recordings for your multimedia products. Some supervisors also handle rights clearance.

Getting Started

If you are planning on using copyrighted music in your multimedia work, clear the rights before you put your multimedia work together. Remember, the Copyright Act gives you no legal basis for demanding that a copyright owner give you a license. If you have a record, tape, or compact disc of a song that you want to use, you may find the name of the copyright owner for the song in the liner notes (for example, Sunny Day, by Susie Songwriter, Copyright 1992 XYZ Music, Inc.). The company named in the sound recording copyright notice—℗—owns the copyright in the sound recording, not the copyrights in the individual songs. You need permission from the record company only if you are planning on copying the actual recording of the song. (This topic is discussed in "Master Recording Licenses," later in this chapter).

To get started, call the music publisher and ask whether it has its own licensing department or uses the Harry Fox Agency for licensing. If the Harry Fox Agency handles the publisher's licensing, call the Harry Fox Agency and ask for the agent who handles multimedia licenses. If you are using a rights clearance agency, the agency will find out who owns the copyrights in the songs you want to use. Make certain that the agent with whom you are dealing understands what multimedia is and what use you will be making of music in your multimedia work. If you do not know who owns the copyright in the song you want, call the Harry Fox Agency or the index department of ASCAP, BMI, or SESAC (the phone numbers are in Appendix C) to find out. You also can look the song up by title in the Catalog of Copyright Entries to find out who registered the copyright. (This catalog is discussed in "Determining Who Owns the Copyright," Chapter 12.)

Searches are discussed in "Determining Who Owns the Copyright," Chapter 12.

If you are planning widespread distribution of your work, you should request Copyright Office registration and assignment searches for each song you want to use—even if you think you have identified the copyright owners. While you should try to get a warranty of noninfringement and an indemnity from all copyright owners who grant you licenses, music publishers generally will give you only a limited indemnity in which their exposure is limited to the amount of the license fee.

Complete the Copyright Office search early, so that you will be able to substitute other works if there are problems with the work's chain of title.

Music publishers that have not previously granted multimedia licenses may be reluctant to grant licenses for this new medium. The reluctance comes from concern that granting licenses for a new medium will somehow have a negative effect on the value of the musical works. You may have to educate the publisher's licensing agent about multimedia works. Explain the technology, explain what role music will play in your multimedia work, and even send the licensing agent a copy of a sample multimedia work. You also might suggest the name of a commercially marketed multimedia work that the agent can view.

Music publishers should be encouraged to view multimedia as a new avenue for the exploitation of music—and a way to increase the public's exposure to their music. Most members of the music publishing business are eager to find new markets for music and for music licenses, and they will work with you to create a good business agreement.

As with other types of works, before you begin negotiating for a license, you should know exactly what use you will make of the licensed music and disclose all your planned uses. You will need to provide detailed information before you are quoted a license fee (music publishers use the information on your planned use in determining their fee).

Remember that while a copyright license is a defense to infringement, a license is no protection for uses of the work that are not authorized in the license.

 Developer obtained a license from Music Publisher to use Music Publisher's copyrighted song, "Windy Hill," in Developer's multimedia work. Although the license did not authorize Developer to change the lyrics, Developer changed them. Developer's license is no defense to an infringement suit charging Developer with unauthorized modification of the song. If Developer wanted to change the words, Developer should have obtained "parody authorization" from Music Publisher (permission to modify the lyrics).

If you want the right to use the music in more than one multimedia work, the license must explicitly give you that right. Consequently, the licensing agent needs to know what you want.

Developer obtained a license to use a five-second excerpt of Music Publisher's copyrighted song in Developer's work, City Tour. Developer later used the same excerpt in another multimedia work, Downtown. Developer's use of the music in Downtown is copyright infringement.

See "Obtaining a License," Chapter 12.

Chain of title complications are discussed in "Determining Who Owns the Copyright," Chapter 12.

See "Determining What Rights You Need," Chapter 12.

What Rights You Need

To use copyrighted music in a multimedia work, you need a license to reproduce the chosen music for use in your multimedia work and to distribute copies of the music as it appears in your finished product. In some cases, you also will need a public performance and public display license. (These rights are discussed in "The Exclusive Rights," Chapter 2, and in "Determining What Rights You Need," Chapter 12). If you plan to modify the music—create new lyrics, for example—you also need a license to do that. The music publisher's contract with the songwriter may require that the songwriter give consent for alterations.

The music industry has its own licensing terminology, and it is helpful to know the terminology when dealing with music publishers:

➤ **Mechanical license.** A license to copy and distribute a song in the form of records, tapes, or compact discs (audio only) is known as a "mechanical" license. This type license doesn't apply to multimedia works.

➤ **Synchronization license.** A license to copy and distribute music in synchronization with an audiovisual work is known as a synchronization license (also called a "synch" license). Because multimedia works contain audiovisual features, the synch license is closest—in terms of traditional licensing categories—to what you need to reproduce music in your multimedia work.

➤ **Parody authorization.** Permission to modify the lyrics to a song is known as parody authorization.

The License

The license should cover the following points:

➤ Definition of the multimedia product or products in which the music can be used (by title or by description or both). Pay careful attention to this provision. To be able to use the licensed music in future versions or in sequels, you must include future versions or sequels in the definition of the multimedia product. Given the rapid advances in technology, you should try to avoid limiting the product definition to a particular format or configuration (CD-ROM, for example).

➤ Authorized uses, including any limitations on the amount of the work that can be copied and used.

➤ Consideration for the license, whether royalties or one-time fee. (See "Fee Considerations," later in this chapter.)

➤ Term (duration) of the license.

➤ Territory limitations, if any. You probably will want a worldwide license, but the United States copyright owner may not own the worldwide rights.

➤ Whether the license is exclusive or nonexclusive. (These terms are defined in "Licenses," Chapter 4).

➤ Warranties and indemnity. (These are discussed in "Obtaining a License," Chapter 12.)

The Harry Fox Agency has created a special multimedia license. A copy of it appears as Form 15 in Appendix B. For another example of a multimedia music license, see Form 16 in Appendix B.

Licenses are discussed in more detail in "Obtaining a License," Chapter 12.

Fee Considerations

If you are planning to use excerpts from a large number of songs in your multimedia work, you may find it useful to bring this to the attention of licensing agents with whom you deal. You cannot afford to pay each music publisher's motion picture rate for hundreds of songs (not to mention other copyrighted works).

If your work is intended for commercial distribution to consumers, tell the licensing agent how many units you expect to sell and what the retail price per unit will be. Otherwise, music publishers and licensing agents are likely to think that the market and the amount of money you will make on your work are much larger than they are likely to be.

In determining license fees, publishers traditionally take into account the importance of the music in the finished work. For example, the fee for using a publisher's song as "theme" music played over a movie's title is generally higher than the fee for using the song as background music. In an interactive multimedia work, the importance of a song or song excerpt will often vary according to how the user interacts with the multimedia work (because the song plays only when a certain segment of the work is accessed, or because the developer made it possible for the user to customize the work). Similarly, length of use (in number of seconds) is generally a factor in determining the license fee. For an interactive multimedia work, the number of seconds a song actually is played during use of the work will vary from one user to the next.

After You Get a License

Once you have obtained a license, stick to its terms. Do only what you are authorized to do. Be careful to comply with all your license obligations, such as royalty payments. Failure to make royalty payments as required by the license may be material breach of contract. If you are required by the license to pay royalties every quarter and you have a quarter in which you

Breach is discussed in "What is a Contract?," Chapter 5.

make nothing and so owe no royalties, tell the licensor that no royalties are due for that quarter.

Master Recording Licenses

If you decide to copy existing sound recordings, you need licenses from the record companies that own the sound recording copyrights. Licenses to copy sound recordings are known in the music industry as master recording licenses or master licenses. Music licenses from music publishers do not authorize you to copy the copyrighted sound recordings.

 Bay Multimedia wants to use an excerpt of Tony Bennett's rendition of "I Left My Heart in San Francisco" in its interactive travel guide. Bay needs a master license to use the recording as well as a license from the music publisher that owns the copyright on the song.

Obtaining a master license is likely to be difficult. If you succeed in obtaining a license, the license fee may be high. However, as the record industry becomes more knowledgeable about multimedia works, it is likely that an increasing number of record companies will begin making their works available to multimedia developers.

The record company's contract with the recording artist may require that the record company obtain the artist's permission before granting you a master license. Even if the contract does not require the artist's permission for the grant of master licenses, you should obtain the artist's consent to avoid violating an artist's right of publicity in his or her voice. See "The Rights of Publicity and Privacy," Chapter 15. This is true unless the artist's contract with the record company waives the right of publicity for all uses of the recording. If the recording was made by a vocalist who belongs to AFTRA (the American Federation of Radio and Television Artists), you also must comply with AFTRA's reuse rules (see "Reuse Provisions," Chapter 16.) Many recording artists belong to AFTRA.

You also may need permission from the American Federation of Musicians (AFM) to use the master recording (see "Reuse Provisions," Chapter 16). The master license should contain a warranty that the record company has paid all applicable AFM fees.

A sample sound recording license is shown in Form 16 in Appendix B. This license authorizes the licensee to use the licensor's musical compositions and sound recordings.

Permission Required

Remember the Ronettes? They recorded the song "Be My Baby" in 1963. In 1989, American Express used the original sound recording of "Be My Baby" in a television commercial. Amex's ad agency got a license to use the song and a master license, but no one contacted the Ronettes to get their permission to use the recording in the commercial. Their suit against American Express is pending.

U.S.-made sound recordings fixed and published before February 15, 1972, are not protected by federal copyright law, but they may be protected under common law copyright or under state unfair competition or antipiracy statutes. It is advisable to get record company consent for the use of pre-1972 sound recordings.

Recording Your Own Version

Given the difficulty and expense of obtaining master licenses from record companies, you may decide to hire your own musicians to record music for your multimedia work (or to use a music production service to do that). Whether you hire musicians or use a production service, you should get a written contract with an appropriate copyright assignment or work made for hire provision. It is also a good idea to get consents from the performers. (See "Option #1: Creating Original Music," earlier in this chapter).

See "Copyright Ownership," Chapter 8.

Musicians' union issues are covered in "Signing Collective Bargaining Agreements" and "Unions and Multimedia," Chapter 16. If you are using a production service, your contract with the service should state whether you or the production service are responsible for paying any applicable American Federation of Musicians union fees.

Sound-Alike Recordings

In 1988, Bette Midler won a $400,000 judgment in federal court in California against an ad agency that used a sound-alike version of her hit, "Do You Want to Dance." *Midler v. Ford Motor Co.,* 849 F.2d 460 (9th Cir. 1988). The singer who recorded the sound-alike version—a back-up singer for Midler—was instructed to sound as much as possible like the Bette Midler record. The court held that the ad agency had appropriated what was not theirs. Because of this case, several similar cases have been filed. You should not create sound-alike recordings for use in your multimedia work without consulting an experienced attorney.

Public Performance Licenses

If you need a public performance license, ASCAP, BMI, or SESAC may be able to help you. This will depend on whether you need a dramatic or nondramatic performance license. A dramatic performance of a composition is a rendition that is woven into and carries forward a plot and its action (for example, an opera). Whether a use is dramatic or nondramatic must be determined on a case-by-case basis.

See "Determining What Rights You Need," Chapter 12.

ASCAP and BMI issue only nondramatic public performance licenses. Copyright owners—music publishers, generally—retain the right to license dramatic performance rights.

If you need a nondramatic performance license because your work will be shown on television or at a public facility that regularly hosts musical entertainment events (a convention center, for example), you may find that you are already covered by a license obtained by the television station or facility. Television stations, nightclubs, concert halls, and even amusement parks generally pay ASCAP and BMI an annual fee for a "blanket license" that permits the licensee to make unlimited nondramatic-performance use of all songs in these organizations' catalogs.

If you need to obtain your own license, you can find out whether ASCAP, BMI, or SESAC handles the songs you want by calling one of those organizations. (Contact information is in Appendix C.) SESAC is much smaller than the other two organizations and has fewer works under its control. If you have album liner notes for a recorded version of the song, the liner notes usually will indicate whether ASCAP or BMI handles performance rights for the song—for example, "1989 Massive Music (BMI)."

If you are obtaining a master license to copy a song from an existing recording, your license may not need to include permission for public performance. There is no public performance right in sound recordings, with one exception: A recent law creates a performance right in the digital audio transmission of sound recordings. This new law, the "Digital Performance Right in Sound Recordings Act of 1995," creates a new exclusive right for sound recording copyright owners—the exclusive right to publicly perform the sound recording by means of "digital audio transmission."

Option #3: Public Domain Music

If you can locate appropriate public domain music for your multimedia work, you are free to use it—that is, you are free to record your own version of the public domain song. You cannot lawfully copy a public domain song as recorded on a copyrighted record, tape, or compact disc unless you get a master license from the record company that owns the sound recording copyright (see "Master Recording Licenses," earlier in this chapter).

 Bay Multimedia plans to use excerpts from a 1987 recording of Bach's *Brandenburg Concerto No. 4* as background music in an interactive mystery. The concerto is in the public domain, but Bay still needs a master license from the record company that owns the sound recording copyright.

Copyrighted Arrangements

While you are free to use a public domain work, you cannot (unless you obtain a license) use a copyrighted arrangement of a public domain work. An arrangement of a public domain work is, if sufficiently original, a separate copyrightable work. If you want to use the public domain elements of a copyrighted arrangement, you may need a musicologist to separate the public domain elements from the arrangement's copyrighted elements.

If you are trying to separate out the public domain elements of a copyrighted arrangement, you may find it helpful to obtain a copy of the arranger's copyright application from the Copyright Office. The application should identify the new matter on which the claim of copyright is based. While the Copyright Office will not send you a copy of someone else's song or other copyrighted work unless litigation is threatened, it will send you a copy of their registration application. To get this, you need the copyright registration number for the arrangement. You can obtain it by looking in the Catalog of Copyright Entries or through a Copyright Office registration search.

See the discussion of derivative works in "Public Domain Works," Chapter 11.

See "Determining Who Owns the Copyright," Chapter 12.

Finding Public Domain Music

You can sometimes find out whether a song is in the public domain by looking at the copyright notice. If the copyright date is greater than 75 years ago, the work is in the public domain. If the composition is less than 75 years old, it could be in the public domain for reasons discussed in "Public Domain Works," Chapter 11.

Every major city has dealers that handle old sheet music. The Lincoln Center Library of the Performing Arts in New York City has an extensive collection of old songs. ASCAP and BMI catalogs—which include many copyrighted arrangements—indicate the public domain status of underlying works for arrangements. The ASCAP booklet, *ASCAP Hit Songs,* is a good source of public domain works. *Kohn on Music Licensing,* a book by Al Kohn and Bob Kohn (Aspen Law and Business), has a list of popular songs that are in the public domain.

In searching for public domain works, don't be fooled by a recent copyright notice and date on what is actually an arrangement of a public domain work. For example, if a new arrangement of a public domain folk tune shows a 1993 copyright date, you cannot—without obtaining a license—use the new arrangement, but you can use the public domain version of the song.

If someone else has written lyrics for a public domain tune, you are free to write your own lyrics for that tune. Both of you are creating new derivative works based on a public domain tune. If you use an arranger or lyricist to create the new lyrics, make certain that your contract with the arranger or lyricist includes a copyright assignment or work made for hire provision.

Option #4: Using Music from Music Libraries

If you don't want to create your own music, deal with rights clearance, or pay license fees, and you can't find suitable public domain music, you may be able to obtain appropriate music from music libraries. A list of music libraries appears in Appendix D.

Music libraries specialize in providing "cleared" music—music in which they own both the musical composition and the master recording copyrights. Many libraries now offer their material in digital audio and MIDI form on CD-ROM. A growing number of companies are now marketing "samplers"—snippets of music, recorded on disks, which are copyright-free.

Make sure that the music library you choose can provide you with all the rights you need. Some music libraries grant only limited licenses to use the works they license. Also be certain that the agent with whom you deal understands how you will be using the licensed music in your multimedia work (see "Option #2: Using Preexisting Music," earlier in this chapter.) If you are using a "copyright-free" sampler, read the fine print (commercial use may not be permitted, for example.) If you are planning widespread distribution of your multimedia product, try to get some proof that the music library (or sampler provider) owns the rights in the music.

Checklists for Clearing Music

Musical Compositons

1. Is the musical composition protected by copyright in the countries in which you wish to use it?

2. Does the musical work include other copyrightable works such as a poem which you also will need to clear?

3. What rights do you need?

   ➤ Mechanical (reproduction)/Synchronization (to use in audio-visual work)

   ➤ Distribution

   ➤ Modification (also known as "parody")

   ➤ Public performance (on-line/advertising/grand performing if it tells a story)

   ➤ Print (for text versions)

4. What geographical areas do you want to cover in your license?

5. Who owns the rights you need in those geographical areas?

6. Do you need sublicensing rights or subsidiary rights such as merchandising or movie rights?

7. How will you define your multimedia product (platforms/media/on-line/sequel)?

8. Do you need a waiver of moral rights of the songwriter?

Sound Recordings

The sound recording (the actual performance of the song) is a separate copyrightable work and generally is owned by a different party (record company) than the owner of the copyright in the musical composition. It needs to be cleared separately.

1. Is the sound recording protected by copyright in the territories in which you wish to use it?

2. What rights do you need?

   ➤ Reproduction/Distribution

   ➤ Modification (if necessary)

   ➤ Digital public peformance (US)/public performance (foreign countries)

3. What geographical areas do you want to cover in your license?

4. Who owns the rights you need in the sound recording in each territory in which you are interested?

5. Do you need sublicensing rights or subsidiary rights such as merchandising or movie rights?

6. How will you define your multimedia product (platforms/media/on-line/sequel)?

7. If you will be using the recording artist's photograph, do you need to obtain a clearance to the right of publicity and clear the photograph?

8. Do you need to pay union reuse fees?

9. Do you need a waiver of moral rights of the performer?

10. Do you need the performer's permission?

11. Do you need permission from the American Federation of Musicians, and have any applicable AFM fees been paid?

15 The Laws of Publicity, Privacy, and Libel

Multimedia developers and publishers must make certain that they don't violate rights of publicity and privacy of individuals appearing in their works. This usually can be accomplished by getting releases from individuals before using illustrations, recordings, photographs, or film or video clips that include those individuals' names, faces, images, or voices.

The law of libel, which protects individuals against the dissemination of falsehoods injurious to their reputation, is generally not a major concern for multimedia developers. Nonetheless, developers and publishers should know enough about libel law to recognize the kind of material that might be libelous.

For a discussion of how these laws are applied in the on-line environment, see Chapter 23.

The Rights of Publicity and Privacy

Most states in the United States recognize that individuals have a right of privacy. The right of privacy gives an individual a legal claim against someone who intrudes on the individual's physical solitude or seclusion, and against those who publicly disclose private facts. It is the individual's right "to be let alone." Remedies for invasion of privacy include injunctions against continued intrusion and damages for mental distress.

The right of privacy cannot be used to prohibit publication of a matter of public or general interest—whether as news or as entertainment. Instead, this right protects the privacy of private life. Liability exists only if the defendant's conduct was such that the defendant should have realized that it would be offensive to persons of ordinary sensibilities.

Almost half the states in the United States recognize that individuals have a right of publicity. The right of publicity gives an individual a legal claim against one who uses the individual's name, face, image, or voice for commercial benefit without obtaining permission. The states recognizing the right are California, Connecticut, Florida, Georgia, Hawaii, Illinois, Kentucky, Massachusetts, Michigan, Minnesota, Missouri, Nebraska, Nevada, New Jersey, New York, Ohio, Oklahoma, Pennsylvania, Rhode Island, Tennessee, Texas, Utah, Virginia, and Wisconsin.

 Developer took a picture of Clint Eastwood standing on a street corner in Carmel. Developer used the picture in a multimedia work that was sold in California. Unless Eastwood gave Developer permission to use Eastwood's image, Developer's use of the image may have violated Eastwood's right of publicity (even though Developer, as "author" of the photo, owned the copyright in the photo).

Remedies for misappropriation of the right of publicity include injunctions against continued use of the misappropriated name, face, image, or voice, and damages based on the fair market value of the use or the profits earned by the infringer.

In recent years, courts have expanded the right of publicity by giving a broad interpretation to the question whether an individual's "image" has been taken. For example, the use of the slogan "Here's Johnny" by a portable toilet provider (with the phrase "The King of the Commodians") was held to violate Johnny Carson's right of publicity. *Carson v. Here's Johnny Portable Toilets, Inc.* 698 F.2d 831 (6th Cir. 1983). A printed ad showing a robot game show hostess in a blonde wig and evening gown was held to violate Vanna White's "identity." *White v. Samsung Electronics America, Inc.* 971 F. 2d 1395 (9th Cir. 1992), *cert. denied,* 113 S. Ct. 2443 (1993).

Newspapers and magazines have a "fair use" privilege flowing from the First Amendment to publish names or images in connection with a newsworthy event. Such use is known as "media use."

One line of cases holds that a publication may use a famous individual's name or likeness so long as that person is used to illustrate a point stemming from a documentary or an article on a subject of general public interest. Another line holds that magazines are permitted to

> **Invasion or Not?**
> An unauthorized photograph of the Gills, in an "affectionate pose" was published in two magazines to illustrate an article on love. The Gills sued the publisher for invasion of privacy. The court found that their privacy was not wrongfully invaded because the Gills had "voluntarily exposed themselves to public gaze" by sitting in a public area outside their ice cream stand. The court hinted that it would have ruled the other way had the photograph been used for advertising purposes. *Gill v. Hearst Publishing Co.*, 40 Cal. 2d 224 (1953).

use photographs of individuals in an article about social issues even though the actual subjects of the photos have only a minimal connection with the article's subject. The right of publicity cannot be used to stifle comment on the lives of public persons (Howard Hughes, Marilyn Monroe), or on the lives of nonpublic persons who are connected to someone famous (the widow of Ernest Heminway, the children of Julius and Ethel Rosenberg).

The "media use" exceptions have been held to apply to nonprint media. For example, when Ginger Rogers sued a film producer for the unauthorized use of her name in a film title (*Frederico Fellini's "Ginger and Fred"*), the court held that motion pictures are a form of expression protected by the First Amendment and that the producer's use of her name was protected artistic expression. *Rogers v. Grimaldi*, 695 F. Supp. 112 (S.D.N.Y. 1988).

In another case, the use of a famous surfer's image and voice in a surfing documentary was held not to violate the surfer's right of publicity.

> **Using Associated Items**
> Just using an item associated with a famous person can get you in trouble—even if you don't use the person's name or photo. When a cigarette manufacturer used a photograph of a well-known racecar driver's distinctively decorated car in a commercial, the driver sued for misappropriation of his "likeness" and invasion of privacy. *Motschenbacher v. R.J. Reynolds Tobacco Co.*, 498 F. 2d. 821 (9th Cir. 1974).

As you can see, the law of publicity is complicated. It also varies from state to state. In some states, the only unauthorized uses that violate the right of publicity are commercial uses (in advertising, for example). Since most multimedia works will be distributed nationwide, you should avoid trying to determine which states' laws you need to worry about. Instead, you should obtain releases (Form 17 in Appendix B) from any person whose name, face, image, or voice is recognizable in your multimedia projects. If you think one of the exceptions to the right applies to your situation, get legal advice.

Experienced performers and models are accustomed to signing these releases. If a person won't sign a release, don't use their name, face, image, or voice in your multimedia project. If you are using a client's employees as actors, models, or narrators, make sure the employees sign releases. If you are using your own employees, make sure they sign releases.

Photographs and Film Clips

If you want to use a photograph of a living person, get the person to sign a statement authorizing you to use his or her face or image as shown in the photograph. You also need a license authorizing you to use the photograph, unless you own the copyright in it.

See "When You Need a License," Chapter 11.

Some photographers routinely obtain releases, but don't assume that this is the case. Even if the photographer did obtain a release, the release may not be broad enough to cover your use of the photograph in a multimedia work.

If you will be obtaining photographs from a stock photo agency (discussed in "Licensing Photographs and Still Images," Chapter 13), tell the agency at the outset that you will need model releases so the agency will only send you photos for which releases are available.

If you want to use a clip from a film or television show, you should obtain releases from all performers shown or heard in the clip. Motion picture producers often require performers to sign releases authorizing the use of the actors' name, face, voice, or image in clips, but the scope of such releases may be too narrow to cover your use (they may cover only the use of clips for publicizing the movie). If the performers shown or heard in the clip belong to SAG or AFTRA, you probably need their consent. See "Reuse Provisions," Chapter 16.

To make the clearance process easier, you may want to eliminate certain individuals from the clip. You'll need the consent of the clip's copyright owner to modify it (see "Determining What Rights You Need," Chapter 12). For example, one multimedia developer wanted to use a television clip of an interview between Isaac Asimov and Jane Pauley. Rather than negotiate with Pauley, the developer eliminated her image and voice from the clip.

The Value of a Release

Here's a case that shows the value of getting a release: A wrestler sued World Championship Wrestling, Inc. for what he claimed was the unauthorized use of his likeness and name in videotapes of a wrestling match in which he had participated. The court granted judgment on the pleadings (without trial) for the defendant, because the wrestler had signed a release giving the match's sponsor exclusive worldwide rights to televise the match and to exploit recordings of the match. *Shreve v. World Championship Wrestling, Inc.,* 216 Ga. App. 387 (Ga. App. 1995).

Sound Recordings

If you want to use an excerpt from a sound recording, get the consent of anyone whose voice is heard in it. In addition, you should get copyright licenses from the musical composition's copyright owner and the master recording copyright owner (see "Option #2: Using Preexisting Music," Chapter 14), and comply with AFTRA and American Federation of Musicians reuse requirements (see "Reuse Provisions," Chapter 16).

Deceased Individuals

In some states, an individual's right of publicity terminates when the individual dies. In other states, the right passes to the heirs of the deceased original owner. In California, Oklahoma, and Texas, the right passes on to the heirs only if the person's likeness has acquired some commercial value at the time of death. In Kentucky, the right is passed on to heirs for public figures only.

The right of publicity lasts 20 years beyond the year of death in Virginia; 40 years in Florida, 50 years in California, Kentucky, Nevada, and Texas; and up to 100 years in Oklahoma. In Tennessee, the right lasts as long as it is continuously exploited by the heirs.

As a rule of thumb, don't use the name, voice, face, or image of a celebrity who has been dead less than 50 years—for example, Marilyn Monroe or Martin Luther King, Jr.—without checking applicable state law on descendability. If state law provides for the right of publicity to descend to heirs, get permission from the current owners of the deceased celebrity's right of publicity before using the celebrity's name, voice, face, or image.

Libel

The law of libel (also known as defamation) protects an individual against the dissemination of falsehoods about the individual. Libel is defined as a false statement about a person, communicated to at least one other person, that injures the defamed person's reputation or subjects the defamed person to hatred, contempt, or ridicule.

To recover damages for libel, a plaintiff must prove that the statement was false and:

➤ Was communicated to others.

➤ Was reasonably understood as referring to the plaintiff.

➤ Injured the plaintiff.

Injury can consist of monetary losses, damage to reputation, or mental anguish. A public figure or official must prove that the publisher or broadcaster made the statement either knowing it was false or entertaining serious doubts about its truth. A private individual only has to prove that the publisher or broadcaster acted negligently in failing to ascertain that the statement was false. The higher burden for public figures and officials flows from the First Amendment.

> **Libel?**
> Apple Computer used the name "Carl Sagan" as an internal code name for a new computer. When Sagan complained, Apple changed the name to "BHA"—for "Butt-Head Astronomer." Sagan sued Apple for libel, invasion of privacy, and misappropriation of the right of publicity. The court dismissed the libel claim, because it found that the new code name did not imply an assertion of objective fact about Sagan and because the statement was protected under the First Amendment. The other claims were settled.

Here are some tips for avoiding libel:

➤ **Original material.** If you plan to use any statements in your multimedia work that could injure someone's reputation, make certain that you can prove that the statements are true. There is often a big difference between "knowing" that something is true and being able to prove that it is true. Journalists are taught to be particularly careful about statements concerning arrests and convictions and statements concerning professionals' qualifications and ethics.

➤ **Photographs.** With digital editing software, it is now easy to edit and merge photographs. Avoid using an edited image that falsely associates an individual with controversial or unsavory events, places, or people. Using an altered image that puts a person in a "false light"—for example, a photograph created by merging a photograph of an elected official with a photograph of a Mafia figure—will expose you to liability for both libel and breach of privacy.

➤ **Licensed material.** If licensed materials include potentially libelous material, don't use the material. If you use it, even though the material didn't originate with you, you could have liability for libel.

➤ **Quotations.** Many people believe that one who merely quotes what someone else said has no liability for libel. This is not true. Don't quote a statement made by someone else if that statement could harm someone's reputation unless you know the statement is true.

➤ **Opinion.** Many people think that you can escape liability for libel by making it clear that you are only stating your opinion. There is no "opinion" exemption to libel. Don't use a statement of opinion that might harm someone's reputation unless you have a factual basis for the opinion.

➤ **Statements about corporations.** Corporations can recover damages for libel. Many executives are zealous about protecting their corporation's reputation. If you make statements that might damage a corporation's reputation, make sure the statements are true.

A truthful statement is not libel, but a truthful statement that discloses private facts about an individual in an objectionable manner may violate the individual's right of privacy.

 Journalist discovered that Sue was abused as a child and reported that fact without Sue's permission in a story on child abuse. Journalist's statement about Sue is not libel, because the statement was true, but Journalist may have violated Sues' right of privacy by publishing the statement.

Permits

If you are going to shoot photographs or video on public property, get a permit from the appropriate government authority (usually a local or state film commission).

If you are going to shoot on private property, get a location release from the property owner that authorizes you to enter and use the premises for shooting and to show the premises in your work. A location release is included in Appendix B (Form 4).

If your shots of public or private places will prominently show a work of fine art that is protected by copyright—a sculpture, for example—you should obtain a license from the copyright owner authorizing you to use the image. Because ownership of the copyright in a work is distinct from ownership of a copy, the owner of the copy of the work that you film or photograph is probably not the owner of the copyright in that work.

See "Owning a Copy of a Work," Chapter 4.

 Mr. Rich has given Developer permission to create a CD-ROM showing Mr. Rich's private art collection. Unless Mr. Rich owns the copyrights in the paintings in the collection, Mr. Rich cannot authorize Developer to use images of the paintings in Developer's multimedia work. If Mr. Rich did not get assignments from the artists who created the paintings, Developer should get permission to use the images of the paintings from the artists (or those to whom the artists assigned the copyrights).

Prop Clearance

One court recently held that it was not copyright infringement to show a copyrighted baby crib mobile in a motion picture without permission from the copyright owner. *Amsinck v. Columbia Pictures Industries, Inc.,* 862 F. Supp. 1044 (S.D.N.Y. 1994). Nonetheless, we recommend that you follow the rules for prop clearance discussed here.

For other copyrighted items that will be shown in photos or video footage in your multimedia product, the general rule on getting permission is that you should get permission if the item will be prominently featured or will be a prominent part of the story. Many copyright owners will be happy to give you permission without any charge. If you get items from a prop house, do not assume that the items have been cleared for use by the copyright owners.

16 Union Issues

Many people who work in the entertainment industry are represented by unions. Performers in the movie and television industries are represented by the Screen Actor's Guild (SAG) and the American Federation of Television and Radio Artists (AFTRA). Recording artists also are represented by AFTRA. Film and television directors are represented by the Directors Guild of America. Screenwriters are represented by the Writers Guild of America and musicians by the American Federation of Musicians. In addition, there are unions for technical workers.

The unions have collective bargaining agreements with many entertainment industry employers. A company that signs a collective bargaining agreement with a union must comply with its numerous rules concerning employee pay, benefits, and working conditions.

This chapter deals with two issues:

➤ Signing collective bargaining agreements.

➤ Reuse of material created by union members.

Signing Collective Bargaining Agreements

If you sign a union's collective bargaining agreement, you will be bound for the duration of the agreement (usually several years) to comply with all provisions of the agreement. The collective bargaining agreement's provisions on hiring, contracts, work conditions, and pay will, in effect, be "written in" to your contracts with union members.

Collective bargaining agreement requirements vary from union to union, because each agreement was negotiated separately by union representatives and industry representatives.

If You Don't Sign

Union members are prohibited from working for those who have not signed the union's collective bargaining agreement. A member of the Writers Guild of America, for example, is prohibited from accepting employment with or selling literary material to a nonsignatory. If you plan to hire screenwriters, performers, directors, or musicians, you may find that the most qualified people in these professions are union members. You will not be able to hire union members unless you sign collective bargaining agreements.

Some unions offer "One Production Only" contracts which permit you to hire union members for the single production covered by the contract. These contracts, also known as "OPOs," are discussed in "Unions and Multimedia," later in this chapter.

If You Sign

If you sign a collective bargaining agreement, you generally will not be permitted to hire nonunion members to do work that is within the scope of the agreement. (This is not true of the Writers Guild, as discussed later in this chapter.) For example, if you sign the Directors Guild agreement, you can hire a director who is not a member of the Guild only if that director joins the Guild.

Signing one union's collective bargaining agreement (SAG's, for example) does not mean that you have to use union members for work not covered by the agreement (electrical work, for example).

Unions and Multimedia

The entertainment industry unions recently have begun to develop collective bargaining agreements for multimedia developers. Those agreements are discussed in the rest of this section.

SAG and AFTRA

SAG and AFTRA, which represent performers, have collective bargaining agreements for multimedia.

If you will be using performers in your multimedia works, you may want to consider signing collective bargaining agreements with SAG or AFTRA. Traditionally, SAG has represented motion picture performers and AFTRA has represented television performers and recording artists. However, over the years, the jurisdictional lines between the two unions have become blurred.

At present, the two unions consider the use of performers in the production of new material for new interactive multimedia works an area of shared jurisdiction. That means you can pick the union you want to join. Most professional performers belong to both SAG and AFTRA, and the compensation scales for the two unions are identical. Some companies sign with both unions.

 Developer plans to hire three performers to act in a video production that will be used in Developer's new multimedia work. If Developer wants to join one of the performers' unions (so he will be able to use union performers), he can join either SAG or AFTRA.

There are exceptions to the "shared jurisdiction" rule:

➤ **SAG jurisdiction.** If you are creating a multimedia work that is based 50 percent or more on preexisting material that originally was shot on film, SAG has exclusive jurisdiction. SAG also has exclusive jurisdiction over traditional animation.

➤ **AFTRA jurisdiction.** If you are creating a multimedia work that is based 50 percent or more on preexisting material that originally was shot for network television on videotape, AFTRA has exclusive jurisdiction. AFTRA also has exclusive jurisdiction over televised game shows, concerts, and news programs.

AFTRA has exclusive jurisdiction over recording artists. If you want to use an AFTRA recording artist in your multimedia work, you will have to sign an agreement with AFTRA.

SAG's Agreement

SAG has a collective bargaining agreement for multimedia developers. This agreement is known as the Screen Actors Guild-Producer Interactive Media Agreement (referred to as the SAG IMA in this chapter). An excerpt from the SAG IMA is in Appendix B (Form 18). This agreement will be in effect through June of 1996.

Michael Prohaska, senior administrator for Interactive Media Contracts at SAG, was instrumental in developing the SAG IMA. In developing the agreement, he talked with a number of multimedia developers about the multimedia industry's special needs and unique features.

Key provisions of the IMA are as follows:

➤ **Employment preference.** A developer who signs the SAG IMA must give preference to "qualified professional performers"—meaning that the developer must hire a "qualified professional performer" rather than someone else unless "no qualified professional performer of the type is reasonably and readily available... through the use of the present hiring practices generally and customarily followed by the Interactive Media industry" (Article I, Section 10).

➤ **Compensation.** The minimum rates of compensation set by the SAG IMA for 1996 are $522 per eight-hour day for a day performer, off-camera performer (narrator), or performer who provides voice-over for animation. The rates for extras are $103 per eight-hour day. "Stars," of course, receive much more than the minimum.

➤ **Rights acquired.** A question that came up when the first version of the SAG IMA was being negotiated was whether multimedia developers would have to pay performers fees when a work was distributed to consumers, in addition to paying the daily performance rates stated in the previous paragraph. (Television producers have to pay performers extra fees when they distribute copies of a show to supplemental markets, such as the videocassette market.) The current SAG IMA makes it clear that a developer does not have to pay again on distribution of the multimedia product. Article I, Section 12 of the IMA gives the developer who pays SAG compensation to a performer the right to exploit the results of the performer's services, in the program for which the performer was employed, in all "Interactive Media," and on all platforms. "Interactive Media" is defined as including personal computers, games, machines, arcade games, CD-interactive machines, and similar devices, whether now known or hereinafter invented.

➤ **Other rights.** A developer can, by paying additional compensation, get "remote delivery" rights, which would cover on-line delivery and delivery over cable television lines, as well as "integration rights" (the right to include the material from the performer's performance in the developer's other interactive programs). If you know that you will want to use the material you are filming in several products, it makes sense to get integration rights (Article I, Section 15C).

➤ **Reuse.** Other than pursuant to the "integration rights" provision, a developer cannot reuse part of the photography or soundtrack of a program produced under the IMA without getting the performer's permission (Article I, Section 13).

➤ **Pension and health plan.** A developer who signs the SAG IMA must contribute 12.65 percent of all gross compensation paid to a performer to the SAG Pension and Health Plans (Article I, Section 31).

➤ **Extras.** A developer who employs more than 10 SAG performers as extras for work on a given day is permitted to employ nonmembers to perform crowd work (Article I, Section 16E).

➤ **Waivers.** SAG recognizes that multimedia production is in its formative stages. It will consider special circumstances that might warrant modifications of the terms of the IMA (Article I, Section 25).

SAG wants to encourage multimedia developers to sign collective bargaining agreements, and Michael Prohaska has indicated that he is flexible and willing to modify the SAG IMA as new situations come up. SAG will, under certain conditions, allow a producer to sign an OPO contract.

If you are interested in signing an agreement with SAG or in finding out more about SAG, you can reach Prohaska at (213) 549-6847.

AFTRA's Agreement

AFTRA's agreement for multimedia developers is called the AFTRA Interactive Media Agreement. An excerpt from the AFTRA IMA is in Appendix B (Form 19).

The AFTRA IMA is similar to the SAG IMA. Compensation rates (set out in Article I, Section 17) are the same as in the SAG IMA. The provisions on employment preference (Article I, Section 12), rights (Article I, Section 14), reuse (Article I, Section 15) and pension and health plan contributions (Article I, Section 32) are much like those provisions in the SAG IMA.

AFTRA will consider waivers regarding the employment of extras when the developer is hiring a large number of extras (Article I, Section 17). Like SAG, it will consider granting waivers modifying the terms of the agreement because of special circumstances (Article I, Section 26).

If you are interested in signing an agreement with AFTRA or in finding out more about AFTRA, call Robert Brown, Director of New Technologies, at (213) 461-8111, extension 219.

Writers Guild of America

The Writers Guild of America (WGA) is currently using a one-page contract with multimedia developers. This contract, known as the Interactive Program Contract, is in Appendix B (Form 20). The contract covers interactive multimedia writing for disk- and cartridge-based platforms and all on-line writing other than on-line news format reporting and other text-only on-line writing.

The WGA contract may be used on a per writer, per project basis. It does not set compensation rates. Compensation is to be determined by the multimedia developer and the member of the WGA that the developer hires. The contract simply requires a multimedia developer who signs it to pay 12½ percent of the agreed-upon compensation to the Guild's pension and health plans for the member who is hired. A developer also can hire a non-WGA designer or writer under the contract, in order to permit the designer or writer to earn membership units toward full WGA membership and become eligible for WGA pension and health benefits.

If you are interested in finding out more about the Writers Guild or in signing a collective bargaining agreement with the WGA, contact the Department of Industry Alliances at (213) 782-4511 or the WGA's multimedia representative, Susan Gerakaris, at (408) 323-1898.

Directors Guild of America

The Directors Guild of America (DGA) is dealing with multimedia developers on a case-by-case basis. The DGA, according to Bryan Unger, has signed up approximately 20 companies involved in multimedia production, primarily for live action production.

The role of directors in multimedia productions is still evolving. The DGA has flexibility in terms of initial compensation for directors, but wants to see directors participate on the back-end through revenue-sharing or royalties. In addition to directors, DGA represents film production managers and assistant directors for film productions, and associate directors and stage managers for videotape productions.

Generally, a signatory must hire a full DGA crew if the project involves work for the whole crew. However, the DGA is flexible about scaling down the hiring requirement for smaller productions.

The DGA prefers that multimedia developers sign long-term agreements. It is resistant to OPOs. However, the Guild occasionally does OPOs.

If you are interested in finding out more about the Directors Guild or in signing a collective bargaining agreement with the DGA, contact Bryan Unger at (310) 209-5330.

American Federation of Musicians

The American Federation of Musicians (AFM) is currently dealing with multimedia developers on a case-by-case basis. According to Sue Collins, three compensation patterns are emerging: revenue-sharing, up-front payment, and "plateau" payment.

A developer who chooses revenue-sharing agrees to make an initial payment to each Federation musician used on a project, and then to pay the musician a percentage of revenues from the project later. This option is appealing to start-ups. (However, the Federation is moving away from this system, according to Collins.) The up-front payment system involves a larger initial payment to the musician but no "back-end" revenue-sharing payments. Under the "plateau" payment, a developer makes an up-front payment which covers the sale of a stated number of units of the title, agreeing to make an additional payment if sales exceed that quantity (the "plateau").

Master recordings are discussed in the "Option #2: Using Preexisting Music," Chapter 14.

If you are interested in finding out more about the American Federation of Musicians or in signing a collective bargaining agreement, contact Collins at (800) 237-0988.

Reuse Provisions

Even if you don't sign a union collective bargaining agreement, the reuse provisions of these agreements will affect you if you want to use an excerpt from a movie or television show or from a master recording of music.

Reuse provisions fall into two categories:

➤ Reuse fees (union fees for using preexisting material).

➤ Consent requirements.

They are discussed in this section.

Reuse Fees

The collective bargaining agreements of the Directors Guild, Writers Guild, and American Federation of Musicians all require that a signatory pay fees to union members involved in creating a work if that work (or a portion of it) is used in a different production.

These fees are referred to as "reuse fees," "new use fees," or "supplemental market fees." In this book, we'll use the term "reuse fee."

 Producer "A," a signatory to the Writers Guild collective bargaining agreement, produced and owns the copyright in *Hotdog,* a motion picture that is based on a screenplay written by Victor, a member of the Writers Guild. Producer "B" wants to use an excerpt from *Hotdog* in a CD-ROM game. Producer "A" must pay reuse fees to Victor (even though Producer already has paid Victor for his work on the *Hotdog* screenplay). Under the reuse provision of the collective bargaining agreement it signed to employ Victor, Producer "A" will need to pay Victor 2% of the aggregate of all monies remitted to it (the interactive rights licensor) by Producer "B" (the interactive rights licensee). Producer "A" may then include this 2% fee in its license fee to Producer "B."

The theory behind the reuse fee provisions is that using existing material takes away jobs that would be available if new material had been created instead. The reuse fees are substantial.

The company for whom the performer did the work actually is responsible for paying the reuse fees. If the copyright has been assigned, the assignee generally assumes this obligation. Your licensor will either require you to pay these fees or add them to your license fee. Your license should include a warranty that any applicable union reuse fees have been paid.

See "Obtaining a License," Chapter 12.

If you want to use an excerpt from a work that was created before the 1950s, you should call the unions whose members were involved in the work and find out when the union's collective bargaining agreement reuse provisions went into effect. You may find that you can use the material without paying reuse fees, because the reuse provisions were not in effect when the work was made. Always check with the appropriate unions on this issue.

Consent Requirements

Several of the entertainment industry unions have consent requirements for the reuse of existing material. Those requirements are discussed in this section.

Performers

The SAG and AFTRA collective bargaining agreements for motion pictures and television state that no part of the photography or soundtrack of a performer can be used in a picture or program in any medium other than the picture or program for which the performer was employed without separately bargaining and reaching an agreement with the performer regarding payment for the reuse. The performer is not permitted to consent to reuse at the time of original employment. Either you or the copyright owner will have to negotiate for the consent of performers who are shown or heard in clips you plan to use. The consent agreement does not apply to AFTRA non-network, non-prime time programs, but reuse fees apply to such programs.

To start the consent process, contact the appropriate union. Contact SAG if the material originally was shot on film and contact AFTRA if it originally was shot on videotape. The union will put you in touch with the performers' agents. If the clip you want to use shows a deceased performer, the union will put you in touch with the performer's executor.

Writers

The Writers Guild's standard contract contains a unique "separation of rights" provision that gives the writer the right to retain certain rights in his or her script. Because of "separation of rights," a Writers Guild member who no longer owns the copyright in a script he or she wrote may own certain rights that you need to license to lawfully use a clip of a movie or television program that is based on that script. Rights retained under the "separation of rights" can include the following rights:

> ➤ **Publication right.** This is the right to publish the work in any book or periodical.

> ➤ **Sequel right.** This is the right to use the leading character or characters of a work for a different story in a television program or a motion picture.

➤ **Merchandising right.** This is the right to manufacture and to sell objects first fully described in the literary material.

If you want to use a clip and the writer has retained any of these rights, you may need to get permission from the writer to use the clip (as well as a license from the copyright owner, as discussed in Chapter 12).

Directors

According to the Directors Guild Basic Agreement, a director must be consulted if a theatrical motion picture made by the director is edited for network television or syndication, or licensed for videodisc or videocassette distribution. In addition, some directors have a contractual right to approve alterations to works they made.

Recording Artists

AFTRA represents recording artists as well as performers. If you want to use an excerpt from a master recording that involves the voice of an AFTRA recording artist, contact AFTRA to start the consent process.

Musicians

The American Federation of Musicians collective bargaining agreements state that use of an existing master recording in a new work requires the union's consent (in addition to the payment of fees for the new use, discussed in "Reuse Fees," earlier in this chapter). If you want to use an existing recording in your multimedia project, contact Colleen Howell at the American Federation of Musicians to get permission for "phono new use." Howell's telephone number is (800) 237-0988.

Other Legal Issues

In addition to dealing with union reuse requirements, if you plan to use film or television clips or excerpts of master recordings in your multimedia work, you must obtain copyright licenses from all copyright owners and you must get right of publicity releases from all performers shown or heard in the clip or excerpt. Clearing these rights can be complicated and expensive.

See "Licensing Film and Television Clips," Chapter 13.

Copyright licenses are discussed in Chapter 12. Music licenses are discussed in "Option #2: Using Preexisting Music," Chapter 14. The right of publicity is discussed in Chapter 15.

If you want to use the leading character from a movie or television series in a multimedia work, you should find out whether the writer has retained the sequel right. (See "Writers," earlier in this chapter.)

Part 4

Post-Production Issues

17 Choosing a Name for Your Product

Trademarks and service marks are words, names, symbols, or devices used by manufacturers of goods and providers of services to identify their goods and services, and to distinguish their goods and services from those sold by others. (For simplicity, the word trademark will serve as a shorthand term in this book for both trademarks and service marks.)

Trademarks can be among your most valuable assets. The value of the *Coca-Cola* trademark has been estimated to be in the billions of dollars.

This chapter covers two main topics:

➤ Choosing a strong trademark for your product that will qualify for the broadest trademark protection.

➤ Clearing a trademark (choosing a trademark that does not infringe another company's trademark or tradename).

We'll also discuss the standards for determining "confusing similarity" between trademarks, and the treatment of titles under trademark law.

Three other topics—dilution law, international trademark protection, and using third-party trademarks in your multimedia projects—are covered briefly at the end of the chapter. The basics of trademark law are covered in "Trademark Law," Chapter 3. The steps that you must take to protect your trademark rights are discussed in "Trademark Protection," Chapter 18.

Choosing a Strong Trademark

Trademarks can be words, symbols, slogans, or devices. They take many forms:

> ➤ **Word.** *Apple* for computers, *Coca-Cola* for soft drinks.

> ➤ **Design.** Prudential's rock for insurance services, Apple's bitten apple for computers.

> ➤ **Phrase.** *Fly the friendly skies* for airline services, *The Weiner the World Awaited* for meat.

> ➤ **Shape.** The pinched scotch bottle for whiskey, the Coca-Cola bottle shape for soft drinks.

> ➤ **Sound.** The roar of the MGM lion for films, the *Star Wars* theme for films and videotapes.

Such words, symbols, and devices can be grouped into four categories depending on their ability to serve as a trademark: generic, descriptive, suggestive, and arbitrary or fanciful. We'll discuss these four categories in this section. Because arbitrary or fanciful terms receive the strongest protection under trademark law, you should choose a trademark that is arbitrary or fanciful.

Generic Terms

A generic term can never function as a trademark because it is a commonly used name of a particular type of good or type of product. Examples of generic terms are *386* for microprocessors and *Softsoap* for hand soap.

Do not choose a generic term for your trademark. Such a term will not qualify for trademark protection.

 Developer chose the trademark Multimedia Software for its software. This trademark is "generic" for this type of software, and Developer will not be able to prevent a competitor from using Multimedia Software for the competitor's own product.

Descriptive Terms

A descriptive term is one which directly describes the characteristics, functions, or qualities of a product. Examples are *Five Minute* for fast-drying glue and *After Tan* for lotion to be used after sunbathing. Surnames—for example, *McDonald's* and *Dupont*—also are considered descriptive.

Although "descriptive" words or symbols may serve as trademarks, they qualify for trademark protection only if they have "secondary meaning." Secondary meaning is a term in trademark law that means that the public already associates the trademark with the goods or services of a particular company.

A federal appellate court found that the word "Fish-fri" was descriptive when used on fish-coating mixes. Because the trademark had acquired secondary meaning in the geographical area in which it was used, the court found that "Fish-fri" was protectable as a trademark. *Zatarains, Inc. v. Oak Grove Smokehouse, Inc.* 698 F. 2d 786 (5th Cir. 1983).

Secondary meaning is achieved through advertising and sales. Market surveys frequently are used to prove secondary meaning. In the "Fish-fri" case, the trademark owner used a market survey that showed that 23 percent of shoppers surveyed identified Fish-fri as a product on the market for use in frying fish.

The problem with choosing a descriptive term as your trademark is that until secondary meaning is established, any competitor could adopt the same "descriptive" term for similar goods. You would not be able to prevent the competitor from using the term on his or her goods.

 Developer picked PC Gallery as its trademark for its multimedia software product. This product is a series of pictures of famous paintings with commentary. However, Developer did not have much money and only sold 100 copies of his program over several years. Two years later, Big Co. started distributing its own collection of paintings for personal computers under the trademark PC Gallery. Big Co. probably is not infringing the rights of Developer because PC Gallery is descriptive and Developer has not sold sufficient copies of his program to create "secondary meaning" in the trademark.

Three varieties of descriptive terms and symbols present particular problems:

➤ **Laudatory terms.** Terms that are laudatory in general (rather than laudatory about a particular product) generally are not protectable as trademarks until you obtain secondary meaning because such terms need to be used by other companies. Examples are *Best* and *Blue Ribbon*.

➤ **Geographically descriptive terms.** If a geographic area is well known for a particular type of product, the area's name is not protectable as a trademark for that type of product without secondary meaning. All sellers of that type of product should be able to use that term. Examples are *New England* for clam chowder and *Cambridge Digital* for computers (Cambridge is the home of a number of computer companies whose products are "digital" in nature).

➤ **Common symbols.** Marks that include commonly used designs and symbols—triangles and squares, for example—will require proof of secondary meaning unless the design is unique.

Suggestive Terms

A suggestive term infers something about the qualities, functions, or characteristics of the goods without directly describing them. Such terms are protectable under trademark law *without* the necessity of proving secondary meaning. (Secondary meaning is discussed in "Descriptive Terms," earlier in this chapter). Examples of suggestive trademarks are *Rapid Shave* for shaving cream and *7-11* for convenience store services.

The distinction between suggestive and descriptive trademarks is one of the most important ones in trademark law, but it also is difficult to draw. If a term requires imagination or thought to reach a conclusion as to the nature of the goods or services—for example, *7-11* for convenience store services—it is considered suggestive rather than descriptive.

Arbitrary and Fanciful Terms

An arbitrary term is a commonly used word that is applied to a product or service with which that term is not normally associated. An example is the word *Apple* for computers. (The term would be generic if used for the fruit.)

A fanciful term is a coined or created word or symbol. *Kodak* for film is an example of a coined term.

If you choose an arbitrary or fanciful term as the trademark for your product, you will receive the broadest possible trademark protection. Because an arbitrary or fanciful term has no relationship to the products or services to which it is applied (unlike generic and descriptive terms), other companies do not need to use such a term on their products. Like suggestive terms, these terms are protectable without proof of secondary meaning, and you receive rights in such trademarks immediately upon use or upon filing a federal intent-to-use application.

Clearing a Trademark

Trademark rights in the United States arise in three different ways: under common law, through state registration, and through federal registration. The three methods of obtaining trademark protection are discussed in "Trademark Law," Chapter 3.

No matter which method of trademark protection you choose, before adopting a trademark, you should ensure that it is available. Clearance of trademarks is a complex but necessary process. It is much cheaper to ensure that the trademark is available before adopting it than to try to purchase the rights of third parties once the trademark is in use and you have invested in packaging and advertising.

Generally, a trademark is cleared in two steps: a federal registrations search, then a state and common law search.

Federal Registrations Search

The purpose of the federal search is to determine if there are any federally registered trademarks that are "confusingly similar" to the trademark that you want to adopt. If you adopt a trademark that is confusingly similar to existing trademarks, the owner of the existing trademark will be able to prevent your use and registration of the trademark. The determination of whether a trademark is confusingly similar to an existing trademark is based on an eight-factor test that is discussed in "Scope of Trademark Rights," later in this chapter. You can use the TrademarkScan database available through Knight-Ridder, Inc.'s Dialog database service to do the federal registrations search yourself, or you can hire one of the trademark search firms listed in Appendix C.

The federal registration search does not indicate whether a term is available for your adoption, only that it is not available (because the term is confusingly similar to a federally registered trademark that is still in use). If the search shows a confusingly similar trademark, you should check to see if the trademark is still in use. If the owner of the trademark registration has ceased using the trademark for more than two years and does not intend to use the trademark again, the trademark may be available for your use despite the federal registration. However you may have to purchase or "cancel" the existing registration (an administrative procedure done through the U.S. Patent and Trademark Office) in order to register your trademark.

Even if the search is "clear," just because someone has not federally registered a trademark does not mean that the trademark (or a similar trademark) is available. Your proposed trademark or a similar one may be in use for similar goods by another company that has superior rights based on common law (the other party also may have rights based on a state trademark registration).

Although you can perform a preliminary review of a trademark search report yourself, you should consider having an experienced trademark attorney review the search report because trademark law includes a number of obscure rules that make it difficult for someone not experienced in the area to interpret a search report. For example, according to the doctrine of "foreign equivalents," all foreign words must be translated into English and then compared with existing trademarks.

 Multimedia, Inc. owns a federal trademark registration for the trademark Vert for multimedia products. The word vert is French for "green." Multimedia, Inc. can prevent another company from using Green for multimedia products. Although Vert and Green are very different in appearance and sound, according to the doctrine of "foreign equivalents," Vert and Green are considered the same word.

State and Common Law Search

The second step is to search for state trademark registrations and common law uses. The common law search will review both "trademark" use (use on products) and "tradename" use (use for company names). The earlier user of a word or device for a tradename (for example, Multimedia Development Company is a tradename) can prevent the use of a similar word or device as a trademark for similar goods or services. A trademark search firm can do this search for you (see Appendix C). However, these firms do not interpret the results for you. For that, you need a trademark attorney.

The state and common law search generally will produce many more potential problems than the federal registrations search. However, you may discover that many of the trademarks listed in the search report are no longer in use (or the companies that own them are out of business).

A trademark search firm generally will take seven to 10 days to provide you with a complete state and common law search report, although you can pay more to get the search completed faster. "Clearance" at the state and common law level can take several weeks as you try to gather information on the current use of the trademarks shown in your search report. You should consider using an experienced trademark attorney to interpret the search report.

Titles

Treatment of titles is a special issue in trademark law. The title of a film or book generally is not protectable under trademark law unless it is part of a series or has obtained secondary meaning through extensive use. For example, *Star Wars* is protectable as a trademark because it is part of a series of films (and due to its fame). *Gone With the Wind* is protectable because the film and novel achieved great fame.

This special rule has not yet been applied to computer or multimedia products, but it might be applied in the future. If it is applied to multimedia products, it will make obtaining trademark rights for single products (as opposed to a series) much more difficult.

Titles are considered to be too short to be protected under copyright law.

Scope of Trademark Rights

Trademark law does not give protection against use of a trademark that is unlikely to cause confusion, mistake, or deception among consumers (but dilution laws, discussed in "Dilution," later in this chapter, may provide protection).

Western Software has a federal registration for the use of Flash on multimedia development tool software. If Giant Co. starts using Flash on desktop publishing software, Giant Co. may be infringing Western Software's trademarks because consumers may think the desktop publishing software and the multimedia development tool software come from the same source. If Giant Co. starts using Flash on fire extinguishers, though, Giant Co. probably is not infringing Western's trademark. Consumers are unlikely to think that the Flash software and the Flash fire extinguishers come from the same source.

A senior party is the first person or company to use the trademark or file a federal "intent to use" application to register the trademark. A junior party is the second (or later) person or company to use the trademark or file a federal "intent to use" application to register the trademark. A senior party can prevent a junior party from using the trademark without proving that consumers are actually confused by the junior party's use of the trademark. The senior party need only show that a "likelihood" of confusion exists.

"Intent to Use" applications are discussed in "Trademark Law," Chapter 3.

Determining "Confusing Similarity"

The test for determining whether two trademarks are confusingly similar varies in minor ways in different parts of the country. The test includes multiple factors, but eight of the most common factors are described in the next sections. (This test is used in the Ninth Circuit, which interprets the law in the states of Washington, Oregon, California, Arizona, New Mexico, and Idaho.)

Trademark Strength

Descriptive trademarks generally have the narrowest scope of protection because other companies need to use these terms on their goods. Suggestive trademarks have a narrower scope of protection than either arbitrary or fanciful trademarks. Arbitrary and fanciful trademarks receive the broadest protection, because other companies do not need to use such trademarks. (The categories of trademarks are described in "Choosing a Strong Trademark," earlier in this chapter.)

A trademark may be strong despite its category because of its use in advertising and sales. For example, *McDonald's* is a descriptive trademark and, thus, normally would be weaker than other types of marks. However, its extensive use in advertising and high visibility have made it one of the strongest trademarks in the United States.

> **Lighten Up!**
> Hormel Foods, the manufacturer of the luncheon meat SPAM, learned that Jim Henson Productions planned to introduce a new Muppet, a wild boar named Spa'am. Hormel sued Henson for trademark infringement. The court ruled for Henson, stating that "Hormel cannot use federal trade laws to enjoin what is obviously a joke at its expense.... [T]he requirement of trademark law is that a likely confusion of source, sponsorship, or affiliation must be proven, which is not the same thing as a 'right' not to be made fun of." *Hormel Foods Corp. v. Jim Henson Productions, Inc.* __F. Supp.__ (S.D.N.Y. 1995).

Difference Between the Goods

Even if two trademarks are identical, there is no confusing similarity (and, thus, no infringement) if the goods are sufficiently different.

> The use of Pomegranate for earth movers would not prevent the use of Pomegranate for a multimedia product. If Pomegranate was being used for graphic design software, though, its use for a multimedia product probably would infringe the rights of the earlier user.

The goods on which similar trademarks are used need not be "competitive" for there to be confusing similarity (and, thus, trademark infringement). Confusing similarity also extends protection against confusion of "association or sponsorship."

> Although clothing is not competitive with films, the owner of the *Star Wars* trademark can prevent the use of *Star Wars* on clothing by Fashion House, Inc. Such use is likely to lead to confusion of "association or sponsorship" because film companies or their licensees frequently sell clothing based on movie titles.

The scope of protection for trademarks in the computer industry is changing. Originally, courts and the U.S. Patent and Trademark Office (PTO) took the position that any use of a trademark in the computer industry would prevent its use for another computer product. Recently, the courts and the PTO have recognized that the computer industry is a series of niche markets. Both are beginning to permit the use of similar trademarks if the goods or services are sufficiently different. For example, the Trademark Trial and Appeal Board at the PTO found that "Information Finder" and "Knowledge Finder" were not confusingly similar because one mark was used to provide on-line medical information services to the general public and the other mark was used to provide on-line medical information services to doctors. This area of law is still evolving. The conservative approach is to avoid adopting a trademark for use on a multimedia product if that trademark is already in use in the computer industry, even if it is used for different goods or services.

Similarity of the Marks

Similarity can be one of the most important factors in determining the potential for confusion. Whether two trademarks are similar is determined by comparing the sight, sound, and meaning of the two trademarks.

In reviewing two trademarks for similarity, you must carefully analyze the common elements of the two. The use of a common suffix such as "tronics" does not make the two marks similar.

You also must consider the visual appearance of the two trademarks. For example, *Rain Barrel* and *Rain Fresh,* although different in immediate appearance, have a similar commercial impression.

If two trademarks are "sound alikes," the fact that the products are sold primarily by phone will increase the chance for confusion and the possibility of infringement. In determining whether the trademarks are "sound alikes," you should consider the number of syllables, the stress pattern, the accent, and possible mispronunciations. For example, *Dramamine* and *Bonamine* were found to be confusingly similar. The key issue is the commercial impression produced by the mark.

Evidence of Actual Confusion
If there are examples of actual confusion, such as misdirected phone calls, it frequently will be the critical evidence against the "junior" party. It is difficult to overcome evidence of actual confusion.

Marketing Channels
If one product is sold only at wholesale and the other only at retail, the likelihood of confusion may be substantially reduced. Similarly, if one product is sold directly to the consumer while the other one is sold through distributors, the likelihood of confusion may be low.

Degree of Care Exercised by Purchasers
There is an assumption that a purchaser will exercise greater care in choosing a more expensive product than in choosing an inexpensive product. Consequently, a trademark used on products that are purchased casually, at a low price, is more likely to be found to infringe a similar trademark than the same trademark used on expensive products would be.

 If Developer adopts the trademark Apiware for his multimedia game that sells for $30, he is likely to be found to infringe Publisher's rights in Apillaware for another computer game that sells for $30. However, if Developer uses the same trademark, Apiware, for his multimedia development software that sells for $10,000, he might not infringe Publisher's rights in Apillaware for a multimedia development product which also sells for $10,000.

Defendant's Intentions
If the junior party adopted the trademark with the intent of emulating the senior party's trademark, this factor will weigh against the junior party. Although it is permissible to emulate another party's trademark, you take an additional risk in doing so because the courts are more willing to protect the senior party.

Likelihood of Expansion
The last factor that must be considered in determining whether two trademarks are confusingly similar is whether the senior party is likely to expand its use of the trademark to the products on which the junior party is using the

mark. Thus, you must analyze not only the current business of the senior party, but also his or her potential for expansion into different product areas.

 Developer has adopted the trademark Attiware for its car game software for young children. If Toy Company adopts Attiware for toy cars, it might be an infringement of Developer's rights because many game software companies also sell toys based on their games.

The analysis of the potential for confusion is one of the most difficult areas in trademark law. Once again, this is one area where it is advisable to obtain the advice of an experienced trademark attorney who is familiar with the court decisions in this area.

Dilution

Although most trademark rights are based on "likelihood of confusion," certain trademarks may qualify for more extensive protection under a theory called "dilution." Dilution is a separate legal theory that exists under the law of approximately half the states and now exists as a federal right.

State dilution laws give owners of strong trademarks the right to prevent a similar mark from being used on completely different products or services.

 The Mercedes trademark is one of the best known trademarks in the world. If Developer adopts Mercedes as the title of his game software program, the Mercedes-Benz Company probably would be able to prevent such use under state dilution laws even though Mercedes-Benz does not distribute game software and is unlikely to start distributing such software.

Lexus/Lexis

When Toyota began selling automobiles under the name Lexus, Mead Data Central—which uses the term Lexis for its computerized legal research service—sued Toyota on a dilution theory. The court ruled against Mead because it found that the strength of the Lexis mark was limited to the market for its services—attorneys and accountants. For the general public, the court said, Lexis had no distinctive quality which Lexus could dilute. *Mead Data Central, Inc. v. Toyota Motor Sales, U.S.A., Inc.*, 875 F. 2d 1026 (2d Cir. 1989).

Dilution laws are meant to address the strong trademark owner's concern that other companies will try to obtain a "free ride" on the trademark's established reputation in fields other than the field in which the owner is using the mark. In the last example, Developer is trying to use the fame of the *Mercedes* trademark to sell his game. Such "free riders" may weaken the distinctiveness of the trademark and damage the reputation of the owner of the original mark.

On January 16, 1996, the President signed into law the Federal Trademark Dilution Act. This new federal statute is expressly limited to "famous" trademarks, but is otherwise similar to most state anti-dilution statutes. Famous trademarks under the new federal law are defined through an eight-part test. Most importantly, the federal statute, unlike state statutes, applies nationwide.

International Trademark Protection

Trademark protection outside the United States varies from country to country. Some countries, such as Japan and Germany, provide few rights for unregistered trademarks. In those countries, only the most famous trademarks, such as *Coca-Cola* and *Mercedes*, will be protected without registration.

Other countries may have a different view of what is confusingly similar. Foreign trademark laws frequently provide broader protection for trademarks in the computer industry than is provided in the United States. You should be aware that registration in the United States will not protect your rights in foreign countries. In fact, in some countries, trademark pirates make a living by registering trademarks in foreign companies and selling them back to the foreign company when its starts to do business in that country.

If you will be selling your product outside the United States, consider registering your trademarks in the countries that are most important to your business. You also should consider registering your trademarks in the countries known for trademark piracy. International trademark registration can be quite expensive. You should analyze the risks and rewards carefully.

> **Foreign Rights**
>
> A British developer opened a Hard Rock Cafe in Argentina after purchasing a franchise and rights to the name for Argentina from Hard Rock Cafe International for $8 million. An Argentine judge issued an order prohibiting the developer from using the name Hard Rock Cafe after a group of local business people claimed they had acquired the name from an Argentine woman who had registered it as a trademark in 1986. The developer was outraged that a judge would grant such an order to people "who clearly have no plans to open a restaurant using the logo." Calvin Sims, "Argentina's Hard Rock Cafe Shuttered in Trademark Dispute," *New York Times*, December 14, 1995.

Using Third-Party Trademarks

You should be careful to avoid using or showing trademarks of other companies in your work without their permission. The trademark owner may object to being associated with your product. For example, Nabisco objected to the use of the *Marlboro* trademark on a billboard in the background of a video game. Similarly, the use of actual car names, such as *Corvette* or *Mustang*, in car-race games has raised objections by the owners of those trademarks.

You should clear the use of third-party trademarks (get permission to use them from their owners) before using them in your multimedia projects. If you cannot clear a trademark, don't use it.

The use of images of actual goods bearing real trademarks in your multimedia product (for example, an airplane with the United Airlines logo) is a gray area. Some trademark owners have taken the position that such use "associates" them with the product in which the images are used and, thus, gives them the right to grant or deny permission to use the images of trademarked goods.

As a general rule, get permission to use an image of a trademarked item if the item will be prominently featured or a prominent part of the story (This is the same rule we give for showing copyrighted products, discussed in "Permits," Chapter 15.) You should be particularly sensitive to such concerns in multimedia products that are viewed as negative or critical about the industry in which the trademark owner is involved (for example, the use of images of airplanes with real logos in a multimedia product that includes plane crashes).

The national sports teams have been aggressive in asserting these rights. If you will be showing a product that includes a national sports team's logo—for example, a "Giants" cap worn by an actor in a video clip—you should contact the team's licensing department about getting a license. Although it is not clear that these organizations have the right, under trademark law, to require a license for merely showing such trademarked products, some of them have taken the position that they do.

18 Protecting Your Intellectual Property Rights

Much of this book has been devoted to how to avoid infringement of others' intellectual property rights. The focus of this chapter is on how you can maximize your own intellectual property protection.

To review the basic principles of copyright law, refer to Chapter 2. The basic principles of patent law, trademark law, and trade secret law are discussed in Chapter 3.

Copyright Protection

For most multimedia works, copyright law is the primary source of intellectual property protection. As a copyright owner, you have the exclusive right to:

➤ Reproduce your work.

➤ Modify your work to create new works (known as derivative works).

➤ Distribute your work.

➤ Publicly display your work.

➤ Publicly perform your work.

> These rights are defined in "The Exclusive Rights," Chapter 2.

Anyone who wants to exercise any of these exclusive rights in your work needs a license from you. For your own multimedia work, you get to be on the other side—the licensor side—of the rights clearance process described in Chapters 11 and 12.

Register Early

Copyright protection attaches automatically when an original work of authorship is "fixed." However, the Copyright Act provides an incentive for "timely" registration: To ensure that you can get statutory damages in an infringement suit, you must register your work within three months after first publication of the work.

"Statutory damages" are damages of $500 to $20,000, "as the court considers just."

"Publication" is defined as distribution of copies to the public by sale, rental, lease, or lending. An offer to distribute copies to a group of persons for further distribution or performance is also publication.

Early registration also makes you eligible to receive an award of attorneys' fees (in the court's discretion).

If you don't register your copyright within three months after first publication, your damages in an infringement suit may be limited to the actual damages that you can prove (how much money you lost as a result of the infringement) and any profits of the infringer that are not taken into account in computing your actual damages. It may be difficult to prove your actual damages and the infringer's profits. You will only be able to get statutory damages if the infringement began before publication of the work.

More importantly, if you don't register your copyright within three months of the first publication, you may not be entitled to recover attorney's fees. Even if you can prove your actual damages and the infringer's profits, the total may be too low to cover your legal fees for the lawsuit. You will only be able to get attorney's fees if the infringement began before publication of the work.

 Defendant used 10 seconds of content from Developer's "published" multimedia work in a new multimedia work. Developer sued Defendant for copyright infringement. Developer had registered the copyright on the multimedia work within three months of first publication of her work. Developer opted for statutory damages and asked the court for attorney's fees. The court awarded Developer $10,000 in statutory damages and the entire cost of her legal fees in the case ($15,000). If Developer had not been eligible to opt for statutory damages and receive attorney's fees, it might not have been worth it to file the lawsuit. Developer would have had difficulty proving that she had any damages from Defendant's use of 10 seconds of her work or that Defendant had profited from using 10 seconds of her work. Additionally, she probably would not have received enough in damages to cover her attorney's fees.

The other reasons to register the copyright in a work are as follows:

➤ You *will* have to register your work before filing a copyright infringement suit. Citizens of foreign countries whose works are protected in the U.S. by the Berne Convention are exempt from this requirement. Expedited registration costs $220. Regular registration costs $20.

➤ If you have registered your work, someone who wants permission to use it or buy it will be able to find you by obtaining a Copyright Office registration search.

➤ If you intend to assign your copyright, give a lender a security interest in your copyright, or grant exclusive licenses, the other party to the transaction probably will want to record the transaction in the Copyright Office and so will insist that the copyright be registered. Recording the transaction gives constructive notice only if the copyright is registered and the copyright registration number or work's title is included on the recorded document.

➤ A certificate of registration made within five years of the first publication of the work is legal evidence of the validity of the copyright and of the facts stated in the certificate of registration. If you registered within five years of first publication, the defendant in an infringement suit has the burden of proof in challenging the validity of your copyright (for example, by claiming that your work was not original) or your ownership of the copyright.

Copyright Office searches are discussed in "Determining Who Owns the Copyright," Chapter 12.

The benefits of recording a transaction are discussed in "Assignments" and "Licenses," Chapter 4.

Registration Procedure

To register your work, you have to fill out a two-page application form and send it along with the required deposit of copies of your work (see "Deposit Requirements," later in this chapter). You must enclose a check for the fee ($20) to the Copyright Office.

You can get an application form from the Copyright Office. For most multimedia works, you should use Form PA, which stands for "performing arts." The PA form is also the form for registering motion pictures and audiovisual works in general. If you are registering only the script or software features of your work, you should use Form TX ("literary works"). Don't file both a Form PA and a Form TX for the same multimedia work.

A sample, filled-out Form PA appears at the end of this chapter.

> **Attorney's Fees for Successful Defendants**
>
> Until recently, a successful defendant in a copyright infringement suit could not get an award of attorney's fees from the plaintiff unless the court found the plaintiff had acted "frivolously or in bad faith" in filing the lawsuit. In a recent case, the Supreme Court held that it was wrong to use a "bad faith" standard for defendants—that the same standard must be applied to plaintiffs and defendants. *Fogerty v. Fantasy, Inc.*, 114 S.Ct. 1023 (1994).

You can get up to 10 free copies of the application forms by calling the Copyright Office's Forms Hotline: (202) 707-9100. Ask for the instructions, "Filling out Application Form PA," too. You also may want to obtain free copies of Copyright Office circulars such as Copyright Basics (Circular 1) and How to Investigate the Copyright Status of a Work (Circular 22). The hotline has an answering machine on which you leave your request, so you should be ready to state what materials you need when you call that number. You should get the material you order within two weeks. If you're not sure what forms and circulars you want, call the Copyright Office's general information number: (202) 707-3000.

The Copyright Office will accept an application made on a photocopied blank form so long as it is clear, legible, and on a good grade of 8½- by 11-inch white paper suitable for automatic feeding through a photocopier. The Copyright Office says that "forms should be printed preferably in black ink, head-to-head (so that when you turn the sheet over, the top of page 2 is directly behind the top of page 1)." A blank form PA is in Appendix G.

How to Fill Out Form PA

Here's how you fill out Form PA. Use black ink or a typewriter to fill out your application form. (Form TX requires basically the same information.)

Front Page

Top right corner

Don't put anything here. This space is for the Copyright Office staff.

Space 1 **Title**

If you already have distributed copies under a particular title—for example, City Tour—use that title. If you haven't chosen a title, chose one and use it on packaging for copies that you distribute in the future. The Copyright Office will register and index your work under this title.

Space 2 **Author**

There are separate instructions for works made for hire and for other types of works.

> Works made for hire. If the work is a work made for hire, list the employer or hiring party as the "author." Don't list contributing employees or independent contractors as authors. For Nature of Authorship, just put "author of entire work (employer for whom work for hire was made)."

> Other types of works. List the individual author or authors and the nature of each author's contribution. Here are some examples: author

See "The Work Made for Hire Rule," Chapter 4.

of the entire work; coauthor of the entire work; author of the software code and user interface; author of the graphics and animation.

If you have licenses to use copyrighted works owned by others, do not put the licensors' names in Space 2. Your licensors are not authors of the work that you are applying to register (and your copyright doesn't cover the work protected by their copyrights). You will mention the types of preexisting works that are included in your work in another section of the application (Space 6).

Space 3 **Year in which creation was completed**
Date and nation of first publication

Give the date of completion of the version of the work that you are applying to register. Publication is defined as distribution to the public by sale, rental, lease, or lending. An offer to distribute copies to a group of persons for further distribution is also publication. If the work has not been published, leave this space blank.

Space 4 **Copyright claimants**

Unless you acquired the copyright in the work by assignment, you are both the author and the claimant. Put your name and address here. This information tells potential licensees where to reach you.

If you acquired the copyright by assignment, explain how you acquired the copyright (for example, "by written assignment from the author"). You must indicate that you acquired all of the author's U.S. copyright rights (not just permission to use the work).

See
"Assignments,"
Chapter 4.

Second Page

Space 5 **Previous registration**

Leave this space blank unless an earlier version of the work has been registered, in which case you have to justify filing a new registration application.

Space 6 **Derivative work or compilation**

If you used preexisting works in your multimedia works—for example, film clips, music, and photographs—you need to fill out Space 6. If you fail to identify preexisting works you have used and you have to sue someone for infringement, the defendant may claim that your copyright registration is unenforceable because you failed to disclaim authorship to the preexistent works. If all of the components of your multimedia work were created for your work, you can skip this space.

➤ *Compilation.* If you created your multimedia work by simply collecting and assembling preexisting materials or data, your work is a compilation and you don't have to fill out "6a." You just have to explain in "6b" what has been compiled—for example, "a compilation of various photographers' photographs of Depression-era poverty scenes with soundtrack consisting of excerpts of musical compositions composed during the Depression." Your goal here is to convince the Copyright Office that there's sufficient originality in your selection, arrangement, and coordination of the material to justify copyright protection.

See "Standards,"
Chapter 2.

➤ *Derivative works.* Most multimedia works are created by editing and combining excerpts of preexisting materials and adding original material (script, soundtrack, and new graphics, for example). Such multimedia works are derivative works (works based on one or more preexisting works). If your multimedia work is a derivative work, you need to fill out "6a" and "6b." In "6a," you need not identify the individual preexisting works that are used in your multimedia work. You can simply state the types of preexisting works that are incorporated in your multimedia work—for example, "previously published film footage, graphics, text, and music." In "6b," state what new material you have added to the preexisting "content" to create your work—for example, "compilation and editing of preexisting material and original text, graphics, and soundtrack."

Spaces 7, 8, and 9   Deposit account, correspondence, and certification

Unless you have a deposit account with the Copyright Office, leave Space 7 blank and attach a check for $20 payable to the Register of Copyrights. You can open a deposit account if you have 12 or more transactions each year with the Copyright Office (get Circular R5).

Put your address in Space 8, unless someone else (a copyright attorney, for example) will be handling any questions the Copyright Office staff might have about your application. Read and fill in the certification, print or type your name, and sign below the typed or printed name. If you are signing as agent of a corporation (president, for example), fill in the corporation's name in the space provided, but sign your own name.

Fill out Space 9, the mailing label for your certificate. It will be several weeks before you receive your certificate.

Deposit Requirements

If your work is in CD-ROM format, the deposit requirement is one complete copy of the CD-ROM package. A complete copy is defined as all of the following items:

➤ The CD-ROM.

➤ The operating software.

➤ Any manuals that go with the material.

➤ A printed version of the work embodied in the CD-ROM, if the work is fixed in print as well as in a CD-ROM.

For other types of works, the deposit requirement is generally two copies of the work (one copy if the work is unpublished).

Separate Registrations for Components

You are not required to file separate copyright registrations for the original individual components of your multimedia work (the music, graphics, video footage, software, and so on). The copyright registration on the multimedia work as a whole covers the components. There are two exceptions to this rule: one for stand-alone components and one for exclusively licensed components.

Stand-Alone Components

Stand-alone components are components that are (or could be) a separate commercial product and that you intend to exploit apart from your multimedia work. An example is a software engine that you use in your multimedia work but also intend to exploit separately by licensing it to other multimedia developers. You should file a separate registration on a stand-alone component to make it easier to identify the component for licensing purposes.

Exclusively Licensed Components

You don't own the copyright in a component for which you have an exclusive license. However, the Copyright Act gives you the right to register a work for which you have an exclusive license. You may wish to do so if you believe that it is likely that the exclusively licensed component will be infringed apart from your work as a whole.

Exclusive licenses are defined in "Licenses," Chapter 4.

Copyright Notice and Warnings

Use copyright notice on your packaging and on the title screen. Copyright notice consists of three elements:

➤ The copyright symbol "©," the word "Copyright," or the abbreviation "Copr."

➤ The year of first publication of the work.

➤ The name of the copyright owner.

The use of copyright notice is optional in the United States. However, there are good reasons for using copyright notice:

➤ Using notice informs the public—and potential infringers—that the work is copyrighted.

➤ Notice tells those who might want to get licenses to use your work who owns the copyright (at the time of the publication of the copy with notice).

➤ In an infringement suit, an infringer who had access to a copy containing notice cannot use an "innocent infringement" defense. This defense, if successful, could result in the court's lowering your statutory damages (discussed in "Register Early," earlier in this chapter) to $200.

➤ It's difficult to prove "willful" infringement (and get increased statutory damages) if copies of your work don't contain the copyright notice.

➤ Using notice will get you protection for your work in the approximately 20 countries that still require the use of notice (countries that are not members of the Berne Convention—Russia, for example).

Many people don't understand the rights of copyright owners under the Copyright Act. For example, some people don't know that buying a copy of a copyrighted work doesn't give them permission to copy the work. You should consider adding your own "warning statement" to copies of your work. For example, you could include on your title screen the statement, "No part of this work may be reproduced in whole or in part in any manner without the permission of the copyright owner."

See "Owning a Copy of a Work," Chapter 4.

International Copyright Protection

As was noted in "International Protection," Chapter 2, American authors automatically receive copyright protection in countries that belong to the Berne Convention and the Universal Copyright Convention. Most major countries belong to one of these conventions. You don't need to register your copyrights in Berne or UCC countries to receive copyright protection in those countries. You do need to use copyright notice on copies of your work that are distributed in countries belonging to the UCC, but not to Berne.

China and Taiwan have not signed either Berne or the UCC. However, the U.S. has bilateral copyright treaties with these countries, and under these treaties, works by U.S. authors are given copyright protection in China and Taiwan. Bolivia and Honduras require a unique form of copyright notice: "All rights reserved." If you plan to distribute your products in these countries, add that phrase at the end of your copyright notice.

Patent Protection

If your product involves technology that is novel and nonobvious, you may be able to patent it. You should see a patent attorney without delay (and certainly before you publicly distribute or display your product). By delaying, you risk losing your right to get a patent.

Trademark Protection

Trademark law provides protection for words, symbols, slogans, and product configurations that are used in marketing products and services.

Although you can obtain trademark ownership and limited trademark protection in the United States simply by using a trademark in connection with your products, you should obtain federal registrations of your trademarks to receive maximum trademark protection. There are several benefits to federal registration:

➤ A federal registration gives you rights in your trademark throughout the United States, even in geographical areas in which you are not currently using your trademark.

➤ A federal registration is legal evidence of your ownership of the mark and your exclusive right to use it in interstate commerce.

➤ Federal registrants can file infringement suits in federal court.

➤ Federal registrants can have U.S. Customs bar the importation of goods bearing infringing trademarks.

➤ Federal registrants enjoy expanded remedies against counterfeited goods, and they are eligible to receive awards of attorney's fees (in the court's discretion) in infringement actions.

If you plan to spend significant amounts of money advertising your product, you should seriously consider federal registration.

If you are planning on coming out with a line of multimedia products, you should consider registering a "house mark" that you can use on your entire product line. "Adobe" is an example of a house mark used by its owner, Adobe Systems, Inc., on the various items in the owner's product line (for example, Adobe Illustrator and Adobe Photoshop).

Trademark protection can be lost by the action or inaction of the trademark owner, whether or not there is a federal registration. To maintain trademark protection, you as the trademark owner must do the following things:

➤ **Continuously use the mark.** A trademark must be used continuously to avoid loss of rights. A federally registered trademark

The basics of patent law are discussed in "Patent Law," Chapter 3.

The basics of trademark law are discussed in "Trademark Law," Chapter 3.

Choosing a trademark is discussed in Chapter 17.

> **Loss of Trademark Protection**
> Judith Rossner's best-selling book, *Looking for Mr. Goodbar,* was made into a movie by Paramount Pictures. A few years later, CBS aired a made-for-television movie based on the same actual murder that had inspired Rossner's book, calling the movie *Trackdown: Finding the Goodbar Killer."* Rossner claimed misappropriation of her title. She lost because she had failed to act to prevent others from using the term "Goodbar" in articles and television programs. *Rossner v. CBS, Inc.,* 612 F. Supp. 334 (S.D.N.Y. 1985).

is assumed to be "abandoned" if it is not used for a period longer than two years. Once a mark has been abandoned, the trademark owner loses the priority date of the original registration or adoption of the mark.

➤ **Monitor third-party use.** A trademark owner has a duty to prevent third parties from using the trademark in a way that is confusing to the public. A trademark owner's failure to prevent confusing use of the trademark can result in the mark becoming "generic" and unprotectible. "Aspirin," "escalator," and "thermos" are examples of trademarks that became generic and lost their protection.

➤ **Exercise quality control over licensees.** Trademarks can be licensed to third parties for their use. However, the trademark owner must exercise quality control over third-party use of the trademark to ensure that the trademark indicates a consistent level of quality of goods or services. The failure to exercise quality control can result in a loss of rights.

➤ **Avoid improper assignment of the mark.** Trademarks can only be assigned with the associated goodwill of the business in which they are used. An attempt to assign a trademark without the goodwill destroys trademark rights.

Trade Secret Protection

Trade secret law protects valuable product and business information that is not generally known.

While developers and publishers don't need to register their trade secrets to establish protection, trade secret protection is lost if reasonable efforts are not made to keep the information from becoming generally known. Measures to maintain secrecy include such steps as marking documents as confidential; restricting employees' and outsiders' access to materials or areas of the company; and requiring employees, independent contractors, and visitors to sign nondisclosure agreements. (Nondisclosure agreements are discussed in "The Contract," Chapter 6, in "Using the Employment Agreement," Chapter 7, and in "Contracts With Independent Contractors," Chapter 8.)

Trade secrets can be licensed to others without losing protection if the licensees are required to maintain the confidentiality of the trade secrets.

The basics of trade secret law are discussed in "Trade Secret Law," Chapter 3.

FORM PA

For a Work of the Performing Arts
UNITED STATES COPYRIGHT OFFICE

REGISTRATION NUMBER

_____

PA _____ PAU

EFFECTIVE DATE OF REGISTRATION

_____

Month _____ Day _____ Year _____

DO NOT WRITE ABOVE THIS LINE. IF YOU NEED MORE SPACE, USE A SEPARATE CONTINUATION SHEET.

1

TITLE OF THIS WORK ▼

City Tour

PREVIOUS OR ALTERNATIVE TITLES ▼

NATURE OF THIS WORK ▼ See instructions

Audiovisual work

2

a

NAME OF AUTHOR ▼

ABC Multimedia, Inc.

DATES OF BIRTH AND DEATH
Year Born ▼   Year Died ▼

Was this contribution to the work a "work made for hire"?
☒ Yes
☐ No

AUTHOR'S NATIONALITY OR DOMICILE
Name of Country
OR { Citizen of ▶ U.S.
Domiciled in ▶

WAS THIS AUTHOR'S CONTRIBUTION TO THE WORK
Anonymous? ☐ Yes ☒ No
Pseudonymous? ☐ Yes ☒ No
If the answer to either of these questions is "Yes," see detailed instructions.

NATURE OF AUTHORSHIP Briefly describe nature of material created by this author in which copyright is claimed. ▼
Entire work

NOTE

Under the law, the "author" of a "work made for hire" is generally the employer, not the employee (see instructions). For any part of this work that was "made for hire" check "Yes" in the space provided, give the employer (or other person for whom the work was prepared) as "Author" of that part, and leave the space for dates of birth and death blank.

b

NAME OF AUTHOR ▼

DATES OF BIRTH AND DEATH
Year Born ▼   Year Died ▼

Was this contribution to the work a "work made for hire"?
☐ Yes
☐ No

AUTHOR'S NATIONALITY OR DOMICILE
Name of Country
OR { Citizen of ▶
Domiciled in ▶

WAS THIS AUTHOR'S CONTRIBUTION TO THE WORK
Anonymous? ☐ Yes ☐ No
Pseudonymous? ☐ Yes ☐ No
If the answer to either of these questions is "Yes," see detailed instructions.

NATURE OF AUTHORSHIP Briefly describe nature of material created by this author in which copyright is claimed. ▼

c

NAME OF AUTHOR ▼

DATES OF BIRTH AND DEATH
Year Born ▼   Year Died ▼

Was this contribution to the work a "work made for hire"?
☐ Yes
☐ No

AUTHOR'S NATIONALITY OR DOMICILE
Name of Country
OR { Citizen of ▶
Domiciled in ▶

WAS THIS AUTHOR'S CONTRIBUTION TO THE WORK
Anonymous? ☐ Yes ☐ No
Pseudonymous? ☐ Yes ☐ No
If the answer to either of these questions is "Yes," see detailed instructions.

NATURE OF AUTHORSHIP Briefly describe nature of material created by this author in which copyright is claimed. ▼

3

a

YEAR IN WHICH CREATION OF THIS WORK WAS COMPLETED This information must be given ◀ Year in all cases.
1996

b

DATE AND NATION OF FIRST PUBLICATION OF THIS PARTICULAR WORK
Complete this information ONLY if this work has been published.
Month ▶ Jan. Day ▶ 19 Year ▶ 1996
U.S. ◀ Nation

4

See instructions before completing this space.

COPYRIGHT CLAIMANT(S) Name and address must be given even if the claimant is the same as the author given in space 2. ▼

ABC Multimedia, Inc.
100 Lake St.
Any City, Ca. 99999

TRANSFER If the claimant(s) named here in space 4 is (are) different from the author(s) named in space 2, give a brief statement of how the claimant(s) obtained ownership of the copyright. ▼

APPLICATION RECEIVED

ONE DEPOSIT RECEIVED

TWO DEPOSITS RECEIVED

FUNDS RECEIVED

DO NOT WRITE HERE OFFICE USE ONLY

MORE ON BACK ▶
• Complete all applicable spaces (numbers 5-9) on the reverse side of this page.
• See detailed instructions.
• Sign the form at line 8.

DO NOT WRITE HERE
Page 1 of _____ pages

EXAMINED BY _____

CHECKED BY _____

☐ CORRESPONDENCE
☐ Yes

FORM PA

FOR
COPYRIGHT
OFFICE
USE
ONLY

DO NOT WRITE ABOVE THIS LINE. IF YOU NEED MORE SPACE, USE A SEPARATE CONTINUATION SHEET.

PREVIOUS REGISTRATION Has registration for this work, or for an earlier version of this work, already been made in the Copyright Office?

☐ Yes ☒ No If your answer is "Yes," why is another registration being sought? (Check appropriate box) ▼

a. ☐ This is the first published edition of a work previously registered in unpublished form.

b. ☐ This is the first application submitted by this author as copyright claimant.

c. ☐ This is a changed version of the work, as shown by space 6 on this application.

If your answer is "Yes," give: **Previous Registration Number** ▼   **Year of Registration** ▼

5

DERIVATIVE WORK OR COMPILATION Complete both space 6a and 6b for a derivative work; complete only 6b for a compilation.

a. **Preexisting Material** Identify any preexisting work or works that this work is based on or incorporates. ▼

Previously published Film footage, graphics, text, music

b. **Material Added to This Work** Give a brief, general statement of the material that has been added to this work and in which copyright is claimed. ▼

Original text, graphics, soundtrack
Compilation and editing of preexisting material

6

See instructions
before completing
this space.

DEPOSIT ACCOUNT If the registration fee is to be charged to a Deposit Account established in the Copyright Office, give name and number of Account.

Name ▼   **Account Number** ▼

7

CORRESPONDENCE Give name and address to which correspondence about this application should be sent. Name/Address/Apt/City/State/ZIP ▼

Susan Something
ABC Multimedia, Inc.
100 Lake St.
Any City, Ca 99999

Area Code and Telephone Number ▶ _(415) 555-1212_

Be sure to
give your
daytime phone
◀ number

CERTIFICATION* I, the undersigned, hereby certify that I am the

Check only one ▼

☐ author

☐ other copyright claimant

☐ owner of exclusive right(s)

☒ authorized agent of ___ _ABC Multimedia, Inc._

Name of author or other copyright claimant, or owner of exclusive right(s) ▲

8

of the work identified in this application and that the statements made
by me in this application are correct to the best of my knowledge.

Typed or printed name and date ▼ If this application gives a date of publication in space 3, do not sign and submit it before that date.

Susan Something   date▶ _Feb. 1, 1996_

Handwritten signature (X) ▼

Susan Something

MAIL CERTIFICATE TO

Name ▼ _Susan Something_
ABC Multimedia, Inc.

Number/Street/Apartment Number ▼
100 Lake St.

City/State/ZIP ▼
Any City, Ca 99999

Certificate
will be
mailed in
window
envelope

YOU MUST
• Complete all necessary spaces
• Sign your application in space 8
**SEND ALL 3 ELEMENTS
IN THE SAME PACKAGE**
1. Application form
2. Nonrefundable $20 filing fee
   in check or money order
   payable to *Register of Copyrights*
3. Deposit material
MAIL TO
Register of Copyrights
Library of Congress
Washington, D.C. 20559-6000

9

The Copyright Office
has the authority to ad-
just fees at 5-year intervals, based on changes
in the Consumer Price
Index. The next adjust-
ment is due in 1996.
Please contact the
Copyright Office after
July 1995 to determine
the actual fee schedule.

*17 U.S.C. § 506(e): Any person who knowingly makes a false representation of a material fact in the application for copyright registration provided for by section 409, or in any written statement filed in connection with the application, shall be fined not more than $2,500.

July 1993—400,000   ☉ PRINTED ON RECYCLED PAPER   ☆U.S. GOVERNMENT PRINTING OFFICE: 1993-342-582/80,018

19 Sales Law

In every state except Louisiana, a statute known as Article Two of the Uniform Commercial Code applies to all contracts for the sale of goods. This chapter highlights some provisions of Article Two that are important for multimedia developers and publishers.

The Uniform Commercial Code

After World War II, legal experts proposed that the states adopt a uniform set of legal rules to simplify, clarify, and modernize the laws regarding the sale of goods and other commercial transactions. These rules, known as the Uniform Commercial Code (UCC), are divided into "articles" that cover different types of commercial transactions.

Article Two of the Uniform Commercial Code applies to "transactions in goods." Forty-nine states, the Virgin Islands, and the District of Columbia have adopted it. Louisiana has not adopted it.

In those states that have adopted Article Two, the rules of Article Two displace general contract law (discussed in Chapter 5) for all transactions in goods. Goods are defined as "all things (including specially manufactured goods) which are movable."

Ironically, Article Two of the UCC is not entirely uniform from state to state. California's version, for example, differs slightly from New York's version. For some provisions, the legal experts who drafted the rules gave the states a choice of several options. In addition, many state legislatures added their own variations for particular provisions.

In international transactions, Article Two may be superseded by the United Nations Convention on the International Sale of Goods. This convention applies to a transaction if both parties are located in countries that have joined the convention, unless the parties have agreed that the convention will not apply. The United States joined the convention on January 1, 1988. Many important commercial states—France and Italy, for example—have joined the convention.

Article Two and Multimedia

For Article Two to apply to a transaction, the transaction must involve "goods." If you are selling copies of your multimedia products in CD-ROM form, you are selling goods because the CD-ROMs that embody your product are movable.

If you are creating a custom multimedia work for a client or for a publisher that will be delivered in CD-ROM form, you probably are selling goods because even though creating a custom work involves services rather than goods, the end product will be movable.

If you are creating a product that will only be provided in intangible form— over a network or interactive television, for example—it is unclear whether Article Two applies. Article Two currently is being revised by a Drafting Committee of the National Conference of Commissioners on Uniform State Laws to cover software licensing and intangibles contracts. It will be several years, at least, before the revised version is adopted by the states.

Merchant

Some of Article Two's provisions apply only to "merchants." A merchant is defined in Article Two as "a person who deals in goods of the kind or otherwise by his occupation holds himself out as having knowledge or skill peculiar to the practices or goods involved in the transaction…" If you are a multimedia developer or publisher, you are probably a merchant for multimedia products.

Important Provisions of Article Two

Article Two governs the substantive rights of the parties to a transaction. Freedom of contract is the guiding principle of Article Two: The parties to a business transaction may, by agreement, modify most of Article Two's rules.

The balance of this chapter covers four provisions of Article Two that are important for multimedia developers and publishers: the writing requirement for contracts, contract formation, warranties, and remedies.

The Writing Requirement

According to Article Two, a contract for the sale of goods for $500 or more is not enforceable "unless there is some writing sufficient to indicate that a contract for sale has been made between the parties" and it is signed by the party against whom enforcement is sought. In negotiating contracts for the sale of your multimedia products, remember that if you do not comply with this writing requirement, you may not be able to enforce your contract in court. (Three exceptions to the writing requirement are discussed in "Exceptions to the Writing Requirement," later in this chapter).

To satisfy Article Two's writing requirement, you don't need to get formal written contracts from those who agree to buy your products. (However, we recommend that you use written contracts for all your business relationships.) All that is required is that the writing be "sufficient to indicate that a contract for sale has been made." The writing need not be signed by both parties, only by the party "against whom enforcement is sought."

See "Written Contracts," Chapter 5.

 West Coast Books, Inc., agreed to buy 300 copies of Developer's multimedia encyclopedia for $40 per copy. When Developer attempted to deliver the copies to West Coast Books, he was told that West Coast had changed its mind about buying Developer's product. West Coast Books and Developer did not have a written contract, but Developer has a letter from West Coast Books' purchasing manager that says, "West Coast Books accepts your offer to sell us 300 copies of your multimedia encyclopedia for $40 per copy." If Developer sues West Coast Books to enforce the contract, the letter will satisfy Article Two's writing requirement. The letter is sufficient to indicate that West Coast Books and Developer made a contract, and it is signed by West Coast Books, the party against whom Developer seeks to enforce the contract.

Something in writing is considered "insufficient" to indicate that a contract was made if it fails to state the quantity term for the sale. If the quantity is stated incorrectly in the writing, the contract can only be enforced for the quantity stated. Make certain that quantity is stated correctly in all written documentation on your sales transactions.

 Developer and West Coast Books agreed orally that West Coast Books would buy 300 copies of Developer's multimedia encyclopedia at $40 per copy. The signed written agreement states that West Coast Books will buy 200 copies. If West Coast Books denies that it actually agreed to buy 300 copies, Developer can only enforce the contract for 200 copies.

Something in writing is considered "sufficient" even if it omits terms that were agreed upon orally by the parties (such as price, delivery date, or payment terms).

If the buyer is a "merchant" as defined in Article Two (see "Merchant," earlier in this chapter), you may be able to satisfy Article Two's writing requirement by sending a "confirmation" of an oral agreement to the buyer within a reasonable time. If the buyer receives the confirmation, has reason to know the contents of the confirmation, and does not object within 10 days of receipt of the confirmation, the confirmation will satisfy the writing requirement.

 Developer and West Coast Books' purchasing manager met and agreed orally that West Coast Books would buy 300 copies of Developer's multimedia encyclopedia at $40 per copy from Developer. The next day, Developer faxed the purchasing manager a letter that said, "I'm writing to confirm our oral agreement, made yesterday, that West Coast will buy 300 copies of my multimedia encyclopedia at $40 per copy." If the purchasing manager does not object to the fax within 10 days, Developer's letter satisfies Article Two's writing requirement.

To avoid disputes about whether or not the buyer is a "merchant," whether the confirmation was sent in a reasonable time, and whether the buyer received the confirmation and had reason to know its contents, you should obtain the buyer's signature on the confirmation. In the example above, Developer could simply add a line to the letter asking that the purchasing manager sign the letter (to indicate that the letter correctly summarized the parties' oral agreement) and send the letter back to the Developer.

Exceptions to the Writing Requirement

There are three exceptions to Article Two's writing requirement that allow an oral agreement to be enforced. They are:

➤ If the other party admits in court testimony or in a court pleading that the contract was made.

➤ If payment has been made or accepted or the goods have been received and accepted.

➤ If the goods are specially manufactured for the buyer and not suitable for sale to others, and the seller has made a substantial beginning on manufacturing the goods before the buyer gives notice that it is repudiating the agreement.

Here's an example of the third exception:

 Big Co. orally agreed to pay Developer $20,000 to create a customized multimedia training work for Big Co. After Developer created the storyboards and script and began production, Big Co. called and cancelled the order. If the training work is not suitable for sale to another client, Developer can enforce the oral contract.

Contract Formation ("Battle of the Forms")

According to the traditional common law of contracts, an offer can be accepted only on its exact terms. If the offeree's response to the offer is not a "mirror image" of the offer—for example, if the response includes terms that were not in the offer—the response becomes a counteroffer. A counteroffer terminates the original offer. A contract can then be formed only if the original offeror accepts the counteroffer.

Article Two does not use the common law "mirror image" rule for contract formation. Instead, Article Two states that a "definite and seasonable expression of acceptance…operates as an acceptance even though it states terms additional to or different from those offered or agreed upon, unless acceptance is expressly conditional on assent to the additional or different terms."

The basics of offer and acceptance are discussed in "Offer and Acceptance," Chapter 5.

 Developer offered to sell West Coast Books 300 copies of Developer's multimedia encyclopedia at $40 per copy. West Coast Books' purchasing manager responded by sending Developer a fax that said, "You've got a deal. Payment due in 120 days." Under the common law of contracts, the parties do not have a contract because the purchasing manager's response contains a new term, "payment due in 120 days," that was not part of the offer. However, because Article Two applies, Article Two's contract formation rule displaces the common law "mirror image" rule. According to Article Two's rule, Developer and West Coast Books formed a contract. The purchasing manager's reply of "you've got a deal" is a "definite and seasonable expression of acceptance."

According to Article Two, when an acceptance contains terms that were not part of the offer, those additional terms are "proposals for addition to the contract." Between merchants (defined earlier in this chapter in "Merchants"), the additional terms become part of the contract unless one of these situations applies:

➤ The offer expressly limited acceptance to the terms of the offer.

➤ The additional terms would materially alter the contract.

➤ The offeror gives notice of objection to the additional terms.

 In the previous example, the "payment due in 120 days" term in the purchasing manager's acceptance is a proposal for addition to the contract. Developer and West Coast Books are both merchants. If Developer does not object to the 120-day payment term, that term is part of the contract unless the term would "materially alter" the contract.

Whether an additional term "materially alters" a contract is a complex factual determination. That determination must be made after considering Article Two's "default rule" for that type of provision (if any), along with the custom in the industry and prior dealings between the parties (if any). In the last example, Article Two's default rule for when payment is due states that "unless otherwise agreed tender of payment is a condition to the seller's duty to tender and complete any delivery." Developer, using that rule, might argue that giving West Coast Books 120 days to pay would materially alter the contract. West Coast Books, however, might have evidence that the custom in the publishing industry is to permit delayed payment by the buyer, or that in a previous contract, Developer gave West Coast Books 120 days to pay.

Disputes arise frequently over whether additional or different terms contained in an acceptance are part of the contract. This is particularly true when contracts are formed by exchanging forms that contain "fine print" or "boilerplate" terms and conditions. For example, sales contracts are frequently formed based on an exchange of the seller's "quotation" and the buyer's "purchase order." Typically, the "quotation" contains terms designed to protect the seller's interests (for example, "payment due on receipt"). The purchase order contains different and additional terms designed to protect the buyer's interests ("payment due 60 days after buyer has had an opportunity to inspect and test the goods"). Try to avoid "battle of the forms" disputes because they are generally difficult and expensive to resolve. (This problem can come up in development agreements as well as in sales contracts.)

See "The Contract," Chapter 6.

If you are the offeror, read the offeree's response to your offer and immediately object to new terms that you do not view as part of your business deal with the offeree. Objections should be made in writing. In the example above, Developer could have avoided a dispute over whether the 120-day payment term proposed by West Coast Books was part of the contract by objecting to that term. If you have sufficient bargaining power, another way to avoid these disputes is to state in your offers that acceptance is limited to the exact terms of your offer.

See "Offer and Acceptance," Chapter 5.

If you are an offeree and it is important to you that a contract include terms that were not in the offer, make your acceptance conditional on assent to your additional or different terms. By doing that, you are making a counteroffer. You will not have a contract unless the offeror accepts your counteroffer.

Developer offered to sell West Coast Books 300 copies of Developer's multimedia encyclopedia for $40 per copy. If West Coast Books' purchasing manager responded by saying, "We've got a deal, but only if you agree to pay shipping," that acceptance would be conditional on Developer's assent to the additional term (it would really be a counteroffer to Developer). If Developer accepts the counteroffer, Developer and West Coast have a contract. If Developer does not accept the offer, the parties do not have an enforceable contract.

Warranties

Article Two provides for four types of warranties in connection with the sale of goods:

> ➤ Express warranty.

> ➤ Implied warranty of merchantability.

> ➤ Implied warranty of fitness for particular purpose.

> ➤ Implied warranties of title and noninfringement.

You should be familiar with the ways in which express warranties arise. These and other warranties are discussed later in this chapter. For the three types of implied warranties, you should be aware that you are making these warranties every time you sell your product unless you take appropriate steps to exclude the warranties. If your products are being sold through a distributor, make certain that your distributor is aware of these warranties.

Many manufacturers and sellers of consumer products exclude all of Article Two's implied warranties. Instead, they warrant only that the product will, for a limited period of time, be free from defects in materials and craftsmanship under normal use and service. These "standard" warranties are poorly suited for multimedia works and should be avoided. State consumer protection laws and the Magnuson-Moss Warranty Act must be considered in drafting warranty language. The Magnuson-Moss Warranty Act is a federal statute that applies to consumer products manufactured after July 4, 1975. Its purpose is to make warranties on consumer products more understandable and enforceable.

Express Warranties

A seller can create express warranties by making statements of fact or promises to the buyer, by a description of the goods, or by display of a sample or model. An express warranty can be created without using formal words such as "warranty" or "guarantee." All that is necessary is that the statements, description, or sample become part of the "basis of the bargain."

 Developer told Client, "All of my multimedia products will run on your laptop computer." Even though Developer did not use the word "warranty," Developer's words created an express warranty. If Client buys one of Developer's products and it will not work on Client's laptop, Developer will be liable to Client for breach of the express warranty.

To avoid making express warranties that you don't mean to make, you must be careful about what you say—and what your marketing representatives say—in marketing your multimedia works. While many written sales contracts include "merger clauses" (language purporting to exclude from the contract any prior promises made by the seller or seller's representatives that

Merger clauses are discussed in "Typical Contract Provisions," Chapter 5.

are not in the written contract), some courts have found that such language does not exclude Article Two express warranties.

An affirmation of the value of the goods or a statement of the seller's opinion or commendation of the goods does not create a warranty.

Developer's ads state that Developer's video game is "the most exciting game currently on the market." That statement does not create an express warranty. It is merely Developer's opinion about the video game.

Implied Warranty of Merchantability

When a merchant (defined in "Merchant," earlier in this chapter) sells goods, a warranty that the goods are "merchantable" is implied in the contract unless that warranty is excluded. To be merchantable, goods must "pass without objection in the trade" and be "fit for the ordinary purposes for which such goods are used."

Big Co. purchased a spreadsheet program that does not add correctly. The program is not "merchantable" because it is not fit for the ordinary purposes for which spreadsheets are used. Unless the seller excluded the implied warranty of merchantability for the sale, the seller gave Big Co. an implied warranty that the program was merchantable. The seller is liable to Big Co. for breaching the implied warranty of merchantability.

For many types of goods, "merchantability" has been defined through cases decided over a number of years. Grain, for example, is "merchantable" only if it contains less than one-half percent in insect parts. For software and multimedia products, though, the standards of "merchantability" have not yet been defined. While it is well known that software and software-based products generally contain "bugs" when they are sold, it is unclear how many "bugs" a product can contain and still be merchantable.

To avoid disputes over whether goods are merchantable, many manufacturers and sellers of goods exclude the warranty of merchantability. Article Two states that this warranty can be excluded only with language that mentions merchantability. If the exclusion is in writing (and it should be, for evidence purposes), the exclusion must be "conspicuous" (in a different typeface, type size, or color from the rest of the contract). This warranty also can be excluded by making it clear in the contract that the goods are sold "as is."

Implied Warranty of Fitness

The "implied warranty of fitness for particular purpose" is made by a seller when two factors are present:

➤ The seller has reason to know of a particular purpose for which the buyer requires the goods.

➤ The buyer relies on the seller's skill or judgment to select suitable goods.

Buyer told Software Vendor, "I'm relying on you to make sure that any software you sell me will run on my present computer, a 486." Unless Software Vendor excluded the implied warranty that the software it sold to Buyer would run on Buyer's computer, Vendor made an implied warranty to Buyer that the software would run on Buyer's 486 computer.

The implied warranty of fitness for particular purpose can be excluded through contract language that explicitly excludes this warranty. It also can be excluded by saying that "there are no warranties which extend beyond the description on the face hereof," or by selling products "as is."

Implied Warranties of Title and Noninfringement

Unless excluded, each contract for the sale of goods includes a warranty by the seller that the seller has the right to transfer title in the goods and that the buyer will get good title. The warranty of title can be excluded only by specific language or by circumstances that give the buyer reason to know that the person selling does not claim full title. This implied warranty is unlikely to be of concern in most multimedia sales transactions (but it could be a problem if you're selling "pirated" copies).

Unless otherwise agreed, a merchant (defined in "Merchant," earlier in this chapter) warrants that the goods sold do not infringe third parties' intellectual property rights. If the buyer furnishes specifications to the seller, the seller is not liable for an infringement claim arising out of the seller's compliance with the specifications.

If you breach the implied warranty of noninfringement, you will have to reimburse the buyer for the damages it pays to the intellectual property owner whose rights are infringed. The damages could far outweigh your profit on the sale.

Clothing Manufacturer sold some dresses to a clothing store for $3,000. The fabric from which the dresses were made infringed a fabric design copyright owned by a third party. The copyright owner sued the clothing store for infringement, and the clothing store had to pay the copyright owner $30,000 in damages (the store's profits from selling the dresses). Because Clothing Manufacturer had sold the dresses to the clothing store with the implied warranty of noninfringement, Clothing Manufacturer had to reimburse the clothing store for the $30,000 in damages and for the costs of the lawsuit. (This example is based on an actual case.)

You can exclude this warranty or modify it, but most manufacturers and vendors do not do that (few are even aware of the existence of this warranty). Rather than exposing yourself to the unlimited liability of Article Two's implied warranty of noninfringement, you should exclude this warranty from your sales contracts, offering instead a limited warranty of noninfringement.

See "The Contract," Chapter 6.

Remedies

Breach of contract is discussed in "What is a Contract?," Chapter 5.

According to Article Two, a buyer can obtain actual damages along with "incidental damages" and "consequential damages" from a seller who breaches a contract. Incidental damages are those resulting from the seller's breach of contract, such as expenses incurred in inspecting and transporting rejected goods and obtaining substitute goods. Consequential damages include any loss that could not reasonably be prevented by the buyer that resulted from the buyer's requirements and needs that the seller knew about (or had reason to know about). Consequential damages also include damages for injury to person or property resulting from a breach of warranty.

 Buyer, a mail-order catalog seller of multimedia products, bought from Seller a telephone system for use in Buyer's mail order business. Seller promised that the system would be installed and operational on January 2. Buyer, relying on that promise, disassembled its old phone system on January 1. The new phone system was not actually operational until February 10. As a result of the delay, Buyer lost $100,000 worth of orders. If Buyer could not reasonably have prevented the loss of the orders (for example, by arranging for an answering service to handle calls), Buyer has consequential damages of $100,000. If Buyer did prevent the loss of orders by having an answering service handle calls between January 2 and February 10, consequential damages are the cost of hiring the answering service.

Article Two states that a contract may provide for remedies "in addition to or in substitution for those provided in this Article and may limit or alter the measure of damages recoverable under this Article." Unless the contract remedy is the buyer's exclusive remedy, the buyer can choose from the Article Two remedies or the contractual remedy. Many manufacturers and sellers of products limit the buyer's remedy to repair of the defect in the product, replacement of the product, or refund of the purchase price.

Most product manufacturers and sellers try to exclude consequential damages because such liability exposes a seller to a risk of having to pay damages far in excess of the product's price. Consequential damages may be limited or excluded unless the limitation or exclusion is "unconscionable." The term "unconscionable" is not defined in Article Two, but many courts have used the definition created by one of the federal appellate courts: "Unconscionability has generally been recognized to include an absence of meaningful choice on the part of one of the parties together with contract terms which are unreasonably favorable to the other party." In the case of consumer goods, limitation of consequential damages for personal injury is assumed to be unconscionable.

If a seller excludes consequential damages or otherwise contractually limits remedies and then "circumstances cause the...remedy to fail of its essential purpose" (that is, leave the buyer with no real remedy), all of Article Two's normal remedies are available to the buyer, possibly even consequential damages. In one case involving a contractual limitation on damages, the buyer, a hospital, had paid the seller, the software supplier Electronic Data Systems Corporation, over $2 million for software systems. The software systems were so defective the hospital could not use them. The contract provision limited the hospital's damages to $4,000, the amount of the average monthly invoice for the transaction. The court found that because the hospital had paid over $2 million for unusable software systems, the $4,000 limit on damages failed to provide the hospital with an adequate remedy and thus "failed of its essential purpose." To avoid such a determination, many manufacturers and sellers who limit the customer's remedy to repair or replacement also promise that they will refund the purchase price if the product cannot be repaired or replaced. The refund promise is a "back-up" remedy.

20 Distribution Agreements

This chapter describes the different forms that multimedia distribution relationships are currently taking. We'll discuss the two choices you have in creating a distribution agreement: assigning the rights or licensing the rights. We'll also cover key issues you'll need to consider in negotiating your agreement, such as what platforms and types of media to include, what the geographic scope of the grant should be, and what ancillary and sequel rights to grant. Other topics include forms of payment, warranties, how to handle credits, and remedies for breach.

On-line distribution of multimedia is discussed in Chapter 23. Product scheduling for retail distribution is discussed in Chapter 22.

Roles

The term "distribution agreements" has a wide range of meanings in the multimedia industry. At the simplest level, a distribution agreement merely provides for the resale of a multimedia work that already has been copied and packaged. Yet the term "distribution agreements" also includes "publishing agreements" in which the publisher creates the packaging and chooses the product's trademark, then reproduces the multimedia work, packages it, and distributes it.

To better understand the relationship of the parties, it is useful to define the roles of the parties involved in distribution. As used in this chapter, "developer" (or "you") means the party who takes the multimedia product from conception to "gold disk." The "publisher" means the company that makes the product ready for market, packages the product, determines the price, reproduces the product and packaging, and chooses the distribution channels. The "distributor" means the company that warehouses the product, ships it, and takes the financial risk of sales to retailers. The allocation of these functions is not absolute. For example, the "publisher" may take on some of the "distributor's" functions. In addition, some companies may take on multiple roles: A "publisher" also may function as a "distributor," and a "developer" may decide to self-publish, and act as a "publisher."

These distinctions can have an important legal effect. In fact, the distinction between a "publisher" and a "distributor" was critical in a case between LucasArts Entertainment Company and Humongous Entertainment Company (HEC). HEC created a video game, "Putt Putt Joins the Parade," based on the SCUMM software tool owned by LucasArts (the SCUMM software had been developed by the principals of HEC when they were employed at LucasArts). HEC's license from LucasArts prohibited HEC from selling the game to other publishers for less than a certain price. LucasArts claimed that HEC breached the license agreement's price restriction when it sold the game to Electronic Arts. The court disagreed, holding that Electronic Arts acted as a distributor rather than as a publisher in the transaction. *LucasArts Entertainment Co. v. Humongous Entertainment Co.*, 815 F. Supp. 332 (N.D. Cal. 1993).

Most of this chapter deals with the relationship between developers and publishers, because that relationship is the most common one. However, many of the issues raised in "Key Issues in License Agreements," such as geographic scope, media, payment, and warranties, also apply to distribution agreements.

Scope of the Agreement

As the owner of the copyright in a multimedia work, you have the exclusive right to reproduce, modify, distribute, publicly peform, and publicly display the work, as discussed in Chapter 2. You also have the right to authorize a publisher to do these things.

The most critical legal issue in the publishing agreement is the scope of the rights being granted. There are two basic choices: assignment (a transfer of ownership) and license (a grant of permission to use the work in ways that otherwise would be copyright infringement).

The choice between these two options will be determined in part by the nature of your multimedia product. For example, if your multimedia product is an interactive training video you specifically designed for a particular company, you may feel comfortable assigning the copyright and other rights in the product to that company. For multimedia products that have more

See "Assignments" and "Licenses," Chapter 4; "The Contract," Chapter 6; and "Compensation Factors," Chapter 9.

general use, the issue becomes more complex because the multimedia industry is young and has not yet established a standard "deal" framework.

Assigning the Rights

The assignment of all rights in the product by the developer to the "publishing" company is quite common in the film and the book publishing industry. This assignment may have certain exceptions (in the book publishing industry, for example, movie and television rights are often retained by the author), or there may be geographic limitations. Such assignments also are common in the multimedia industry for single or narrow-use applications. You also may find assignment of all rights appropriate for multimedia products with more general applications, depending on the roles of the parties.

 Developer has completed an interactive training program for the sales staff of Big Co. on how to sell their earth moving equipment. Big Co. demands an assignment of all rights in the product. Developer should be willing to assign the rights to Big Co. unless the product includes a software "engine" or other component that Developer wishes to use in a future product.

For a mass market product in which you assign all rights, a publishing agreement frequently provides that compensation is an initial payment (generally, an advance against royalties) with continuing royalties paid to you. The amount of the royalties will depend on the nature of the product, the market, and your involvement in the product's development. For example, the royalties for the original product on CD-ROM may be quite different than the royalties on clothing or other merchandise articles. (Royalties for these other products are generally one quarter to one half the royalty for the original CD-ROM product.) This structure can be quite satisfactory for you if you understand its consequences.

In other industries, such as music and book publishing, a limited assignment extending only to certain countries or media is common. However, this approach has not yet been frequently used in the multimedia industry. When an assignment is quite limited, many of the issues discussed in "Licensing the Rights," later in this chapter, become important.

Currently, most assignments in multimedia publishing agreements are for all rights in the work. Once you have assigned all of your rights to the publisher, you will not be able to port the work to a different platform or "reuse" either the multimedia work or its component parts in another multimedia project (because the copyright owner's exclusive rights will belong to the publisher). Component parts include the underlying software, the storyline, the characters, the user interface, and the source art (which can include photographs; two-dimensional, hand-drawn art; three-dimensional rendered

This topic also is discussed in "Developer Compensation," Chapter 9.

Reuse of material protected by assigned copyrights is discussed in more detail in "The Contract," Chapter 6.

images; and video), preproduction materials such as scripts and storyboards, and sound effects and music.

If you wish to use those components in other multimedia products, you must obtain a "license back" from the publisher. As a licensee, you will need to address many of the same issues (such as scope of the rights) as a publisher who is a licensee (see "Licensing the Rights," later in this chapter). However, some issues that apply to the publisher, such as performance warranties, would not be relevant to you because you created the multimedia product and are familiar with its performance.

Another option, if you wish to use a component in other projects, is to retain ownership of the component, granting the publisher a nonexclusive, perpetual right to use the component. This arrangement, called a "technology trade" or "technology transfer," is becoming common for technology engines such as a 3D display engine or video playback engine, because of the huge time and manpower investment required to create these engines.

Licensing the Rights

If you license the rights in your multimedia products instead of assigning them, you must carefully define the scope of the license. The issues can be quite complicated. The multimedia industry is young, and there is uncertainty about the ways in which multimedia products will be used and distributed. For example, will the products be distributed on CD-ROMs or supplied over networks? Failure to properly define these rights can lead to problems similar to those in the movie industry: In that industry, disputes continue to the present day about the right to distribute films in videocassette form (in contrast to the "core" right to distribute films for performances in movie theaters). For example, Time Warner lost a suit about its right to distribute the Beatles' film, *Yellow Submarine*, in videocassette form. The court ordered Time Warner to pay the owner of the copyright $2.3 million dollars as damages for distributing videocassette copies.

Consequently, you should expect that the publisher will wish to obtain the broadest possible grant of rights to avoid uncertainties about product distribution. The most important issues that will arise in the license form of publishing agreements are discussed in "Key Issues in License Agreements," later in this chapter.

Exclusive and Nonexclusive Licenses

See "Licenses,"
Chapter 4.

Although license agreements take many forms, the first critical issue is whether the license is exclusive or nonexclusive. In most publishing agreements, the publisher will want exclusivity. Unless the publisher is acting only as a simple distributor (such as Merisel, a company that buys and sells finished products), such a request is not unreasonable. Exclusivity ensures the publisher that money spent on promotion will result in revenues to the publisher and not to a second "free riding" publisher. It also prevents confusion regarding pricing and returns (for example, with two publishers of the same product, a distributor might not know to whom to return products). However, you may wish to limit the exclusivity to the markets in which the publisher is best able to exploit the product.

 Developer developed an interactive history of the Korean War. She granted an exclusive license to distribute the work in CD-ROM and diskette form to Book Publisher Company. However, she granted the exclusive rights to create a television documentary to Film Development Company because Film Development Company had more experience in the television industry.

In exclusive agreements, make sure that the publisher has a strong incentive to distribute the product. If the publisher changes its corporate strategy or simply fails to market your product, your expected revenues (which are generally based on royalties arising from sales) will be lower than you expected. Such incentives can take a variety of forms: legal obligations (with the rights reverting to you, if the publisher fails to meet the obligations) or minimum payments, for example.

The legal obligation to market a product traditionally requires one of four types of effort from the publisher:

➤ Best efforts.

➤ Reasonable commercial efforts.

➤ Efforts in comparison to other types of products.

➤ More detailed effort requirements (such as advertising budgets and so on).

One problem with this legal obligation to exploit is that most publishers will not agree to employ "best efforts" because the legal standard for "best efforts" is so high that it is difficult to meet. Unfortunately, the "reasonable commercial efforts" standard is less precise and could be difficult to enforce. The latter two forms of effort may require difficult predictions about what amount of advertising and other promotion efforts are appropriate.

Rather than rely solely on such legal standards, you should ensure that the publisher has a clear economic incentive to market your product and recover its "investment." This can take the form of a large nonrefundable advance to you, minimum royalties, or a combination of the two.

In exclusive agreements, you also should be alert to the remedies for the lack of performance by the publisher. If your only remedy for any failure of performance by the publisher is to terminate the publisher, you may face a difficult choice. Termination probably will be costly for you because you must find a new publisher and restart an advertising campaign. A new publisher may be reluctant to take on a product that it believes has "failed." Termination also could result in other problems, such as a "flooding" of the market with your product as the original publisher sells off its inventory at discount prices. (Intermediate remedies are discussed in "Remedies," later in this chapter.)

Key Issues in License Agreements

We'll discuss the key issues for license agreements—platforms, types of media, and so on— in this section. These issues also may be important for "license back" of rights in components (if you have assigned all of your rights in the work to your client), or if you are granting a "limited" assignment of rights to the client or publisher.

Platforms

The publishing agreement should clearly state the platform or platforms for which you are granting distribution rights. Currently, the Macintosh and IBM platforms are the two most important for most multimedia products. However, some products may be exploited on a variety of other platforms, including Sony Playstation, Nintendo, Sega Saturn, CD-I, and 3DO. You may even divide the platforms among "home" video console systems (such as Super Nintendo Entertainment System), "arcade" ("coin-op") systems, and handheld systems (such as GameBoy). You should be confident that the publisher has the ability to exploit your multimedia product on all of the platforms granted in the license.

Another way of splitting fields of use is by operating systems, such as DOS, Windows, Mac, Windows '95, Windows NT, and Sun's Solaris. This type of splitting is becoming less meaningful due to the number of operating systems that permit "emulation" of other operating systems. For example, Apple Computer has introduced a computer that also runs Windows programs.

The publisher will want the broadest possible rights to maximize the return on its investment in the product. You should recognize that the publisher needs rights on certain minimum platforms to make the distribution of the product economically profitable. One common solution is to give the publisher the right to exploit the rights on certain platforms, with a "right of first refusal" to exploit the work on other platforms. A right of first refusal is a right to match a proposed offer or an actual offer from a third party. You can then exploit your product on other platforms if the publisher chooses not to do so.

If your contract with a publisher includes a right of first refusal for the publisher, make certain that it contains a time limit—for example, ten days from the date the publisher is notified of the other offer. Also, make certain that the provision requires the publisher to match all terms of the other offer—for example, minimum royalties, marketing commitments, and revision rights—and not just the compensation term.

Another possibility is to grant the publisher broad platform rights, but to have specific platform rights revert to you if the publisher does not exploit them by a stated date.

A weaker form of the right of first refusal is a "right of first negotiation." This right requires you to negotiate in good faith with the publisher for a limited time period.

 Developer has developed an interactive "edutainment" product to teach mathematics to first grade students. She granted Publisher an exclusive license to distribute the product on the IBM and Mac platforms. She granted Publisher a right of first refusal to distribute the work on the 3DO, Sega Genesis, and Nintendo platforms. She ported the product to the Sega Genesis platform and got an offer from Sega to distribute this version. Because Publisher had a right of first refusal for distribution of the Sega Genesis version, she offered the same terms to Publisher. When Publisher failed to accept the terms within the 30-day acceptance period in the original agreement, Developer was free to enter into the distribution agreement with Sega for the Sega version of the product. This grant of an exclusive right to Sega will be limited to the Sega platform and will not interfere with the rights granted to Publisher. (Rights of first refusal can be structured in many different ways and this example only describes one of them.)

Types of Media

The publishing agreement should define the types of media upon which your product can be exploited by the publisher. Some examples of current media include CD-ROMs, diskettes, and cartridges. Many licenses currently include rights in all media. The clear definition of the scope of these rights is important because of the uncertainty about the way in which multimedia products will be distributed in the future. As mentioned in "Licensing the Rights," earlier in this chapter, film companies are still involved in disputes about their rights to distribute films in the "new" medium of videocassette. You should try to avoid similar problems.

You and the publisher should carefully determine what restrictions are appropriate and define them carefully. You also need to consider other forms of media such as distribution via cable or telephone companies and use on interactive television and computer networks.

Geographic Scope

Most multimedia publishing agreements currently give worldwide rights to the publisher. However, it may be appropriate to grant more limited rights if you believe that the publisher does not have the capability to distribute your product worldwide. If you decide to include such limits, it is important to describe the exact nature of the geographic rights. The "leakage" of products outside of distribution territories is not uncommon. For example, many software vendors were surprised to discover their products were being sold in South American countries even though they had not established any publishers or distributors in those countries. They discovered that it was common for computer software dealers in Florida to purchase products for further distribution in South America. To avoid such problems, the publishing agreement should carefully limit distribution of the product to distribution for use in a particular country or area.

 Developer granted Publisher an exclusive United States right to distribute his game software. Developer may find that his game software is being sold in the United States by Publisher for use in arcades in South America with the Publisher's knowledge. It is not clear that Developer can stop such resales without a more limited distribution right in the original agreement with the Publisher. To avoid this problem, Developer should have granted Publisher an exclusive right to distribute his game software for use in arcades located in the United States (instead of the exclusive right to distribute the game software in the United States). Then, Developer would have the legal right to prevent such distribution outside of the United States.

License terms are discussed in "Obtaining a License," Chapter 12.

If the multimedia product can be broadcast by television (or satellite) or used on a network, you should impose appropriate geographic restrictions on this type of distribution. You also should be aware of any geographic limitations imposed by content licenses authorizing your use of third-party works.

 Developer created an education game to teach French to high school students. He licensed French songs for use in his game to help the students learn the language. His song license is limited to reproduction and distribution in Canada and the United States (the music publisher that granted the license only has the right to license the songs in the United States and Canada). If Developer distributes the product in the United Kingdom and Ireland, he will be violating his license with the music publisher. The music publisher may terminate the license agreement for breach. The Developer also may be sued by the owner of the copyrights in the songs in the United Kingdom and Ireland.

Ancillary Rights

Your multimedia product may have the potential for significant revenue from "ancillary" rights. Ancillary rights are rights to exploit the storyline, characters, or settings in other media, such as books, television, merchandising, and films. For example, sale of "hint books" for video games can be lucrative. Many Hollywood films now make more from merchandising the characters in their films than they make from the actual box office receipts. For example, the original *Batman* movie grossed approximately $400 million worldwide from performance in movie theaters, but earned over $500 million through merchandising sales of clothing, toys, games, and videocassettes.

Sequel Rights

If the multimedia work is one that lends itself to sequels, sequel rights are important to you and the publisher. Many game programs, because of the characters in their games, present rich opportunities for sequels. Frequently, each sequel will outsell the previous product. For example, Brøderbund has been successful in exploiting sequels of Carmen Sandiego. In fact, Brøderbund has expressly stated that its corporate strategy is to "develop products that may be expanded into families of related sequel or complementary products that achieve sustained consumer appeal and brand name recognition." In the film industry, the *Star Wars* trilogy has been extremely successful.

You must decide if you wish to grant sequel rights to the publisher and what the terms will be. You may decide to use the terms of the original license agreement for the sequel, or you can provide for a separate negotiation at the time the sequels are ready for development. A common solution is to give the publisher a "right of first refusal" to distribute sequels (see the explanation of this term in "Platforms," earlier in this chapter). This compromise is advantageous for both parties because the publisher is already familiar with the original work and its marketing, and you avoid the expense of working with a new publisher. At the same time, you can feel comfortable that the right of first refusal ensures that you will receive market value for your sequel.

If you grant sequel rights, pay careful attention to the definition of the scope of sequel rights. Is a sequel a product that includes the use of a single character, theme, or setting, or must it include the entire ensemble of characters

> ### A "Right of First Refusal" Dispute
>
> Saban International granted a book publisher the right to publish six books based on Saban's Mighty Morphin Power Ranger characters. A rider to the publishing agreement provided that if Saban decided to grant publishing rights for additional books, Saban would submit the additional titles to the publisher for consideration. After Saban licensed other publishers to publish various books based on the Power Rangers, the publisher sued Saban for breach of contract. Saban maintained that the rider only covered books published in the same format as the initial six books (8 x 8 in size). The judge ruled for the publisher. *Tom Doherty Associates Inc. v. Saban Entertainment,* 869 F. Supp. 1130 (S.D.N.Y. 1994).

as well as identical themes and settings in the original product? The contract provision on sequel rights also should deal with the publisher's rights to propose sequels, and the terms for the creation and distribution of such sequels by the publisher.

This issue takes a different form when you have assigned all of your rights to the publisher. In that structure, the publisher has the right to create sequels because one of the rights that you assigned is the "modification" right. You then need to include contract provisions to give you the right to participate in creating and distributing sequels.

See "The
Exclusive Rights,"
Chapter 2.

Foreign Language and Other Platforms

The distribution agreement should address the "porting" of the original multimedia product to other platforms and "localizing" to foreign languages. You should consider how much control you wish to retain over such new versions. For example, you may want the right to create such new versions both for economic and quality control reasons (necessary to protect your trademarks). However, you should recognize that the publisher also needs the ability to create such new versions to maximize the return on its investment. If you cannot or do not wish to create such new versions, the publisher should have the right to do so (subject to your right to approve the new versions).

A common solution gives you, the developer, a right of first refusal to create such versions upon the request of the publisher. If you fail to exercise your right of first refusal, the publisher can create such works directly or through third parties. However, if the publisher creates such a work, it will own the copyright in the translation, and you should obtain an assignment of such rights to you. If your trademark or tradename is used on publisher-created versions, it is important that you ensure that these products meet your quality standards.

See "Trademark
Protection,"
Chapter 18.

Unrelated Works

You may want to enter into a broader relationship with a publisher. In such a relationship, the publisher has an option to develop and distribute a limited number of your future projects (or any projects that you create during a certain period), whether or not they are related to one another. (This type of agreement is common in the film industry.) The distribution agreement should state clearly what information you must provide to the publisher about a future project and what procedure the publisher must follow to exercise its option on a project. You should clearly define the term of the "acceptance period" during which the publisher must make the decision—frequently it is a period after receipt of the project's description. The agreement also should describe the scope of the publisher's obligations once it has exercised the option for a proposal.

Trademarks

As we said in Chapter 18, you should obtain federal registrations of your trademarks to receive maximum trademark protection. If you don't register your marks, the publisher may try to do so.

You should remember that the use of your trademarks or tradenames on a product requires you to exercise quality control over the product. If the relationship permits the publisher to develop new versions of the products (whether they are multimedia works or merchandising articles, such as clothes), you must ensure that such products meet the quality control standards that you have established for your trademarks. Failure to exercise quality control could result in you losing your right to enforce your trademarks.

Payment

You should ensure that the calculation and timing of payments are clearly described in the distribution agreement. Generally, payment is divided into two categories: advances and royalties. You also may receive separate payment of "expenses" to license content.

Advances

Advances are the initial payment that you receive from the publisher before distribution of the product. Advances can be paid in a lump-sum payment or a series of payments tied to milestones in the development of a product.

Advances are determined in a variety of ways: They can be arbitrary amounts set to encourage the publisher to exploit the product, or they can be tied to the expense of developing a particular product. These expenses can include traditional costs, such as employee and independent contractor salaries, and third-party license fees. They also can include less traditional expenses, such as the premiums for "errors and omission" insurance or purchase of needed equipment.

Milestones and budget categories are discussed in "The Funding Process" and "Preparing the Budget," Chapter 9.

 Developer is a small company that is negotiating its first transaction with Publisher. Publisher is willing to pay Developer an advance to cover the expenses of developing the product. However, Developer needs a Silicon Graphics computer and a scanner to create the new product. Publisher may be willing to increase the size of the advance to permit Developer to purchase or lease the necessary equipment.

One of the most important issues for you is whether the advances are refundable or nonrefundable. Refundable means you may have to repay the advances to the publisher for certain defined reasons. It may be appropriate to repay the advances if you are unsuccessful in creating the multimedia product for certain reasons under your control, such as loss of employees or accepting additional work, or if the development project is terminated and you sell the product to another publisher. However, a requirement to refund the advances if your multimedia product is not successful in the marketplace is unreasonable. Such a requirement would mean that you would lose both the money and the time that you spent in developing the product.

Frequently, advances are nonrefundable, but recoupable from the royalties due to you. Recoupment can take many forms. The most common form requires withholding of all your royalties until all of the advances from the publisher have been repaid. The potential problem with this approach is that you will not have any cash flow from royalties after the delivery of the multimedia product until all of the advances are repaid. Depending on the amount of the advances, this repayment could take months or even years. One compromise is to permit recoupment of a designated percentage of your royalties so that the publisher receives repayment of advances (although more slowly than under the prior structure) and you receive revenue immediately from the distribution of the multimedia product.

Publisher paid Developer a $200,000 advance which is recoupable from a 10 percent royalty on net revenues from the sale of the product. The royalties due to Developer were $50,000 in the first quarter, $70,000 in the second quarter, $100,000 in the third quarter, $120,000 in the fourth quarter, and $170,000 in the fifth quarter. If all advances are recouped from royalties before any payment of royalties to Developer, Publisher will be repaid its advances by the third quarter. Developer will not be paid royalties until the third quarter. The first payment will be $20,000.

If the Publisher agrees that recoupment will be limited to 50 percent of the royalties due to Developer, Developer will receive payments immediately: $25,000 in the first quarter, $35,000 in the second quarter, $50,000 in the third quarter, $60,000 in the fourth quarter, and $140,000 in the fifth quarter. Publisher will not be repaid until the fifth quarter (instead of in the third quarter).

When you are contemplating a publishing agreement for a series of products, the issue of cross-recoupment (sometimes referred to as "cross-collateralization") frequently arises. Cross-recoupment is the right of the publisher to obtain repayment of advances on one product from royalties for another product. Cross-recoupment permits the publisher to spread its risk among several products, some of which may be less successful than others. This request is generally reasonable because it permits the parties to share the risks and rewards more equally.

Royalties

Royalties can take many forms. In fact, they represent one of the most flexible means of allocating a financial return between the parties. The balance of this section will discuss the most common issues that arise in determining royalties.

Royalty Base

Although many developers focus on what "percentage" they will get of the royalty base, the definition of the royalty base is the more important issue. The initial question in this definition is whether royalties will be paid on gross or net revenues. Gross revenues are all revenues received from the distribution of the product, without any deductions. The problem with the use of gross revenues is that they don't reflect the profits of the publisher. The multimedia industry is young, and many of the distribution expenses are not yet well defined. The publisher is likely to be conservative in setting royalties based on gross revenues because of uncertainties about what the actual profit will be. This problem can be particularly acute for the publisher if the multimedia product includes significant amounts of "third-party" content for which the publisher is responsible for paying license fees. In this situation, the publisher may have great difficulty in estimating its profits on the product in advance.

See "Obtaining a License," Chapter 12.

The advantage to you of royalties paid on gross revenues is that gross revenues are relatively easy to calculate. Unlike "net profits," gross revenues are not really subject to manipulation. The recent dispute between Art Buchwald and a major movie studio regarding a "net profits" agreement illustrates the manipulation problem. Art Buchwald contributed a brief story idea to the studio for an initial $10,000 payment. He was to get a fixed fee and a share in the "net profits" if the idea was used in a film. Eventually, the idea was used for the Eddie Murphy movie, *Coming to America*. The studio denied that the idea was the basis for the movie, but a judge disagreed. The studio then stated that though the movie grossed over $350 million worldwide, the movie had a deficit of $18 million under the net profits definition. Art Buchwald challenged the studio over their calculation of net profits. The trial revealed many examples of the studio marking up the costs of services it provided to cover its overhead and make further profits. For example, the deductions included a 10 percent advertising overhead that was not related to actual costs, and a 15 percent overhead charge that was found not even "remotely" to correspond to actual costs. The judge described a 15 percent overhead charge on an operational allowance for Eddie Murphy Productions as "charging overhead on overhead."

Nonetheless, net revenue is the most frequent royalty base in multimedia publishing agreements. If properly defined, this royalty base poses little risk to you. The use of net revenues may actually mean a greater return to you: The publisher may be willing to pay a higher percentage of the net revenue. The critical issue is the list of what items are deducted from gross revenues to calculate net revenue. The most common deductions are:

➤ Sales and use taxes.

➤ Shipping charges.

➤ Shipping insurance.

➤ Returns and stock balancing.

➤ Discounts (including cooperative advertising, credits, and rebates).

➤ Costs of manufacturing.

For multimedia products that will have significant international sales, net revenues also may include a deduction for royalty payments that cannot be brought back into the United States because of currency control or similar laws of foreign countries. (Some countries do not permit revenues earned in that country to be converted into dollars and transferred out of the country.) If the publisher creates a "ported" or "localized" version of the product, the royalty rate on such a version may be reduced to reflect the publisher's greater investment.

You should review the components of net revenue carefully for deductions that are controlled by affiliates or subsidiaries of the publisher. These types of deductions may not reflect the market costs of the goods or services being provided.

To reflect the true price of your product, the price used to calculate gross revenues or net revenues should be fixed in a market transaction. Avoid having this price based on sales by the publisher to its related companies, such as sales subsidiaries, because that price may be quite different from market price due to taxes and other concerns.

Payment Mechanics

The royalty provision also should state when the royalties become due. The two most common choices are the date products are shipped and the date the payment is received. These choices involve different risks for you and for the publisher.

The date of shipment is an easy date to determine. However, the publisher's distributors will not pay the publisher immediately for the product—they may take an additional 30 to 90 days (or even 120 days for some foreign sales) after receipt of the product to pay. Consequently, the publisher may be reluctant to adopt the date of shipment as the date royalties are due. This is because it requires that the publisher finance your royalty payments on products for which it has not yet received payment (and will not receive payment for several months).

On the other hand, if the payment becomes due on the date of receipt of payment by the publisher, you share the collection risk with the publisher. Publishers prefer this payment method because it reduces their risk. Moreover, if multimedia products are treated like books, retail distributors will have the right to return all of the copies they have "bought." Such a return policy could make the payment of royalties that are based on "sales" erratic when the royalty payments are reduced to reflect returns. (You should ensure that if returns exceed shipments, you do not have an obligation to repay any of your prior royalty payments.) Under this method, you risk not receiving a royalty payment for copies sent by the publisher to a distributor who sells the product but doesn't pay the publisher, or who enters bankruptcy before payment. Nonetheless, this arrangement is the most common one.

The publishing agreement also should state how frequently payments are to be made, and the nature of reports that will accompany the payment. At a minimum, the report should indicate the period of the report, the amount of sales, and the calculation of royalties. If the publishing agreement covers more than one product, the report should provide this information for each product by stock balancing unit (SKU) (e.g., 5.25" and 3.5" versions). The most common time periods for payment for many game products is monthly (quarterly or semiannually for many CD-ROM products). For more complex agreements, you also may wish to have the report include geographic information on sales, if it is available. You should recognize that such information may not be available, particularly due to the relative newness of the distribution channels.

Bundled Products

"Bundled" products are those that are distributed with the hardware or software of the publisher or a third party. They need to be handled differently in the royalty provision than "retail" products. The compensation the publisher receives from bundled products may be difficult to calculate. For example, a publisher could provide a "free" product for bundling with another product for premiums or a preloaded game on a computer. The amount of payment, if any, received per bundled copy is generally much less than the amount received for a retail sale. One common solution is to provide for payment of a fixed dollar amount per bundled copy rather than a percentage of royalties or a different percentage.

Bundling also is discussed in "Price Pressures," Chapter 22.

Minimum Unit Royalties

You may wish to consider a per-unit minimum royalty on retail copies. If the royalty is set as a percentage of the publisher's net revenues, your royalty payments may be much lower than you expect if the publisher sells the product for less than you expect. On the other hand, this reduced price may reflect the true market price of your product.

Both you and the publisher share a desire to maximize the revenue from the distribution of the product. In many cases, such per-unit minimums will not be necessary. If you decide to request such minimums, set them carefully to take into account the publisher's potential return and the realities of the marketplace. For example, multimedia products are rarely sold at the "suggested retail price." Minimum royalties based on the assumption that the publisher is receiving the suggested retail price are likely to be unrealistic because the publisher typically receives between 50–60 percent of the "suggested retail price" from the distributors. You can use the suggested retail price as the basis for this calculation, but you should recognize that the publisher will not be receiving the full amount. You also may wish to provide for a reduction in the per-unit royalty if the distribution price is reduced over time. Finally, you should recognize that the publisher may need to sell off older versions at less than normal retail prices.

Developers occasionally have tried to get the same per-copy royalty for both bundled and retail copies. This either sets the royalty rate too low for retail sales or too high for bundled sales. Generally, the result is a high per-copy royalty that deters the publisher from distributing bundled copies of the product.

Annual Minimums

The requirement of minimum royalty payments is one of the most effective devices to ensure that the publisher remains committed to exploiting the product. Such minimums may be less necessary if you have received a sufficiently large advance. Minimum royalty payments set clear expectations between you and the publisher. Generally, such minimums are set on a calendar-year basis. The amount varies depending on the price of the product and the sales expectations. On the other hand, you and the publisher may have different expectations for the product, and it may be difficult to agree on an amount acceptable to both parties. Annual minimums are rarely used in nonexclusive licenses.

Warranties

A "warranty" is simply a legal promise that certain facts are true. Most distribution agreements include a warranty section in which the publisher asks you to warrant certain facts. You can provide a warranty even for facts that are not within your control.

As discussed in "The Contract," Chapter 6, warranties come in different levels of certainty. The most common types of warranties are:

➤ Absolute.

➤ Know or should know.

➤ Actual knowledge.

"Absolute" warranties have the highest degree of certainty. These warranties have no exceptions and do not depend on your actual knowledge. Publishers prefer this type of warranty because proving that you had knowledge of a certain matter may be difficult.

Other warranties are qualified by statements such as "know or should have known" or "actual knowledge." Such qualifiers try to limit your duty to investigate the facts. The "know or should have known" warranty imposes on the warrantor a greater duty to investigate and "know" the status of the facts warranted than the "actual knowledge" warranty.

Whether to provide an absolute or a qualified warranty will depend on the subject of the warranty. For example, an absolute warranty that there are no pending lawsuits about the multimedia product is quite reasonable because you should know such information. However, a qualified warranty may be more appropriate for a warranty of noninfringement of third-party patents because you can infringe a patent innocently without any knowledge of the patent or the infringement.

The term "warranty" has a different meaning under the Uniform Commercial Code.

See "Important Provisions of Article Two," Chapter 19.

The warranties most commonly requested by a publisher are discussed in the balance of this section.

Ownership or Right to Grant the License

Depending on the nature of the multimedia product, the publisher may demand a warranty that you are the sole and exclusive owner of all intellectual property rights in the product, or simply that you have the right to grant the licenses in the distribution agreement. For example, for a work that has significant third-party content, you would not be able to warrant that you are the owner of the copyright of the entire work because it includes copyrightable material owned by third parties. However, a publisher will want to ensure that you have obtained the right to distribute third-party materials contained in your work. If you haven't gotten appropriate licenses from third parties, the publisher will infringe third-party copyrights by distributing your work. In fact, the publisher is likely to request copies of licenses and other contracts with third parties to ensure that you have the rights you need. This process is called "due diligence."

See "Due Diligence," Chapter 21.

If you are granting an assignment or an exclusive license, the publisher wants to be certain that you can actually grant exclusive rights in the product.

See "Using the Employment Agreement," Chapter 7, and "Copyright Ownership," Chapter 8.

See "Joint
Authorship and
Ownership,"
Chapter 4.

The publisher does not want "free riders" who also have the right to distribute the product and take advantage of the publisher's advertising. If you have failed to obtain appropriate assignments from the individuals who helped to create the product, those individuals may have "joint" ownership of the copyright in the product. This joint ownership will permit them to grant other publishers the right to distribute the product. Such "parallel" rights would undermine the exclusivity of the original publisher.

Noninfringement of Third-Party Rights

A warranty of noninfringement of third-party rights is one of the most important ones for a publisher because of the complex nature of multimedia products and the frequent use of third-party content. The publisher wants to ensure that you have obtained all of the rights necessary to distribute the product and that the product, as created, does not infringe third-party rights. Even though the publisher receives these warranties from you, it is still liable to third parties for infringement of their rights if you are wrong.

Different types of intellectual property call for different levels of certainty in the warranty. You should be willing to provide strong warranties regarding noninfringement of trade secrets and copyrights because these types of infringements are within your control.

The most difficult issue for you is the warranty about the noninfringement of patents. Unlike the infringement of copyrights or misappropriation of trade secrets, you can infringe patents without your knowledge. The problem is complicated by the youth of the multimedia industry and the lack of information about potentially applicable patents. In addition, patent applications in the United States are maintained in confidence until they actually are issued, a period of secrecy that may last several years. On the other hand, you are clearly more knowledgeable about how the product was developed than the publisher. The appropriate allocation of this risk requires careful negotiation between the parties.

Performance

See "Important
Provisions of
Article Two,"
Chapter 19.

Warranties about the performance of the product arise under Article Two of the Uniform Commercial Code. Most multimedia products would be considered "goods" under the Uniform Commercial Code and, therefore, would be subject to the rules imposed by that statute. You should be familiar with Article Two's "express" and "implied" warranties to determine the scope of your obligations.

Although you should be prepared to provide limited performance warranties, you should describe carefully the scope of your responsibilities for correcting errors in your product. You also will want to disclaim the "implied" performance warranties of "fitness for a particular purpose" and "merchantability" because of their ambiguity for software products. Virtually all software products have bugs, and the question of how many bugs are permitted in "merchantable" software is still open. Finally, you probably will be providing an express indemnity for infringement of third-party intellectual property rights, so you should disclaim the statutory warranty of noninfringement. Otherwise you would be providing two separate indemnities.

Credits

If the publisher has the right to reproduce your product or is providing packaging, you should ensure that you receive appropriate credit. Credits are important. The Writers Guild of America has established elaborate rules in the movie and television industries regarding appropriate credits for writers and others involved in the creation of films and television programs, but no such rules currently exist in the multimedia industry. The most frequent form of credits are "written by" and "developed by" on the title screen, the packaging, and the manual. Spell out what you want in your contract with the publisher.

You also should recognize that the publisher will be interested in maintaining control of the packaging of its products. Consequently, you should not make unrealistic demands about size and placement of credits. If you are providing only one part of a larger work, you should ensure that you review the final placement of credits prior to duplication to avoid having your credits buried in optional screens.

Remedies

Remedies are the relief for the failure ("breach") of a party's obligations under the distribution agreement. Pay careful attention to the remedies in the distribution agreement. Termination of the agreement is a "blunt" remedy. It may not be an effective remedy for many lesser breaches of obligations under the distribution agreement. If you terminate the distribution agreement, you must then find a new publisher and start the advertising and distribution process once again.

You should consider what type of "intermediate" remedies should be available to you for a less than complete failure on the part of the publisher. For example, if the publisher is successfully distributing your multimedia product in the United States but not in Europe, you will have a difficult decision if your choices are limited to taking no action or terminating the entire agreement. Instead, you should consider an "intermediate" remedy that permits termination in the countries in which the publisher is not performing successfully. Intermediate remedies should be put in place at the time the agreement is drafted.

You also should be aware of remedies that may be imposed on you for the breach of your obligations. One of the most common and most important remedies is an indemnity of the publisher for infringements of third-party intellectual property rights. The costs of defending and paying damages in an infringement case could far exceed the revenues you receive under the distribution agreement. The most efficient way of avoiding this liability is to properly clear any third-party content before using it (see Chapters 11, 12, 13, and 14).

One basis for allocating risks under a contract is to allocate them to the party best able to reduce them. As the developer, you are best able to assess the risk of infringement of third-party intellectual property rights and to reduce the risk. If you have a dispute with third parties, you can reduce your liability by including a requirement in the distribution agreement that permits you to demand that the publisher suspend distribution of the product in countries where challenges by third parties have been brought. For example, if a foreign corporation has brought a trademark infringement claim against the publisher in France based on your trademark, you should be able to demand that the publisher cease distributing the product in France (or remove the trademark for copies distributed in France) to avoid increasing your liability for damages.

In addition, you may wish to try to limit your liability for damages under this obligation. For example, you could ask to limit your liability under the agreement to the amount of your royalties. However, the publisher may be reluctant to permit such a limit. This is because the publisher's liability is likely to be significantly greater than the sum of all of the royalties paid to you. (The publisher's liability will be based on its profits, not on royalty payments to you.) Two potential compromises are to set a limit of a large amount based on the predicted sales or obtain insurance against this risk. Unfortunately, at the current time, it is difficult to obtain insurance for this type of risk. The issue of limiting your liability for infringement of third-party intellectual property rights may be one of the most contentious ones in your negotiations with the publisher.

21 Publishers' Concerns

The structure of transactions between multimedia developers and publishers is still in flux. The still-young multimedia industry draws on conflicting traditions from the book publishing, television, film, and software industries. There is currently no industry framework to use as a guide.

The multimedia publisher must deal with the same issues that face the developer (discussed in Chapter 20), but will have a different perspective. This chapter will describe key issues from the publisher's point of view.

Other chapters also discuss a number of issues that are relevant to the publisher—for example: Chapter 7, Employees; Chapter 8, Contractors and Consultants; Chapter 9, Creating a Multimedia Title for a Publisher; Chapter 10, Writing for Multimedia; Chapter 12, Clearing Rights and Obtaining Licenses; Chapter 22, The Business of Multimedia; and Chapter 23, On-line Issues.

Scope of Rights

The question of whether the distribution agreement should be structured as an assignment or a license is probably the most difficult and important issue between publishers and developers.

See "Scope of the Agreement" and "Assigning the Rights," Chapter 20.

The advantage of an assignment is that it provides the publisher with all rights in the product, and it does not require the publisher to predict which rights will be most valuable in the future. Even a general assignment should state clearly whether it includes an assignment of rights in the characters and settings in the product. Characters and settings could have significant value in sequels and other media.

If the publisher does not have the negotiating leverage to obtain an assignment, it will have to be satisfied with a license. In that case, the publisher should ensure that it gets a right of first refusal to exploit the multimedia product in media other than the "core" product form which it has licensed. The most common core product forms are CD-ROM and diskette. The most common noncore product rights, discussed in the balance of this section, are:

➤ Right to port to other platforms.

➤ Right to localize for other languages.

➤ Right to develop publisher-originated sequels.

➤ Right to distribute developer-originated sequels.

➤ Right to complete an unfinished work.

➤ Merchandising and ancillary rights.

Rights to Porting and Localization

In many cases, the publisher may only receive the right to reproduce and distribute the product. However, the publisher should be careful to obtain the right to modify the multimedia product for other platforms and other languages, even if the developer is not currently interested in such modifications. The current uncertainty about which platform will be the most important reinforces the importance of the porting and localization right. The publisher also should try to ensure that localization is made easier by having easy access to text files and text fields large enough for translations which are longer than English text.

The modification right and other exclusive rights are discussed in "The Exclusive Rights," Chapter 2.

As discussed in "Assignments," Chapter 4, copyright rights are divisible. If the publisher does not obtain the right to modify the product to create ported versions or foreign language versions of the product, the publisher will not have porting or localization rights. In that case, the publisher may miss significant opportunities for increased revenue.

See "Key Issues in License Agreements," Chapter 20.

On the other hand, the developer may wish to control the creation of such ports and localized products. A frequent compromise is to provide the developer with a "right of first refusal" to create such works. However, to avoid a separate negotiation for each new version, the publisher should try to establish the terms upon which it will be able to distribute such new versions (generally, the publisher will prefer the same terms as those for the original version).

The publisher also should consider whether the developer should be permitted to make these modifications for platforms with which the developer is not familiar. In other words, does the publisher wish to subsidize the developer's learning to create a product for a new platform? The publisher also should establish what materials—such as source code, graphics files, and camera-ready art—the developer will provide if the publisher (or the publisher's contractor) creates the modifications. Access to the developer's materials could substantially reduce the cost of creating these new versions.

Rights to Sequels

Many multimedia products offer significant opportunities to create a series of products based on the same theme, characters, or settings. The ability to market a series instead of a single product can substantially increase the return for the publisher. Consequently, the right to distribute sequels is critical for the publisher.

The publisher should establish the terms on which such sequel rights will be made available in as much detail as possible. If the publisher cannot obtain an absolute right to distribute sequels, a "right of first refusal" is the next best alternative, preferably based upon the same terms as those for distribution of the initial product. The disadvantage to the publisher of simply getting a right of first refusal is that it creates an "auction" with third parties, a situation that may not recognize the publisher's contribution to the value of the original product.

The publisher should try to get the following minimum information from the developer to decide whether to exercise its right of first refusal to distribute sequels:

➤ A written proposal (including a budget) from the developer to create the sequel.

➤ The royalty percentage for the sequel (if not already established).

➤ The advances for the sequel (if not already established).

➤ Other appropriate distribution terms.

If the publisher decides not to exercise the right of first refusal on a proposal, the developer should be allowed to offer rights in the sequel on the same terms to a third party for a limited period of time—typically from 30 to 120 days. If this time period is not limited, the publisher takes the risk that over time the initial product will become more successful and the original terms for the sequel will become more attractive. To ensure that the publisher and third parties compete on an equal basis for the sequel rights, the period during which the developer can offer such terms should be limited.

As an alternative, the publisher should try to include a "right of last look." This right gives the publisher a final opportunity to obtain rights in the sequel if the developer is about to enter into an agreement with a third party. A "right of last look" generally offers the publisher the opportunity to obtain the rights on the same terms as the third party. It is usually of very short duration (frequently five or fewer business days).

The publisher also should try to ensure that it has the right to develop sequels based on its own ideas. For example, the developer may decide not to create any further sequels, for reasons not based on the economic success of the original product. The publisher may believe that a sequel would be successful, and the publisher should have the right to invest in such a sequel. To avoid conflict with the developer, the publisher should consider offering the developer the right of first refusal to create that sequel based on the publisher's ideas. However, if the developer does not exercise that right, the publisher should be able to make the sequel. Naturally, the royalties paid to the developer for a sequel based on the publisher's ideas should be less than those for the original product.

Rights to Complete

Many developers are thinly capitalized organizations that may not be able to complete a project if a key person leaves. Consequently, the publisher should ensure that it has the right to complete a multimedia product if the developer is unsuccessful. Completion rights also should apply to ported versions, foreign language versions (localizations), and sequels whose development was begun by the developer. Once again, if the publisher does not have an assignment of rights in the product or the explicit right to modify the product, the publisher will not have the right to complete a product. At the same time, the developer may not have the resources to repay any advances. Thus, the publisher will be left with an unfinished product and an unrecoverable advance. This potential problem emphasizes the importance of having an escrow with source code and other components.

Rights to Merchandising and Ancillary Products

Depending on the type of multimedia product, the rights to ancillary products—books, clothing, television, and film—may be more valuable than the rights to the original multimedia product on CD-ROM or diskette. If the multimedia product creates popular characters, the potential returns in the ancillary products market may be enormous. The publisher should obtain the exclusive rights to license these characters, or at least a right of first refusal to exploit them.

Due Diligence

"Due diligence" is the shorthand term for the investigation of facts and legal issues undertaken by lawyers (or others) as part of a business transaction. In publishing agreements, the most important part of the publisher's due diligence is ensuring that the developer has properly done two things:

➤ Cleared any rights to third-party content used in the product. (See Chapters 11, 12, 13, and 14.)

➤ Obtained the necessary assignments from the individuals who helped to create the product. (See Chapters 7 and 8.)

The publisher will be liable for infringement if it distributes a product that includes third-party material without appropriate permission. Ignorance of the infringement is not a defense for the publisher, nor are developer warranties. The publisher will have a substantially greater liability for infringement than the developer. Damages awards to third parties will be calculated on the publisher's profits, not on those of the developer (or the royalties paid by publisher to developer).

Damages are discussed in "Copyright Protection," Chapter 18.

 Developer used a videoclip from the film *Terminator* in a multimedia product on sales training without clearing the rights to use the clip. Publisher got a warranty from Developer of ownership of all rights in the product and a warranty of noninfringement of third-party rights in the publishing agreement. The Publisher distributed the product to retail stores. The studio probably will sue both Developer and Publisher. Even though Publisher got a warranty that the product did not infringe third-party rights, both parties will be liable for copyright infringement. Publisher also may have a claim against Developer for its damages.

In addition, the third party whose intellectual property rights are infringed may obtain a court order to prevent distribution of the product and destroy existing copies of the product. In October 1993, Berkeley Systems obtained an injunction against Delrina for the use of Berkeley Systems' famous "Flying Toasters" in a "spoof" screen saver in which Delrina's Opus character shot down "Flying Toasters." One Delrina officer stated that complying with the order to cease distribution and destroy existing copies of the Delrina product cost the company hundreds of thousands of dollars.

Although the publisher can obtain warranties from the developer that no intellectual property infringement problems exist, warranties will not protect the publisher against embarrassment and business problems arising from the unauthorized use of third-party materials. The publisher also may find that the developer does not have the resources to defend or reimburse the publisher for damages paid to such a third party, despite having a legal obligation to do so.

Warranties are discussed in "Warranties," Chapter 20.

To avoid "buying" a lawsuit, the publisher or its attorney should understand how the multimedia product was developed, review third-party content licenses, and review the developer's agreements with its employees and independent contractors. It is much cheaper to discover and resolve problems before beginning distribution of the product.

License terms are discussed in "Obtaining a License," Chapter 12.

Publisher performed "due diligence" on a golf game it wanted to distribute. Publisher reviewed the assignment agreements with the individuals who created the game and the golf celebrity who licensed his name to be used on it. Publisher discovered that several of the individuals involved in the development of the game were not full-time employees of Developer at the time they worked on the game and they had not executed assignment agreements. The golf celebrity has licensed his name only for a year, and the license is limited to IBM computers. Before licensing the product, the Publisher should ensure that the individuals have executed appropriate assignment agreements. Publisher also may wish to extend the term of the celebrity license and broaden its scope.

This topic is discussed in "Determining What Rights You Need," Chapter 12.

Once again, because the legal issues are complicated and the industry is new, there are no industry standards about exactly what rights are needed. The burden is on the publisher to ensure that the developer has taken appropriate steps to obtain the rights necessary to develop and distribute the work.

Payment

See "Payment," Chapter 20.

Most multimedia distribution agreements provide for the payment of an advance against royalties, and for royalties on per-copy sales. The publisher's perspective on payment is discussed in this section.

Royalties

The publisher should ensure that the method of calculating royalties is clearly defined. As discussed in "Payment," Chapter 20, the publisher generally will prefer royalties based on net revenues rather than on gross revenues because it is less risky for the publisher.

In most cases, advances will be recouped against royalties. Recoupment is the repayment to the publisher of the advance previously paid to the developer. The procedure for recoupment of advances requires a careful balance of developer and publisher concerns. The publisher will want its advance repaid as rapidly as possible, a goal best achieved by withholding all of the royalty payments due to the developer until the advance is repaid. However, the publisher should recognize the potential problem this may create for the developer. Many developers are thinly capitalized and may depend on the revenue from the product being distributed while they work on other projects. By simply decreasing the percentage of the royalty payments used to recoup the advance from 100 percent to a lower percentage, the publisher can ensure that the developer continues to have a revenue stream. (For an example, see "Payment," Chapter 20. If the publishing agreement includes the right to distribute multiple products from the same developer, the publisher should ensure that it can "cross-recoup" (sometimes referred to as "cross-collateralize") its advances—recoup advances for one product against royalties due on another product.

Bundling

Bundling may be an important distribution channel for the publisher. There are a wide variety of financial arrangements in bundling—ranging from small payments to nonmonetary accommodations, such as cross licenses of other products. The publisher should ensure that royalties for bundling are calculated in a way that does not prevent bundling by requiring too high a payout. Minimum royalties per copy can be dangerous in bundling if not set realistically. Some publishers use a fixed-dollar-per-copy royalty. A fixed-dollar royalty is attractive for its simplicity when compared with the difficulty of attempting to calculate the value of "nonmonetary" compensation to determine the amount of a "percentage of revenue" royalty.

Completed Versions and New Versions

Obviously, the royalty for derivative products developed by the publisher and for products completed by the publisher should be less than the royalties for those products that the developer has successfully completed. The publisher should try to establish in advance the reduction in royalties for derivative products that it develops on its own or on products that it must complete. These concerns extend to ported and foreign language versions created by the publisher, as well as to new "sequels" developed by the publisher.

Bankruptcy

If the publisher has received an assignment of all rights in the intellectual property of a product, then it is relatively well protected against the consequences of the developer's bankruptcy. However, a problem could arise in identifying the materials (source code, graphics files, and so forth) to which the publisher has rights if the developer is also simultaneously creating other products when bankruptcy occurs. To avoid this problem, the publisher should consider an escrow arrangement in which all materials are deposited on a regular basis with a third-party escrow agent. Banks and law firms also act as escrow agents.

> ### The Publisher's Obligation
>
> In print publishing contracts, the author typically has the obligation to deliver a manuscript "satisfactory to the publisher in form and content." In a contract of that kind, the publisher has an implied obligation to engage in appropriate editorial work with the author. *Harcourt Brace Jovanovich, Inc. v Goldwater*, No. 79 Civ. 4863 (S.D.N.Y. 1982) (Slip opinion). The same may be true for multimedia publishers. In the HBJ case, a writer and Barry Goldwater contracted with the publisher for the publication of Goldwater's memoirs. HBJ returned the manuscript to the writer, stating that it was unacceptable and demanding the return of the advance. The court held that HBJ had no right to reject the manuscript because it had not engaged in any editorial work.

Bankruptcy of a developer poses potentially serious problems for the publisher if the publisher has a license rather than an assignment. Many developers are thinly capitalized and, thus, the chances of bankruptcy are real.

Generally, a United States bankruptcy court can terminate a license agreement if it is considered to be "executory"—one in which both parties have continuing obligations. Virtually every multimedia license agreement would be considered executory. For example, the publisher's obligation to pay royalties and the developer's indemnity of the publisher for intellectual property infringement is sufficient to make the license agreement executory. If the trustee in bankruptcy determines that the license is "burdensome" on the bankrupt company, the trustee can terminate the license and make the licensee (in this case, the publisher) an unsecured creditor with no further rights under the agreement and only a claim for damages. An unsecured creditor generally is paid only a small percentage of the amount of its claim.

In addition, the trustee can then relicense the product to a third party. In the United States, this problem was partially solved by amendment to the Bankruptcy Code in 1988. This amendment (found in 11 U.S.C. § 365[n] in the United States Code) provides that a licensee can retain its right under a license agreement so long as it continues to pay royalties and waives the right to future performance from the bankrupt party (for example, correction of errors) and certain other rights.

Unfortunately, this amendment solves only part of the problems for a publisher. Three other problems exist:

➤ First, this amendment applies only to intellectual property rights arising under United States law. Thus, if the publishing agreement includes the right to distribute the product outside of the United States, such rights would be subject to bankruptcy laws of each foreign country.

➤ Second, this amendment does not apply to trademark licenses. At the request of the United States Trademark Association (now the International Trademark Association), trademarks were excluded from this provision. Thus, the trustee in bankruptcy is still able to terminate the trademark license if the trustee can convince the bankruptcy court that the license is burdensome.

➤ Third, the amendment may not apply to exclusive copyright licenses in the United States. Such licenses are a "transfer of interest in copyright" and not a mere license. The most effective way of protecting an exclusive copyright license is to register the copyright and record the existence of the exclusive license against the registration. Once such a transfer is recorded, it will give "constructive notice" of the transfer and prevent future assignees or licensees from obtaining superior rights. Although

See "Licenses" and "Assignments," Chapter 4.

the effect of a bankruptcy on an exclusive copyright license is not clear at the present time, an exclusive copyright license that is properly recorded should survive bankruptcy.

The solution to the problem of possible developer bankruptcy is difficult and will vary depending on the nature of the rights granted and your negotiating leverage. You should contact your legal counsel on how to deal with this problem.

Recording of transfers is discussed in "Assignments" and "Licenses," Chapter 4.

Right to Sue Third-Party Infringers

Once the publisher has paid for the right to distribute the product, it should be able to stop third-party infringers or require the developer to do so by requiring that the developer sue third parties to stop the sale of infringing products. The right to sue "offensively" generally belongs to the owner of the copyright (or trademark). Thus, unless the publisher has received an assignment of all rights in the product, this right to sue will reside with the developer. An important exception to this rule in the United States permits an exclusive *copyright* licensee to sue third parties for infringement. However, the right of an exclusive licensee to sue varies depending on the country and the type of intellectual property (patent, trade secret, copyright, or trademark). Consequently, the publisher should deal with this issue expressly in the publishing agreement.

Another problem in the right to sue third parties for infringement arises for components of the product that the developer does not own, such as photographs or characters. If the developer has only licensed such rights and those licenses are nonexclusive, then the developer (and, consequently, the publisher) will not have the right to sue for infringement of rights in those components. Unless the developer obtained the right to sue for infringement of components in its license agreements, the developer will only have the right to sue third parties for copying of the "whole work," not for copying of components. (These rights under trademark law are a little different because they are based on "confusing similarity," discussed in "Scope of Trademark Rights," Chapter 17.)

 Developer has nonexclusively licensed a photograph of Marilyn Monroe for her celebrity trivia game. She used the photograph prominently on the front package of her game. A competitor with a similar game used the same photograph on the front of the package of his game, but without a license. Developer will not be able to sue her competitor for copyright infringement without the permission of the copyright owner of the photograph because she only has a nonexclusive license.

Generally, the publishing agreement should state whether the publisher or the developer has the first right to sue a third party for infringement. If that party decides not to bring suit within a limited time period, the other party should have the right to bring the suit. The agreement also should provide that the party not bringing the suit will assist the other party. Finally, the publishing agreement should allocate the division of any damages received from such a lawsuit. The failure to do so can lead to litigation between the developer and the publisher. One common solution provides that the damages, after deductions for the expense of the lawsuit (including attorneys' fees), should be split in some fixed percentage between the parties.

If the developer retains ownership of the intellectual property in the multimedia product, the developer may wish to have authority to approve any lawsuit settlements to avoid settlements that would adversely affect its rights. If the developer refuses to approve the settlement, the developer should have the obligation to take over the litigation and pay the publisher for the amounts spent in the litigation. Otherwise, the developer could block settlement of the lawsuit and force the publisher to continue the lawsuit without the developer bearing any expense for the continued litigation.

22 The Business of Multimedia

by Joanna Tamer

In this chapter, multimedia consultant Joanna Tamer discusses CD-ROM pricing strategies and the calendar which multimedia publishers must follow to get retail shelf space.

Price Pressures and New Channel Opportunities Demand New Product Planning

From the earliest days of multimedia, the price points of CD-ROM titles have progressed downward to a mass market level. From an introductory point of $129 per title in 1992, we have now reached a street price of $29 and $39. This price descent will not stop until we reach true consumer pricing—$24.95 or lower, preferably $19.95, $14.95, and below. We should see these consumer prices established by the end of 1996.

It is important that title publishers anticipate this market change, and adjust their distribution and marketing strategies to meet the reality of this price point and the broader channels which it opens. As prices continue to decline, all products ride the downward curve. At the moment, products priced at $12.95, $14.95, and $19.95 may be mostly old or failed product, but this will be the price point for new and quality product within the next 18 months.

Falling prices are not bad news. The advantage is that product priced below $24.95 can reach much broader channels than titles priced higher.

Newly-emerging channels—from mass merchants like WalMart and Target to discount clubs like Price Club and Costco, and industry-specific channels such as music stores and bookstores—are price-sensitive: they understand their target market, the expected spending level of their retail customers, and prefer to treat CD-ROM titles as a similar stock-keeping unit (SKU) to their other products.

This means the optimum price is $19.95 or below.

From SRP to Net Pricing

In the last several months, the wholesale price—the price at which the distributor sells to the retailer—has shifted from a discount off suggested retail price (SRP) to "net pricing." In a net pricing scheme, distributors set a fixed price for the title for retailers, and retailers have the flexibility to adjust their "street price" or "sticker price" to meet fluctuating consumer demand and competitive situations. You will notice that the listed suggested retail price is now rarely printed on the CD-ROM titles' box. What price might once have been listed, we can refer to as "the fictitious SRP."

Street prices are 15 percent to 20 percent below the fictitious SRP. So a $49 SRP will sell at $38 to $44. By Christmas 1995, most titles will sink to a fictitious SRP of $39, with a street price between $29 and $34. Although action-adventure games (because of their high concept and expensive production) may maintain a somewhat higher price point and street price, the majority of consumer CD-ROM titles will sell between $29 and $39 by this coming Christmas.

By Christmas 1996, street prices for most consumer CD-ROM titles are very likely to be $24.95 or less. It is a very sensible assumption that products will be forced to the new pricing regardless of their development costs.

The Price-wise Product-Planning Strategy

This combination of descending price points and the opening of broader channels seeking these lower price points offers a unique opportunity to create an aggressive product planning strategy that anticipates the new market position of 1996. This product strategy involves developing products that can be justifiably priced at $19.95 and below.

It is possible, with careful planing, to create a series of products that are aesthetically compelling and robust in their content and interactivity, but are "narrow" in their breadth. For example, a travel guide to Europe, which might cost $350,000 to develop, could be divided into four or five titles, with each title devoted to a specific region. The content among the titles would contain the same depth, interactivity and richness, but the breadth of the product would be narrowed. The publisher, having developed a five-title series, priced per title at $19.95, would fragment the product to allow each title to be sold for a price point that anticipates the decline in pricing by a full year, which in turn helps open new channels to welcome this price point. This "fragmentation" also provides the publisher a variety of marketing options appropriate to the "smaller" titles.

The Nuts & Bolts and Dollars & Cents

Lower prices are only part of the equation. The $350,000 in development cost that might have been spent on the single, broad title, can, with the series approach, be spread over each title, after the development cost of the engine and template is established and amortized. When seeking funding, the publisher presents a product series plan, with each title costing less than $100,000 to develop. This attracts the funding sources, who can understand that the break-even point is within reach of edutainment titles' sales volumes.

To create this product planning, new products must be developed which are rich, robust, and deep, but also sufficiently narrow. A series of products in the same genre must define a title series or product line. Multiple products in a line during an initial release allow many opportunities for marketing. One title could be "sacrificed" to extensive bundling, functioning as a preview mechanism or advertising for the other titles. A five-product line also reassures retailers that stock balancing is available from the publisher. In addition, the publisher may mix and match various titles in new configurations for retail: two-for-ones, three packs, and a deluxe five-disc set, priced at $49.95 for the five discs, for instance. This approach generates value through product merchandising; the same content, created as a single title, could not sell over $39 per unit.

The publisher who develops two such products into two five-title series, now has a ten-product line, which is a substantial market entry. The mass merchants, bookstores, and other channels welcome product at this price point, as they welcome product series; the net effect of each series for publishers is to allow access into much broader channels, creating greater coverage throughout retail, as well as supporting repeatable marketing and merchandising opportunities and expanded sales through catalog selling. Under these circumstances, multiple bundling deals are now available.

This low price/product series strategy is especially applicable to children's titles, and particularly with titles for young children. One common children's title design flaw is that they incorporate too much content for the target age group's typical attention span, even with repeat playings. It is not necessary—or even desirable—to create so full a product for young children.

Parents are happier buying multiple titles at a lower price; this $19.95 price point is indeed a magic number.

Will Publishers Pay the Price?

The buying public is fickle and price-conscious. The consumer has too often paid top dollar for a bad title, and would much prefer to risk his or her discretionary dollars on a less expensive title. With no previewing mechanism, the consumer does not know what he or she will receive, and the lower price point brings comfort.

Packaging is, as always, critical, but spending big money on packaging is not always the right answer. Many of the channels seeking this lower-priced CD-ROM product would prefer jewel case packaging, without the expensive and cumbersome software box. Not only does this reduce the cost of packaging—where often disproportionately high costs can occur relative to the lower product price—but creative packaging, using some of the new alternatives to jewel cases, can be an effective marketing tool.

This narrow-focus, series-oriented CD-ROM title strategy has proven effective in creating profitability for small companies. This strategy spreads the risk of the companies' launch into the industry over multiple products and creates a viable balance sheet for initial and continued funding of products.

Christmas in July: A New Consumer-driven Title Marketing Calendar

As consumer CD-ROM titles push ever further into retail's entertainment mainstream, the CD-ROM title business increasingly resembles the toy business, and title publishers must accordingly mimic the behavior of consumer products manufacturers and marketers as they gird themselves for frenzied holiday buying sprees. Like their newfound role-model marketers in the consumer products industry, CD-ROM consumer title publishers must be ready for Christmas in July.

In the spring of 1995, the CD-ROM title industry's retail calendar finally fell into line and followed the model of other consumer products. The spring trade shows created the initial deals for shelf space for the Christmas season, and the spring show of special note was E3, in May 1995. The retail buyers arrived, hunting for product and making up their initial stocking lists for Christmas. Deals were initiated in May, reiterated in June, and finalized in July. Products setting out to find shelf space for the holiday selling season after July were mostly out of luck.

For publishers, this early to-market rush means that products must be ready for presentation at RetailVision in April and in a fully demonstrable, nearly final form, for showing in May and June for E3, and the Spring Consumer Electronics Show. For products with distinct segments, such as children's book titles, full chapters with all appropriate interactivity and hot spots must be ready for showing at these spring events. And the production schedule must be nearing completion, since beta testing must begin in July.

With July reserved for testing, August can be spent replicating the disc, manufacturing the packaging, and assembling the finished product into retail-ready shape. Product then ships to retail in September, preferably during the month's first week.

Packaging Protocol of the Spring Show Set-ups

Product demonstrations represent only the beginning of what title publishers must prepare for as they accommodate the new "Christmas in July" retail regimen. The packaging prototypes must also be ready for the spring shows, even if there are only one or two boxes made, although it is best not to finalize or produce the packaging until distributors and retailers have approved it for their shelves. Distributors and retailers have significant authority over package design, and they will be clear about their demands about how packaging must be changed. But they always need to see a prototype first.

Finished, assembled, and shrink-wrapped titles must be shipped into distribution in September, so that they can reach the retail shelves in October for the selling season. Although replication, assemblage, and shipping are becoming faster and smoother operations for replication plants, publishers who are late getting product to their replicators may lose their place in line and have to be squeezed into the schedule, often with a significant time delay or "rush" charges. It is important to understand that replication facilities run 24 hours a day, and are fully booked during the third and fourth quarters, not only with multimedia product for the consumer market, but with business products and with audio CD replication. Consequently, it is important to schedule the replication date early on and stick to it.

Marketing plans must also be ready for the spring shows, with at least "top line" advertising and public relations budgets assigned to each product and marketing plan. Cooperative marketing dollars and market development funds must be clearly budgeted per product or product line, and per retailer. Distributors and retailers are extremely interested in the number of marketing dollars which will flow into their organizations for each product. They are also concerned that a publisher's marketing budget and plan for promotion and advertising will create significant "pull" marketing to bring the customers into the store to buy the products. And they want to know that there are enough co-op and market development funds available to "push" the product through their channel.

Planning the Perfect Pitch

This combination of compelling product, savvy packaging, marketing plans, and co-op budgets are a publisher's sales pitch to retail and to distribution. The pitch must be highly evolved and quickly and clearly presentable in time for the spring shows. Distributors and retailers may spend as much as half an hour in a scheduled meeting, but little or no time with publishers on the show floor who have not made an appointment. The pitch must be succinct, thorough, and available to be left with the retailer or distributor in a written and visual form, preferably as a CD-ROM.

Distributors and buyers will negotiate with publishers at these shows, outlining their preliminary interest in stocking the product in certain volumes, assigning appropriate shelf space, and considering the "depth" which they will stock on each title (how many "deep" each title goes in the retail shelf stacks). These preliminary commitments are made per product, and sometimes in a mix-and-match strategy across a product line.

In July, everyone follows up to finalize their commitments. Publishers commit to shipping deadlines, co-op marketing dollars, market development funds, and discounts to the channel. Distributors and retailers commit to product mixes, depth of product, programs available to use with the cooperative marketing dollars, and final approval of packaging. Execution of the marketing plan must begin in July and August to be ready for release in September and October.

Public relations which launch a product or a product line must be set in motion no later than June, because magazine advertising and critical reviews are developed with at least three months' lead time before publication. A publisher's PR company must leave two or three months available to get the attention of a trade magazine reviewer, obtain his commitment to look at and review the product, make certain the product is reviewed, and see that the review is written no later than June for publication in September, October, and November.

Photos of the box design must be ready, even if it will change some, and then, of course, new photos must be taken when and if a change occurs. Once the reviewer is lined up, finished product must be sent to him or her, post-beta, for review in July if the review is to show up in the October issue. The product must not be buggy, and should be fully finished by this time. Reviewers rarely look at demonstration copies.

Credo for a New Calendar: *Don't* Wait Til Next Year

So, if the calendar demands product and marketing strategies to be finalized in July, publishers must begin fully funded development during the previous year. If publishers are using an existing template and engine, and simply putting new content into it, they might be able to begin as late as January. The development of a new engine and template would require three to six months of additional time, or at least 12 to 18 months' development time prior to release. First product attempts always take longer than the traditional development schedule.

If funding is required before product is developed, a publisher may face up to a two-year development cycle in order to secure funding, build an engine and template, create the product, and have it ready for July dealmaking.

Independently developed products looking for a publishing deal and Christmas shelf space should be in circulation during the early months of the calendar year, when publishers are planning their product lines for the Christmas season. At this time, publishers can plan which products they will acquire, which they will develop in-house, and what marketing monies will be required for public relations throughout the year in preparation for the Christmas release. Finished titles, pressed and packaged, seeking shelf space after the mid-summer months will face considerable difficulty.

More and more, publishers will find they must tighten their discipline in planning, product completion, and timeliness to market in order to compete in new media's increasingly market-driven, consumer-oriented retail environment.

Joanna Tamer, President of S.O.S., has specialized in distribution and business development strategies for new media developers, publishers, distributors, platform manufacturers and retailers since 1990. Communications may be addressed to Joanna Tamer, S.O.S., Inc., 100 Driftwood, Suite 1, Marina del Rey, CA 90292. Telephone 310/306-1814; fax 310/306-4681; email joeytamer@aol.com.

The material in this chapter was previously published in *CD-ROM Professional* (October 1995 and January 1996 issues). The material is used here with permission.

Part 5

On-line and
Educational Issues

23 On-line Issues

In this chapter, we'll discuss a number of on-line legal issues with emphasis on the Internet and the World Wide Web.

Law and Cyberspace

Some people think that copyright law and other laws do not apply in cyberspace—because cyberspace is a "new frontier," because ideas and information should flow freely in cyberspace, or because laws do not apply to transmissions made possible by technology that was not in existence when the laws were enacted.

Do not make the mistake of thinking that the laws discussed in other chapters in this book do not apply to material distributed over the Internet. The laws *do* apply. For example:

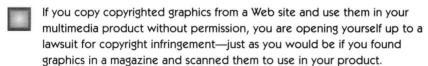 If you copy copyrighted graphics from a Web site and use them in your multimedia product without permission, you are opening yourself up to a lawsuit for copyright infringement—just as you would be if you found graphics in a magazine and scanned them to use in your product.

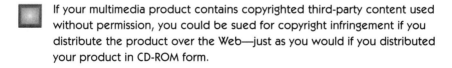 If your multimedia product contains copyrighted third-party content used without permission, you could be sued for copyright infringement if you distribute the product over the Web—just as you would if you distributed your product in CD-ROM form.

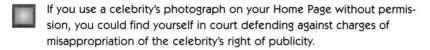 If you use a celebrity's photograph on your Home Page without permission, you could find yourself in court defending against charges of misappropriation of the celebrity's right of publicity.

If you write an article saying unflattering, untrue things about the CEO of the company that's your main competitor and post the article to Usenet Newsgroups, you will be setting yourself up for a lawsuit for defamation—just as you would if you published and distributed a newsletter containing the article.

There are certainly questions about how particular laws should be applied to Internet transactions, and some of these questions are discussed in later sections of this chapter. However, if you are using the Internet, you should assume that the laws that apply to traditional transactions and traditional media apply in cyberspace—both the laws discussed in this book and other laws, such as criminal laws.

Myths

Much public domain material is available on the Net—government reports and uncopyrightable factual information, for example. However, much of the material that is on the Internet is protected by copyright.

There are a number of myths about how copyright law applies to copying material from the Internet and posting material on the Internet. We'll discuss some of them in this section.

Copying Material from the Net

Don't make the mistake of believing these myths about copying material from the Net:

Myth #1: If I find something on the Net, it's okay to copy it and use it without getting permission.

While you are free to copy public domain material that you find on the Net, generally you should not copy copyrighted material without getting permission from the copyright owner—whether you find the material on the Net or in a more traditional medium (book, music CD, software disk, etc.) This topic (and exceptions to the copyright owner's rights) is covered in Chapter 11.

Myth #2: Material on the World Wide Web is in the public domain if it's posted without a copyright notice.

Do not assume that material is uncopyrighted just because it does not contain a copyright notice. Under current law, the use of copyright notice is optional. This topic is discussed in "Procedure for Getting Protection," Chapter 2.

Myth #3: Anyone who puts material on a Web server wants people to use that material, so I can do anything I want with material that I get from a Web server.

Individuals and organizations put material on a Web server to make it accessible by others. They do not give up their copyright rights by putting material on a Web server. Also, the person who posted the material may not own it.

Myth #4: It's okay to copy material from a Home Page or Web site without getting permission.

Much of the material that appears in Web sites and Home Pages is protected by copyright. If you want to use something from someone else's Home Page or Web site, get permission—unless permission to copy is granted in the text of the Home Page or Web site (see "Taking Material from the Net," later in this chapter).

Posting Material

And don't believe these myths about how copyright law applies to putting copyrighted material owned by others on the Net:

Myth #5: It's okay to use copyrighted material in my Web site so long as no one has to pay to visit my Web site.

Unless your use of the copyrighted work is fair use (see "Fair Use," later in this chapter), you need a license to copy and use the work in your Web site even if you won't be charging people to view your Web site. (You also need a public display license.) This topic is covered in Chapter 11.

Myth #6: It's okay to make other people's copyrighted material available on my Web server so long as I don't charge people anything to get the material.

Copying and distributing copyrighted material without permission can be copyright infringement even if you don't charge for the copied material. Making material available for others to copy can be contributory infringement (discussed in "Operator Liability," later in this chapter).

Myth #7: My Web site will be a wonderful showcase for the copyright owner's song/graphics/text, so I'm sure the owner will not object to my use of the material.

Don't assume that a copyright owner will be happy to have you use his or her work. The owner may, for example, be concerned that the reproduction quality of your Web site will not do the work justice. Even if the owner is willing to let you use the work, the owner may want to charge you a license fee.

The "White Paper"

In 1993, the Clinton Administration's Working Group on Intellectual Property Rights, chaired by the Commissioner of Patents and Trademarks, studied the issue of whether the needs of the global information society would warrant changes in the intellectual property laws. The group issued a preliminary report for public comment in July 1994; it issued a final report—known as the "White Paper"—in September 1995. The White Paper can be found on-line at http://iitf.doc.gov/.

Conclusions

Copyright is the most important of the four intellectual property laws for Internet users (just as it is the most important of the four laws for multimedia developers and publishers). The Working Group concluded that the Copyright Act is "fundamentally adequate and effective"—with a few changes to take proper account of current technology—to carry us into the Information Age. The group recommended that revision of the other three intellectual property laws (patent, trademark, and trade secret law) not be undertaken at this time.

According to the White Paper, copyright protection is an essential component to the success of the National Information Infrastructure (NII), not an obstacle to the success of the NII. Although some of the individuals who testified before the Working Group or filed comments felt that copyright protection should be reduced in the on-line world, the White Paper's authors rejected this approach. They believed that unless authors and owners of works have copyright protection for their works on the Internet, they will not make their works available for others to use.

Proposed Changes in Copyright Law

The changes in copyright law proposed by the Working Group included the following:

> ➤ **Distribution right.** They recommended that the Copyright Act be amended to expressly recognize that copies can be distributed to the public by transmission and to state that transmissions fall within the copyright owner's exclusive distribution right. (Under current law, a transmission by computer is arguably not a distribution, because "distribution" is defined in terms of physical copies.)

> ➤ **Prohibition on devices to defeat anti-copying systems.** The Working Group believes that, in the future, copyright owners probably will use anti-copying technology to protect their works on the Internet. The group recommended prohibiting the manufacture of devices or methods whose primary purpose or effect is to defeat anti-copying systems.

> ➤ **Library exemption.** The Working Group proposed that the current statutory exemption for library photocopying be expanded. The current exemption and the proposed expansion are discussed in "Library Photocopying," Chapter 24.

➤ **Sound recording performance right.** The Working Group recommended adding a public performance right for sound recordings. (Congress already has added this right for digital audio transmissions. See "Option #2: Using Preexisting Music," Chapter 14.)

➤ **Criminal violations.** Under current law, it is a crime to willfully infringe a copyright for commercial advantage or private financial gain. The Working Group recommended changing the criminal statute to make it a crime to reproduce or distribute copies with a retail value of greater than $5,000. The change grew out of a case against a bulletin board owner who encouraged others to use his bulletin board to upload copyrighted software for downloading by others. The bulletin board operator was indicted, but the court dismissed the indictment because the bulletin board operator did not charge for the software. *United States v. LaMacchia*, 871 F. Supp. 535 (D. Mass. 1994).

Criticism

The White Paper has been criticized for showing too much concern for copyright owners' rights and too little concern for fair use. Some critics say that the White Paper overstates the extent to which current law supports the Working Group's "copyright maximalist" viewpoint (for an example, see "Operator Liability," later in this chapter)—and that the "minor" changes it proposes are really major changes to the law in favor of copyright owners.

For a good statement of the anti-White Paper sentiment, see an article by Pamela Samuelson, "The Copyright Grab," in the January 1996 issue of *Wired*. (You can locate a copy of this article on the Web at http://www.hotwired.com/wired/whitepaper.html.)

Fair Use

Under U.S. copyright law, you don't need a license to use a copyrighted work if your use is "fair use." The fair use exception was created to allow limited use of copyrighted material for purposes such as criticism, comment, news reporting, teaching, scholarship, and research. Examples of fair use are quoting passages from a book in a book review; summarizing an article, with brief quotations, for a news report; and copying a small part of a work to give to students to illustrate a lesson.

> **Fair Use Defense Raised in On-line Copying Case**
>
> Dennis Erlich, a former minister of the Church of Scientology, posted 154 pages of copyrighted and confidential Church of Scientology teachings to a Usenet Newsgroup. When the church sued him for copyright infringement, Erlich claimed that the posting was fair use. The court, using the four-factor analysis described here, ruled against the defense, primarily because Erlich had copied large portions of the works (some unpublished) with only minimal added criticism or commentary. *Religious Technology Center v. Netcom On-Line Communication Services, Inc.*, __F. Supp.__ (N.D. Ca. 1995). (Another aspect of this case is discussed in "Operator Liability," later in this chapter.)

Fair use is discussed in "When You Don't Need a License," Chapter 11. However, because there's some confusion about how fair use applies to material on the Internet, we'll discuss it briefly here.

Posting Copyrighted Material

Some people think that posting someone else's copyrighted material on the Internet or putting it on a Web server is fair use, because the "culture" of the Net is that it's okay to do these things.

Under current law, there is no absolute fair use right to post someone else's copyrighted material on the Internet. If copyrighted material is used on the Internet without the permission of the copyright owner, whether the posting is fair use will be decided by considering four factors: the purpose and character of the use, the nature of the copyrighted work, the amount and substantiality of the portion used, and the effect on the potential market for or value of the protected work.

This is the same fair use analysis that is applied to decide whether the use of copyrighted material in a book (or other traditional product) is fair use. There is no special fair use exemption for the Internet. Posting copyrighted material *may* be fair use. It is not necessarily fair use. Compare these two examples:

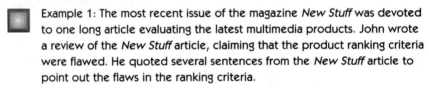

Example 1: The most recent issue of the magazine *New Stuff* was devoted to one long article evaluating the latest multimedia products. John wrote a review of the *New Stuff* article, claiming that the product ranking criteria were flawed. He quoted several sentences from the *New Stuff* article to point out the flaws in the ranking criteria.

Example 2: John scanned the *New Stuff* article described in Example 1 and posted it to several Usenet Newsgroups so that Usenet members could have the article for free.

In the first example, John's use of several sentences from the *New Stuff* article to support his criticism of the article is probably fair use—just as it would be if John had quoted the article in a review published in a newspaper or magazine. All four factors point toward fair use—John's use of the article was for a traditional fair use purpose (criticism or comment); the article was published and factual; he used only a small part of the article; and his review was not a substitute for the *New Stuff* article.

In the second example, John's use of the *New Stuff* article is probably not fair use. It's true that even in this example, two of the fair use factors point toward fair use—John's use of the *New Stuff* article was noncommercial (he didn't charge for access to the copy of the article), and the article was a published, factual work. However, the other two factors point the other way—

John copied the whole article, and he created a substitute for the copyrighted work. This sort of "nontransformative" use is not likely to be fair use.

Taking Material from the Net

There are people who think that there's a fair use right to copy and use material found on the Net. "The owner put the material up," they reason. "It must be okay to copy it and use it."

Copying copyrighted material from the Internet—like posting copyrighted material on the Net—*can* be fair use, but the usual fair use analysis applies. Copying several sentences from a copyrighted document that you find on-line to give to students to illustrate a lesson is probably fair use. Copying an entire document that you find on-line to give to a large number of friends and colleagues may not be fair use.

Common Sense

"But everyone does these things," you may be thinking. "Everyone who uses the Net probably has posted copyrighted material owned by others or copied copyrighted material from the Net. Surely these things cannot be copyright infringement."

Use common sense. How many of us photocopy newspaper or magazine articles to share with friends or colleagues? This is technically copyright infringement. Similarly, if you copy entire articles and post them on the Net to "share" them, you will not necessarily be sued by the copyright owner. Historically, those who copy for personal use (as opposed to resale) have rarely been sued. The same may prove true for on-line copying. However, publishers and content owners may be more likely to pursue individuals for on-line copying than for photocopying, because many publishers and content owners see the Internet—where the push of a button can disseminate multiple copies of their material—as the ultimate threat to their operations and ownership rights.

The Future of Fair Use on the Net

The Clinton Administration's Working Group on Intellectual Property Rights has appointed a committee of educators and content owners to discuss Internet fair use issues and, if possible, to develop guidelines for uses of copyrighted works by libraries and educators. Topics include multimedia, library preservation of materials, browsing rights, and distance learning. The committee, known as the Conference on Fair Use (CONFU), began meeting in September 1994. To date, no guidelines have been adopted.

Nontransformative use as fair use is discussed in "When You Don't Need a License," Chapter 11.

Implied Licenses

Some people think that putting copyrighted material on the Internet is implied consent to copying and using the material for any purpose. Don't believe it.

Copyright law *does* recognize that permission to use copyrighted material can be implied from a copyright owner's conduct or from custom. Here are three examples of how the doctrine of implied license applies in cyberspace:

1. When you want to access a document a copyright owner has placed on a Web server, your computer will have to make a temporary copy of the document in its random access memory (RAM). By posting the document without a limitation on such copying, the copyright owner has implicitly given you permission to make that temporary copy, since you cannot otherwise view the document.

2. When the user of an on-line service provider sends a message to a public message board, many attorneys believe that the author of the message implicitly gives the on-line service provider permission to display the message.

3. It's customary, when replying to an email message or a message board message, to repeat the message (or part of it). The message's author implicitly gives others permission to copy the message for the purpose of replying to it (copying for the purpose of reply could also be fair use).

The doctrine of implied license is a narrowly applied "gap filler" that's used when implied permission makes sense—based on circumstances (Examples 1 and 2), or on custom (Example 3). At the present, people familiar with Net usage have different opinions about the scope of the implied license that arises from posting material on the Net. For example, some people think that posting a document gives an implied license to Net users to print out a "hard" copy of the document (in addition to making a temporary copy in the computer's RAM). Others would say the implied license is limited to permission to make a temporary copy in the computer's RAM.

Be cautious about relying on an implied license while Net custom is still developing (after all, mass usage of the World Wide Web only goes back a few years). Don't try to stretch the implied license doctrine—for example, relying on the doctrine to justify printing out several hundred messages from a message board and selling them as a compilation of views on the topic.

Taking Material from the Net

Licensing is discussed in Chapter 12.

Much of the material that is on the Internet is copyrighted. If you find material on the Net that you want to use in your own work—whether in your multimedia product, your Web site, or some other project—do not make the mistake of believing that you are free to use the material without going through the normal licensing process. Putting a document on the Net is not a waiver of copyright or a dedication of the document to the public domain.

When you find something on the Net that you want to use, go through the same analysis that you would if the material appeared in a more traditional medium (in a book, software diskette, or music CD, for example). If the material is in the public domain, you are free to use it. If it is copyrighted, you need a license if your intended use of the work would, without a license, infringe any of the copyright owner's exclusive rights.

See "When You Need a License," "When You Don't Need a License," and "Public Domain Works," Chapter 11.

Limited Permission Grants

A number of documents available on the Internet contain a statement that it's permissible to copy the document for certain purposes. Here are three examples:

➤ "This article may be copied in its entirety for personal or educational use (the copy should include a License Notice at the beginning and at the end). It may be posted on gopher and FTP sites, but please provide notice of such posting to the authors at the addresses below. It may not be modified without the written permission of the authors."

➤ "Permission is granted to freely copy this document in electronic form, or to print for personal use."

➤ "All the text and pictures on this Web server are copyrighted. You may use the pictures for any noncommercial purpose if you attribute the source."

Authors place these limited permission grants on their documents because they want the documents to be shared and used for certain purposes (and they don't want to be bothered with requests for permission for such uses). Don't confuse a limited permission grant with a waiver of copyright. A limited permission grant is just a license to use the work in ways stated in the grant—and only in those ways.

Licenses are discussed in Chapter 4 and Chapter 12.

Uses Not Covered

If you want to use a work in a way that is not covered by the document's limited permission grant, contact the copyright owner and get permission. If you don't, you will be infringing the copyright on the work.

Developer found some images she liked on a Web page. The Web page stated, "You may use these images for any noncommercial purpose if you attribute the source." If Developer uses those images in a commercial CD-ROM product without getting permission from the owner, she will be infringing the copyrights on the images. Developer should go through the normal licensing process if she wants to use those images in her commercial product.

Don't assume that a copyright owner who puts a limited permission grant on a document will be happy to have you use the work for purposes other than those stated in the grant. If you want to use a work that comes with a "limited permission grant" in a way not covered by the grant, follow the procedure that you would use with copyrighted works from traditional media: Get permission before you use the work. Once you have stepped outside the bounds of the grant, you are on dangerous ground.

Use Caution

When you want to use a work from the Net that comes with a limited permission grant, be cautious about concluding that the use you want to make of the work is within the scope of the grant. If there's any doubt about whether the grant covers your planned use, contact the copyright owner to discuss your plans and get written permission giving you the right to use the material in your project. If you assume the grant covers your use and you go ahead and use the work, the copyright owner may disagree and sue you, possibly getting an injunction that will hold up distribution of your product.

See "Determining What Rights You Need," Chapter 12.

 Developer found a short geography quiz on the Net. The quiz stated that it could be copied for educational purposes. Developer, relying on the limited permission grant, used the quiz in an edutainment CD-ROM. The copyright owner sued Developer for copyright infringement, claiming that Developer's use of the quiz was commercial use rather than educational use. While the case was pending, the copyright owner got a preliminary injunction against the sale of Developer's product pending resolution of the lawsuit.

In the example immediately above, it is possible that Developer ultimately will win the lawsuit. However, in the meantime, she cannot sell her product. It would have been wiser to have contacted the copyright owner and requested, for a reasonable fee, permission to use the quiz. If the owner refused to give permission or if the owner's license fee was too high, the Developer then could have substituted other material and continued to market her product without delay.

Written Permission

If you are planning on using material from the Net in a multimedia product that will be widely distributed, it's best to obtain written permission for all third-party content, even if your use of the material is clearly within the scope of a limited permission grant. Publishers often require written licenses for all third-party content.

Who Is the Owner?

If you want to use material put up by someone other than the copyright owner, but with the owner's permission, you need permission from the owner, not from the poster.

 On-line Service Provider got Author's permission to post a chapter from Author's book on OSP's commercial on-line service. If Developer wants to use the chapter in Developer's CD-ROM encyclopedia, Developer needs permission from Author (not from OSP).

Getting permission to use material you find on the Net is complicated by the fact that some people post copyrighted material they do own or have permission to use. If someone has posted copyrighted material in violation of the copyright owner's exclusive rights, getting the poster's permission to use the copyrighted material will do you no good. The person posting it has no right to authorize you to use the material. You need the owner's permission.

 John, a fan of the cartoon strip "Peanuts," used a picture of Snoopy on his Web site without getting permission from the copyright owner. Developer downloaded the picture to use in her CD-ROM product, with John's permission. Getting permission from John is worthless, since John does not own the copyright (and is himself probably an infringer of the owner's exclusive rights).

Do not assume that the person who posted the document is the owner. Ask questions: Who created the document? What is its origin? If there's any doubt about whether the person who put the document up is the owner, don't use the document. It is always a good idea to ask for warranties of ownership and noninfringement.

See "Warranties and Indemnities," Chapter 8, and "Obtaining a License," Chapter 12.

Finally, when getting permission, be wary of people who mistakenly think they own the rights in material they have commissioned in the past.

 Developer saw some photographs she liked in Z Company's Web site. Developer contacted Z Company's president and got permission to use the photographs on her Web site. If the copyrights in the photographs are owned by the photographer who took them (likely, if the photographer was a free-lancer), Z Company cannot authorize Developer to use the photographs. Only the photographer can.

Copyright ownership rules are discussed in Chapter 4. Ownership of works created by independent contractors is discussed in "Copyright Ownership," Chapter 8.

Developing Your Own Web Site

In this section, we'll discuss some legal issues you should consider in developing your own Web site.

Copyright Law

See "When You Don't Need a License," Chapter 11.

Don't use copyrighted material owned by others on your Web site unless you get permission or unless one of the exceptions to the copyright owner's exclusive rights applies. Copyright owners are increasingly vigilant about "policing" the Web to find infringers.

It is tempting to use images of copyrighted cartoon or television characters to add appeal to your Web site. Don't, unless you get a license. The owners of this type of material are particularly diligent about going after unauthorized users. For example, an individual who used a picture of Winnie-the-Pooh on his Web site got a "cease and desist" letter from the book publisher that owns the rights to Winnie-the-Pooh, and Star Trek fans who used photos from the television series and the movies got "cease and desist" letters from Paramount Pictures.

It's also tempting to use music clips to jazz up your Web site. Some people think it's okay to use three or four bars of a song without getting permission. This is a myth. Copying a small amount of a work can be copyright infringement, and there is no "safe harbor" involving the number of bars copied.

Previously Licensed Material

See "Option #2: Using Preexisting Music," Chapter 14.

If you want to use copyrighted material which you licensed to use in the past, don't assume that the old license will cover your use of the material on your Web site. You may need a new license. Use of licensed material in a way not authorized in the license is copyright infringement.

> Multimedia Publisher used ten seconds of a music clip from a recording in a kiosk product, "Standout," after getting the necessary licenses (from the music publisher and the record company). If those licenses were limited to the use of the clip in the single product "Standout," Publisher will need new licenses to use the clip in Publisher's Web site.

Using Licensed Content on the Net

If you plan to use a Web site to publicize your CD-ROM products, you probably will want to include clips of your products on-line. If you want to use a clip that contains licensed third-party content, be careful. Your license to use that content may not give you the right to use it on the Internet.

If you plan to publicize your products on your Web site in the future, your licenses to use third-party content should include language authorizing you to use a clip of the licensed content on the Net to publicize your multimedia product (in addition to language authorizing you to use the content in your CD-ROM product itself).

Material You Own

If you own the copyright in a work, you can use the work on your Web site.

What works do you own? If you are an employer, according to U.S. law, you own the copyright in works created by employees acting within the scope of their employment.

 Five years ago, Karen, a graphic designer employed by Multimedia Co., created Multimedia's logo. Multimedia Co. is free to use the logo in any manner—including on its Web site—without Karen's permission.

If you want to use material created for you in the past by an independent contractor, you may need the contractor's permission. In this country, a hiring party does not own the copyright in work created by an independent contractor unless the hiring party got an assignment or unless that work had "specially commissioned work made for hire" status.

 High Tech Co.'s public relations department has in its files a photograph of the company headquarters taken several years ago by a free-lance photographer for a company brochure. Unless High Tech Co. got an assignment from the photographer, High Tech Co. should get the photographer's permission before using the photograph in the company's Web site.

Don't assume that you own a work just because you've used it before. The prior use may have been unauthorized—or it may have been authorized based only on a limited license grant. Check your documentation for the earlier use. If you don't have any documentation, check with the owner of the work.

Other Material You Can Use

You can avoid obtaining licenses to use third-party material on your Web site if you use public domain material.

Further, you don't need a license to make fair use of copyrighted material, to copy facts or ideas, or to parody the work.

You also can avoid licensing by creating your own content. For material that is created in-house by employees, follow the suggestions in Chapter 7 to ensure that you have copyright ownership throughout the world. For material that is created by an independent contractor, follow the suggestions described in "Copyright Ownership," Chapter 8.

Ownership of works created by employees is discussed in "The Work Made for Hire Rule," Chapter 4, and in "Works Made by Employees," Chapter 7.

Ownership of works made by independent contractors is discussed in "Copyright Ownership," Chapter 8.

Public domain works and fair use are discussed in Chapter 11.

Other Laws

Privacy, publicity, and defamation are discussed in Chapter 15.

The laws of privacy, publicity, and defamation apply to the use of material on the Web. Elvis Presley Enterprises is not likely to be amused if you scan an image of Elvis from a Graceland postcard and use it on your Web page. By scanning the postcard, you are violating the right of publicity in the Elvis likeness (owned by Elvis's heirs), in addition to infringing the copyright on the postcard.

Patent law and trade secret law also apply to activities on the Internet. CompuServe caused quite a stir in late 1994 when it announced that all providers of software using the ".gif" format (a common data compression format for images) would have to be licensed by CompuServe due to a patent held by Unisys on a data compression algorithm. Currently RSA Data Security and Cylink both are licensing patents related to public key encryption.

The principles of trademark law also apply. The *Playboy* case and the *Sega* case (discussed in "Operator Liability," later in this chapter) both included claims of trademark infringement because the material copied included the owner's trademarks.

Copying Existing Web Sites

Original Web sites and original material on Web sites (logos, images, etc.) are protected by copyright. As with other copyrighted material, the copyright does not extend to the ideas used in a Web site or to facts presented in the Web site. You are free to copy the ideas and uncopyrightable facts, but you should not copy the page as a whole or the protected expression.

 Recycling Co.'s competitor, MoCo, has a Web site that consists of four components—information about MoCo, information about MoCo's services, statistics about the growing popularity of recycling in the U.S., and a "request" form that users can email in to get more information on the company's services. Recycling Co. is free to put together its own Web site with company information, service information, statistics, and an email request form. It also is free to use the facts from MoCo's statistics page. However, if Recycling Co. copies MoCo's graphics or Web page text and layouts, that's probably copyright infringement.

Whether you can copy an existing Web site's network of links to other Web sites is unclear. While a Web site owner presumably cannot claim copyright protection in an individual link to another site, the selection involved in setting up a network of links could be protected by copyright.

Legality of Other Web Site Features

In this section, we'll discuss legal issues raised by "pointing" at other Web sites, "mirroring" other Web sites, and including "chat functions" in a Web site.

Pointing

Attorneys familiar with copyright law and the Internet currently are debating whether you need permission from the owner of another Web site to "point" (link) to that site. The majority view is currently that pointing to another site doesn't infringe the copyright on the linked site. Linking does not involve copying or displaying the "pointed at" page at the Web site that contains the pointer. When someone who is browsing a Web site containing pointers "clicks" on a pointer, the pointer itself is transferred to that individual's computer and sent to the source to retrieve the "pointed at" object.

Nonetheless, it is a good idea to ask permission before including pointers to other Web sites. Generally, permission will be granted (most other Web site owners will be happy to have the increased visibility that linking offers them). Some owners may ask you not to point to their sites if they don't want to be associated with your site or if they fear this will somehow result in the loss of their copyright rights.

Don't use a graphic image from the "pointed at" Web site as a pointer to that site unless you have permission to use the image (the .gif file). Use text instead. Copying a .gif file from someone else's Web site without permission is probably copyright infringement, even if you have permission to point to the site.

Mirroring

Some Web sites "mirror" another site by copying the other site's files and storing an exact copy of those files for users to access. Mirroring is done to minimize the load at the original site, or for the convenience of the users of the Web site containing the "mirrored" files. Because the copying involved in mirroring could be copyright infringement, you shouldn't mirror other sites without getting permission from the copyright owner for that site.

Chat Functions

If your Web site offers a chat function (real-time conversation) or includes a bulletin board, you may be liable for copyright infringement and other wrongs committed by users of these functions. This topic is discussed in "Operator Liability," later in this chapter.

Hiring a Web Developer

Many companies hire Web developers to create their Web sites. If you hire a Web developer, you should have a written contract with the Web developer

See "Copyright Ownership," Chapter 8.

Warranty provisions are discussed in "The Contract," Chapter 6, and in "Obtaining a License," Chapter 12.

with an appropriate copyright assignment provision giving you copyright ownership. A sample Web site development agreement is included in Appendix B (Form 11).

If the Web developer uses copyrighted third-party content in your Web pages, you'll need licenses to use that material. You also should get a warranty from the developer that the material the developer creates for you does not infringe any third-party copyrights or other rights.

Copyright Protection for Your Site

Although it is not necessary to use a copyright notice on your Web site, using a notice may deter people from copying it without permission (and may help dispel the myth that copyright doesn't apply to material on the Internet). See "Copyright Notice and Warnings," Chapter 18.

Although it is not necessary to register your copyright with the Copyright Office, there are advantages to doing so. This topic is discussed in "Copyright Protection," Chapter 18.

Fair use gives others limited permission to copy your site—for example, displaying your site on a "worst sites" or "best sites" feature may be fair use, because it is copying for the purpose of criticism or comment. See "Fair Use," earlier in this chapter.

Domain Names

A domain name is the way that people can identify and find you and your company on the Internet. You don't have to get a domain name—people can reach you on the Net by sending email for you to an "Internet Protocol" address consisting of eight numbers. However, domain names are easier for people to remember than a string of numbers.

You may want to register a domain name for your use on the Internet. A domain name is a mnemonic description of an Internet address (the actual address of a computer on the Internet is a string of numbers). Here are two examples:

➤ "aol.com" (the domain name for America Online)

➤ "gcwf.com" (the domain name for Gray Cary Ware & Freidenrich, the law firm of one of the authors of this book)

In the two examples, the "com" suffix is called a "top level domain" and indicates a commercial entity. Other top level domains in use are:

➤ "edu" for educational institutions

➤ "net" for computers belonging to network providers

➤ "org" for miscellaneous organizations

➤ "gov" for federal government offices (in the U.S. only)

➤ "mil" for military organizations

➤ "int" for international organizations

In a domain name, the name or initials to the left of the suffix identify the host computer (America Online in the first example, the law firm in the second one). For email address purposes, a third name is usually added to the domain name to identify an individual—for example, laderapres@aol.com (the email address for the publisher of this book, found at America Online), or mradcliffe@gcwf.com.

How to Register

Domain name registration for "com," "edu," "net," "org," and "gov" domain names is under the authority of a nonprofit agency called InterNIC. The actual registration process is run by Network Solutions, Inc. (NSI), of Herndon, Virginia.

Generally, businesses have their Internet access providers (such as Netcom or Pipeline) register their domain name. If you want to contact InterNIC yourself to register your domain name, the phone number is (703) 742-4777; the fax number is (703) 742-4811; and the email address is hostmaster@rs.internic.net. (You must have already gotten an Internet Protocol address from your Internet service provider.) The initial registration fee is $100 (for two years) and the annual renewal fee is $50. (This money is used to pay the cost of administering the domain name registration system.)

Choosing a Name

Most companies choose a domain name that is readily associated with the company's name—an acronym or shortened version of the name, such as "aol" for America Online. However, the fact that you have incorporated under a name or filed a trademark application for it does not automatically give you the right to get a domain name registration for it.

See "Trademark
Law," Chapter 3.

The basic registration rule is "first come, first served." If you are the first to apply for a name, you'll generally get it, unless another party complains that your use of the name violates their rights under trademark law. In that case, NSI's conflict resolution policy (described below) will apply.

Abuse and Conflicts

In July 1995, NSI issued a policy statement to limit potential abuses of the domain name registration system and resolve conflicts where more than one party claims the right to a given domain name.

Policy Against Abuse

In your application, you must warrant that you intend to use the name on a regular basis, that your use of the name will not violate any trademark or other intellectual property right of a third party, and that you are not seeking the use of the name for the purpose of confusing or misleading anyone.

Conflicts

NSI has stated that it does not have the legal resources to screen applications to determine if the use of a domain name by an applicant could infringe on the rights of a third party. However, if a court or an arbitrator issues an order that a domain name rightfully belongs to a third party, NSI will transfer the domain name to the winner.

When a domain name applicant's right to use a name is challenged by another party—for example, by a company that has a U.S. trademark registration on the name—NSI's conflict resolution rules are applied to determine whether the applicant or registrant may use the name pending resolution of the dispute.

The NSI policy can be found at ftp://rs.internic.net/policy/internic/domain4.txt.

Warehousing Names

"Warehousing" of names—registering them to save them for future use or to prevent others from using them—is not permitted. The prohibition against warehousing and the warranties are designed to prevent abuse of the domain name registration system (such as standardized test preparation company Princeton Review's registration of the name "kaplan.com" in order to block its competitor, Kaplan Education Centers, from registering that domain name).

Trademark Registration of Domain Name

The Patent and Trademark Office has indicated that it will not register a domain name unless the name satisfies the traditional standard of trademark use, which is use to distinguish the owner's goods or services from the goods or services of others. The top level domain name ("com," for example) cannot qualify for federal trademark registration.

Many companies that generally are diligent about protecting their trademark rights have not bothered to reserve the domain name equivalent of their trademarks. If you own trademarks, register your important trademarks as domain names. Even if you don't own trademarks, if you plan to do business on the Net, go ahead and register your company name as a domain name.

Operator Liability

In this section, we'll discuss whether a system operator or service provider is liable when someone using the operator's or provider's facilities or services commits copyright infringement or a tort through those facilities or services. We will first discuss the view of the authors of the White Paper (discussed earlier in this chapter), then consider recent court decisions.

Copyright Infringement

The White Paper's Position

The White Paper's authors believe that current law makes system operators and service providers liable for infringement by system and service users. Booksellers, record stores, newsstands, and computer software retailers are liable for copyright infringement if they sell infringing works. The White Paper's authors concluded that on-line service providers and systems operators, as "electronic publishers," also must have such liability.

The White Paper's authors noted that some people think that an on-line service provider should be exempt from liability for infringement on its system—or at least given a higher standard for liability (liability only where the service provider had actual knowledge of the infringing activity, and the ability and authority to terminate it). The White Paper, however, rejects the call for an exemption or a different standard, stating that "it is—at best—premature to reduce the liability of any type of service provider." Service provider liability for user infringement is appropriate, the White Paper states, because service providers have a business relationship with their subscribers and are in a position to know the activities of their subscribers and to stop unlawful activities. The risk of liability for infringement by a system user is a legitimate cost of engaging in a business that causes harm to others.

Cases

At the time this book goes to press, there are three reported court decisions on the issue of system operator liability for infringement by a subscriber or user of the system: the *Netcom, Playboy, and* Sega cases.

The Netcom Case

In *Religious Technology Center v. Netcom Online Communication Services, Inc.,* _F. Supp. _ (N.D. Cal. 1995), the individual defendant, Dennis Erlich, uploaded messages containing 154 pages of copyrighted Church of Scientology materials to the Usenet Newsgroup alt.religion.scientology. The church asked Erlich to stop his postings, but he refused.

The church then asked the BBS system used by Erlich, to reach the Usenet to deny access to the Internet to Erlich, because Erlich was infringing the church's copyrights. It made the same request of Netcom, the BBS's Internet access provider. The BBS and Netcom refused the request.

The church sued Erlich, the bulletin board operator, and Netcom for copyright infringement. The court found that Netcom and the bulletin board operator were not liable for direct infringement but that they could have liability for contributory infringement.

In considering whether Netcom had liability for direct infringement, the judge noted that copying of the church's materials took place within Netcom's computer each time Erlich posted a message to the Newsgroup, since a copy of each message was automatically made on Netcom's computer and stored there for several days. However, the judge held that Netcom was not liable for direct infringement because Netcom did not take any affirmative act that directly resulted in copying the Church of Scientology's works (aside from setting up a system that copies and stores messages to get them from the sender to the Usenet). The judge stated that even though copyright is a strict liability statute, "there should still be some element of volition or causation which is lacking where a defendant's system is merely used to create a copy by a third party." As to whether Netcom was liable for infringing the public display and distribution rights of the copyright owner, the court held that no purpose would be served by holding Netcom liable, even though Netcom was a "link" that helped Erlich distribute the infringing material to Newsgroup members.

Contributory copyright infringement is established when a defendant, with knowledge of another party's infringing activity, causes or materially contributes to the infringing conduct. The court found that Netcom could be liable for contributory infringement for postings made by Erlich after the church notified Netcom that Erlich was posting infringing material. If Netcom had knowledge of Erlich's infringement, as the church claimed, and failed to cancel infringing messages while there was still time to do so, that would constitute substantial participation in the distribution of the message. Netcom would then be liable for contributory infringement.

As for the BBS operator, because there were no allegations of volitional or causal elements—only automatic copying within the BBS operator's computer, as part of getting Erlich's messages to the Usenet—the court held that the BBS operator was not liable for direct infringement. The BBS operator would be liable for contributory infringement, however, if the BBS operator knew or should have known of Erlich's infringing actions and materially contributed the infringement by failing to stop it.

Playboy and Sega Cases

Two cases, *Playboy Enterprises v. Frena*, 839 F. Supp. 1552 (M.D. Fla. 1993), and *Sega Enterprises Ltd. v. MAPPHIA*, 857 F. Supp. 679 (N.D. Ca. 1994), address the issue of whether a bulletin board operator is liable for copyright infringement when bulletin board users upload and download infringing material.

In *Playboy v. Frena*, the system operator ("sysop") operated a bulletin board containing "adult subject matter" images, including a number of photographs scanned in from *Playboy* magazine. Subscribers to the bulletin board could browse the images on-line or download them. When *Playboy* sued the sysop for infringing its copyrights in the photographs, the sysop claimed that *subscribers* were the infringers (they were allowed to upload whatever they wanted). However, because the sysop's descriptions for these files contained the words "Playboy" or "Playmate," it appears that he knew of the infringements. In holding the sysop liable for infringement, the court stated that sysops of BBSs that contain infringing files are liable to a copyright owner for direct infringement, regardless of whether the sysop is aware of the infringement.

In *Sega v. MAPPHIA,* the sysops ran a BBS on which unauthorized copies of plaintiff Sega's video game programs were uploaded and downloaded by subscribers. The court found that the copies were uploaded with the knowledge of the sysops and that the downloading of copies by subscribers was facilitated and encouraged by the sysops. The court held that the sysops had committed both direct and contributory infringement.

Liability for Libel

Whether system operators, on-line service providers, and Internet access providers should be held liable for libel when defamatory content is posted by users is being debated.

Libel is discussed in "Libel," Chapter 15.

Defamation law distinguishes between original publishers, distributors, and common carriers. Here are the basic rules:

> ➤ **Publishers:** Actual publishers of books, magazines, and newspapers generally are liable for republication of defamatory material, because they are deemed to have acquired knowledge of the content provided by third parties through the process of editing and producing their publications for sale.

> ➤ **Distributors:** Those who merely deliver or transmit defamatory material previously published by someone else are liable for having published defamatory material only if they knew or had reason to know that the material was false and defamatory. Libraries and booksellers fall into this category.

> ➤ **Common carriers:** Common carriers—a telephone company, for example—are immune from liability for defamatory content carried by their equipment.

It is difficult to apply these rules to cyberspace because many of the players perform multiple functions (for example, an on-line news service with an interactive Web page and a bulletin board). Legislation recently passed by Congress as part of the Telecommunications Reform Act of 1995 appears to resolve this issue, stating that "[n]o provider or user of an interactive computer service shall be treated as the publisher or speaker of any information provided by another information content provider." 47 U.S.C. Sec. 330(c)(1).

At the time the legislation went into effect, there were two cases dealing with system operator/service provider liability for defamation by users.

Stratton Oakmont

In *Stratton Oakmont, Inc. v. Prodigy Services Co.*, 1995 N.Y. Misc. LEXIS 229 (N.Y.S.Ct. 1995), the plaintiff, a securities investment bank, sought to hold Prodigy liable for allegedly defamatory statements made about Stratton by an unknown Prodigy subscriber on Prodigy's financial bulletin board, "Money Talk." The court held that Prodigy was liable as a "publisher" because Prodigy exercised content control. (The new legislation referred to earlier will prevent this result in future cases.) Money Talk discussions were facilitated by "bulletin board leaders" who participated in discussions and had the ability to delete posted messages believed to be in bad taste or grossly repugnant to community standards or harmful to maintaining a harmonious on-line community. Stratton Oakmont withdrew the suit in October 1995 in exchange for a statement from Prodigy that Prodigy was sorry that a subscriber had posted messages accusing Stratton Oakmont of fraud.

Cubby

In *Cubby v. CompuServe*, 776 F. Supp. 135 (S.D.N.Y. 1991), CompuServe was sued for allegedly defamatory statements made about the plaintiffs on CompuServe's "Rumorville" bulletin board. The court held that CompuServe was merely a distributor, because it had no more editorial control over bulletin board material than does a public library, book store, or newsstand (CompuServe contracted with another company to review and control the contents of the bulletin board). The court granted summary judgment for CompuServe, because the plaintiffs failed to show that there was a genuine issue as to whether CompuServe knew or had reason to know of the allegedly libelous statements.

Liability for Other Wrongs by Users

Whether system operators and service providers will be held liable for user wrongs other than copyright infringement and defamation is being debated currently.

The Federal Trade Commission's current view on liability for unfair and deceptive practices is that a third party (such as a system operator or service provider) should be held liable for a user's unfair or deceptive message only when the third party "knew or should have known" that the message was unfair or deceptive and failed to take appropriate action. In 1994, the FTC investigated fraudulent ads posted on American Online (AOL) by a credit repair operation and prosecuted the author of those messages, not AOL. (AOL cooperated with the FTC.)

The Web site Hollywood Network recently shut down a chat lounge after employees discovered a number of messages describing plans for attacking and murdering actress Jodie Foster. Police investigating a New Jersey murder obtained a criminal search warrant to search America Online's records after learning that the defendant had met the victim in a "men for men" chat room on AOL and used the help of people he met in the chat room to dispose of the body.

Distributing Your Multimedia Products Over the Net

If you will be distributing your multimedia products over the Net, there are a number of issues you should consider (in addition to the issues raised in earlier chapters of this book). In this section, we'll discuss four issues—licensing third-party content for products to be distributed over the Net, acquiring international rights, complying with foreign laws, and using "net wrap" agreements.

Please don't consider this brief discussion of these four issues an exhaustive treatment of the law of electronic commerce. That law is still developing, and it's worthy of its own book.

Licensing Third-Party Content

If you will be distributing your products over the Net, your licenses to use third-party content should include the public display right, the distribution right, and the public performance right.

Acquiring International Rights

Because the Net is international in scope, you will need a worldwide license for third-party content. If the copyright rights in the content have been split up geographically—as is common for music—you will need licenses from several different rights holders to get worldwide rights.

If material for your product is to be created by employees, make certain that you will have worldwide ownership rights to the material. If material for your product is to be created by independent contractors, get assignments from the contractors even if the work can be treated as a "specially commissioned" work for hire. A work made for hire agreement probably won't get you foreign rights in the commissioned works, because most countries' copyright ownership rules do not have anything comparable to the "specially commissioned works" branch of the Copyright Act.

Complying with Foreign Laws

Because your distribution will be international, you may need to consider whether your product contains material that violates laws of other countries.

Exclusive rights are discussed in "The Exclusive Rights," Chapter 2. Licensing these rights is discussed in "Determining What Rights You Need," Chapter 12.

See "Using the Employment Agreement," Chapter 7, and "Copyright Ownership," Chapter 8.

For example, "adult subject matter" that can lawfully be distributed here may be considered pornographic in other countries (as CompuServe recently learned, when a prosecutor in Munich informed CompuServe that it was breaking German law by giving Germans access to Usenet discussion groups on sexuality.)

You also need to consider whether aspects of your marketing program and customer information collection program are illegal under foreign laws. Germany, for example, has strict data-protection legislation. Personal information that is freely given and used in the U.S. for marketing purposes is off limits in Germany. Citibank AG found this out recently when it set up a program to link its Visa card to the German national railroad's Bahncard. Citibank mailed out joint application forms for both cards. The form had to be changed so that customers who wanted only a Bahncard would not have to disclose information about their income, and Citibank had to agree to respect German data-protection laws when it processed the application forms at its credit card centers in the United States. None of that data can be given out to other companies.

Using "Web-wrap" Agreements

Some companies are beginning to use "Web-wrap" agreements to try to protect their intellectual property rights, to define the terms and conditions of customer access and use, to disclaim implied warranties of merchantability and fitness, and to limit liability. Software sellers have long used "shrink-wrap" agreements on packages for these purposes.

See "Important Provisions of Article 2," Chapter 19.

In a typical software shrink-wrap, terms of use and warranty limitations are printed on the outside of the packaging for the software, along with a statement that tearing open the wrapping will constitute acceptance of those terms and limitations. A user generally finds a Web-wrap for a Web site by clicking on a link connected to the copyright notice at the end of the first page of a Web site. However, the user usually is not required to take any action to show assent to the Web terms, other than continued use of the Web site.

Under current law, whether Web-wraps and shrink-wraps are enforceable is uncertain. Some attorneys have argued that shrink-wraps are unenforceable because they are "unconscionable" contracts of adhesion (contracts which consumers are powerless to reject, because consumers cannot effectively bargain with the manufacturer of the shrink-wrapped product). If the purchaser does not have the opportunity to review the terms of the shrink-wrap prior to purchase, the enforceability of the shrink-wrap is particularly questionable.

The Uniform Commercial Code is discussed in the first section of Chapter 19.

Under a proposed revision to the Uniform Commercial Code, Web-wraps and shrink-wraps are enforceable only if the user *actively manifests assent* after having had an *opportunity to review* the license terms. A user has an "opportunity to review" the license terms if the license is available before the user gets access, such that the user's attention is called to the terms or provided in a conspicuous manner during normal first use of the work. A user "manifests assent" if, having had an opportunity to review a license that states what conduct would constitute acceptance and having had the opportunity not to take such action, he or she engages in such conduct.

Although the proposed revision is not yet law, it does provide some guidance on steps to take to help make a Web-wrap enforceable. To meet the "opportunity to review" standard, don't just provide a link to the Web-wrap at the end of the Home Page. Instead, make it clear on the Home Page, in a conspicuous manner, that the link to the Web-wrap connects to a license providing terms for use of the Web site. To meet the "manifestation of assent" standard, provide a second link at the conclusion of the license for the user to click on to show acceptance of the terms. Clicking on the "acceptance" link should be a prerequisite to going beyond the Home Page.

24 Educational and Distance Learning Issues

In this chapter, we'll cover five topics of interest to educators:

➤ Educational use of copyrighted materials.

➤ Ownership of educational materials.

➤ Legal issues presented by various forms of "distance learning."

➤ Distribution agreements for materials created by educators.

➤ Using copyrighted material for fund-raisers.

Copyright law basics are covered in Chapter 2, and the rules of copyright ownership are covered in Chapter 4.

Myths

There are a number of myths about how copyright law applies to educational use of copyrighted materials. Don't make the mistake of believing these myths:

Myth #1: "Educators and libraries are exempt from the copyright law."

There is no general exemption from the copyright law for educators or libraries. There *are* two narrow statutory exceptions to the copyright owner's exclusive rights that permit libraries and educators to use copyrighted material without permission in certain ways and under certain conditions (these exceptions are discussed later in this chapter). However, these exceptions are limited.

> ### Educational Use as Fair Use
>
> Educational use is not necessarily fair use. In *Marcus v. Rowley*, a public school teacher who owned the copyright on a booklet on cake decorating sued another public school teacher who had used a substantial portion of the plaintiff's booklet in her own booklet. The court found that the use was not fair use. 695 F. 2d 1171 (9th Cir. 1983). In *Encyclopedia Britannica Educational Corp. v. Crooks*, a public school system's taping of off-the-air broadcasts of educational programs (for permanent retention and use by the school system) was held to not be fair use. 542 F. Supp. 1156 (W.D.N.Y. 1982).

Myth #2: "Any educational use is fair use."

Educational use *may* be fair use, but it is not *necessarily* fair use. (See "Educational Use as Fair Use" in the box and "Fair Use," later in this chapter.)

Myth #3: "Copyright owners never sue educators."

This is not true. (See "Educational Use as Fair Use" in the box.)

Myth #4: "It's okay to photocopy copyrighted materials for classroom use."

There is no general exception to the Copyright Act's reproduction right for teacher copying. Copying for classroom use may be fair use, but it is not necessarily fair use.

Myth #5: "Copyright law doesn't apply to nonprofit organizations."

There is no general exemption from the copyright law for nonprofit organizations.

The Reality

Educators need to be familiar with copyright law and to respect the rights of copyright owners. If an educator wants to use copyrighted material in a way that would be an exercise of the copyright owner's exclusive rights, the educator should get permission from the copyright owner if the narrow statutory exceptions do not apply and the use is not fair use.

Educators do not need permission to:

➤ Make fair use of copyrighted material (discussed later in this chapter).

➤ Use copyrighted material in noninfringing ways (see "When You Don't Need a License," Chapter 11).

➤ Use material that is in the public domain (see "Public Domain Works," Chapter 11).

➤ Use works created by federal government officers and employees as part of their official duties (see "Types of Works Protected by Copyright," Chapter 2).

Exceptions for Educators

Two provisions of the Copyright Act give educators the right to use copyrighted material without getting permission from the copyright owner. These provisions are:

➤ **Section 108,** which permits libraries to copy copyrighted material for certain purposes (an exception to the copyright owner's reproduction right).

➤ **Section 110,** which permits instructors in nonprofit educational institutions to publicly perform and display copyrighted material without permission in classroom teaching and instructional broadcasts (an exception to the copyright owner's public performance and display rights).

Library Copying Exception

The Copyright Act gives a copyright owner the exclusive right to reproduce the copyrighted work in copies. Section 108 of the Copyright Act creates a narrow exception to the reproduction right for libraries, giving them a limited right to reproduce copyrighted works for archival purposes and replacement purposes and to fulfill a user's request for a copy.

Conditions

Section 108 applies only if three conditions are met: (1) the reproduction is without any purpose of direct or indirect commercial advantage; (2) the library's collections are open to the public or are available to persons doing research in a specialized field (not just to researchers affiliated with the library); and (3) the copy of the work includes a notice of copyright. A library in a profit-making institution can rely on Section 108 so long as the reproduction itself is not commercially motivated.

These conditions apply to copying for all three purposes covered by the statute, which are as follows:

➤ **Preservation of unpublished work**. A library may make a copy of an unpublished work from its collections "in facsimile form" for the purposes of preservation and security or for deposit for research use in another library that meets the "open collection" requirement. Section 108(b). Unpublished works are works that have not been distributed to the public by sale or other transfer of ownership, or by rental, lease, or lending (dissertations and student papers, for example).

➤ **Replacement of published work**. A library may make a copy of a published work "in facsimile form" for the purpose of replacing a copy that is damaged, deteriorated, lost, or stolen—but only, if the library has, after reasonable efforts, determined that a replacement cannot be obtained at a fair price. Section 108(c).

➤ **At the request of a user**. A library may make a copy of one article from a periodical issue or a collection (or a small part of any other copyrighted work such as a book) at the request of a library user if three additional conditions are met: (1) the copy becomes the property of the user; (2) the library has had no notice that the copy would be used for any purpose other than private study, scholarship, or research; and (3) the library displays prominently at the place where orders are accepted, and includes on its order form, a warning of copyright. Section 108(d). A library may make a copy of an entire work at a user's request if it has determined, after a reasonable investigation, that a copy cannot be obtained at a fair price. Section 108(e). According to the legislative history for Section 108, a "reasonable investigation" would include inquiries to commonly known U.S. trade sources (wholesalers, distributors, book stores) and to the publisher or author.

Types of Works

The exception permitting library copying at the request of a user does not apply to musical works, pictorial works, graphic works, sculptural works, or motion pictures or other audiovisual works (except for audiovisual news programs). It is primarily applied to literary and dramatic works (but also is applicable to pantomimes and choreographic works, sound recordings, and architectural works). There is no limitation on the type of work that can be copied for purposes of preservation or replacement.

Systematic Reproduction

The reproduction right given to libraries under Section 108 is limited to "the isolated and unrelated reproduction or distribution of a single copy... on separate occasions." A library cannot rely on Section 108 to justify systematic reproduction or distribution of single or multiple copies.

Taken literally, the prohibition against systematic reproduction and distribution could be read to prohibit copying for interlibrary loan arrangements (the lending of materials or copies of materials by one library for use by patrons of another library). However, Congress added a proviso to the prohibition against systematic reproduction; it states that the prohibition does not prevent a library from participating in interlibrary arrangements that do not have the effect of substituting for a subscription or purchase of copyrighted works.

To determine what should constitute requesting journal articles (the most commonly requested material) in such quantities as to substitute for a subscription, Congress sought the help of the National Commission on New Technological Uses of Copyright Works (CONTU). CONTU decided that the rule should be that the requesting library may not ask for more than five copies of an article published in a given periodical during the five years prior to the date of the reproduction request. This rule is known as the "suggestion of five."

New Copying Technologies

When Section 108 was enacted, "reproduction" meant photocopying. There are a number of questions about how Section 108 applies to copying made possible by new technologies:

1. **Can a library rely on Section 108 to create a machine-readable copy of a print work by scanning?** Not if the copying is for archival or replacement purposes. The reproduction for those two purposes must be "in facsimile form." A machine-readable copy may be made to satisfy the request of a library user for a copy of the work, because there is no requirement that such a copy be "in facsimile form" (although some people might take the position digital copies are not within the scope of Section 108 because that provision focused on the *photocopying* needs of libraries).

2. **Can a library—anticipating that it will get a number of requests for a copy of a particular work—make a machine-readable "master" copy on disk that it keeps in it files, so that copies can be quickly printed out (or the disk duplicated) when users request copies?** No. Section 108 does not authorize a library to make a copy *before* it gets a user request (other than for archival or replacement purposes). A library is allowed to make copies only to *satisfy* a user's request. Also, Section 108 does not authorize a library to keep a copy of the material requested by a user; the copy must become the property of the user.

3. **Does Section 108 permit a library to scan a copyrighted article and put it on a server (computer), so that library users can access the article over a network (viewing it on library or home computer monitors) when they want to?** No, for the reasons stated in the answer to #2.

4. **Does Section 108 permit a library to create an "electronic reserve room" by scanning articles a professor wants to put on reserve and making the scanned compilation available to students in the professor's course by computer network or on disks?** No, for the reasons stated in the answer to #2. (Reserve room copying also is discussed in "Teacher Photocopying," later in this chapter.)

5. **Does Section 108's "user request" aspect permit a library to fax a copy of an article to a user who has requested the article?** Technically, the answer is no. Section 108 authorizes the making of only a single copy. Sending material from bound books or journals by fax normally requires making two copies (you have to make a photocopy of the requested book or journal pages to feed through the fax

machine a page at a time, and a second copy is made by the fax equipment in the process of transmission). If the library destroys the photocopy once the transmission has been made, that may fulfill the "spirit" of Section 108 (if not the "letter" of the provision).

6. **Does Section 108 permit a library system with several branches to order one copy of a journal subscription and make copies for branch libraries?** No. Section 108 does not permit copying to substitute for the purchase of multiple subscriptions. Such copying would not be "isolated and unrelated" reproduction, but "systematic reproduction."

7. **Does Section 108 permit libraries to reach "subscription sharing" agreements with other libraries ("We'll subscribe to journal A, you subscribe to journal B. You give us copies of articles from B when we request them, and we'll give you copies of articles from A when you request them")?** No. This also would be "systematic reproduction" and a substitute for subscriptions.

8. **How can a library give the warning of copyright that is required for Section 108 "user request" copying when the users make their requests for copies by email, fax, or telephone?** One law librarian suggests finding the "functional equivalent" of placing a warning sign at the order desk and on the order form—faxing a warning of copyright back to those whose requests come in by fax; reading it to those whose requests are made by telephone; and, on an email request system, placing the warning on the screen at which the user initiates the request (Laura Gassaway, "Document Delivery," *Computers in Libraries*, May 1994, page 25).

Recommendations for Change
The Working Group on Intellectual Property Rights—created by the Clinton Administration in 1994 to examine the intellectual property implications of the National Information Infrastructure—has recommended that Section 108 be amended to: (1) allow the preparation by a library of three copies of any work that is in digital form, with no more than one copy in use at any time; (2) authorize the making of digital copies for preservation purposes; and (3) recognize that the use of copyright notice on a published copy of a work is no longer mandatory (under the current statute, a copy made pursuant to Section 108 at the request of a user must include a notice of copyright).

As for interlibrary loan, according to the Working Group, "publication on demand"—getting permission from a publisher to download material made available by the publisher on a server—may become an effective and economic substitute for interlibrary loan. The group stated that the CONTU

Guidelines' "suggestion of five"—while remaining effective for print materials—cannot be generalized to cover interlibrary loan of electronic publications. Instead, new scenarios must be considered to protect both the interests of copyright owners and to continue to provide libraries with a safe "borrowing" guide. The Conference on Fair Use (discussed in "The Future of Fair Use on the Net," Chapter 23) was given the task of working on this issue.

Exceptions to the Performance Right

The Copyright Act gives the copyright owner the exclusive right to publicly perform and display the copyrighted work. However, Section 110 of the Copyright Act gives educators narrow exceptions to the owner's public performance and display rights—for face-to-face teaching and for instructional broadcasts.

Section 110's exceptions for educators apply only to nonprofit educational institutions. For-profit schools cannot rely on the exception, nor can corporations or trade associations which conduct educational programs.

Face-to Face Teaching

Section 110(1) states that the performance or display of a copyrighted work in the course of face-to-face teaching activities by a nonprofit educational institution in a classroom or similar setting devoted to instruction is not infringement. This exception applies to all types of copyrightable works. It permits an educator in a nonprofit educational institution to do the following things in classroom teaching:

➤ Act out a drama.

➤ Read a poem or prose work.

➤ Play or sing a musical work.

➤ Show a motion picture.

➤ Show an interactive multimedia CD-ROM.

➤ Display text or pictorial material by a projector.

Without Section 110(1), an educator would need the owner's permission to do these things (unless the use is fair use). The first five activities are exercises of the copyright owner's public performance right (discussed in "The Exclusive Rights," Chapter 2, and in "Determining What Rights You Need," Chapter 12). The last activity is an exercise of the public display right.

(Display also is covered by another exception, Section 106(5), which gives the owner of a copy lawfully made, or any person authorized by the owner, the right to display the copy publicly, either directly or by projection of no

Other aspects of the Working Group's report are discussed in "The White Paper," Chapter 23.

Other Section 110 exemptions from the public performance right are discussed in "Determining What Rights You Need," Chapter 12.

more than one image at a time, to viewers present at the place where the copy is located.)

In the case of a motion picture or other audiovisual work, the Section 110(1) exception does not apply if the copy was not lawfully made and the person responsible for the performance knew or had reason to believe that it was not lawfully made. Generally, an educator who acquires a videotaped copy of a motion picture from a legitimate source will have no difficulty with this element of the exception.

The Section 110(1) exception applies to the public performance right only. It does not authorize a nonprofit school to copy a copyrighted work into "fixed" instructional materials created by the school.

 John, a high school music and drama teacher at a nonprofit school, made a video for use in his classes. In the video, John performs several copyrighted songs on various instruments and acts out a copyrighted monologue. Section 110(1) does not authorize John's use of the songs or the monologue in the video, just in a "live" class.

Face-to-face teaching, according to the legislative history, requires that the instructor and pupils be in the same building, but not necessarily in the same room (amplification devices or visual enhancing equipment may be used within the building). The exception does not apply to the use of copyrighted material in instructional television broadcasts, fixed videos, long-distance videoconferencing, or on-line instruction.

The performance cannot be open to outsiders, but must be limited to the pupils and the instructors (including guest instructors). The exception does not apply to performances by actors, singers, or instrumentalists brought in from outside the school to put on a program.

Because the teaching activities must take place in "a classroom or similar place devoted to instruction," performances in an auditorium or stadium during assembly, graduation ceremony, class play, or sporting event (where the audience is not confined to members of a particular class) are outside the scope of the exception. The exception applies to use of the material in teaching activities only—not for entertainment or as a reward for good behavior.

Instructional Broadcasts

Section 110(2) of the Copyright Act states that the performance of a nondramatic literary or musical work or display of any type of work, by or in the course of a transmission, is not infringement if three conditions exist: (1) the performance or display is a regular part of the systematic instructional activities of a nonprofit educational institution or governmental body; (2) the performance or display is directly related to and of material assistance to the teaching content of the transmission; and (3) the transmission is made primarily for reception in classrooms or similar places normally devoted to instruction, or reception by persons to whom the transmission is directed because their disabilities or other special circumstances prevent their attendance in classrooms or similar places normally devoted to instruction, or reception by government officers or employees as part of their duties.

The legislative history indicates that this provision was intended to cover instructional television courses aimed at students who are unable to attend daytime classes because of employment, distance from campus, or other reasons. It also would appear to apply to videoconferencing and on-line instruction, because these two activities are within the Copyright Act's definition of "transmission." (According to Section 101, to "transmit" a performance or display is to communicate it by any device or process whereby images or sounds are received beyond the place from which they are sent.") It also applies to transmissions within the campus (from the building where the instructor is located to a different building on the campus where students are located).

Section 110(2), like Section 110(1), does not authorize a nonprofit educational institution to copy a copyrighted work into "fixed" instructional materials (such as a videotape or CD-ROM) for transmission later. The exception covers the public performance right only, not the reproduction right. However, an institution that is entitled to transmit a performance or display without permission from the copyright owner under Section 110(2) may make up to 30 copies of the transmission program if the copies are destroyed within seven years from the date the transmission program was first transmitted to the public. Section 112(b).

Teacher Photocopying

There is no statutory exception in the Copyright Act that authorizes teachers to photocopy copyrighted material for research or for classroom use. However, in 1976, representatives of educational institutions and the Association of American Publishers reached agreement on the "Guidelines for Classroom Copying." These guidelines are intended to state the minimum standards of educational fair use. While they are not law, courts are highly likely to respect them, holding that copying which is within the limits of the Guidelines is fair use.

The guidelines cover two topics: single copying for teachers and multiple copies for classroom use. They apply only to "not-for-profit" educational institutions.

The guidelines do not permit copying to create or replace or substitute for anthologies or to substitute for the purchase of books, reprints, or periodicals. They do not permit copying of "consumable" materials (such as workbooks, tests, and test answer sheets). They do not permit copying that is ordered by a higher authority (such as the school superintendent); they only permit copying at the "instance and inspiration" of a teacher. A teacher cannot rely on the guidelines to continue to copy the same item from term to term. (For repeated use, the teacher should request permission to copy the material.)

A copy of the Guidelines for Classroom Copying appears in Appendix A.

Single Copying for Research

The guidelines state that a teacher may reproduce, for research or for use in teaching or preparation for teaching, any of the following:

➤ A chapter from a book

➤ An article from a periodical or newspaper

➤ A short story, short essay, or short poem

➤ A chart, graph, diagram, drawing, cartoon, or picture from a book, periodical, or newspaper

Multiple Copies for Classroom Use

A teacher may make copies of copyrighted material for classroom use (no more than one copy per pupil in the course) if each copy includes a copyright notice and the copying meets three requirements: brevity, spontaneity, and cumulative effect.

Brevity

The "brevity" requirement states how much material the teacher may copy. The limits are as follows:

➤ **Poetry:** A complete poem, if less than 250 words; from a longer poem, an excerpt of not more than 250 words.

➤ **Prose**: A complete article, story, or essay, if less than 2,500 words; from a longer work, an excerpt of not more than 1000 words or 10% of the work (whichever is less), but in any event, a minimum of 500 words.

➤ **Illustrations**: One chart, graph, diagram, drawing, cartoon, or picture per book or per periodical issue.

➤ **Works combining language with illustrations (such as children's books):** These cannot be reproduced in their entirety, even if under 2,500 words. Instead, an excerpt of not more than two published pages and not more than 10% of the words may be reproduced.

Spontaneity

The "spontaneity" requirement is that the copying "is at the instance and inspiration of the individual teacher" and "the inspiration and decision to use the work and the moment of its use for maximum teaching effectiveness are so close in time that it would be unreasonable to expect a timely reply to a request for permission."

Cumulative Effect

The "cumulative effect" requirement puts a limit on how much copying the teacher can do in one class term. No more than one short poem, article, story, essay, or two excerpts may be copied from the same author during one class term, and no more than three may be copied from the same collective work or periodical volume. There cannot be more than nine instances of multiple copying for one course during the term. (These two limitations do not apply to current news periodicals, newspapers, and current news sections of other periodicals.) Finally, the copying must be for only one course in the school in which the copies are made.

Copying Not Covered by Guidelines

The guidelines have been criticized as being too restrictive for classroom situations at the university and graduate level. The American Library Association recommends that university-level faculty members needing to exceed the guideline's limits "not feel hampered" by the guidelines (although the ALA recommends that faculty members attempt a "selective and sparing" use of photocopied, copyrighted material). *American Library Association, "Model Policy Concerning College and University Photocopying for Classroom, Research, and Library Reserve Use"* (1982).

The ALA takes the position that most single-copy photocopying for a teacher's personal use in research "may well constitute fair use"—even when it involves a substantial portion of a work. As for multiple copying for classroom use, the ALA takes the position that an instructor's photocopying practices should not have a significant detrimental impact on the market for the copyrighted work (the fourth fair use factor). The ALA recommends restricting the use of an item to one course. It warns against repeatedly copying excerpts from one periodical or author without getting permission.

Getting Permission

Copying that is not within the guidelines may be fair use (discussed later in this chapter). However, a teacher's safest course of action when the guidelines don't apply is to ask permission from the copyright owner.

A sample "permission request" letter appears in Appendix B (Form 5). The American Library Association recommends sending the request, with a self-addressed return envelope, to the permissions department of the publisher well in advance of the time when the material will be needed for class.

The Copyright Clearance Center (CCC) handles permission grants for photocopying rights for many publications. Permission to copy material for which the CCC handles permissions is obtained simply by sending a set fee to the CCC. To obtain a list of publications for which the CCC handles permission, contact the CCC (contact information is in Appendix C). Blanket licenses (licenses to copy all works for which the CCC handles permissions) also are available.

Commercial Photocopying

The copyright law applies to all forms of photocopying, whether it is done by the teacher, at an educational institution's copy center, or at a commercial copy center. Most commercial copiers will require that you provide them with permission from publishers whose works you want copied. If copying is done by a commercial copy center without permission, the copy center may be liable for infringement (an example, the *Kinko's* case, is discussed later in this chapter).

Some commercial copy centers will help you obtain permission to photocopy copyrighted material.

Copying for the Library's Reserve Shelf

The American Library Association takes the position that the Guidelines for Classroom Copying apply to the library reserve shelf, to the extent that the reserve shelf functions as an extension of the classroom. If the faculty member who requested that material be placed on reserve meets the guidelines' requirements for making multiple copies of that material, the ALA takes the position that libraries are permitted to put photocopies of copyrighted works on reserve.

The ALA has developed its own guidelines for copying for reserve room purposes:

➤ If the request calls for one copy to be placed on reserve, the library may photocopy an entire article, an entire chapter from a book, or an entire poem.

➤ Requests for multiple copies should be honored if the amount of the material is reasonable in relation to the total amount of the material assigned for the course; the number of copies is reasonable in light of the number of students enrolled, the difficulty and timing of assignments, and a number of other courses which may assign the same material; the material contains a notice of copyright; and the effect of copying the material would not be detrimental to the market for the work (the library should own at least one copy of the work).

The ALA's view is that copying within these guidelines is fair use. Publishers apparently have not objected to these guidelines on reserve room copying (at least, not to the extent of filing lawsuits). However, electronic reserve rooms are a different story. The Association of American Publishers is concerned about electronically stored copies, because it considers digital copies to be particularly susceptible to infringing use. *Association of American Publishers, Inc., "An AAP Position Paper on Scanning" (1994)*. According to the AAP, "scanning technology allows the creation of digital collections and services that function in a very different manner from a print-based reserve room. Campus terminal locations could become sites for a variety of potentially infringing uses in a digital environment."

Fair Use

When copyrighted material is used for educational purposes without the permission of the copyright owner and neither the narrow "educational use" statutory exceptions nor the Guidelines for Classroom Copying apply, the question is whether the use is fair use.

The mere fact that use is nonprofit educational use does not require a finding of fair use. Whether a use—educational or otherwise—is fair use is determined by considering four factors: (1) the purpose and character of the use; (2) the nature of the copyrighted work; (3) the amount and substantiality of the portion used in relation to the copyrighted work as a whole; and (4) the effect of the use upon the potential market for or value of the copyrighted work. (These are the same four factors discussed in "When You Don't Need a License," Chapter 11, and in "Fair Use," Chapter 23.)

Nonprofit Educational Use

If the use is nonprofit educational use, the first factor favors a finding of fair use. However, if two of the other factors go the other way—for example, if most of a copyrighted work is copied to create a market substitute for the copyrighted work, as in the *Marcus v. Rowley* case (discussed earlier in this chapter)—the use may not be fair use.

A teacher's use of a small part of a copyrighted work for traditional fair use purposes of comment or criticism on the work or to illustrate a lesson is probably fair use. Beyond that, it is often difficult to tell whether a particular use of a work is fair or unfair. If a copyrighted work is being used in such a way as to have a significant negative effect on the potential market for or value of the protected work (the fourth factor), the use is likely to be found to be unfair.

Why you are using the copyrighted work may be important in the fair use determination. If you are using a music clip in an instructional video on music theory to illustrate a point, that may be fair use. If you use the same clip as background music to add "sex appeal" to a video on geography, a court could characterize your use as use for entertainment rather than educational use.

This case is discussed in "When You Don't Need a License," Chapter 11.

Videotaping Educational Broadcasts

Many teachers tape educational television programs to use in class later. Several years ago, the Supreme Court held that home videotaping for time-shifting purposes was fair use. The same is probably true of teacher taping for time-shifting purposes. However, keeping the tape to show again and again is much less likely to be fair use, especially if copies of the program are available for purchase. In *Encyclopedia Britannica Educational Corp. v. Crooks*, 542 F. Supp. 1156 (W.D.N.Y. 1982), a school system's taping for permanent retention and use was held to not be fair use.

Fair Use & Commercialism

In *American Geophysical Union v. Texaco*, the question was whether it is unlawful for a profit-seeking corporation, Texaco, to make unauthorized copies of copyrighted scientific journal articles for use by the company's scientists. (Texaco's library circulated original copies of a number of scientific journals and invited researchers to make their own photocopies.) Texaco claimed the researchers were copying for research purposes. The court, however, viewed the use as commercial use (a researcher's copying served to facilitate his or her research, which led to the creation of new products and to profits for Texaco). The court concluded that the copying was not fair use. *American Geophysical Union v. Texaco*, 37 F. 3d 881 (2d. Cir. 1994)

Commercial Setting

If the use is educational in some sense but there's a commercial motive involved as well, the court may put more emphasis on the commercial motive than on the educational aspect in analyzing the first fair use factor. (See "Fair Use and Commercialism" on this page.)

If you teach for a for-profit educational institution or a for-profit seminar provider and rely on fair use to use copyrighted material, you should not assume that a court's finding on the first fair use factor—purpose and nature of the use—will be in your favor. This also is true if you are creating educational material that will be distributed through commercial channels—an educational CD-ROM product for home use, for example. If commercial distribution is a possibility, don't use copyrighted material owned by others without getting licenses (see Chapter 12). Any publisher interested in distributing your product will expect to see licenses authorizing you to use third-party content.

Materials Created by Teachers and Faculty Members

In this section, we'll discuss copyright ownership for materials created by teachers and faculty members. This includes traditional material such as lesson plans, tests, "handouts" for class, and research papers. It also includes "new media" materials such as instructional videos, educational CD-ROMs (interactive multimedia), and materials for on-line instruction.

Works Created by Employees

When a teacher is employed by an institution and creates material within the scope of the employment, according to copyright law, the institution owns the copyright. (See "The Work Made for Hire Rule," Chapter 4, and "Works Made by Employees," Chapter 7).

> Helen, a professor employed at Gavel Law School, created a set of instructional materials for students in her copyright course at Gavel. According to copyright law, Gavel owns the copyright in the materials. To date, though, few institutions have asserted ownership claims against teacher-employees.

There's a different rule for works created by independent contractors (discussed later in this section); for ownership of patents, trademarks, and trade secrets (see Chapter 3); and for government contracts.

Full-time teachers under contract are probably employees. Part-timers and adjuncts may not be. Whether a worker is an employee or an independent contractor must be determined by weighing 13 factors (see "Who is an Employee," Chapter 7, and "Who is an Independent Contractor," Chapter 8). As a general rule, if the institution does not treat the instructor as an employee for tax and employee benefits purposes, it will be difficult for the institution to establish that the instructor is an employee for copyright ownership purposes.

Even if an instructor is an employee, the institution does not own the copyright for material created outside the scope of employment.

> If Helen, the Gavel Law School professor, wrote a science fiction novel on weekends and evenings, Gavel probably does not own the copyright in the novel, because writing the novel probably was outside the scope of Helen's employment with Gavel.

The Business of Course Packets

In *Basic Books v. Kinko's*, a number of publishers claimed that Kinko's infringed their copyrights when Kinko's copied excerpts from their copyrighted books (chosen by professors) for course packets for college students. Kinko's claimed its use of the excerpts was fair use and that the copying was for educational purposes. The court noted that the use of the course packets by the students was educational. However, it held that the use of the packets in the hands of Kinko's employees was commercial, because Kinko's made money on the packets. The court found that the first factor favored the publishers, and it concluded that the copying was not fair use. *Basic Books, Inc. v. Kinko's Graphics Corp.*, 758 F. Supp. 1522 (S.D.N.Y. 1991).

For instructors and faculty members who are employees, whether material was created within the scope of employment or outside the scope may be a difficult question. Job descriptions in academia tend to be vague (if they exist at all). Educational institutions—unlike proprietary companies—rarely ask employees to sign assignment agreements (such as Form 6, Appendix B) when they are hired. Particularly where "new media" material is involved—instructional videotapes and interactive multimedia CD-ROMs—a faculty member may take the position that the creation of the material was not within the scope of the employment. There are few reported cases on this issue. One case held that a word processing manual written by high school teachers may have been created outside the scope of the employment (*Hays v. Sony Corp. of America*, 817 F. 2d 412 (7th Cir. 1988).

Complicating the situation still further, some people argue that academic tradition allows faculty members to own copyrighted works not necessary for classroom instruction (for example, textbooks, scholarly articles, musical compositions, and works of fine art). And some believe that there may have been a "teacher exception" to the work for hire rule under the 1909 Copyright Act which is still in effect under the current Copyright Act. (This viewpoint is discussed in the *Hays* case.)

Some universities have written policies allowing faculty members to own the copyrights in works they create within the scope of the employment. It is unclear whether a policy manual statement to that effect meets the Copyright Act's requirements for transfers of copyright ownership or for giving ownership of a work made for hire to an employee.

Works Created by Contractors

When a teacher works as an independent contractor for an institution, a different rule applies: The teacher, as an independent contractor, owns the copyright unless the institution gets an assignment of the copyright or unless the parties agree in writing to treat the work as a work made for hire (this only works for certain types of works).

See "Assignments," Chapter 4, and "Giving Ownership to an Employee," Chapter 7.

Sometimes a teacher who is an employee of an academic institution is asked by the institution to take on a separate project for additional pay—for example, to make an instructional video over the summer. Such a teacher may be an independent contractor for the separate project (under the 13-factor test, as applied to the hiring for the separate project). If so, the teacher would own the copyright in the work created for that project, unless the institution got an assignment of the copyright or a written agreement to treat the work as a work made for hire. If work is owned by an independent contractor, the institution—like any other third party—will need

See "Copyright Ownership," Chapter 8.

a license (permission) from the contractor to use the work if the use is an exercise of the exclusive rights of copyright owner.

 John, an independent contractor who teaches one course a year as an adjunct for Gavel Law School, has created an interactive multimedia CD-ROM that helps students learn the rules of evidence. If Gavel's Dean wants to get copies of the CD-ROM for other evidence professors at Gavel to use with their students, the Dean needs permission from John.

Licensing is discussed in Chapter 12.

Joint Ownership

If a work is created within the scope of employment by two or more teachers who are employees of the same institution, the institution is the owner of the copyright under the work made for hire doctrine discussed above. However, if teachers who are independent contractors work together to create a work, they may jointly own the copyright.

Resolving Uncertainties

In many instances, uncertainty over ownership rights for materials created by instructors or faculty members will not cause any problems. For example, for most materials created by teachers, an institution is unlikely to try to prevent the teacher from continuing to use the materials after the teacher has left the institution's employment (even though, under copyright law, the institution probably has a right to do so if the teacher was an employee who created the materials within the scope of employment). Many of these materials may not even have value in the hands of someone other than the creator.

See "Joint Authorship and Ownership," Chapter 4.

However, for those materials that *do* have value for use by other teachers—or value for commercial exploitation—the copyright ownership issue should be addressed by the teacher and the institution, in writing. The ownership rules described here (and in Chapters 7 and 8) are default rules that apply when the parties have not reached their own agreement on ownership. They are free to reach their own agreement.

If it is important to an educational institution to have worldwide ownership of a copyrighted work created in the scope of employment by an employee, the institution should get the employee to sign an employment agreement, rather than just relying on the work made for hire rule. If the institution wants to give ownership of a work created by an employee within the scope of employment to the employee, how to do that is explained in "Giving Ownership to an Employee," Chapter 7. If an institution wants to own a work created by an independent contractor, it should get an assignment.

See "Using the
Employment
Agreement,"
Chapter 7.

See "Copyright
Ownership,"
Chapter 8.

Conversely, if a teacher or faculty member wants copyright ownership for a work created within the scope of employment, he or she should try to get the institution's representative to sign a written agreement stating that the employee owns the work. If the teacher works as an independent contractor, the copyright belongs to the teacher unless the institution has taken steps to acquire ownership (an assignment or, for certain types of works, a work made for hire agreement). Nonetheless, if ownership could be an important issue, the teacher should still get the institution's representative to acknowledge in writing that the teacher owns the copyright (to avoid misunderstandings and expensive litigation).

Distance Learning

In this section, we'll discuss how the legal principles discussed earlier in this chapter and in other chapters of this book apply to the various forms of distance learning—correspondence courses with written material, instructional videos, interactive multimedia, instructional television, and on-line instruction. We'll also discuss instructor concerns about these materials, consultants, and agreements with distributors.

Correspondence Courses

Correspondence courses, in which written materials are sent out to students for home study, are the earliest form of distance learning.

Schools are free to buy copyrighted materials, such as textbooks, from publishers and authorized distributors and distribute them to students. Doing this does not infringe the copyright owner's exclusive distribution right, because one who has bought a copy of a work has the right to resell it.

Photocopying copyrighted material for distribution to students requires getting permission from the copyright owner, unless the use is fair use (as discussed in "Teacher Photocopying," earlier in this chapter).

It is unclear whether the Guidelines for Classroom Copying (discussed in "Teacher Photocopying") apply to correspondence courses offered by not-for-profit institutions. The guidelines authorize copying for "classroom use or discussion." An argument could be made that there is no classroom in the correspondence course situation. The guidelines do not apply to for-profit institutions offering correspondence courses.

See "Owning a
Copy of a Work,"
Chapter 4.

As to the "educational use" statutory exceptions to the copyright law, if the institution offering a correspondence course has a library, the library can rely on Section 108 to make copies of copyrighted material at the requests of students (assuming the library meets the general conditions for relying on Section 108). Section 110(1) and (2) are inapplicable, because correspondence courses do not involve the public performance of copyrighted works.

Instructional Videos

Making an instructional video requires attention to copyright law and other laws. It may require getting film permits and model releases.

Copyright Law

If you will be using copyrighted content owned by third parties in your video—music clips and film clips, for example—unless your use is fair use, you need to clear the right to use that content, just as a commercial multimedia developer would (see Chapters 11, 12, 13, and 14).

If you perform (play) a copyrighted musical composition in a work, unless fair use applies, you need permission from the copyright owner. You may be able to find suitable public domain music.

The Section 110(1) and (2) "educational use" statutory exceptions discussed earlier in this chapter do not apply to the production of instructional videos, since the videos are neither face-to-face teaching (Section 110(1)) or performances in the course of transmissions (Section 110(2)).

Other Laws

To avoid claims that your video violates an individual's right of privacy and publicity, get a release from any person whose image, name, or voice is used. This includes students (for minors, get a parent to sign the release). If a teacher is making the video but the institution is to own the copyright (see "Copyright Ownership" earlier in this chapter), the institution should get a release from the teacher. To avoid libel claims, follow the suggestions made in "Libel," Chapter 15.

See "Option #2: Using Preexisting Music," and "Option #3: Public Domain Music," Chapter 14.

If you are going to shoot photographs or video on private property, get a location release from the property owner. If you will be shooting on public property, you may need a permit from a government authority. If your shots will show a work that is protected by copyright—a painting, for example—you may need permission from the copyright owner. If your video will show trademarks, you may need permission from the owner of the trademark.

If you will be distributing copies of the video on your own or through a distributor, see "Distribution Agreements," later in this chapter, and Chapter 19 (Sales Law).

See "The Rights of Publicity and Privacy," Chapter 15.

Interactive Multimedia

Creating an educational interactive multimedia product requires attention to the same legal issues involved in instructional video production (and, in

Permits are discussed in "Permits," Chapter 15.

See "Using Third-Party Trademarks," Chapter 17.

general, to all the legal issues that commercial multimedia developers must address, as discussed in the earlier chapters of this book).

Today's technology makes it easy to combine third-party content—text, graphics, film clips, and music clips—into an interactive multimedia product. Unless fair use applies, you need a license to do that. Right now, there are no guidelines (like the Guidelines for Classroom Copying) to help you determine whether your use of copyrighted material in an educational multimedia product is fair use.

As with instructional videos, neither the Section 110(1) exception (face-to-face teaching) nor the Section 110(2) exception (performances in the course of a transmission) applies.

Videoconferencing

Videoconferencing probably will become a popular form of distance learning in the next few years, as equipment gets cheaper, because it allows the teacher to interact with students during the class.

Videoconferencing (like traditional classroom teaching) can involve the public performance of copyrighted material—for example, the instructor whose teaching is being transmitted to students by videoconferencing equipment could read from a prose work or recite a poem or play a musical composition on the piano. When the performance in the videoconferenced course is a regular part of the systematic instructional activities of a government body or a nonprofit educational institution, the copyright owner's permission is not needed for this public performance if Section 110(2)'s conditions are met (these are discussed in "Exceptions to the Performance Right," earlier in this chapter).

Videoconferencing is within the Copyright Act's definition of transmission (to "transmit" a performance is "to communicate it by any device or process whereby images or sounds are received beyond the place from which they are sent"). The Section 110(2) exception is limited to nondramatic literary works and nondramatic musical works, however. It would not permit the instructor to act out a play (a *dramatic* work), perform an opera (a *dramatic* musical work), show a motion picture, perform a choreographic work, or display a pictorial, graphic, or sculptural work or an architectural work.

If Section 110(b) applies, you also can make up to 30 copies of the particular transmission program embodying the performance or display without infringing the copyright owner's reproduction right (as long as the copies are destroyed within seven years from the date of the program). Section 112(b).

Videoconferenced courses may involve the use of photocopied copyrighted materials. As with correspondence courses, it is unclear whether the Guidelines for Classroom Copying apply (because there is no "classroom" in the traditional sense of a teacher and students being physically present in one room). Unless the copying is fair use, permission from the copyright owners is needed (see "Teacher Photocopying," earlier in this chapter).

Instructional TV

Instructional television can be one way (teacher to students) or two way (with response from the students).

As with videoconferencing, public performances of copyrighted works do not require the permission of the copyright owner if the institution is a governmental body or a nonprofit educational institution, if the performance is a regular part of the systematic instructional activities of a governmental body or nonprofit educational institution, and if the other requirements for relying on Section 110(2) are met (these are discussed in "Instructional Broadcasts," earlier in this chapter). Remember, this is true only for nondramatic literary works and nondramatic musical works.

If Section 110(2) doesn't apply, a "compulsory license" (license for which the fee is set by the Copyright Royalty Tribunal) may be available under Section 118(d) if you are a nonprofit organization and the program is being transmitted over a noncommercial educational broadcast station. Section 118(d) states that a public broadcasting entity may, by paying the compulsory license fee established by the Copyright Royalty Tribunal, publicly perform or display certain types of works—published nondramatic musical works and published pictorial, graphic, and sculptural works—on a noncommercial educational broadcast station.

A "public broadcasting entity" is defined in Section 118(g) as "a noncommercial educational broadcast station" or any nonprofit institution engaged in noncommercial educational broadcasting. A "noncommercial educational broadcast station" is defined as a television or broadcast station eligible to be licensed—or licensed—by the FCC, as a noncommercial educational broadcast station and which is owned and operated by a public agency or a nonprofit foundation, or a television or radio broadcast station owned and operated by a municipality which transmits only noncommercial programs for educational purposes.

On-line Instruction

On-line instruction uses material posted on servers, email, and "chat" functions (on the World Wide Web, through on-line service providers such as America Online and CompuServe, and through private networks). For example, the University of California at Los Angeles (UCLA) is currently offering writing courses on-line.

Many of the special issues raised by on-line instruction are covered in Chapter 23. As stated in that chapter, the copyright law applies to on-line usage.

Electronic "field trips" may require releases from individuals who will be shown, location releases and permits for filming on private and public property, and permission to show copyrighted works.

Teacher Concerns

Some teachers who are asked by their institutions to make "fixed" distance learning materials, such as instructional videos and interactive multimedia CD-ROMs, may be concerned that these materials will be used to replace "live" teachers (in these days of shrinking financial resources for education).

If you are a teacher who is in this position, consider asking your institution to agree in writing to restrictions on how the material can be used and for how long. For example, you may be happy to have the material used off-site in locations far from your campus, but not on your campus.

See "Permits," Chapter 15.

In the absence of such an agreement, if the institution owns the copyright in the material (see "Copyright Ownership," earlier in this chapter), the institution probably can do whatever it wants with the material. It's possible, though, that in some states, your right of publicity would give you a right to limit the institution's use of the material, unless you signed a broad release.

Consultants

If outside consultants or free-lancers will be used to create materials of any type for distance learning, follow the suggestions in "Copyright Ownership," Chapter 8, to ensure that you have ownership of material created by the free-lancer. If you don't do this, the free-lancer will own his or her material.

See "The Rights of Publicity and Privacy," Chapter 15.

John asked Sue, a graphic artist, to create some graphics for his interactive multimedia CD-ROM on U.S. geography. He asked Sam to design the software for the CD-ROM. Unless John got assignments or work made for hire agreements from Sue and Sam, Sue owns the copyright in her graphics and Sam owns the copyright in his software.

Student Contributions

If you will be selling copies of distance learning materials which you and your students have created, you also should follow the suggestions in

"Copyright Ownership," Chapter 8, for student contributions (for minors, a parent must sign). A student is not an employee of the school, so the work made for hire doctrine (discussed in "Copyright Ownership," earlier in this chapter) does not apply. Make certain that the students have not incorporated third-party material into their work in violation of the rights of the copyright owners (the fact that they have the technology to do so doesn't mean that they have the right, under copyright law, to do so).

Distribution Agreements

If you are interested in finding a distributor or publisher for educational materials that you (or instructors affiliated with your educational institution) have created, here are some points to consider:

➤ **Copyright ownership.** If there's doubt as to whether an institution or instructor owns the materials, the publisher will want this issue clarified (or will require assignments or licenses from both parties, possibly with royalty splitting). The same is true if several individuals have helped create the materials (creating conflicting claims of ownership or claims of joint ownership).

➤ **Use of third-party material**. The publisher will want to see licenses to use third-party material and warranties of noninfringement. If you relied on fair use (or were unaware that you might need licenses), the publisher may lose interest unless you can get licenses (and it's much better to get them before you use the material). Licensing is discussed in Chapters 12 and 13.

➤ **Releases and permits**. If you didn't get releases from individuals whose image, name, or face are shown, or didn't get filming permits for locations or permission to show copyrighted objects, the publisher may lose interest. These topics are discussed in Chapter 15.

➤ **Rights granted**. Be cautious about granting an assignment of your copyright to a publisher. An assignment is a complete transfer of copyright ownership. If you assign the copyright and a better deal comes along, you're stuck (even if the publisher to whom you granted the assignment is not pushing your product and you're getting zero in royalties). You will not be able to use components of the product in other projects unless you get a license from the publisher. You won't even be able to use the product in your own courses without a license (that would be an exercise of the public performance right for a work that you no longer own). Be cautious about a broad exclusive license for the same reasons. A narrow exclusive license generally will often be better for you (for example, an exclusive license to distribute a

See "Warranties," Chapter 20.

See "Assignments," Chapter 4.

CD-ROM version of the product to consumers for home use in the U.S.). In any event, if you want to continue to use the product in your own classes or other ways and to show it at professional conferences, make certain you put that in the agreement.

You also should read Chapter 20 (Distribution Agreements), Chapter 21 (Publisher Concerns), and Chapter 22 (The Business of Multimedia).

See "Assigning the Rights," Chapter 20.

Using Copyrighted Materials for Fund-raisers

Section 110(4) of the Copyright Act provides a limited exception to the public performance right for educational, religious, and charitable fund-raising events. This provision applies only to nondramatic literary or musical works (not to dramatic works, such as plays; or to dramatic musical works, such as operas; or to audiovisual works). It does not apply to transmissions.

Because the former copyright law—the 1909 Act—contained an exception from the copyright owner's public performance right for any non-profit performance, many people think that nonprofit performance of a work still does not require the permission of the copyright owner (or they think that permission is not required unless an admission fee is charged for the performance). Section 110(4) is much more limited than the prior law. It requires careful reading.

For Section 110(4) to apply, the performance must be without any purpose of direct or indirect commercial advantage and without payment of any fee or compensation to the performers, promoters, or organizers. If there is a direct or indirect admission charge, the proceeds, after deducting the reasonable costs of the performance, must be used exclusively for educational, religious, or charitable purposes.

If there is an admission charge, the provision does not apply—even if the proceeds are to be used for educational, religious, or charitable purposes—if the copyright owner serves notice of objection to the performance on the person responsible for the performance seven days before the date of the performance.

Appendices

A The Copyright Act of 1976, Selected Provisions

§ 101. Definitions

"Audiovisual works" are works that consist of a series of related images which are intrinsically intended to be shown by the use of machines or devices such as projectors, viewers, or electronic equipment, together with accompanying sounds, if any, regardless of the nature of the material objects, such as films or tapes, in which the works are embodied.

A "collective work" is a work, such as a periodical issue, anthology, or encyclopedia, in which a number of contributions, constituting separate and independent works in themselves, are assembled into a collective whole.

A "compilation" is a work formed by the collection and assembling of preexisting materials or of data that are selected, coordinated, or arranged in such a way that the resulting work as a whole constitutes an original work of authorship. The term "compilation" includes collective works.

A "computer program" is a set of statements or instructions to be used directly or indirectly in a computer in order to bring about a certain result.

"Copies" are material objects, other than phonorecords, in which a work is fixed by any method now known or later developed, and from which the work can be perceived, reproduced, or otherwise communicated, either directly or with the aid of a machine or device. The term "copies" includes the material object, other than a phonorecord, in which the work is first fixed.

A "derivative work" is a work based upon one or more preexisting works, such as a translation, musical arrangement, dramatization, fictionalization, motion picture version, sound recording, art reproduction, abridgment, condensation, or any other form in which a work may be recast, transformed, or adapted. A work consisting of editorial revisions, annotations, elaborations, or other modifications which, as a whole, represent an original work of authorship, is a "derivative work. "

To "display" a work means to show a copy of it, either directly or by means of a film, slide, television image, or any other device or process or, in the case of a motion picture or other audiovisual work, to show individual images nonsequentially.

A work is "fixed" in a tangible medium of expression when its embodiment in a copy or phonorecord, by or under the authority of the author, is sufficiently permanent or stable to permit it to be perceived, reproduced, or otherwise communicated for a period of more than transitory duration. A work consisting of sounds, images, or both, that are being transmitted, is "fixed" for purposes of this title if a fixation of the work is being made simultaneously with its transmission.

A "joint work" is a work prepared by two or more authors with the intention that their contributions be merged into inseparable or interdependent parts of a unitary whole.

"Literary works" are works, other than audiovisual works, expressed in words, numbers, or other verbal or numerical symbols or indicia, regardless of the nature of the material objects, such as books, periodicals, manuscripts, phonorecords, film, tapes, disks, or cards, in which they are embodied.

"Motion pictures" are audiovisual works consisting of a series of related images which, when shown in succession, impart an impression of motion, together with accompanying sounds, if any.

To "perform" a works means to recite, render, play, dance or act it, either directly or by means of any device or process or, in the case of a motion picture or other audiovisual work, to show its images in any sequence or to make the sounds accompanying it audible.

"Phonorecords" are material objects in which sounds, other than those accompanying a motion picture or other audiovisual work, are fixed by any method now known or later developed, and from which the sounds can be perceived, reproduced, or otherwise communicated, either directly or with the aid of a machine or device. The term "phonorecords" includes the material object in which the sounds are first fixed.

"Pictorial, graphic, and sculptural works" include two-dimensional and three-dimensional works of fine, graphic, and applied art, photographs, prints and art reproductions, maps, globes, charts, diagrams, models, and technical drawings, including architectural plans. Such works shall include works of artistic craftsmanship insofar as their form but not their mechanical or utilitarian aspects are concerned; the design of a useful article, as defined in this section, shall be considered a pictorial, graphic, or sculptural work only if, and only to the extent that, such design incorporates pictorial, graphic, or sculptural features that can be identified separately from, and are capable of existing independently of, the utilitarian aspects of the article.

"Publication" is the distribution of copies or phonorecords of a work to the public by sale or other transfer of ownership, or by rental, lease, or lending. The offering to distribute copies or phonorecords to a group of persons for purposes of further distribution, public performance, or public display, constitutes publication. A public performance or display of a work does not of itself constitute publication.

To perform or display a work "publicly" means—

(1) to perform or display it at a place open to the public or at any place where a substantial number of persons outside of a normal circle of a family and its social acquaintances is gathered; or

(2) to transmit or otherwise communicate a performance or display of the work to a place specified by clause (1) or to the public, by means of any device or process, whether the members of the public capable of receiving the performance or display receive it in the same place or in separate places and at the same time or at different times.

"Sound recordings" are works that result from the fixation of a series of musical, spoken, or other sounds, but not including the sounds accompanying a motion picture or other audiovisual work, regardless of the nature of the material objects, such as disks, tapes, or other phonorecords, in which they are embodied.

A "transfer of copyright ownership" is an assignment, mortgage, exclusive license, or any other conveyance, alienation, or hypothecation of a copyright or of any of the exclusive rights comprised in a copyright whether or not it is limited in time or place of effect, but not including a nonexclusive license.

A "useful article" is an article having an intrinsic utilitarian function that is not merely to portray the appearance of the article or to convey information. An article that is normally a part of a useful article is considered a "useful article."

A "work of visual art" is—

(1) a painting, drawing, print, or sculpture, existing in a single copy, in a limited edition of 200 copies or fewer that are signed and consecutively numbered by the author, or, in the case of a sculpture, in multiple cast, carved, or fabricated sculptures of 200 or fewer that are consecutively numbered by the author and bear the signature or other identifying mark of the author; or

(2) a still photographic image produced for exhibition purposes only, existing in a single copy that is signed by the author, or in a limited edition of 200 copies or fewer that are signed and consecutively numbered by the author.

A work of visual art does not include—

(A) (i) any poster, map, globe, chart, technical drawing, diagram, model, applied art, motion picture or other audiovisual work, book, magazine, newspaper, periodical, data base, electronic information service, electronic publication, or similar publication;

(ii) any merchandising item or advertising, promotional, descriptive, covering, or packaging material or container;

(iii) any portion or part of any item described in clause (i) or (ii);

(B) any work made for hire; or

(C) any work not subject to copyright protection under this title.

A "work made for hire" is—

(1) a work prepared by an employee within the scope of his or her employment; or

(2) a work specially ordered or commissioned for use as a contribution to a collective work, as a part of a motion picture or other audiovisual work, as a translation, as a supplementary work, as a compilation, as an instructional text, as a test, as answer material for a test, or as an atlas, if the parties expressly agree in a written instrument signed by them that the work shall be considered a work made for hire. For the purpose of the foregoing sentence, a "supplementary work" is a work prepared for publication as a secondary adjunct to a work by another author for the purpose of introducing, concluding, illustrating, explaining, revising, commenting upon, or assisting in the use of the other work, such as forewords, afterwords, pictorial illustrations, maps, charts, tables, editorial notes, musical arrangements, answer material for tests, bibliographies, appendixes, and indexes, and an "instructional text" is a literary, pictorial, or graphic work prepared for publication and with the purpose of use in systematic instructional activities.

§ 102. Subject matter of copyright: In general

(a) Copyright protection subsists, in accordance with this title, in original works of authorship fixed in any tangible medium of expression, now known or later developed, from which they can be perceived, reproduced, or otherwise communicated, either directly or with the aid of a machine or device. Works of authorship include the following categories:

(1) literary works;

(2) musical works, including any accompanying words;

(3) dramatic works, including any accompanying music;

(4) pantomimes and choreographic works;

(5) pictorial, graphic, and sculptural works;

(6) motion pictures and other audiovisual works;

(7) sound recordings; and

(8) architectural works.

(b) In no case does copyright protection for an original work of authorship extend to any idea, procedure, process, system, method of operation, concept, principle, or discovery, regardless of the form in which it is described, explained, illustrated, or embodied in such work.

§ 103. Subject matter of copyright: Compilations and derivative works.

(a) The subject matter of copyright as specified by section 102 includes compilations and derivative works, but protection for a work employing preexisting material in which copyright subsists does not extend to any part of the work in which such material has been used unlawfully.

(b) The copyright in a compilation or derivative work extends only to the material contributed by the author of such work, as distinguished from the preexisting material employed in the work, and does not imply any exclusive right in the preexisting material. The copyright in such work is independent of, and does not affect or enlarge the scope, duration, ownership, or subsistence of any copyright protection in the preexisting material.

§ 106. Exclusive rights in copyrighted works

Subject to sections 107 through 120, the owner of copyright under this title has the exclusive rights to do and to authorize any of the following:

(1) to reproduce the copyrighted work in copies or phonorecords;

(2) to prepare derivative works based upon the copyrighted work;

(3) to distribute copies or phonorecords of the copyrighted work to the public by sale or other transfer of ownership, or by rental, lease, or lending;

(4) in the case of literary, musical, dramatic, and choreographic works, pantomimes, and motion pictures and other audiovisual works, to perform the copyrighted work publicly; and

(5) in the case of literary, musical, dramatic, and choreographic works, pantomimes, and pictorial, graphic, or sculptural works, including the individual images of a motion picture or other audiovisual work, to display the copyrighted work publicly.

§ 106A. Rights of certain authors to attribution and integrity

(a) RIGHTS OF ATTRIBUTION AND INTEGRITY. Subject to section 107 and independent of the exclusive rights provided in section 106, the author of a work of visual art—

(1) shall have the right—

(A) to claim authorship of that work, and

(B) to prevent the use of his or her name as the author of any work of visual art which he or she did not create;

(2) shall have the right to prevent the use of his or her name as the author of the work of visual art in the event of a distortion, mutilation, or other modification of the work which would be prejudicial to his or her honor or reputation; and

(3) subject to the limitations set forth in section 113(d), shall have the right—

(A) to prevent any intentional distortion, mutilation, or other modification of that work which would be prejudicial to his or her honor or reputation, and any intentional distortion, mutilation, or modification of that work is a violation of that right, and

(B) to prevent any destruction of a work of recognized stature, and any intentional or grossly negligent destruction of that work is a violation of that right.

(b) SCOPE AND EXERCISE OF RIGHTS. Only the author of a work of visual art has the rights conferred by subsection (a) in that work, whether or not the author is the copyright owner. The authors of a joint work of visual [art] are coowners of the rights conferred by subsection (a) in that work.

(d) DURATION OF RIGHTS

(1) With respect to works of visual art created on or after the effective date set forth in section 9(a) of the Visual Artists Rights Act of 1990, the rights conferred by subsection (a) shall endure for a term consisting of the life of the author.

(2) With respect to works of visual art created before the effective date set forth in section 9(a) of the Visual Artists Rights Act of 1990, but title to which has not, as of such effective date, been

transferred from the author, the rights conferred by subsection (a) shall be coextensive with, and shall expire at the same time as, the rights conferred by section 106.

(3) In the case of a joint work prepared by two or more authors, the rights conferred by subsection (a) shall endure for a term consisting of the life of the last surviving author.

(4) All terms of the right conferred by subsection (a) run to the end of the calendar year in which they would otherwise expire.

(e) TRANSFER AND WAIVER.

(1) The rights conferred by subsection (a) may not be transferred, but those rights may be waived if the author expressly agrees to such waiver in a written instrument signed by the author. Such instrument shall specifically identify the work, and uses of that work, to which the waiver applies, and the waiver shall apply only to the work and uses so identified. In the case of a joint work prepared by two or more authors, a waiver of rights under this paragraph made by one such author waives such rights for all such authors.

(2) Ownership of the rights conferred by subsection (a) with respect to a work of visual art is distinctive from ownership of any copy of that work, or of a copyright or any exclusive right under a copyright in that work. Transfer of ownership of any copy of a work of visual art, or of a copyright or any exclusive right under a copyright, shall not constitute a waiver of the rights conferred by subsection (a). Except as may otherwise be agreed by the author in a written instrument signed by the author, a waiver of the rights conferred by subsection (a) with respect to a work of visual art shall not constitute a transfer of ownership of any copy of that work, or of ownership of a copyright or of any exclusive rights under a copyright in that work.

§ 107. Limitations on exclusive rights: Fair use

Notwithstanding the provisions of sections 106 and 106A, the fair use of a copyrighted work, including such use by reproduction in copies or phonorecords or by any other means specified by that section, for purposes such as criticism, comment, news reporting, teaching (including multiple copies for classroom use), scholarship, or research, is not an infringement of copyright. In determining whether the use made of a work in any particular case is a fair use the factors to be considered shall include—

(1) the purpose and character of the use, including whether such use is of a commercial nature or is for nonprofit educational purposes;

(2) the nature of the copyrighted work;

(3) the amount and substantiality of the portion used in relation to the copyrighted work as a whole; and

(4) the effect of the use upon the potential market for or value of the copyrighted work.

§ 108. Limitations on exclusive rights: Reproduction by libraries and archives

(a) Notwithstanding the provisions of section 106, it is not an infringement of copyright for a library or archives, or any of its employees acting within the scope of their employment, to reproduce no more than one copy or phonorecord of a work, or to distribute such copy or phonorecord, under the conditions specified by this section, if —

(1) the reproduction or distribution is made without any purpose of direct or indirect commercial advantage;

(2) the collections of the library or archives are (i) open to the public, or (ii) available not only to researchers affiliated with the library or archives or with the institution of which it is a part, but also to other persons doing research in a specialized field; and

(3) the reproduction or distribution of the work includes a notice of copyright.

(b) The rights of reproduction and distribution under this section apply to a copy or phonorecord of an unpublished work duplicated in facsimile form solely for purposes of preservation and security or for deposit for research use in another library or archives of the type described by clause (2) of subsection (a), if the copy or phonorecord reproduced is currently in the collections of the library or archives.

(c) The right of reproduction under this section applies to a copy or phonorecord of a published work duplicated in facsimile form solely for the purpose of replacement of a copy or phonorecord that is damaged, deteriorating, lost, or stolen, if the library or archives has, after a reasonable effort, determined that an unused replacement cannot be obtained at a fair price.

(d) The rights of reproduction and distribution under this section apply to a copy, made from the collection of a library or archives where the user makes his or her request or from that of another library or archives, of no more than one article or other contribution to a copyrighted collection or periodical issue, or to a copy or phonorecord of a small part of any other copyrighted work, if—

(1) the copy or phonorecord becomes the property of the user, and the library or archives has had no notice that the copy or phonorecord would be used for any purpose other than private study, scholarship, or research; and

(2) the library or archives displays prominently, at the place where orders are accepted, and includes on its order form, a warning of copyright in accordance with requirements that the Register of Copyrights shall prescribe by regulation.

(e) The rights of reproduction and distribution under this section apply to the entire work, or to a substantial part of it, made from the collection of a library or archives where the user makes his or her request or from that of another library or archives, if the library or archives has first determined, on the basis of a reasonable investigation, that a copy or phonorecord of the copyrighted work cannot be obtained at a fair * price, if—

*So in original.

(1) the copy or phonorecord becomes the property of the user, and the library or archives has had no notice that the copy or phonorecord would be used for any purpose other than private study, scholarship, or research; and

(2) the library or archives displays prominently, at the place where orders are accepted, and includes on its order form, a warning of copyright in accordance with requirements that the Register of Copyrights shall prescribe by regulation.

(f) Nothing in this section—

(1) shall be construed to impose liability for copyright infringement upon a library or archives or its employees for the unsupervised use of reproducing equipment located on its premises: *Provided*, That such equipment displays a notice that the making of a copy may be subject to the copyright law;

(2) excuses a person who uses such reproducing equipment or who requests a copy or phonorecord under subsection (d) from liability for copyright infringement for any such act, or for any later use of such copy or phonorecord, if it exceeds fair use as provided by section 107;

(3) shall be construed to limit the reproduction and distribution by lending of a limited number of copies and excerpts by a library or archives of an audiovisual news program, subject to clauses (1), (2), and (3) of subsection (a); or

(4) in any way affects the right of fair use as provided by section 107, or any contractual obligations assumed at any time by the library or archives when it obtained a copy or phonorecord of a work in its collections.

(g) The rights of reproduction and distribution under this section extend to the isolated and unrelated reproduction or distribution of a single copy or phonorecord of the same material on separate occasions, but do not extend to cases where the library or archives, or its employee—

(1) is aware or has substantial reason to believe that it is engaging in the related or concerted reproduction or distribution of multiple copies or phonorecords of the same material, whether made on one occasion or over a period of time, and whether intended for aggregate use by one or more individuals or for separate use by the individual members of a group; or

(2) engages in the systematic reproduction or distribution of single or multiple copies or phonorecords of material described in subsection (d): *Provided*, That nothing in this cause prevents a library or archives from participating in interlibrary arrangements that do not have as their purpose or effect, that the library or archives receiving such copies or phonorecords for distribution does so in such aggregate quantities as to substitute for a subscription to or purchase of such work.

(h) The rights of reproduction and distribution under this section do not apply to a musical work, a pictorial, graphic or sculptural work, or a motion picture or other audiovisual work other than an audiovisual work dealing with news, except that no such limitation shall apply with respect to rights granted by subsections (b) and (c), or with respect to pictorial or graphic works published as illustrations, diagrams, or similar adjuncts to works of which copies are reproduced or distributed in accordance with subsections (d) and (e).

(i) Five years from the effective date of this Act, and at five-year intervals thereafter, the Register of Copyrights, after consulting with representatives of authors, book and periodical publishers, and other owners of copyrighted materials, and with representatives of library users and librarians, shall submit to the Congress a report setting forth the extent to which this section has achieved the intended statutory balancing of the rights of creators, and the needs of users. The report should also describe any problems that may have arisen, and present legislative or other recommendations, if warranted.

§ 109. Limitations on exclusive rights:

Effect of transfer of particular copy or phonorecord

(a) Notwithstanding the provisions of section 106(3), the owner of a particular copy or phonorecord lawfully made under this title, or any person authorized by such owner, is entitled, without the authority of the copyright owner, to sell or otherwise dispose of the possession of that copy or phonorecord.

§ 110. Limitations on exclusive rights: Exemption of certain performances and displays

Notwithstanding the provisions of section 106, the following are not infringements of copyright:

(1) performance or display of a work by instructors or pupils in the course of face-to-face teaching activities of a nonprofit educational institution, in a classroom or similar place devoted to instruction, unless, in the case of a motion picture or other audiovisual work, the performance, or the display of individual images, is given by means of a copy that was not lawfully made under this title, and that the person responsible for the performance knew or had reason to believe was not lawfully made;

(2) performance of a nondramatic literary or musical work or display of a work, by or in the course of a transmission, if—

(A) the performance or display is a regular part of the systematic instructional activities of a governmental body or a nonprofit educational institution; and

(B) the performance or display is directly related and of material assistance to the teaching content of the transmission; and

(C) the transmission is made primarily for —

(i) reception in classrooms or similar places normally devoted to instruction, or

(ii) reception by persons to whom the transmission is directed because their disabilities or other special circumstances prevent their attendance in classrooms or similar places normally devoted to instruction, or

(iii) reception by officers or employees of governmental bodies as a part of their official duties or employment;

§ 201. Ownership of copyright

(a) INITIAL OWNERSHIP. Copyright in a work protected under this title vests initially in the author or authors of the work. The authors of a joint work are coowners of copyright in the work.

(b) WORKS MADE FOR HIRE. In the case of a work made for hire, the employer or other person for whom the work was prepared is considered the author for purposes of this title, and, unless the parties have expressly agreed otherwise in a written instrument signed by them, owns all of the rights comprised in the copyright.

(c) CONTRIBUTIONS TO COLLECTIVE WORKS. Copyright in each separate contribution to a collective work is distinct from copyright in the collective work as a whole, and vests initially in the author of the contribution. In the absence of an express transfer of the copyright or of any rights under it, the owner of copyright in the collective work is presumed to have acquired only the privilege of reproducing and distributing the contribution as part of that particular collective work, any revision of that collective work, and any later collective work in the same series.

(d) TRANSFER OF OWNERSHIP.

(1) The ownership of a copyright may be transferred in whole or in part by any means of conveyance or by operation of law, and may be bequeathed by will or pass as personal property by the applicable laws of intestate succession.

(2) Any of the exclusive rights comprised in a copyright, including any subdivision of any of the rights specified by section 106, may be transferred as provided by clause (1) and owned separately. The owner of any particular exclusive right is entitled, to the extent of that right, to all of the protection and remedies accorded to the copyright owner by this title.

§ 202. Ownership of copyright as distinct from ownership of material object

Ownership of a copyright, or of any of the exclusive rights under a copyright, is distinct from ownership of any material object in which the work is embodied. Transfer of ownership of any material object, including the copy or phonorecord in which the work is first fixed, does not of itself convey any rights in the copyrighted work embodied in the object; nor, in the absence of an agreement, does transfer of ownership of a copyright or of any exclusive rights under a copyright convey property rights in any material object.

§ 204. Execution of transfers of copyright ownership

(a) A transfer of copyright ownership, other than by operation of law, is not valid unless an instrument of conveyance, or a note or memorandum of the transfer, is in writing and signed by the owner of the rights conveyed or such owner's duly authorized agent.

(b) A certificate of acknowledgement is not required for the validity of a transfer, but is prima facie evidence of the execution of the transfer if—

(1) in the case of a transfer executed in the United States, the certificate is issued by a person authorized to administer oaths within the United States; or

(2) in the case of a transfer executed in a foreign country, the certificate is issued by a diplomatic or consular officer of the United States, or by a person authorized to administer oaths whose authority is proved by a certificate of such an officer.

§ 205. Recordation of transfers and other documents

(a) CONDITIONS FOR RECORDATION. Any transfer of copyright ownership or other document pertaining to a copyright may be recorded in the Copyright Office if the document filed for recordation bears the actual signature of the person who executed it, or if it is accompanied by a sworn or official certification that it is a true copy of the original, signed document.

(b) CERTIFICATE OF RECORDATION. The Register of Copyrights shall, upon receipt of a document as provided by subsection (a) and of the fee provided by section 708, record the document and return it with a certificate of recordation.

(c) RECORDATION AS CONSTRUCTIVE NOTICE. Recordation of a document in the Copyright Office gives all persons constructive notice of the facts stated in the recorded document, but only if

(1) the document, or material attached to it, specifically identifies the work to which it pertains so that, after the document is indexed by the Register of Copyrights, it would be revealed by a reasonable search under the title or registration number of the work; and

(2) registration has been made for the work.

(d) PRIORITY BETWEEN CONFLICTING TRANSFERS. As between two conflicting transfers, the one executed first prevails if it is recorded, in the manner required to give constructive notice under subsection (c), within one month after its execution in the United States or within two months after its execution outside the United States, or at any time before recordation in such manner of the later transfer. Otherwise the later transfer prevails if recorded first in such manner, and if taken in good faith, for valuable consideration or on the basis of a binding promise to pay royalties, and without notice of the earlier transfer.

(e) PRIORITY BETWEEN CONFLICTING TRANSFER OF OWNERSHIP AND NONEXCLUSIVE LICENSE. A nonexclusive license, whether recorded or not, prevails over a conflicting transfer of copyright ownership if the license is evidenced by a written instrument signed by the owner of the rights licensed or such owner's duly authorized agent; and if

(1) the license was taken before execution of the transfer; or

(2) the license was taken in good faith before recordation of the transfer and without notice of it.

§ 302. Duration of copyright: Works created on or after January 1, 1978

(a) IN GENERAL. Copyright in a work created on or after January 1, 1978, subsists from its creation and, except as provided by the following subsections, endures for a term consisting of the life of the author and fifty years after the author's death.

(b) JOINT WORKS. In the case of a joint work prepared by two or more authors who did not work for hire, the copyright endures for a term consisting of the life of the last surviving author and fifty years after such last surviving author's death.

(c) ANONYMOUS WORKS, PSEUDONYMOUS WORKS, AND WORKS MADE FOR HIRE. In the case of an anonymous work, a pseudonymous work, or a work made for hire, the copyright endures for a term of seventy-five years from the year of its first publication, or a term of one hundred years from the year of its creation, whichever expires first.

§ 401. Notice of copyright: Visually perceptible copies

(a) GENERAL PROVISIONS. Whenever a work protected under this title is published in the United States or elsewhere by authority of the copyright owner, a notice of copyright as provided by this section may be placed on publicly distributed copies from which the work can be visually perceived, either directly or with the aid of a machine or device.

(b) FORM OF NOTICE. If a notice appears on the copies, it shall consist of the following three elements:

(1) the symbol © (the letter C in a circle), or the word "Copyright," or the abbreviation "Copr. "; and

(2) the year of first publication of the work; in the case of compilations or derivative works incorporating previously published material, the year date of first publication of the compilation

or derivative work is sufficient. The year date may be omitted where a pictorial, graphic, or sculptural work, with accompanying text matter, if any, is reproduced in or on greeting cards, postcards, stationery, jewelry, dolls, toys, or any useful articles; and

(3) the name of the owner of copyright in the work, or an abbreviation by which the name can be recognized, or a generally known alternative designation of the owner.

(c) POSITION OF NOTICE. The notice shall be affixed to the copies in such manner and location as to give reasonable notice of the claim of copyright. The Register of Copyrights shall prescribe by regulation, as examples, specific methods of affixation and positions of the notice on various types of works that will satisfy this requirement, but these specifications shall not be considered exhaustive.

(d) EVIDENTIARY WEIGHT OF NOTICE. If a notice of copyright in the form and position specified by this section appears on the published copy or copies to which a defendant in a copyright infringement suit had access, then no weight shall be given to such a defendant's interposition of a defense based on innocent infringement in mitigation of actual or statutory damages, except as provided in the last sentence of section 504(c)(2).

§ 408. Copyright registration in general

(a) REGISTRATION PERMISSIVE. At any time during the subsistence of the first term of copyright in any published or unpublished work in which the copyright was secured before January 1, 1978, and during the subsistence of any copyright secured on or after that date, the owner of copyright or of any exclusive right in the work may obtain registration of the copyright claim by delivering to the Copyright Office the deposit specified by this section, together with the application and fee specified by sections 409 and 708. Such registration is not a condition of copyright protection.

§ 411. Registration and infringement actions

(a) Except for actions for infringement of copyright in Berne Convention works whose country of origin is not the United States and an action brought for violation of the rights of the author under section 160A(a), and subject to the provisions of subsection (b), no action for infringement of the copyright in any work shall be instituted until registration of the copyright claim has been made in accordance with this title. In any case, however, where the deposit, application, and fee required for registration have been delivered to the Copyright Office in proper form and registration has been refused, the applicant is entitled to institute an action for infringement if notice thereof, with a copy of the complaint, is served on the Register of Copyrights. The Register may, at his or her option, become a party to the action with respect to the issue of registrability of the copyright claim by entering an appearance within sixty days after such service, but the Register's failure to become a party shall not deprive the court of jurisdiction to determine that issue.

§ 412. Registration as prerequisite to certain remedies for infringement

In any action under this title, other than an action brought for a violation of the rights of the author under section 106a(a) or an action instituted under section 411(b), no award of statutory damages or of attorney's fees, as provided by sections 504 and 505, shall be made for

(1) any infringement of copyright in an unpublished work commenced before the effective date of its registration; or

(2) any infringement of copyright commenced after first publication of the work and before the effective date of its registration, unless such registration is made within three months after the first publication of the work.

§ 501. Infringement of copyright

(a) Anyone who violates any of the exclusive rights of the copyright owner as provided by sections 106 through 118 or of the author as provided in section 106A, or who imports copies or phonorecords into the United States in violation of section 602, is an infringer of the copyright or right of the author, as the case may be. For purposes of this chapter (other than section 506), any reference to copyright shall be deemed to include the rights conferred by section 106A(a).

§ 504. Remedies for infringement: Damages and profits

(a) IN GENERAL. Except as otherwise provided by this title, an infringer of copyright is liable for either

(1) the copyright owner's actual damages and any additional profits of the infringer, as provided by subsection (b); or

(2) statutory damages, as provided by subsection (c).

(b) ACTUAL DAMAGES AND PROFITS. The copyright owner is entitled to recover the actual damages suffered by him or her as a result of the infringement, and any profits of the infringer that are attributable to the infringement and are not taken into account in computing the actual damages. In establishing the infringer's profits, the copyright owner is required to present proof only of the infringer's gross revenue, and the infringer is required to prove his or her deductible expenses and the elements of profit attributable to factors other than the copyrighted work.

(c) STATUTORY DAMAGES.

(1) Except as provided by clause (2) of this subsection, the copyright owner may elect, at any time before final judgment is rendered, to recover, instead of actual damages and profits, an award of statutory damages for all infringements involved in the action, with respect to any one work, for which any one infringer is liable individually, or for which any two or more infringers are liable jointly and severally, in a sum of not less than $500 or more than $20,000 as the court considers just. For the purposes of this subsection, all the parts of a compilation or derivative work constitute one work.

(2) In a case where the copyright owner sustains the burden of proving, and the court finds, that infringement was committed willfully, the court in its discretion may increase the award of statutory damages to a sum of not more than $100,000. In a case where the infringer sustains the burden of proving, and the court finds, that such infringer was not aware and had no reason to believe that his or her acts constituted an infringement of copyright, the court in its discretion may reduce the award of statutory damages to a sum of not less than $200.

§ 505.   Remedies for infringement: Costs and attorney's fees

In any civil action under this title, the court in its discretion may allow the recovery of full costs by or against any party other than the United States or an officer thereof. Except as otherwise provided by this title, the court may also award a reasonable attorney's fee to the prevailing party as part of the costs.

Agreement on Guidelines for Classroom Copying in Not-for-Profit Educational Institutions With Respect to Books and Periodicals

The purpose of the following guidelines is to state the minimum standards of educational fair use under Section 107 [of the Copyright Act]....

Guidelines

I. Single Copying for Teachers

A single copy may be made of any of the following by or for a teacher at his or her individual request for his or her scholarly research or use in teaching or preparation to teach a class:

A. A chapter from a book;

B. An article from a periodical or newspaper

C. A short story, short essay or short poem, whether or not from a collective work;

D. A chart, graph, diagram, drawing, cartoon or picture from a book, periodical, or newspaper.

II. Multiple Copies for Classroom Use

Multiple copies (not to exceed in any event more than one copy per pupil in a course) may be made by or for the teacher giving the course for classroom use or discussion; *provided that:*

A. The copying meets the tests of brevity and spontaneity as defined below; and

B. Meets the cumulative effect test as defined below; and,

C. Each copy includes a notice of copyright.

Definitions

Brevity

(i) Poetry: (a) A complete poem if less than 250 words and if printed on not more than two pages, or (b) from a longer poem, an excerpt of not more than 250 words.

(ii) Prose: (a) Either a complete article, story, or essay of less than 2,500 words, or (b) an excerpt from any prose work of not more than 1,000 words or 10% of the work, whichever is less, but in any event a minimum of 500 words.

[Each of the numerical limits stated in "i" and "ii" above may be expanded to permit the completion of an unfinished line of a poem or of an unfinished prose paragraph.]

(iii) Illustration: One chart, graph, diagram, drawing, cartoon or picture per book or per periodical issue.

(iv) "Special" works: Certain works in poetry, prose or in "poetry prose" which often combine language with illustrations and which are intended sometimes for children and at other times for a more general audience fall short of 2,500 words in their entirety. Paragraph "ii" notwithstanding, such "special works" may not be reproduced in their entirety; however, an excerpt comprising not more than 10% of the words found in the text thereof, may be reproduced.

Spontaneity

(i) The copying is at the instance and inspiration of the individual teacher, and

(ii) The inspiration and decision to use the work and the moment of its use for maximum teaching effectiveness are so close in time that it would be unreasonable to expect a timely reply to a request for permission.

Cumulative Effect

(i) The copying of the material is for only one course in the school in which the copies are made.

(ii) Not more than one short poem, article, story, essay or two excerpts may be copied from the same author, nor more than three from the same collective work or periodical volume during one class term.

(iii) There shall not be more than nine instances of such multiple copying for one course during one class term.

[The limitations stated in "ii" and "iii" above shall not apply to current news periodicals and newspapers and current news sections of other periodicals].

III. Prohibitions as to I and II Above

Notwithstanding any of the above, the following shall be prohibited:

(A) Copying shall not be used to create or to replace or substitute for anthologies, compilations, or collective works. Such replacement or substitution may occur whether copies of various works or excerpts therefrom are accumulated or reproduced and used separately.

(B) There shall be no copying of or from works intended to be "consumable" in the course of study or of teaching. These include workbooks, exercises, standardized tests and test booklets and answer sheets and like consumable material.

(C) Copying shall not:

(a) substitute for the purchase of books, publishers' reprints or periodicals;

(b) be directed by higher authority;

(c) be repeated with respect to the same item by the same teacher from term to term.

(D) No charge shall be made to the student beyond the actual cost of the photocopying.

Agreed March 19, 1976

B Form Contracts

These contracts have been used for actual transactions. However, they should be considered samples rather than "model" agreements that will fit all of your needs. You should review them (and the chapters to which they relate) to understand the issues that you need to address.

The contracts included here may not fit your needs in a particular transaction. Consult with an experienced attorney prior to using any of these contracts.

These contracts are provided for your personal use in your business or law practice or use by your company. They may not be reproduced or modified for use by third parties without the permission of the authors.

You'll find these contracts in electronic form on the disk that came with this book. Forms 15, 18, 19, and 20 are not on the disk, as these forms were provided by other organizations. Form 21 is not on the disk, but you have permission to photocopy the form from the book.

System requirements for using the disk are as follows: Wordperfect Version 5.1 word processing software (or word processing software capable of reading ASCII formatted files).

If you have an Apple computer that does not read PC files, you can get a MAC version of the disk (in MS Word 3 for MAC) by sending $12 to Ladera Press, c/o Port City Fulfillment Services, P.O. Box 5030, Port Huron, MI 48061. You can use the order form from the end of the book (if the order form is missing, just include a note, with your name and address, telling us you want a MAC disk). Make your check payable to Ladera Press. If you prefer, you can fax the order form or request (include your VISA or MASTERCARD number and expiration date). The The fax number is (810) 987-3562. To order by phone, call (800) 523-3721.

Extra copies of the PC (IBM) version of the disk are also available for $12.

Forms

1. Nondisclosure Agreement (Protecting Developer's Confidential Information)
2. Short-Form Assignment by Developer
3. Quitclaim
4. Location Release
5. Permission Request
6. Employee Nondisclosure and Assignment Agreement
7. Independent Contractor Agreement
8. Work Made for Hire Agreement
9. Assignment Agreement (To Developer—Includes Representations)
10. Distribution Agreement
11. Web Site Development and Maintenance Agreement
12. Footage, Photo, and Text License (Nonexclusive, to Developer)
13. Short-Form Assignment to Developer
14. Software Component License
15. Music License Used by Harry Fox Agency for Multimedia
16. Music and Sound Recording License
17. Release
18. Screen Actors Guild Interactive Media Agreement
19. AFTRA Interactive Media Agreement
20. Writers Guild Agreement
21. Budget Preparation Form
22. Development and Publishing Agreement

1. Nondisclosure Agreement (Protecting Developer's Confidential Information)

This agreement is used when the developer is disclosing confidential information during discussions of a potential business project. The agreement permits the information to be used only for evaluation.

NONDISCLOSURE AGREEMENT
(Protecting Developer's Confidential Information)

This nondisclosure agreement ("Agreement") is entered into as of _____ ("Effective Date") by and between Development Company _____ ("Devco") and _____ ("Recipient"). Devco and Recipient are engaged in discussions in contemplation of or in furtherance of a business relationship. In order to induce Devco to disclose its confidential information during such discussions, Recipient agrees to accept such information under the restrictions set forth in this Agreement.

1. **Disclosure of Confidential Information.** Devco may disclose, either orally or in writing, certain information which Recipient knows or has reason to know is considered confidential by Devco relating to _____ ("Devco Confidential Information"). Devco Confidential Information shall include, but not be limited to, trade secrets, know-how, inventions, techniques, processes, algorithms, software programs, schematics, software source documents, contracts, customer lists, financial information, sales and marketing plans and business plans.

2. **Confidentiality.** Recipient agrees to maintain in confidence Devco Confidential Information. Recipient will use Devco Confidential Information solely to evaluate the commercial potential of a business relationship with Devco. Recipient will not disclose the Devco Confidential Information to any person except its employees or consultants to whom it is necessary to disclose the Devco Confidential Information for such purposes. Recipient agrees that Devco Confidential Information will be disclosed or made available only to those of its employees or consultants who have agreed in writing to receive it under terms at least as restrictive as those specified in this Agreement. Recipient will take reasonable measures to maintain the confidentiality of Devco Confidential Information, but not less than the measures it uses for its confidential information of similar type. Recipient will immediately give notice to Devco of any unauthorized use or disclosure of the Devco Confidential Information. Recipient agrees to assist Devco in remedying such unauthorized use or disclosure of the Devco Confidential Information. This obligation will not apply to the extent that Recipient can demonstrate that:

   (a) the Devco Confidential Information at the time of disclosure is part of the public domain;

   (b) the Devco Confidential Information became part of the public domain, by publication or otherwise, except by breach of the provisions of this Agreement;

   (c) the Devco Confidential Information can be established by written evidence to have been in the possession of Recipient at the time of disclosure;

   (d) the Devco Confidential Information is received from a third party without similar restrictions and without breach of this Agreement; or

(e) the Devco Confidential Information is required to be disclosed by a government agency to further the objectives of this Agreement, or by a proper court of competent jurisdiction; provided, however, that Recipient will use its best efforts to minimize the disclosure of such information and will consult with and assist Devco in obtaining a protective order prior to such disclosure.

3. **Materials.** All materials including, without limitation, documents, drawings, models, apparatus, sketches, designs and lists furnished to Recipient by Devco and any tangible materials embodying Devco Confidential Information created by Recipient shall remain the property of Devco. Recipient shall return to Devco or destroy such materials and all copies thereof upon the termination of this Agreement or upon the written request of Devco.

4. **No License**. This Agreement does not grant Recipient any license to use Devco Confidential Information except as provided in Article 2.

5. **Term.**

(a) This Agreement shall terminate ninety (90) days after the Effective Date unless terminated earlier by either party. Devco may extend the term of the Agreement by written notice to Recipient. Either party may terminate this Agreement, with or without cause, by giving notice of termination to the other party. The Agreement shall terminate immediately upon receipt of such notice.

(b) Upon termination of this Agreement, Recipient shall cease to use Devco Confidential Information and shall comply with Article 3 within twenty (20) days of the date of termination. Upon the request of Devco, an officer of Recipient shall certify that Recipient has complied with its obligations in this Section.

(c) Notwithstanding the termination of this Agreement, Recipient's obligations in Article 2 shall survive such termination.

6. **General Provisions.**

(a) This Agreement shall be governed by and construed in accordance with the laws of the United States and of the State of California as applied to transactions entered into and to be performed wholly within California between California residents. Except as provided in Section 6(b), any dispute arising out of or relating to this Agreement, or the breach, termination or validity thereof, will be submitted by the parties to arbitration, to take place in _____, by the American Arbitration Association under the commercial rules then in effect for that Association except as provided in this Section. All proceedings will be held in English and a transcribed record prepared in English. Depositions may be taken and discovery obtained in any such arbitration proceedings in accordance with California Code of Civil Procedure Sections 1283.05 and 1283.1, which is incorporated herein by this reference. Judgment upon the award rendered by the arbitrator(s) may be entered in any court having jurisdiction thereof.

(b) Notwithstanding Section 6(a), Devco shall have the right to obtain a preliminary relief on any equitable claim in any court of competent jurisdiction, where such judgment is necessary to preserve its property and/or proprietary rights under this Agreement.

(c) Any notice provided for or permitted under this Agreement will be treated as having been given when (a)delivered personally, (b)sent by confirmed telex or telecopy, (c)sent by commercial overnight courier with written verification of receipt, or (d)mailed postage prepaid by certified or registered mail, return receipt requested, to the party to be notified, at the address set forth below, or at such other place of which the other party has been notified in accordance with the provisions of this Section. Such notice will be treated as having been received upon the earlier of actual receipt or five (5) days after posting.

(d) Recipient agrees that the breach of the provisions of this Agreement by Recipient will cause Devco irreparable damage for which recovery of money damages would be inadequate. Devco will, therefore, be entitled to obtain timely injunctive relief to protect Devco's rights under this Agreement in addition to any and all remedies available at law.

(e) Neither party may assign its rights under this Agreement.

(f) This Agreement may be amended or supplemented only by a writing that is signed by duly authorized representatives of both parties.

(g) No term or provision hereof will be considered waived by either party, and no breach excused by either party, unless such waiver or consent is in writing signed on behalf of the party against whom the waiver is asserted. No consent by either party to, or waiver of, a breach by either party, whether express or implied, will constitute a consent to, waiver of, or excuse of any other, different, or subsequent breach by either party.

(h) If any part of this Agreement is found invalid or unenforceable, that part will be amended to achieve as nearly as possible the same economic effect as the original provision and the remainder of this Agreement will remain in full force.

(i) This Agreement constitutes the entire agreement between the parties relating to this subject matter and supersedes all prior or simultaneous representations, discussions, negotiations, and agreements, whether written or oral.

IN WITNESS WHEREOF, the parties have executed this Agreement as of the Effective Date.

"RECIPIENT":   "DEVCO":

_____   DEVELOPMENT COMPANY

By: _____   By: _____

_____   _____
Typed name   Typed name

_____   _____
Title   Title

Address: Address:

_____   _____

_____   _____

_____   _____

2. Short Form Assignment by Developer

This agreement is used to record the transfer of a copyright by the developer in the Copyright Office. The assignee, generally the client, must include either the registration number or title of the copyrightable work to have "constructive notice" of the transfer (see "Obtaining a License" Chapter 12). This short form assignment can also be used to record an assignment of less than all rights in the work (for example, an assignment of audio visual rights or motion picture rights). It can be modified to use in recording an exclusive license.

SHORT FORM ASSIGNMENT BY DEVELOPER

The developer, _____, ("Developer") for good and valuable consideration, the receipt of which is acknowledged, grants to Client Company ("Client"), its successors and assigns all right, title and interest in the copyrightable work named _____ ("Work") owned by Developer. Developer authorizes the recordation of this notice with the Copyright Office. The [registration number/name] of the Work is _____.

CLIENT: DEVELOPER:

CLIENT COMPANY   _____

By: _____   By: _____

_____   _____
Typed name   Typed name

_____   _____
Title   Title

Address: Address:

_____   _____

_____   _____

_____   _____

_____   _____

3. Quitclaim

This letter is used in community property states to "quitclaim" any rights which a spouse may have in a copyright. It should be used when obtaining a copyright assignment from a married individual in a community property state. (see "Community Property," Chapter 4.)

QUITCLAIM

_____

_____

_____

Dear [Husband/Wife]:

Your [Husband/Wife] is assigning all rights (including the copyright) in _____ ("Work") to Developer Company ("Devco"). Under certain interpretations of the law, you may have partial ownership rights in the Work. In order to avoid any doubt and in consideration for our payment to [Husband/Wife], you agree to assign all of such rights, if any, in the Work to Devco and to quitclaim all rights in the Work. Please indicate your agreement by signing below. Thank you for your assistance.

Sincerely yours,

Developer Company

Read and Agreed:

_____

4. Location Release

This agreement is used to obtain the right to enter onto property to photograph it or film it and the right to use the photographs or film in a motion picture.

LOCATION AGREEMENT

_____ ("Grantor") hereby grants to _____ ("Company") and its employees, contractors, agents, independent producers, and suppliers, permission to enter upon and use the property, both exterior and interior, located at: _____
_____

("Property"); and also the right to reproduce the Property, elsewhere, including the name, signs and identifying features thereof, accurately or otherwise, for the purpose of photographing by means of film, videotape, or otherwise, and recording certain scenes for a motion picture.

The permission herein granted shall be for one or more days beginning on or about _____ (subject to change on account of weather conditions or changes in production (schedule)) and continuing until completion of all scenes and work required and shall include permission to reenter the Property for the purpose of making added scenes and retakes ("Additional Use").

Company may place all necessary facilities and equipment, including temporary sets, on the Property and agrees to remove same after completion of work and leave the Property in as good condition as when received, reasonable wear and tear from uses permitted herein excepted. Signs on the Property may, but need not be, removed or changed, but, if moved or changed, must be replaced.

Company agrees to use reasonable care to prevent damage to the Property, and will indemnify the owner and all other parties lawfully in possession of the Property and hold each of them harmless from any claims and demands of any person or persons arising out of, or based upon personal injuries, death or property damage resulting directly from any act of negligence on Company's part in connection with the work hereunder.

All rights of every kind in and to all photographs and sound records made hereunder (including but not limited to the right to exhibit any and all scenes photographed or recorded at and of the Property or reproduction of the Property throughout the world) shall be and remain vested in Company, its successors, assigns and licensees, and neither the owner nor any tenant, or other party now or hereafter having an interest in the Property, shall have any right of action against Company or any other party arising out of any use of said photographs and/or sound recordings whether or not such use is or may be claimed to be defamatory, untrue, or censurable in nature and hereby waives any and all rights of privacy, publicity, or any other rights of a similar nature in connection with the exploitation of any such photography or soundtrack.

In full consideration of the above, Company shall pay Grantor the sum of _____ and for Additional Use, if any, the sum of _____. If the charge herein is on a daily rate, such charge shall be made only for days on which photography actually occurs on the Property. Payment will be made on or before the date of filming.

The commencement date above contemplated and any obligations of the parties shall be postponed for a period equal to the period of any act of God, fire, strike or other labor controversy, law or other governmental regulation which hinders or prevents Columbia's normal business operations or production of the Picture, plus such additional period of time as Companymay reasonably require to recommence production of the Picture.

Should Company elect not to use said Property for filming purposes, written notice will be given prior to filming date releasing all parties from any obligations mentioned above.

The provisions, if any, contained in Schedule "A" attached hereto shall be deemed a part of this Agreement.

The undersigned warrants that the undersigned has the full right to enter into this Agreement and that the consent of no other party is necessary to effectuate the full and complete permission granted therein.

Signed: _____
    [Grantor]

For Company: _____

SCHEDULE "A"

Company shall have the right to use the Property for the following number of days and purposes commencing on or about _____.

DAYS	PURPOSE
_____	Preparation
_____	Photography
_____	Striking/Clean Up

Should Company require additional days' use of the Property for any of the purposes set forth, Grantor grants Company the right to use the Property for such additional days.

5. Permission Request Letter

A teacher or faculty member can use this letter to request permission to photocopy material for classroom use.

April 5, 1996

Permissions Department

Ladera Press

3130 Alpine Road

Menlo Park, Ca. 94025

Dear Sir or Madam:

I would like permission to copy the following for use in my classes at _____ (school name) in _____ (city and state):

> Title: Multimedia Law and Business Handbook
>
> Copyright: J. Dianne Brinson and Mark F. Radcliffe
>
> Author: J. Dianne Brinson and Mark F. Radcliffe
>
> Material to be duplicated: Chapter 23
>
> Number of Copies: 50
>
> Distribution: The material will be distributed to students in my classes and they will pay only the cost of the photocopying.
>
> Type of reprint: Photocopy
>
> Use: The chapter will be used as supplementary teaching materials.

I have enclosed a self-addressed envelope for your convenience in replying to this request.

Sincerely,

Faculty Member

6. Employee Nondisclosure and Assignment Agreement

This agreement is used to ensure that the developer's employee maintains the developer's information in confidence and assigns to developer all proprietary rights developed during the term of his or her employment. This agreement prohibits the employee from engaging in employment, consulting or other activity in a business competitive with the developer. It should be signed on an employee's first day of work for the developer. The "employee" is referred to in the first person (as "I"). The developer is referred to as Development Company ("Devco").

EMPLOYEE NONDISCLOSURE AND ASSIGNMENT AGREEMENT

This Agreement is intended to set forth in writing my responsibility to Development Company ("Devco"). I recognize that Devco is engaged in a continuous program of research, development, and production respecting its business, present and future. As part of my employment with Devco, I have certain obligations relating to inventions that I develop during my employment.

In return for my employment by Devco, I acknowledge and agree that:

1. **Effective Date.** This agreement ("Agreement") shall be effective on _____, 19___, the first day of my employment with Devco.

2. **Confidentiality.** I will maintain in confidence and will not disclose or use, either during or after the term of my employment, any proprietary or confidential information or know-how belonging to Devco ("Confidential Information"), whether or not in written form, except to the extent required to perform duties on behalf of Devco. Confidential Information refers to any information, not generally known in the relevant trade or industry, which was obtained from Devco, or which was learned, discovered, developed, conceived, originated or prepared by me in the scope of my employment. Such Confidential Information includes, but is not limited to, software, technical and business information relating to Devco's inventions or products, research and development, production processes, manufacturing and engineering processes, machines and equipment, finances, customers, marketing, and production and future business plans and any other information which is identified as confidential by Devco. Upon termination of my employment or at the request of my supervisor before termination, I will deliver to Devco all written and tangible material in my possession incorporating the Confidential Information or otherwise relating to Devco's business. These obligations with respect to Confidential Information extend to information belonging to customers and suppliers of Devco who may have disclosed such information to me as the result of my status as an employee of Devco.

3. **Work Products.**

    3.1 Definition of Work Products. As used in this Agreement, the term "Work Product" means any new work of authorship, new or useful art, discovery, contribution, finding or improvement, whether or not patentable, and all related know-how. Work Product includes, but is not limited to, all storylines, characters, computer software, designs, discoveries, formulae, processes, manufacturing techniques, inventions, improvements, and ideas.

3.2 *Disclosure of Work Products and Assignment of Proprietary Rights.*

(a) The "Devco Work Product" is defined as any Work Product that I may solely or jointly conceive, develop or reduce to practice during the period of my employment, (i) that relates, at the time of conception, development, or reduction to practice of the Work Product, to Devco's business or actual or demonstrably anticipated research or development; (ii) that was developed, in whole or in part, on Devco's time or with the use of any of Devco's equipment, supplies, facilities, or trade secret information; or (iii) that resulted from any work I performed for Devco. I will promptly disclose and describe to Devco all Devco Work Product.

(b) (i) I hereby irrevocably assign, convey and otherwise transfer to Devco, and its respective successors and assigns, all rights, title, and interests worldwide in and to the Devco Work Product and all proprietary rights therein, including, without limitation, all copyrights, trademarks, design patents, trade secret rights, moral rights, and all contract and licensing rights, and all claims and causes of action of any kind with respect to any of the foregoing, whether now known or hereafter to become known.

(ii) In the event I have any right in and to the Devco Work Product that cannot be assigned to Devco, I hereby unconditionally and irrevocably waive the enforcement of all such rights, and all claims and causes of action of any kind with respect to any of the foregoing against Devco, its distributors and customers, whether now known or hereafter to become known and agree, at the request and expense of Devco and its respective successors and assigns, to consent to and join in any action to enforce such rights and to procure a waiver of such rights from the holders of such rights.

(iii) In the event I have any rights in and to the Devco Work Product that cannot be assigned to Devco and cannot be waived, I hereby grant to Devco, and its respective successors and assigns, an exclusive, worldwide, royalty-free license during the term of the rights to reproduce, distribute, modify, publicly perform and publicly display, with the right to sublicense and assign such rights in and to the Devco Work Product including, without limitation, the right to use in any way whatsoever the Devco Work Product.

(iv) I retain no rights to use the Devco Work Product and agree not to challenge the validity of the ownership by Devco of the Devco Work Product.

(v) I do not assign or agree to assign any Work Product created by me prior to my employment by Devco.

(c) Unless I specifically state such an exception in Exhibit A, if I use Work Product that I created prior to my employment with Devco during my employment with Devco, I grant an irrevocable, nonexclusive, royalty-free, worldwide license to Devco, with the right to sublicense, to reproduce, modify, distribute, publicly perform and publicly display such works as part of Devco's products.

(d) I recognize that Work Product relating to my activities while working for Devco and conceived or made by me, alone or with others, within one year after termination of my employment may have been conceived in significant part while employed by Devco. Accordingly, I agree that such Work Products shall be presumed to have been conceived during my employment with Devco and are to be assigned to Devco as a Devco Work Product unless and until I have established the contrary. I agree to disclose promptly in writing to Devco all Work Product made or conceived by me for one (1) year after my term of employment, whether or not I believe such Work Product is subject to this Agreement, to permit a determination by Devco as to whether or not the Work Product should be the property of Devco. Any such information will be received in confidence by Devco.

3.3 Nonassignable Work Products. This Agreement does not apply to any Work Product which qualifies fully as a nonassignable invention under the provisions of Section 2870 of the California Labor Code.

4. **Devco's Materials.** Upon termination of my employment with Devco or at any other time upon Devco's request, I will promptly deliver to Devco, without retaining any copies, all documents and other materials furnished to me by Devco or prepared by me for Devco.

5. **Competitive Employment.** During the term of my employment with Devco, I will not engage in any employment, consulting, or other activity in any business competitive with Devco without Devco's written consent.

6. **Non-solicitation.** During the term of my employment with Devco and for a period of two (2) years thereafter, I will not solicit or encourage, or cause others to solicit or encourage, any employees of Devco to terminate their employment with Devco.

7. **Acts to Secure Proprietary Rights.**

    7.1 Further Acts. I agree to perform, during and after my employment, all acts deemed necessary or desirable by Devco to permit and assist it, at its expense, in perfecting and enforcing the full benefits, enjoyment, rights and title throughout the world in the Devco Work Product. Such acts may include, but are not limited to, execution of documents and assistance or cooperation in the registration and enforcement of applicable patents and copyrights or other legal proceedings.

    7.2 Appointment of Attorney-In-Fact. In the event that Devco is unable for any reason whatsoever to secure my signature to any lawful and necessary document required to apply for or execute any patent, copyright or other applications with respect to any Work Product (including improvements, renewals, extensions, continuations, divisions or continuations in part thereof), I hereby irrevocably appoint Devco and its duly authorized officers and agents as my agents and attorneys-in-fact to execute and file any such application and to do all other lawfully permitted acts to further the prosecution and issuance of patents, copyrights or other rights thereon with the same legal force and effect as if executed by me.

8. **No Conflicting Obligations.** My performance of this Agreement and as an employee of Devco does not and will not breach any agreement to keep in confidence proprietary information, knowledge or data acquired by me prior to my employment with Devco. I will not disclose to Devco, or induce Devco to use, any confidential or proprietary information or material belonging to any previous employer or other person or entity. I am not a party to any other agreement which will interfere with my full compliance with this Agreement. I

will not enter into any agreement, whether written or oral, in conflict with the provisions of this Agreement.

9. **Survival.** Notwithstanding the termination of my employment, Section 3.2 and Articles 2, 6, and 7 shall survive such termination. This Agreement does not in any way restrict my right or the right of Devco to terminate my employment at any time, for any reason or for no reason.

10. **Specific Performance.** A breach of any of the promises or agreements contained herein will result in irreparable and continuing damage to Devco for which there will be no adequate remedy at law, and Devco shall be entitled to injunctive relief and/or a decree for specific performance, and such other relief as may be proper (including monetary damages if appropriate).

11. **Waiver.** The waiver by Devco of a breach of any provision of this Agreement by me will not operate or be construed as a waiver of any other or subsequent breach by me.

12. **Severability.** If any part of this Agreement is found invalid or unenforceable, that part will be amended to achieve as nearly as possible the same economic effect as the original provision and the remainder of this Agreement will remain in full force.

13. **Governing Law.** This Agreement will be governed by and construed in accordance with the laws of the United States and the State of California as applied to agreements entered into and to be performed entirely within California between California residents.

14. **Choice of Forum.** The parties hereby submit to the jurisdiction of, and waive any venue objections against, the United States District Court for the Northern District of California, San Jose Branch and the Superior and Municipal Courts of the State of California, Santa Clara County, in any litigation arising out of the Agreement.

15. **Entire Agreement.** This Agreement, including all Exhibits to this Agreement, constitutes the entire agreement between the parties relating to this subject matter and supersedes all prior or simultaneous representations, discussions, negotiations, and agreements, whether written or oral. This Agreement may be amended or modified only with the written consent of both me and Devco. No oral waiver, amendment or modification will be effective under any circumstances whatsoever.

16. **Assignment.** This Agreement may be assigned by Devco. I may not assign or delegate my duties under this Agreement without Devco's prior written approval. This Agreement shall be binding upon my heirs, successors, and permitted assignees.

EMPLOYEE:

_____   _____
Date   Signature

                                  _____
                                  Printed Name

                                  DEVCO:

_____   DEVELOPMENT COMPANY
Date:

                                  By: _____

                                  Title: _____

                                  Address:

                                  _____

                                  _____

                                  _____

LIMITED EXCLUSION NOTIFICATION

THIS IS TO NOTIFY you in accordance with Section 2872 of the California Labor Code that the above Agreement between you and Devco does not require you to assign to Devco, any invention for which no equipment, supplies, facility or trade secret information of Devco was used and which was developed entirely on your own time, and (a) which does not relate (1) to the business of Devco or (2) to Devco's actual or demonstrably anticipated research or development, or (b) which does not result from any work performed by you for Devco. This limited exclusion does not apply to any patent or invention covered by a contract between Devco and the United States or any of its agencies requiring full title to such patent or invention to be in the United States.

I ACKNOWLEDGE RECEIPT of a copy of this notification.

_____

Signature

_____

Printed Name of Employee

_____

Date

WITNESSED BY:

DEVELOPMENT COMPANY

_____

Representative

_____

Date

EXHIBIT A
Prior Work Products

7. Independent Contractor Agreement

This agreement is used when the independent contractor will perform a project for a multimedia company. The agreement assumes that the project is a simple one that does not include detailed milestones and acceptance provisions.

INDEPENDENT CONTRACTOR AGREEMENT

THIS AGREEMENT ("Agreement") is entered into by and between Development Company ("Devco"), a _____ corporation, and the undersigned (the "Contractor").

1. **Engagement of Services.** Contractor agrees to perform services for Devco as follows:

   _____

   _____

   _____

   ("Project"). Devco selected Contractor to perform these services based upon Devco receiving Contractor's personal service and therefore Contractor may not subcontract or otherwise delegate its obligations under this Agreement without Devco's prior written consent. Contractor agrees to perform the services in a professional manner.

2. **Compensation.**

   2.1 *Fees and Approved Expenses.* Devco will pay Contractor the fee set forth in Exhibit A for services rendered by Contractor pursuant to this Agreement. Contractor will not be reimbursed for any expenses incurred in connection with the performance of services under this Agreement, unless those expenses are approved in advance and in writing by Devco.

   2.2 *Timing.* Devco will pay Contractor for services and will reimburse Contractor for previously approved expenses within thirty (30) days of the date of Contractor's invoice.

3. **Independent Contractor Relationship.** Contractor and Devco understand, acknowledge, and agree that Contractor's relationship with Devco will be that of an independent contractor and nothing in this Agreement is intended to or should be construed to create a partnership, joint venture, or employment relationship.

4. **Trade Secrets—Intellectual Property Rights.**

   4.1 *Disclosure.*

   (a) Contractor agrees to disclose promptly in writing to Devco, or any person designated by Devco, all work product, including but not limited to computer programs, processes, know-how and other copyrightable material, that is conceived, developed, made or reduced to practice by Contractor within the scope of the Project.

   (b) Contractor represents that his performance of all of the terms of this Agreement does not and will not breach any agreement to keep in confidence proprietary information, knowledge or data of a third party and Contractor will not disclose to Devco, or induce Devco to use, any confidential or proprietary information belonging to third parties unless such use or disclosure is authorized in writing by such owners.

(c) Contractor represents that any inventions or copyrighted works relating to Devco's actual or anticipated business or research and development which Contractor has conceived, developed, made, or reduced to practice at the time of signing this Agreement, have been disclosed in writing to Devco and attached to this Agreement as Exhibit B. These inventions and copyrighted works are not assigned to Devco. However, if Contractor uses such inventions or copyrighted works in the Project, Contractor grants to Devco a royalty-free, worldwide, perpetual, irrevocable, non-exclusive license, with the right to sublicense, to reproduce, distribute, modify, publicly perform and publicly display such inventions and copyrighted works in Devco's products based on the Project.

4.2 *Confidential Information.* Contractor agrees during the term of this Agreement and thereafter to take all steps reasonably necessary to hold in trust and confidence information which he knows or has reason to know is considered confidential by Devco ("Confidential Information"). Contractor agrees to use the Confidential Information solely to perform the project hereunder. Confidential Information includes, but is not limited to, technical and business information relating to Devco's inventions or products, research and development, manufacturing and engineering processes, and future business plans. Contractor's obligations with respect to the Confidential Information also extend to any third party's proprietary or confidential information disclosed to Contractor in the course of providing services to Devco. This obligation shall not extend to any information which becomes generally known to the public without breach of this Agreement. This obligation shall survive the termination of this Agreement.

4.3 *No Conflict of Interest.* Contractor agrees during the term of this Agreement not to accept work or enter into a contract or accept an obligation, inconsistent or incompatible with Contractor's obligations or the scope of services rendered for Devco under this Agreement.

4.4 *Assignment of Work Product.*

(a) "Work Product" means the storyline, characters, computer software, designs, discoveries, works of authorship, formulae, processes, manufacturing techniques, inventions, improvements and ideas solely or jointly conceived, developed or reduced to practice during the Project. Contractor hereby irrevocably assigns, conveys and otherwise transfers to Devco, and its respective successors and assigns, all rights, title and interests worldwide in and to the Work Product and all proprietary rights therein, including, without limitation, all copyrights, trademarks, design patents, trade secret rights, moral rights, and all contract and licensing rights, and all claims and causes of action of any kind with respect to any of the foregoing, whether now known or hereafter to become known. In the event Contractor has any rights in and to the Work Product that cannot be assigned to Devco, Contractor hereby unconditionally and irrevocably waives the enforcement of all such rights, and all claims and causes of action of any kind with respect to any of the foregoing against Devco, its distributors and customers, whether now known or hereafter to become known and agrees, at the request and expense of Devco and its respective successors and assigns, to consent to and join in any action to enforce such rights and to procure a waiver of such rights from the holders of such rights. In the event Contractor has any rights in and to the Work Product that cannot be assigned to Devco and cannot be waived, Contractor hereby grants to Devco, and its respective successors and assigns, an exclusive, worldwide, royalty-free license during the term of the rights to reproduce, distribute, modify, publicly perform and publicly display, with the right to sublicense and assign such rights in and to the Work Product including, without limitation, the right to use in any way whatsoever the Work Product. Contractor retains no rights to use the Work Product and agrees not to challenge the validity of the ownership by Devco in the Work Product.

(b) Contractor agrees to assist Devco in any reasonable manner to obtain and enforce for Devco's benefit patents, copyrights, and other property rights covering the Work Product in any and all countries. Contractor agrees to execute, when requested, patent, copyright, or similar applications and assignments to Devco, and any other lawful documents deemed necessary by Devco to carry out the purpose of this Agreement. Contractor further agrees that the obligations and undertaking stated in this Section 4.4(b) will continue beyond the termination of Contractor's service to Devco. If called upon to render assistance under this Section 4.4(b), Contractor will be entitled to a fair and reasonable fee in addition to reimbursement of authorized expenses incurred at the prior written request of Devco.

(c) In the event that Devco is unable for any reason whatsoever to secure Contractor's signature to any lawful and necessary document required to apply for or execute any patent, copyright or other applications with respect to any Work Product (including improvements, renewals, extensions, continuations, divisions or continuations in part thereof), Contractor hereby irrevocably designates and appoints Devco and its duly authorized officers and agents as his agents and attorneys-in-fact to act for and in his behalf and instead of Contractor, to execute and file any such application and to do all other lawfully permitted acts to further the prosecution and issuance of patents, copyrights or other rights thereon with the same legal force and effect as if executed by Contractor.

4.5 *Return of Devco's Property.* Contractor acknowledges that Devco's sole and exclusive property includes all documents, such as drawings, manuals, notebooks, reports, sketches, records, computer programs, employee lists, customer lists and the like in his custody or possession, whether delivered to Contractor by Devco or made by Contractor in the performance of services under this Agreement, relating to the business activities of Devco or its customers or suppliers and containing any information or data whatsoever, whether or not Confidential Information. Contractor agrees to deliver promptly all of Devco's property and all copies of Devco's property in Contractor's possession to Devco at any time upon Devco's request.

4.6 *Warranties.* Contractor represents and warrants that:

(a) the Work Product was created solely by him, his full-time employees during the course of their employment, or independent contractors who assigned all right, title and interest in their work to Contractor;

(b) Contractor is the owner of all right, title and interest in the tangible forms of the Work Product and all intellectual property rights protecting them The Work Product and the intellectual property rights protecting them are free and clear of all encumbrances, including, without limitation, security interests, licenses, liens, charges or other restrictions except as set forth in Exhibit C;

(c) Contractor has maintained the Work Product in confidence;

(d) the use, reproduction, distribution, or modification of the Work Product does not and will not violate the rights of any third parties in the Work Product including, but not limited to, trade secrets, trademarks, publicity, privacy, copyrights, and patents;

(e) the Work Product is not in the public domain;

(f) Contractor has full power and authority to make and enter into this Agreement.

4.7 Performance. Contractor represents and warrants that for a period of following acceptance of the Work Product (i) the will be free from defects in workmanship and materials under normal use, and (ii) that the will perform in accordance with the specifications in Exhibit A.

4.8 Indemnification. Contractor agrees to defend, indemnify, and hold harmless Devco, their officers, directors, sublicensees, employees and agents, from and against any claims, actions or demands, including without limitation reasonable legal and accounting fees, alleging or resulting from the breach of the warranties in Section 4.6. Devco shall provide notice to Contractor promptly of any such claim, suit, or proceeding and shall assist Contractor, at Contractor's expense, in defending any such claim, suit or proceeding.

5. **Termination—Noninterference with Business.**

5.1 Termination by Devco. Devco may terminate this Agreement for material breach at any time upon fifteen (15) days prior written notice to Contractor. Devco also may terminate this Agreement immediately in its sole discretion upon Contractor's material breach of Article 4 and/or Section 5.3 of this Agreement and/or upon any acts of gross misconduct by Contractor directly affecting this Agreement or the independent contractor relationship.

5.2 Termination by Contractor. Contractor may terminate this Agreement for material breach at any time upon fifteen (15) days prior written notice to Devco.

5.3 Noninterference with Business. During and for a period of two (2) years immediately following termination of this Agreement by either party, Contractor agrees not to solicit or induce any employee or independent contractor to terminate or breach an employment, contractual or other relationship with Devco.

6. **General Provisions.** This Agreement will be governed by and construed in accordance with the laws of the United States and the State of California as applied to agreements entered into and to be performed entirely within California between California residents. This Agreement, including all Exhibits to this Agreement, constitutes the entire agreement between the parties relating to this subject matter and supersedes all prior or simultaneous representations, discussions, negotiations, and agreements, whether written or oral. No term or provision hereof will be considered waived by either party, and no breach excused by either party, unless such waiver or consent is in writing signed on behalf of the party against whom the waiver is asserted. No consent by either party to, or waiver of, a breach by either party, whether express or implied, will constitute a consent to, waiver of, or excuse of any

other, different, or subsequent breach by either party. Contractor may not assign its rights or obligations arising under this Agreement without Devco's prior written consent. Devco may assign its rights and obligations under this Agreement. This Agreement will be for the benefit of Devco's successors and assigns, and will be binding on Contractor's heirs, legal representatives and permitted assignees. If any dispute arises between the parties with respect to the matters covered by this Agreement which leads to a proceeding to resolve such dispute, the prevailing party in such proceeding shall be entitled to receive its reasonable attorneys' fees, expert witness fees and out-of-pocket costs incurred in connection with such proceeding, in addition to any other relief to which it may be entitled. All notices, requests and other communications required to be given under this Agreement must be in writing, and must be mailed by registered or certified mail, postage prepaid and return receipt requested, or delivered by hand to the party to whom such notice is required or permitted to be given. Any such notice will be considered to have been given when received, or if mailed, five (5) business days after it was mailed, as evidenced by the postmark. The mailing address for notice to either party will be the address shown on the signature page of this Agreement. Either party may change its mailing address by notice as provided by this Section. The following provisions shall survive termination of this Agreement: Article 4 and Section 5.3. This Agreement is effective as of , 19, and will terminate on , 19, unless terminated earlier in accordance with Section 5 above.

"DEVCO":   "CONTRACTOR":

DEVELOPMENT COMPANY

By: _____   By: _____

_____   _____
Typed name   Typed name

_____   _____
Title   Title

Address: Address:

_____   _____

_____   _____

_____   _____

EXHIBIT A
Project and Specifications
EXHIBIT B
Prior Work Product Disclosure
EXHIBIT C
Exceptions

8. Work Made For Hire Agreement (To Developer—Includes Representations)

This agreement is used to give the developer ownership of products which are eligible for treatment as "commissioned works made for hire" (discussed in "The Work Made for Hire Rule," Chapter 4, and in "Copyright Ownership," Chapter 8.) To be effective, the agreement must be signed before the commencement of work on the product.

The agreememt includes a "back-up" assignment to ensure transfer of rights in copyright if the product does not fall within the limited categories of "commissioned works for hire" and to assure that the developer has ownership of the work in in foreign countries. It also includes representations about ownership and other important issues.

WORK FOR HIRE AGREEMENT
(To Developer-Includes Representations)

THIS AGREEMENT ("Agreement") is dated as of _____ by and between _____("Author") and Development Company, _____ with its principal place of business at _____("Devco").

WHEREAS, Devco is a developer of interactive art, literature, and entertainment products; and

WHEREAS, Author will contribute certain material to Devco for the multimedia product _____ ("Work") and the parties intend that Devco be the owner of all rights in Work. The agreement will confirm such understanding.

NOW THEREFORE, the parties agree as follows:

1. The Work is a commissioned "work for hire" which will be owned by Devco. If the Work is determined not to be a "work for hire" or such doctrine is not effective, the Author hereby irrevocably assigns, conveys and otherwise transfers to Devco, and its respective successors, licensees, and assigns, all right, title and interest worldwide in and to the Work and all proprietary rights there-in, including, without limitation, all copyrights, trademarks, design patents, trade secret rights, moral rights, and all contract and licensing rights, and all claims and causes of action of respect to any of the foregoing, whether now known or hereafter to become known. In the event, I have any right in the Work which cannot be assigned, I agree to waive enforcement worldwide of such right against Devco, its distributors, and customers or, if necessary, exclusively because such right, worldwide to Devco with the right to sublicense. These rights are assignable by Devco.

2. Author represents and warrants that: (a)the Work will be created solely by him, his full-time employees during the course of their employment, independent contractors who will assign all right, title and interest in their work to Author;(b) Author will be the owner of all right, title and interest in the tangible forms of the Work and all intellectual property rights protecting them. (c) the Work and the intellectual property rights protecting them will be free and clear of all encumbrances, including, without limitation, security interests, licenses, liens, charges or other restrictions; (d) the use, reproduction, distribution, or modification of the Work will not violate the rights of any third parties in the Work including, but not limited to, trade secrets, publicity, privacy, copyrights and patents; (e) the Work will not be in the public

domain; and (f) Author has full power and authority to make and enter into this Agreement. Author agrees to defend, indemnify and hold harmless Devco, its officers, directors and employees for any claims, suits or proceedings alleging a breach of these warranties.

3. Author agrees that he or she will take all actions and execute any and all documents as may be requested by Devco, at Devco's expense, from time to time to fully vest in Devco all rights, title and interests worldwide in and to the Work.

4. In consideration of the foregoing, Devco agrees to pay to Author the sum of Dollars ($).

DEVCO: AUTHOR:

DEVELOPMENT COMPANY   _____

                                               Printed name

By: _____   By: _____

_____

Printed name

_____

Title

Address: Address:

_____   _____

_____   _____

_____   _____

9. Assignment Agreement (To Developer—Includes Representations)

This agreement is used for an assignment of copyright to the developer. It includes standard representations about ownership and other important issues.

ASSIGNMENT AGREEMENT
(Includes Representations)

THIS AGREEMENT ("Agreement") is dated as of _____ by and between _____ _____ ("Assignor") and Development Company, _____ with its principal place of business at _____ ("Devco").

WHEREAS, Devco is a developer of interactive art, literature, and entertainment products; and

WHEREAS, Assignor has contributed certain material to Devco for the multimedia product _____ ("Work"), and the parties intended that Devco be the owner of all rights in Work. The agreement will confirm such understanding.

NOW THEREFORE, the parties agree as follows:

1. Assignor hereby irrevocably assigns, conveys and otherwise transfers to Devco, and its respective successors, licensees, and assigns, all right, title and interest worldwide in and to the Work and all proprietary rights therein, including, without limitation, all copyrights, trademarks, design patents, trade secret rights, moral rights, and all contract and licensing rights, and all claims and causes of action of respect to any of the foregoing, whether now known or hereafter to become known. In the event, Assignor has any right in the Work which cannot be assigned, Assignor agrees to waive enforcement worldwide of such right against Devco, its distributors, and customers or, if necessary, exclusively license such right worldwide to Devco, with the right to sublicense. These rights are assignable by Devco.

2. Assignor represents and warrants that: (a) the Work was created solely by Assignor, Assignor's full-time employees during the course of their employment, or independent contractors who assigned all right, title and interest in their work to Assignor; (b) Assignor is the owner of all right, title and interest in the tangible forms of the Work and all intellectual property rights protecting them; (c) the Work and the intellectual property rights protecting them are free and clear of all encumbrances, including, without limitation, security interests, licenses, liens, charges or other restrictions; (d) the use, reproduction, distribution, or modification of the Work does not and will not violate the rights of any third parties in the Work including, but not limited to, trade secrets, publicity, privacy, copyrights, and patents; (e) the Work is not in the public domain; and (f) Assignor has full power and authority to make and enter into this Agreement. Assignor agrees to defend, indemnify, and hold harmless Devco, its officers, directors and employees for any claims, suits or proceedings alleging a breach of these warranties.

3. Assignor agrees that he or she will take all actions and execute any and all documents as may be requested by Devco, at Devco's expense, from time to time, to fully vest in Devco all rights, title and interests worldwide in and to the Work.

4. In consideration of the foregoing, Devco agrees to pay to Assignor the sum of _____ Dollars ($_____).

DEVCO:

DEVELOPMENT COMPANY

By: _____

_____
Printed name

_____
Title

Address:

_____

_____

_____

_____

ASSIGNOR:

_____
Printed name

By: _____

Address:

_____

_____

_____

_____

10. Distribution Agreement

This agreement is a bundling agreement used by a multimedia publisher where the OEM intends to manufacture from a golden master provided by the publisher.

At the end of the agreement is a checklist for distribution agreements.

DISTRIBUTION AGREEMENT

This Agreement, effective _____, 19___, is made between _____, a _____ Corporation with its principal place of business at _____ ("Publisher") and Distributor, a _____ corporation with its principal place of business at _____ ("Distributor").

Recitals:

Publisher has expended considerable time, effort, and resources in the development and/or publishing of certain unique, copyrighted and proprietary interactive multimedia products and software, and the documentation and packaging materials related thereto (the "Publisher Products" as defined below);

Distributor desires to act as a distributor of the Publisher Products bundled together with the products of Distributor or of third parties, and represents to Publisher that Distributor has sufficient expertise, resources, and personnel to perform its obligations under this Agreement;

Distributor further desires to manufacture the Publisher Products for purposes of such distribution; and Publisher desires to have Distributor act as a manufacturing distributor of the Publisher Products on the terms and conditions set forth herein.

Therefore, in consideration of the mutual covenants and promises contained herein, the parties hereto agree as follows:

A. **DEFINITIONS**
   1. *"Publisher Products"* shall mean the products identified in Exhibit A attached hereto, together with any accompanying documentation, packaging, or other materials identified on Exhibit A (if any). Publisher, in its sole discretion, reserves the right to add Publisher Products to or delete Publisher Products from Exhibit A on thirty (30) days notice.
   2. *"Bundles"* shall mean the combination of the Publisher Products with hardware and/or software distributed as a unit by Distributor, as described in Exhibit C.
   3. *"Proprietary Rights"* shall mean all rights of Publisher and its licensors in the Publisher Products including, without limitation, copyright, patent, design patent, trademark, trade dress, trade secret, and publicity rights, arising under applicable law and international conventions.
   4. *"Territory"* shall be defined as the world.

B. GRANT OF LICENSES

1. ***Distribution License.*** Publisher grants to Distributor a nontransferable and non-exclusive license during the term of this Agreement to include the Publisher Products in Bundles and to distribute Bundles directly or through distributors and retailers to end-users located in the Territory. In addition to the other terms and conditions of this Agreement, these licenses to distribute are expressly subject to the following conditions:

   a. Distributor's distribution to end-users, whether directly or through distributors and retailers, shall be made only pursuant to the end-user license included with the Publisher Products, and each license of an Publisher Product by Distributor to an end-user will be allowed only in jurisdictions where an enforceable copyright covering the Publisher Products exists; and

   b. Distributor's distribution to any entity other than end-users, including without limitation distribution to retailers or other distributors or sub-distributors, shall be made pursuant to written agreement(s) with Distributor which (i) comply with all of the terms of this Agreement, (ii) are no less protective of Publisher's rights than the terms of this Agreement, and (iii) expressly make Publisher a third party beneficiary.

   c. Distributor shall be entitled to distribute only those Publisher Products manufactured by Distributor.

2. ***Manufacturing License.*** Subject to the terms of this Agreement, Publisher grants to Distributor and Distributor accepts, for the term of this Agreement, the nonexclusive right to manufacture the Publisher Products only in the United States and only for distribution as otherwise provided in this Agreement, subject to the following limitations:

   a. Distributor may manufacture the Publisher Products, provided that such manufacturing is at Distributor's own cost and in accordance with this Agreement and otherwise prudent in protecting Publisher's and its Licensors' Proprietary Rights. Any and all copies of the Publisher Products manufactured by Distributor shall contain security coding in a form acceptable to Publisher. Distributor shall indemnify and pay Publisher for any unauthorized copies of the Publisher Products manufactured by Distributor or at its authorized facilities at the full retail price of such Publisher Products.

   b. Distributor shall manufacture the Publisher Products in accordance with strict security procedures and shall keep detailed manufacturing and distribution records for all units manufactured. Distributor's manufacturing facilities and manufacturing and distribution records shall be open to Publisher's inspection without notice.

   c. Distributor shall include with all copies of the Publisher Products manufactured by Distributor an end-user license in the form provided by Publisher. Changes to the terms of the end-user license shall be subject to approval by Publisher, in its sole discretion.

   d. Distributor shall manufacture the Publisher Products from production masters of the Publisher Products (including without limitation production masters of packaging and related materials) provided by Publisher in accordance with the schedule set forth on Exhibit B. Distributor agrees not to alter the Publisher Products (including without limitation their packaging) without Publisher's prior written consent.

3. **Prohibited Acts.** Neither Distributor nor anyone to whom Distributor distributes the Publisher Products has the right to distribute or sell the Publisher Products except as part of Bundles within the Territory, without the express prior written approval of Publisher. Anyone who unbundles any Publisher Products shipped to Distributor for inclusion in Bundles shall be liable for the full wholesale price of all such unbundled Publisher Products plus all applicable attorneys' fees and costs incurred in investigating and prosecuting an action against the unbundling party. Distributor shall notify those to whom it distributes the Publisher Products in Bundles that unbundling is specifically prohibited, and that anyone who unbundles any Bundled Publisher Products shipped to or through Distributor shall be liable for the full wholesale price of all such unbundled Publisher Products plus all applicable attorneys' fees and costs incurred in investigating and prosecuting an action against the unbundling party.

4. **Limitations.** Title to the Publisher Products and all associated patents, copyrights, trademarks, trade dress, trade secrets and other proprietary rights shall remain with Publisher and its licensors. Except as expressly authorized by Publisher in writing, Distributor will not, and will cause its employees, agents and distributors not to: (i) modify, translate, reverse engineer, decompile, disassemble, create derivative works of or copy the Publisher Products or related documentation; (ii) remove, alter, or cover any copyright or trademark notices or other proprietary rights notices placed or embedded by Publisher on or in the Publisher Products.

5. **Non-Exclusivity.** The licenses granted in this Agreement are non-exclusive. Accordingly, nothing in this Agreement shall be construed as limiting in any manner Publisher's marketing or distribution activities (including without limitation the distribution of Publisher Products upgrades and Publisher Products to end users of Bundles) or Publisher's appointment of other dealers, distributors, value-added resellers, original equipment manufacturers, licensees or agents in the Territory.

6. **Packaging, Advertising and Promotion.**

   a. Packaging. Distributor shall not alter the packaging in which the Publisher Products are provided, including without limitation production masters for manufacturing of packaging.

   b. Promotion and Advertising. Publisher shall have the right to approve any advertising or promotional materials regarding or including the Publisher Products which incorporates any original artwork not provided by Publisher. Any such advertising or promotional materials shall be submitted to Publisher for approval, in its sole discretion, and Publisher shall have seven (7) business days in which to approve or disapprove the advertising or promotional materials. Publisher's failure to approve or disapprove the materials within seven (7) business days shall constitute approval of the materials. Distributor shall not provide any copies of the Publisher Products or other materials to magazines, newspapers or other publications for review purposes.

7. **Reserved Rights.** Except as expressly provided in this Agreement, Publisher does not grant any right to Distributor to (a) use, print, copy, or display (except for promotional purposes) the Publisher Products; (b) assign, sublicense, or otherwise transfer its rights or delegate its obligations under this Agreement or any of the rights, licenses, software,

Publisher Products, or materials to which it applies; or (c) modify, amend, rewrite, translate to another language or otherwise vary the Publisher Products. Publisher shall at all times retain all right, title and interest to the Publisher Products. Publisher reserves the right at any time to terminate Distributor's rights to manufacture or distribute any particular Publisher Product on thirty (30) days notice. Upon the receipt of such notice, Distributor shall cease its manufacturing, marketing, selling, distribution, import and export of such Publisher Product within the time period specified in such notice.

C. COMPENSATION and STATEMENTS

1. *License Fees.* For each copy of the Publisher Products which Distributor manufactures, Distributor shall pay Publisher the license fees set forth in Exhibit B. Payment shall be made by Distributor within thirty (30) days of purchase order date.

2. *Minimum License Fees.* At a minimum, Distributor shall be obligated to pay Publisher the minimum license fees set forth in Exhibit B, in the amounts and on the schedule and terms set forth in Exhibit B.

3. *Purchase Orders.* Distributor shall use its standard form purchase orders to indicate to Publisher the number of copies of the Publisher Products that Distributor will manufacture. Distributor shall be entitled to manufacture no more than the number of units of the Publisher Products shown on the Distributor purchase orders received by Publisher. No other term or condition of the Distributor purchase orders shall have any force or effect. Distributor shall be obligated to pay license fees for all units indicated on the purchase orders. The first three purchase orders, totaling 30,000 units, are attached to this Agreement as Exhibit E. Distributor shall pay license fees for these units based on the dates of the purchase orders.

4. *Content Royalties.* The initial payment and additional license fees shall include all royalties to be paid to third parties ("content royalties"). It will be Publisher's responsibility to ensure that all content royalties are paid when due.

5. *Audit.* Publisher shall have the right, upon reasonable request, to review those records of Distributor necessary to verify the units manufactured and license fees paid. Any such audit will be conducted at Publisher's expense and at such times and in such a manner as to not unreasonably interfere with Distributor's normal operations; provided, however, that if any such audit reveals an error of at least 5% in the payment of royalties, then Distributor shall pay the costs of the audit. If a deficiency is shown by such audit, Distributor shall immediately pay that deficiency. Non-payment of any deficiency within thirty (30) days of the date on which Distributor receives notice of such deficiency shall constitute a material breach of this Agreement.

D. WARRANTY

1. *Warranty.* Publisher warrants to Distributor that, for a period of one (1) year from the shipment to Distributor (or, if earlier, termination of this Agreement), the Publisher Product masters will conform substantially to Publisher's published specifications. If Distributor discovers a material defect in the master for the Publisher Products within the warranty period, Distributor will promptly notify Publisher. Publisher's entire obligation and Distributor's sole remedy will be for Publisher to use its best efforts promptly

to correct any discovered defect and provide Distributor with a corrected version of the master for the Publisher Products.

2. *Limited Warranty on Media.* Publisher warrants the diskettes and/or compact disc on which the masters of the Publisher Products are recorded to be free from defects in materials and workmanship under normal use for a period of ninety (90) days from the date of delivery. Publisher's entire liability and Distributor's exclusive remedy regarding master diskettes and/or compact discs not meeting Publisher's limited warranty and which are returned to Publisher shall be replacement of the master disk or diskette or credit against future orders of Publisher Products, at Publisher's option. Publisher will have no responsibility to replace or credit a diskette/disc damaged by accident, abuse or misapplication.

3. *Disclaimer.* EXCEPT FOR THE ABOVE EXPRESS LIMITED WARRANTIES, Publisher MAKES AND DISTRIBUTOR RECEIVES NO WARRANTIES ON THE Publisher PRODUCTS, EXPRESS, IMPLIED, STATUTORY, OR IN ANY OTHER PROVISION OF THIS AGREEMENT OR COMMUNICATION WITH DISTRIBUTOR, AND Publisher SPECIFICALLY DISCLAIMS ANY IMPLIED WARRANTIES OF MERCHANTABILITY OR FITNESS FOR A PARTICULAR PURPOSE. Publisher DOES NOT WARRANT THAT THE OPERATION OF THE Publisher PRODUCTS WILL BE UNINTERRUPTED OR ERROR FREE.

E. TRADEMARKS

1. *Use.* During the term of this Agreement, Distributor shall have the right to indicate to the public that it is an authorized distributor of the Publisher Products and to advertise (within the Territory and solely in connection with Bundles) the Publisher Products under the trademarks, marks, and trade names that Publisher and its licensors may adopt from time to time for the Publisher Products ("Trademarks"). Distributor will not, and will ensure that its distributors and dealers will not, alter or remove any Trademark, or affix, without the prior written permission of Publisher, any other trademarks, marks or other logos on the Publisher Products. Nothing herein shall grant to Distributor any right, title or interest in the Trademarks. At no time during or after the term of this Agreement shall Distributor challenge or assist others to challenge the Trademarks or the registration thereof or attempt to register any trademarks, marks or trade names confusingly similar to those of Publisher and its licensors for the Publisher Products.

2. *Approval.* All representations of the Publisher Trademarks that Distributor intends to use shall first be submitted to Publisher for approval (which shall not be unreasonably withheld) of design, color, and other details relating to the Trademarks.

F. INTELLECTUAL PROPERTY INDEMNITY

1. Publisher will defend at its expense any action brought against Distributor to the extent that it is based on a claim that the Publisher Products or any part thereof, when used within the scope of this Agreement, infringes a United States copyright or a United States patent issued and known to Publisher as of the date of this Agreement, and Publisher will pay any settlements and any costs, damages and attorneys' fees finally awarded against Distributor in such action which are attributable to such claim; provided, the foregoing obligation shall be subject to Distributor notifying Publisher promptly in writ-

ing of the claim, giving Publisher the exclusive control of the defense and settlement thereof, and providing all reasonable assistance in connection therewith. Publisher shall have no liability for any claim of infringement arising out of (i) the use of other than a current unaltered release of the Publisher Products or (ii) the use or combination of the Publisher Products with non-Publisher programs, data or equipment if such infringement was caused by such use or combination, and (iii) Publisher shall have the right, upon either the occurrence of or the likelihood (in the opinion of Publisher) of the occurrence of a finding of infringement to: (a) procure for Distributor the right to continue distributing the Publisher Products or (b) replace the relevant portions of the Publisher Products with other equivalent, non-infringing portions. If Publisher is unable to accomplish either (iii)(a) or (b) above, then at Publisher's option, Publisher shall remove the Publisher Product in issue and refund to Distributor the amount paid to Publisher under this Agreement relating to that Publisher Product. THE FOREGOING IS IN LIEU OF ANY WARRANTIES OF NONINFRINGEMENT, WHICH ARE HEREBY DISCLAIMED, AND SETS FORTH Publisher'S ENTIRE LIABILITY FOR ANY INFRINGEMENT BY THE Publisher PRODUCTS OR ANY PART THEREOF.

G. TERMINATION

1. This Agreement shall terminate automatically without notice, one year from the effective date first set forth above, unless the parties have mutually agreed in writing to renew it for an additional term.

2. Publisher may terminate this Agreement for any reason or no reason on thirty (30) days' written notice. Until Distributor has fulfilled its minimum purchase commitment for the term of this Agreement as set forth in Section C above, Distributor shall be entitled to terminate this Agreement only upon Publisher's breach of a material provision of this Agreement, which breach has not been cured within thirty (30) days of Distributor giving written notice of such breach. After Distributor has satisfied its minimum purchase commitment for the term of this Agreement, Distributor may terminate this Agreement for any reason or no reason on thirty (30) days' notice.

3. This Agreement may be terminated automatically, without notice, (i) upon the institution by or against Distributor of insolvency, receivership or bankruptcy proceedings or any other proceedings for the settlement of Distributor's debts, (ii) upon Distributor's making an assignment for the benefit of creditors, or (iii) upon Distributor's dissolution.

4. ***Effect of Termination.*** Upon the termination of this Agreement, the rights and licenses granted to Distributor pursuant to this Agreement (including without limitation the right to manufacture and the right to distribute the Publisher Products through distributors) will automatically cease, provided that all existing sublicenses to end users will continue for the duration of such sublicense. All payments owing from Distributor to Publisher shall become immediately due and payable upon termination. All Publisher trademarks, marks, trade names, patents, copyrights, designs, drawings, formulae or other data, photographs, samples, literature, and sales aids of every kind shall remain the property of Publisher. Within thirty (30) days after the termination of this Agreement, Distributor shall prepare all such items in its possession for shipment, as Publisher may direct, at Publisher's expense. Distributor shall not make or retain any copies of any

confidential items or information which may have been entrusted to it. Effective upon the termination of this Agreement, Distributor shall cease to use the Trademarks.

5. **Sell-Off Period.** Notwithstanding the provisions of section G.4 above, if termination occurs because the term set forth in section G.1 above has expired, and not because of any breach of material provisions of this Agreement by Distributor or any other reason, Distributor shall be entitled to sell-off remaining Publisher Products manufactured in the ordinary course of business and currently in Distributor's inventory as of the date of termination as part of Bundles according to the terms of this Agreement for a period of thirty (30) days, provided that Distributor has paid any additional license fees owed for the manufacture of such Publisher Products. At the end of this sell-off period, Distributor shall, at Publisher's sole option, destroy all remaining copies of the Publisher Products in its inventory or return such copies to Publisher for a refund of license fees paid or payment of manufacturing costs (as may be applicable) for the copies returned in saleable condition. If termination occurs because of a breach of any material provision of this Agreement, or for any other reason other than expiration of the term of the license set forth in section G.1 above (including termination by Publisher at its option under section G.2 above), then all of Distributor's rights under this Agreement shall immediately terminate as provided in section G.4, and Distributor shall have no right to sell off remaining Publisher Products in its inventory, which shall, at Publisher's sole option, be destroyed or returned to Publisher for a refund of license fees paid or payment of manufacturing costs (as may be applicable) for the copies returned in saleable condition.

6. **Survival Provisions.** If this Agreement is terminated for any reason, those provisions which by their nature would survive such termination will survive termination. Termination shall not effect any other rights which either party may have at law or in equity.

H. CUSTOMER SUPPORT

1. Publisher will be responsible for providing reasonable and customary customer and technical support for the Publisher Products.

I. LIMITATION OF LIABILITY

1. IN NO EVENT WILL Publisher BE LIABLE FOR COSTS OF PROCUREMENT OF SUBSTITUTE PRODUCTS OR SERVICES, LOST PROFITS, OR ANY SPECIAL, INDIRECT, CONSEQUENTIAL, OR INCIDENTAL DAMAGES, HOWEVER CAUSED AND ON ANY THEORY OF LIABILITY, ARISING IN ANY WAY OUT OF THIS AGREEMENT OR THE TERMINATION THEREOF, WHETHER OR NOT Publisher HAS BEEN ADVISED OF THE POSSIBILITY OF SUCH DAMAGE, AND NOTWITHSTANDING ANY FAILURE OF ESSENTIAL PURPOSE OF ANY LIMITED REMEDY PROVIDED IN THIS AGREEMENT.

J. INDEMNIFICATION OF Publisher

1. Except for the warranty and infringement claims based on the Publisher Products discussed above, Distributor agrees to indemnify and hold Publisher and its licensors harmless against any cost, loss, liability, or expense (including attorneys' fees) arising out of third party claims against Publisher as a result of Distributor's or its distributors' or retailers' promotion or distribution of the Publisher Products or Bundles, including, without limitation, providing unauthorized representations or warranties to its customers regard-

ing the Publisher Products or breaching any term, representation or warranty of this Agreement.

K. GENERAL TERMS

1. **Nonassignability and Binding Effect.** Distributor agrees that its rights and obligations under this Agreement may not be transferred or assigned directly or indirectly without the prior written consent of Publisher. Publisher may assign its rights and obligations under this Agreement without Distributor's consent. Subject to the foregoing, this Agreement shall be binding upon and inure to the benefit of the parties hereto, their successors and assigns.

2. **Notices.** Notices under this Agreement shall be sufficient only if personally delivered, delivered by a major commercial rapid delivery courier service, delivered by facsimile transmission confirmed by first class mail, or mailed by certified or registered mail, return receipt requested, to a party at its address first set forth above or as amended by notice pursuant to this subsection. If not received sooner, notice by any of these methods shall be deemed to occur seven (7) days after deposit.

3. **Import and Export Controls.** Distributor will comply with all export laws and restrictions and regulations of the Department of Commerce or other United States or foreign agency or authority, and will not export, or allow the export or reexport of any Publisher Products in violation of any such restrictions, laws or regulations.

4. **Governing Law and Legal Actions.** This Agreement shall be governed by and construed under the laws of the State of California without regard to choice of laws principles. The parties consent to the jurisdiction of the state and federal courts located in San Francisco, California, and agree that process may be served in the manner provided herein for giving of notices or otherwise as allowed by law.

5. **Partial Invalidity.** If any provision of this Agreement is held to be invalid, then the remaining provisions shall nevertheless remain in full force and effect, and the invalid or unenforceable provision shall be replaced by a term or provision that is valid and enforceable and that comes closest to expressing the intention of such invalid or unenforceable term or provision.

6. **No Agency.** The parties hereto are independent contractors. Nothing contained herein or done in pursuance of this Agreement shall constitute either party the agent of the other party for any purpose or in any sense whatsoever, or constitute the parties as partners or joint venturers.

7. **No Waiver.** No waiver of any term or condition of this Agreement shall be valid or binding on either party unless the same shall have been mutually assented to in writing by both parties. The failure of either party to enforce at any time any of the provisions of this Agreement, or the failure to require at any time performance by the other party of any of the provisions of this Agreement, shall in no way be construed to be a present or future waiver of such provisions, nor in any way effect the ability of either party to enforce each and every such provision thereafter.

8. **Force Majeure.** Nonperformance by either party shall be excused to the extent that performance is rendered impossible by strike, fire, flood, earthquake, or governmental

acts, orders or restrictions; provided that any such nonperformance shall be cause for termination of this Agreement by the other party if the nonperformance continues for more than sixty (60) days.

9. **Attorneys' Fees.** The prevailing party in any legal action brought by one party against the other and arising out of this Agreement shall be entitled, in addition to any other rights and remedies it may have, to reimbursement for its expenses, including costs and reasonable attorneys' fees.

10. **Entire Agreement.** This Agreement sets forth the entire agreement and understanding of the parties relating to the subject matter herein and merges all prior discussions between them. No modification of or amendment to this Agreement, nor any waiver of any rights under this Agreement, shall be effective unless in writing signed by the parties.

11. **Counterparts.** This Agreement may be executed in two or more counterparts and all counterparts so executed shall for all purposes constitute one agreement, binding on all parties hereto.

PUBLISHER

By: _____

DISTRIBUTOR

By _____

Print Name: _____

Title: _____

EXHIBIT A
Publisher Products

(with documentation, packaging, and other materials, if any, as identified herein)

Publisher reserves the right to add Publisher Products to or delete Publisher Products from this Exhibit on thirty (30) days' notice.

EXHIBIT B
Licensed Manufacturing Quantities Schedule

Publisher shall deliver the Production Masters of the Publisher Products as follows:

Publisher Product

Delivery Date for Production Masters On or Before

Subject to the terms and conditions of the Agreement and provided that Distributor attaches purchase orders to this Agreement in Exhibit E for the units set forth below, Distributor shall be entitled to manufacture the Publisher Products as follows:

Publisher Product

Quantity Authorized for Manufacture

License Fee Per Copy Manufactured

Minimum manufacturing commitments for subsequent months shall be as follows:

Month

Products available for Manufacturing

Quantity of Each Product

Total Minimum License Fees to be Paid

EXHIBIT C
Approved Bundles

EXHIBIT D
Territory

EXHIBIT E
Purchase Orders

CHECKLIST FOR DISTRIBUTION AGREEMENTS

This checklist covers all types of distribution agreements. However, a particular distribution agreement may not include each provision. Some of the provisions are alternatives and cannot all be included in a particular agreement. We have included cross-references to the accompanying distribution agreement.

I. Define what is being distributed. The definition should be as specific as possible and may be included in an exhibit.
   A. Definition of product (Section A.1)
      1. Material included
      2. Appearance of graphic user interface
      3. Run time version of software
      4. Performance specifications
      5. Hardware or operating software platforms
   B. Definition of additional materials (Section A.1)
      1. Customer documentation
      2. Advertising "trailers" and/or package design

II. Scope of Distribution Rights.
   A. Ownership, unusual except in entertainment industry (see assignment)
   B. Exclusive license
      1. Territory
         a. End users in territory
         b. Distributors, but can they only sell to end users in the territory
         c. Deal with "cross" territory sales, either due to multi-national users or other orders
      2. Hardware (IBM-compatible, Mac, Sun)
      3. Operating system (be careful of computers which run multiple operating systems or which have "emulation" programs to permit them to run programs for other operating systems)
      4. Distribution channel (retail, bookstore, direct)
      5. Media (such as CD-ROM, CD-I, diskette)
      6. Language
      7. Field of Use
      8. Anti-trust concerns
      9. House accounts (reserved customers)
   C. Non-exclusive license (Section B.1)
      1. Territory
         a. End users in territory
         b. Distributors, but can they only sell to end users in the territory
         c. Deal with "cross" territory sales, either due to multi-national users or other orders
      2. Hardware (IBM-compatible, Mac, Sun)
      3. Operating system (be careful of computers which run multiple operating systems or which have "emulation" programs to permit them to run programs for other operating systems)
      4. Distribution channel (retail, bookstore, direct)

     5. Media (such as CD-ROM, CD-I, diskette)

     6. Language

     7. Field of Use

     8. House accounts (reserved customers)

  D. Scope of rights (Section B.1/B.2)

     1. Distribution

     2. Reproduction and distribution

     3. "Localization" (such as translation)

  E. Advertising (Section B.6)

     1. Right to use developer name, image, likeness and biography

     2. Use of developer trademark (mandatory or voluntary)

III. Payment

  A. Purchase for fixed price (Section C)

  B. Royalty

     1. Fixed royalty per unit

     2. Gross receipts (occasionally includes some deductions of "costs" such as taxes, shipping and returns)

     3. Net receipts

     4. Royalty due

       a. Upon shipment

       b. Upon receipt of payment

       c. Frequency

     5. Advances

       a. Refundable/non-refundable

       b. Recoupable against future royalties and rate of crediting (i.e. 100% which is "dollar for dollar")

       c. Cross-recoupment (recoupment against more than one product)

       d. Minimums

     6. Other Provisions

       a. Reports with payment

       b. Record keeping

         1. What records

         2. How long need they be retained

       c. Audit rights

         1. Who can audit the records

         2. How often can the audits be performed

         3. Who pays if an underpayment is found

  C. Right to return unsold inventory (Section G.5)

  D. Liability for sales or use taxes

IV. Scope of Obligations

  A. For "reproducting distributors", need to identify the "tangible" materials which will be delivered and the format (Section B.2/G.3)

     1. Golden Master

     2. Customer documentation

        3. Advertising material

        4. Trademark policy

    B. Distribution only: order procedure

        1. Lead time for order

        2. Procedure for acceptance of order

          a. Written confirmation

          b. Default rule

        3. Remedy for cancellation

    C. Acceptance (Section G.2)

        1. Standards

          1. Conformance with specifications

          2. Completion of certain tests

        2. Person or entity which decides

        3. Form of Notice

          1. Written notice

          2. "Default" (i.e. failure to give noticeafter certain period is deemed approval)

    D. Future rights and obligations (Section D/H)

        1. Right of first refusal/negotiation for porting to other languages or   platforms

        2. Right of first refusal/negotiation for sequels

        3. Error correction

        4. Maintenance of underlying software

    F. Confidentiality

        1. Define "confidential information"

          a. Marked information

          b. Know or reason to know

          c. Specified information, such as business plans or product design

        2. Disclosure by both parties or only one

        3. Limits on use to purposes of agreement

        4. Period during which information must be maintained in confidence

        5. Limits

          a. Enters public domain

          b. Written permission from disclosing party

          c. Court or administrative proceedings

V. Warranties

    A. No warranties (sometimes called "AS-IS" or quitclaim; it is rather rare)

    B. Ownership

    C. No conflicting transfers

    D. No liens or other encumbrances

    E. No infringement of third party rights (including patent, copyright, trade secret, trademark, publicity and privacy) (Section F)

    F. Performance (Section D)

        1. Specification

        2. Free of defects in materials and workmanship

        3. Development work by professionals

        4. No viruses, time-bombs or other similar devices

        5. Disclaimer of "implied warranties"

     G. Special trademark issues (most important for "reproducing distributors")

  (Section E)

        1. Continued use

        2. No uncontrolled licensing

        3. No abandonment

        4. No registration by distributor

    H. Term of performance warranties (Section D.1)

    I. Maintenance (Section H)

        1. Developer supplies, with direct relationship to customer

        2. Distributor provides help desk, but relies on developer

        3. Distributor provides maintenance

    J. Limitation of remedies (Section D.1)

        1. Repair

        2. Replace

        3. Terminate

VI. Indemnity

    A. Scope (Section F)

        1. Defend-pay for the defense

        2. Indemnify-pay damages

        3. Hold harmless-pay for other expenses

    B. Terms (Section F)

        1. Notice

        2. Co-operation

        3. Payment of expenses

    C. Limits (Section F)

        1. Territory

        2. Combinations with other materials

        3. No settlement without permission

          4. Remedies

          a. Replace

          b. License

          c. Terminate

        5. Amount

VII. Limitations

    A. Separate limits on amount for specific liabilities (for example, performance or indemnity for intellectual property infringement)

    B. Disclaimer of consequential damages (Section I)

VIII. Remedies

    A. Failure of performance (Section D.1/D.2)

        1. Suspend payment/withhold royalty

        2. Suspend performance

        3. Terminate agreement

       4. Sue for monetary damages only

       5. Injunctive relief (order by a court to do or cease doing something)

   B. Procedure (Section G)

       1. Notice

       2. Right to cure

   C. Termination for convenience (Section G.2)

   D. Effect of Termination (Section G.5)

       1. Right to sell off

       2. Limited right to order new products after of termination

   E. Survival of Obligations after Termination (Section G.6)

       1. Warranties

       2. Indemnity

       3. Confidentiality

       4. Payments

IX. Other Issues

   A. Governing law (Section K.4)

       1. Substantive

       2. Procedural

   B. Dispute Resolution

       1. Mediation

       2. Court litigation

       3. Arbitration

          a. Rules

          b. Governing authority (American Arbitration Association, International Chamber of Commerce)

          c. Number of arbitrators

          d. Limitation on authority to grant certain damages

   C. Assignment (Section K.1)

       1. No assignment

       2. Prohibited assignees

       3. Permitted assignees (merger, sale of assets)

11. Web Site Development and Maintenance Agreement

This Web site development and maintenance agreement is used to have a Web site developed and maintained on the Internet. It provides that the access to the Internet will be provided by a separate Internet service provider who is not party to this agreement.

WEB SITE DEVELOPMENT AND MAINTENANCE AGREEMENT

This Agreement is made as of _____, 199__ (the "Effective Date") by and between _____, a _____ corporation with offices at _____("Corporation") and _____, Inc., a _____ corporation with offices at _____ ("Developer").

RECITALS

A. Corporation wishes to have Developer create a Web site and maintain such Web site for Corporation on the Internet. Corporation shall employ a separate entity to provide access to the Internet.

B. Corporation wishes to retain Developer to develop the Web site.

NOW, THEREFORE, in consideration of the premises and mutual covenants and agreements set forth herein, Corporation and Developer agree as follows:

Section 1
DEFINITIONS

1.1 ***Beta Version*** means a working version of the Web site recorded in executable form on the specified medium with any necessary supporting software and data, which has been fully tested by Developer prior to delivery and which Developer believes in good faith to be bug free and to fully implement all functions called for in the Specifications.

1.2 ***Corporation Content*** means the material provided by Corporation to be incorporated into the Web site.

1.3 ***Development Schedule*** shall be as set forth in Schedule "B" to this Agreement which lists the deliverable items contracted for ("Deliverables") and the deadlines for their delivery. "Payment Schedule" shall be as also set forth in Schedule "B".

1.4 ***Developer Tools*** means the software tools of general application, whether owned or licensed to Developer, which are used to develop the Web site.

1.5 ***Documentation*** means the documentation for the software and other material which implement the Web site.

1.6 ***Enhancements*** means any improvements to the Web site to implement new features or add new material Enhancements shall include modifications to the Web site Content to make the Web site operate on a Server System of a new ISP.

1.7 ***Error*** means any failure of the Web site (i) to meet the Specifications and/or (ii) to operate with the Server System.

1.8 *Final Version* means a non-copy protected and unencrypted disk master of the final version of the Web site, recorded in executable form on the specified medium with any necessary supporting software and data, as to which all development work hereunder, and corrections to the Beta Version, have been completed and which meets the Specifications.

1.9 *ISP* means an Internet Service Provider which maintains the Web site on the World Wide Web portion of the Internet. The ISP may change from time to time.

1.10 *Specifications* for the Web site shall be as set forth in Schedule "A" to this Agreement.

1.11 *Source Materials* means (i) all documentation, notes, development aids, technical documentation and other materials provided to Developer by Corporation for use in developing the Web site, and (ii) the source code, documentation, notes and other materials which are produced or created by Developer during the development of the Web site, in such internally documented form as is actually used by Developer for development and maintenance of the Web site.

1.12 *Server System* means the hardware and software systemowned or licensed by the ISP.

1.13 *Web site Content* shall mean (i) the graphic user interface, text, images, music and other material of the Web site developed by Developer under this Agreement which is visible to World Wide Web browsers and (ii) software (including cgi scripts and perl scripts) developed by Developer under this Agreement to implement the Web site. Web site Content shall not include the Developer Tools.

1.14 *Web site* means the site to be developed for Corporation on the graphic portion of the Internet known as the World Wide Web which is described in the Specifications at the following address:_____.

Section 2
DEVELOPMENT AND DELIVERY OF DELIVERABLES

2.1 *Development; Progress Reports.* Developer shall use commercially reasonable efforts, to develop each Deliverable in accordance with the Specifications. Developer shall first prepare a design for the Web site. This design shall include drawings of the user interface, a schematic of how to navigate the Web site, a list of hyperlinks and other components. All development work will be performed by Developer or its employees at Developer's offices or by approved independent contractors who have executed confidentiality and work-for-hire/assignment agreements which are acceptable to Corporation. Developer agrees that no development work shall be performed by independent contractors without the express written approval of Corporation. Each week following execution of this Agreement during which any development and/or testing hereunder remains uncompleted, and whenever else Corporation shall reasonably request, Developer shall contact, or meet with Corporation's representative, and report all tasks completed and problems encountered relating to development and testing of the Web site. During such discussion or meeting, Developer shall advise Corporation in detail of any recommended changes with respect to remaining phases of development in view of Developer's experience with the completed development. In addition, Developer shall contact Corporation's representative promptly by telephone upon discovery of any event or problem that will materially delay development work, and thereafter, if requested, promptly confirm such report in writing.

2.2 *Delivery.* Developer shall deliver all Deliverables for the Program within the times specified in the Development Schedule and in accordance with the Specifications. All Deliverables shall comply with the Submission Guidelines set forth in Schedule "A".

2.3 *Manner of Delivery.* Developer agrees to comply with all reasonable requests of Corporation as to the manner of delivery of all Deliverables, which may include delivery by electronic means.

2.4 *Delivery of Source Materials.* Upon request by Corporation, but in no event later than the delivery of the Final Version, Developer shall deliver to Corporation all Source Materials.

Section 3
TESTING AND ACCEPTANCE; EFFECT OF REJECTION

3.1 *Testing and Acceptance Procedure.* All Deliverables shall be thoroughly tested by Developer and all necessary corrections as a result of such testing shall be made, prior to delivery to Corporation. Upon receipt of a Deliverable, Corporation will, in its sole discretion either: i) accept the Deliverable and make the milestone payment set forth in Schedule "B"; or, ii) provide Developer with written notice of the aspects in which the Deliverable contains Errors and request that Developer correct said Deliverable.

3.2 *Additional Quality Assurance.* If Corporation requests that Developer correct the Deliverable, Developer shall within five (5) calendar days of such notice, or such longer period as Corporation may allow, submit at no additional charge a revised Deliverable in which such Errors have been corrected. Upon receipt of the corrected Deliverable Corporation may, in its sole discretion: i) accept the corrected Deliverable and make the milestone payment set forth in Schedule "B"; or, ii) request that Developer make further corrections to the Deliverable and repeat the correction and review procedure set forth in this Paragraph **3.2**. In the event Corporation determines, in its sole discretion, that the Deliverable is still not acceptable after three attempts at correction by Developer, Corporation may terminate this Agreement.

Section 4
OTHER OBLIGATIONS OF DEVELOPER

4.1 *Web site Quality.* Developer agrees that the Web site will be of high quality and will be free of defects in material and workmanship in all material respects. The Web site will conform in all respects to the functional and other descriptions contained in the Specifications. For a period of one year after the date of acceptance of the Final Version by Corporation, Developer agrees to fix at its own expense any Errors ("Warranty Period"). DEVELOPER DISCLAIMS ALL IMPLIED WARRANTIES, INCLUDING WITHOUT LIMITATION, THE WARRANTIES OF MERCHANTABILITY AND FITNESS FOR A PARTICULAR PURPOSE.

4.2 Web site Maintenance. Developer also agrees to provide Corporation with reasonable technical support and assistance to maintain and update the Web site on the World Wide Web during the Warranty Period at no cost to Corporation. Such assistance shall not exceed _ hours per calendar month. After the expiration of the Warranty Period, Developer agrees to provide Corporation with reasonable technical support and assistance to maintain and update the Web site on the World Wide Web for $___ annual fee for five years after the last day of the Warranty Period ("Maintenance Period"). Such maintenance shall include correcting any Errors or any failure of the Web site to conform to the Specifications. Maintenance shall not include the development of Enhancements at the time of the notice.

4.3 Enhancements. During the Maintenance Period, if Developer wishes to modify the Web site, it may request that Developer provide a bid to provide such Enhancements. Developer shall provide Corporation a first priority on its resources to create the Enhancements over any other third party with the exception of obligations under contracts with third parties existing on the date of the notice. Such services shall be provided on a time and materials basis at the most favored price under which Developer provides such services to third parties.

Section 5
PROPRIETARY RIGHTS

5.1 Corporation's Ownership Rights. Developer acknowledges and agrees that the Web site Content and Documentation, including but not limited to images, graphic user interface, source and object code, and any documentation and notes associated with the Web site are and shall be the property of Corporation. Title to all property rights including but not limited to copyrights, trademarks, patents and trade secrets in the Web site Content and Documentation is with, and shall remain with, Corporation.

5.2 Assignment of Rights. Developer agrees to transfer and assign, and hereby transfers and assigns to Corporation its entire right, title and interest worldwide, if any, including without limitation all copyright ownership therein, no matter when acquired, in the Web site Content and Documentation. Developer agrees to cooperate with Corporation in perfecting any such assignment of rights, including without limitation by executing and delivering such documents as Corporation may request. During and after the term of this contract, Developer will assist Corporation in every reasonable way, at Corporation's expense, to establish original ownership of all such rights on the part of Corporation. Developer hereby waives any and all claims that Developer may now or hereafter have in any jurisdiction to so-called "moral rights" with respect to the results of Developer's work and services hereunder.

5.3 License to Web site Content. Corporation grants to Developer a non-exclusive, worldwide license to reproduce and modify the Corporation Content to develop and maintain the Web site.

5.4 Internet Access. Corporation shall be responsible for obtaining access to the Internet through an ISP. Developer shall not be responsible for such access and shall not be considered a party to the agreement between ISP and Corporation. Although the Web site will be hosted by the ISP, the ISP will not be a party to this Agreement nor will it be a third party beneficiary of this Agreement.

*5.5 **Liability for Corporation Content.*** Developer shall not be liable for the modification, display or other use of the Corporation Content.

Section 6
PAYMENT

*6.1 **Payment Schedule.***The development fees set forth in Schedule "B" shall be paid as provided in such Schedule.

*6.2 **Maintenance Fees.*** Maintenance fees shall be due thirty (30) days prior to the commencement date of each year of the Maintenance Period.

*6.3 **Taxes.*** Developer shall be responsible for the payment of all sales, use and similar taxes.

Section 7
CONFIDENTIALITY

*7.1 **Confidential Information.*** The terms of this Agreement, the Source Materials and technical and marketing plans or other sensitive business information, including all materials containing said information, which are supplied by the Corporation to Developer or developed by Developer in the course of developing the Web site is the confidential information ("Confidential Information") of Corporation.

*7.2 **Restrictions on Use.*** Developer agrees that except as authorized in writing by Corporation: (i) Developer will preserve and protect the confidentiality of all Confidential Information; (ii) Developer will not disclose to any third party, the existence, source, content or substance of the Confidential Information or make copies of Confidential Information; (iii) Developer will not deliver Confidential Information to any third party, or permit the Confidential Information to be removed from Developer's premises; (iv) Developer will not use Confidential Information in any way other than to develop the Web site as provided in this Agreement; (v) Developer will not disclose, use or copy any third party information or materials received in confidence by Developer for purposes of work performed under this Agreement; and (vi) Developer shall require that each of its employees who work on or have access to the materials which are the subject of this Agreement sign a suitable confidentiality and work-for-hire/assignment agreement and be advised of the confidentiality and other applicable provisions of this Agreement.

*7.3 **Limitations.*** Information shall not be considered to be Confidential Information if Developer can demonstrate that it (i) is already or otherwise becomes publicly known through no act of Developer; (ii) is lawfully received from third parties subject to no restriction of confidentiality; (iii) can be shown by Developer to have been independently developed by it without use of the Confidential Information; or (iv) is authorized in writing by Corporation to be disclosed, copied or used.

*7.4 **Return of Source Materials.*** Upon Corporation's acceptance of the Final Version, or upon Corporation's earlier request, Developer shall provide Corporation with all copies and originals of the Web site Content, Corporation Content and Source Materials, as well as any other materials provided to Developer, or created by Developer under this Agreement. Not later than seven (7) days after the termination of this Agreement for any reason, or if sooner requested by Corporation, Developer will return to Corporation all originals and copies of the Confidential Information, Web site Content, Corporation Content and Source Materials, as well as any other materials provided to Developer, or created by Developer under this Agreement except that Developer may retain one copy of the Web site Content and Source Materials, which will remain the Confidential Information of Corporation, for the sole purpose of assisting Developer in maintaining the Web site. Developer shall return said copy to Corporation promptly upon request by Corporation.

Section 8
WARRANTIES, COVENANTS AND INDEMNIFICATION

8.1 Warranties and Covenants of Developer. Developer represents, warrants and covenants to Corporation the following:

(a) Developer has the full power to enter into this Agreement and perform the services provided for herein, and that such ability is not limited or restricted by any agreements or understandings between Developer and other persons or companies;

(b) Any information or materials developed for, or any advice provided to Corporation, shall not rely or in any way be based upon confidential or proprietary information or trade secrets obtained or derived by Developer from sources other than Corporation unless Developer has received specific authorization in writing to use such proprietary information or trade secrets;

(c) Except to the extent based on the Corporation Content, the Web site Content and Documentation do not infringe upon or misappropriate, any copyright, patent right, right of publicity or privacy (including but not limited to defamation) trade secret or other proprietary rights of any third party.

(d) Its performance of this Agreement will not conflict with any other contract to which Developer is bound, and while developing the Web site, Developer will not engage in any such consulting services or enter into any agreement in conflict with this Agreement.

8.3 Developer's Indemnity. Developer agrees to indemnify, hold harmless and defend Corporation and its directors, officers, its employees and agents from and against all claims, defense costs (including reasonable attorneys' fees), judgments and other expenses arising out of or on account of such claims, including without limitation claims of:

(a) alleged infringement or violation of any trademark, copyright, trade secret, right of publicity or privacy (including but not limited to defamation), patent or other proprietary right with respect to the Web site Content or Documentation to the extent Developer has modified or added to the materials provided by Corporation;

(b) any use of confidential or proprietary information or trade secrets Developer has obtained from sources other than Corporation;

(c) Any negligent act, omission, or willful misconduct of Developer in the performance of this Agreement; and

(d) the breach of any covenant or warranty set forth in Section 8.1 above.

8.4 ***Conditions to Indemnity.*** Developer's obligation to indemnify is conditioned on Corporation's notifying Developer promptly of any claim as to which indemnification will be sought and providing Developer reasonable cooperation in the defense and settlement thereof.

8.5 ***Corporation's Indemnification.*** Corporation agrees to indemnify, hold harmless and defend Developer and its directors, officers, its employees and agents from and against all claims, defense costs (including reasonable attorneys' fees), judgments and other expenses arising out of the breach of the following covenants and warranties:

(a) Corporation possesses full power and authority to enter into this Agreement and to fulfill its obligations hereunder.

(b) The performance of the terms of this Agreement and of Corporation's obligations hereunder shall not breach any separate agreement by which Corporation is bound.

(c) The Corporation Content does not infringe or violate any trademark, copyright, trade secret, right of publicity or privacy (including but not limited to defamation), patent or other proprietary right.

8.6 ***Conditions to Indemnity.*** Corporation's obligation to indemnify is conditioned on Developer's notifying Corporation promptly of any claim as to which indemnification will be sought and providing Corporation reasonable cooperation in the defense and settlement thereof.

Section 9
TERMINATION

9.1 ***Termination for Non-Performance or Delay.*** In the event of a termination of this Agreement by Corporation pursuant to Paragraph **3.2** hereof, Corporation will have no further obligations or liabilities under this Agreement. Corporation will have the right, in addition to all of its other rights, to require Developer to deliver to Corporation all of Developer's work in progress, including all originals and copies thereof, as well as any other materials provided to Developer, or created by Developer under this Agreement. Payment of any Development Schedule milestones under Schedule "B" which have been met shall be deemed payment in full for all obligations of Corporation under this Agreement, including full payment for all source code, object code, documentation, notes, graphics and all other materials and work relating to the portion of the Program which has been completed as of the time of termination.

9.2 ***Termination for Convenience.*** Corporation shall have the right at any time to terminate this Agreement on twenty one (21) days written notice. In the event of such termination, Corporation's entire financial obligation to Developer shall be for then accrued payments due under the Development Schedule, plus the pro-rated portion of the next payment, if any, due with respect to items being worked on up to the time of termination.

Section 10
GOVERNING LAW AND DISPUTE RESOLUTION

10.1 *Arbitration.* The parties agree to submit any dispute arising out of or in connection with this Agreement to binding arbitration in San Francisco, California before the American Arbitration Association pursuant to the provisions of this Section 10.1, and, to the extent not inconsistent with this Section 10.1, the rules of the American Arbitration Association. The parties agree that such arbitration will be in lieu of either party's rights to assert any claim, demand or suit in any court action, (provided that either party may elect either binding arbitration or a court action with respect to a breach by the other party of such party's proprietary rights, including without limitation any trade secrets, copyrights or trademarks). Any arbitration shall be final and binding and the arbitrator's order will be enforceable in any court of competent jurisdiction.

10.2 *Governing Law; Venue.* The validity, construction, and performance of this Agreement shall be governed by the laws of the state of _____, and all claims and/or lawsuits in connection with agreement must be brought in _____.

Section 11
MISCELLANEOUS PROVISIONS

1 1.1 *Notices.* For purposes of all notices and other communi cations required or permitted to be given hereunder, the addresses of the parties hereto shall be as indicated below. All notices shall be in writing and shall be deemed to have been duly given if sent by facsimile, the receipt of which is confirmed by return facsimile, or sent by first class registered or certified mail or equivalent, return receipt requested, addressed to the parties at their addresses set forth below:

If to Developer:

_____

_____

_____

Attn: _____

If to Corporation:

_____

_____

Attn: _____

11.2 *Designated Person.* The parties agree that all materials exchanged between the parties for formal approval shall be communicated between single designated persons, or a single alternate designated person for each party. Neither party shall have any obligation to consider for approval or respond to materials submitted other than through the Designated Persons. Each party shall have the right to change its Designated Persons from time to time and to so notify the other.

11.3 *Entire Agreement.* This Agreement, including the attached Schedules which are incorporated herein by reference as though fully set out, contains the entire understanding and agreement of the parties with respect to the subject matter contained herein, supersedes all prior oral or written understandings and agreements relating thereto except as expressly otherwise provided, and may not be altered, modified or waived in whole or in part, except in writing, signed by duly authorized representatives of the parties.

11.4 *Force Majeure.* Neither party shall be held responsible for damages caused by any delay or default due to any contingency beyond its control preventing or interfering with performance hereunder.

11.5 *Severability.* If any provision of this Agreement shall be held by a court of competent jurisdiction to be contrary to any law, the remaining provisions shall remain in full force and effect as if said provision never existed.

11.6 *Assignment.* This Agreement is personal to Developer. Developer may not sell, transfer, sublicense, hypothecate or assign its rights and duties under this Agreement without the written consent of Corporation. No rights of Developer hereunder shall devolve by operation of law or otherwise upon any receiver, liquidator, trustee, or other party. This Agreement shall inure to the benefit of Corporation, its successors and assigns.

11.7 *Waiver and Amendments.* No waiver, amendment, or modification of any provision of this Agreement shall be effective unless consented to by both parties in writing. No failure or delay by either party in exercising any rights, power, or remedy under this Agreement shall operate as a waiver of any such right, power, or remedy.

11.8 *Agency.* The parties are separate and independent legal entities. Developer is performing services for Corporation as an independent contractor. Nothing contained in this Agreement shall be deemed to constitute either Developer or Corporation an agent, representative, partner, joint venturer or employee of the other party for any purpose. Neither party has the authority to bind the other or to incur any liability on behalf of the other, nor to direct the employees of the other. Developer is an independent contractor, not an employee of Corporation. No employment relationship is created by this Agreement. Developer shall retain independent professional status throughout this Agreement and shall use his/her own discretion in performing the tasks assigned.

11.9 *Limitation on Liability; Remedies.* Except as provided in Section 8 above with respect to third party indemnification, neither party shall be liable to the other party for any incidental, consequential, special, or punitive damages of any kind or nature, including, without limitation, the breach of this Agreement or any termination of this Agreement, whether such liability is asserted on the basis of contract, tort (including negligence or strict liability), or otherwise, even if either party has warned or been warned of the possibility of any such loss or damage.

IN WITNESS WHEREOF, this Agreement is executed as of the Effective Date set forth above.

[Corporation]   [Developer]

By: _____   By: _____
    Name   Name

Its: _____   Its: _____
    Title   Title

SCHEDULE A
SPECIFICATIONS

SCHEDULE B
DEVELOPMENT AND PAYMENT SCHEDULE

Item	Due Date	Payment Upon Acceptance
Contract Signing	_____	_____
Delivery of Web site Design	_____	_____
Delivery of Beta Version	_____	_____
Delivery of Final Version and Source Materials	_____	_____
Acceptance of Final Version		
by		

TOTAL: _____

Each of the foregoing milestone payments shall be payable upon Corporation's acceptance of an acceptable Deliverable.

Bonus. Corporation agrees to pay Developer a bonus of $_____ which shall be payable to Developer in the event Developer delivers a Final Version of the Web site which is acceptable to Corporation prior to _____.

12. Footage, Photo, and Text license (Nonexclusive, to Developer)

This form is used to obtain permission to use prerecorded film or video footage, photographs, and text on a nonexclusive basis in a multimedia title. It was provided by Renée Chernus, an attorney in private practice in San Rafael, California.

FOOTAGE, PHOTO AND TEXT LICENSE AGREEMENT
(With Credit)

LICENSOR: _____

ADDRESS: _____

CITY/STATE: _____

This agreement is made and entered into this ___ day of _____, 19__ by and between _____ ("Licensor") and _____ ("Producer").

1. GRANT OF RIGHTS: For good and valuable consideration, the receipt and sufficiency of which are hereby acknowledge, Licensor hereby grants to Producer a nonexclusive license to incorporate the Work, as hereinafter defined, into the Production, as hereinafter defined. The license granted hereunder includes the right to edit, telecast, cablecast, rerun, reproduce, use, digitize, modify without destroying the historical integrity or compromising the images and distribute in perpetuity the Work, in whole or in part, as incorporated in the Production and any advertising and promotion related to the Production. This license shall not include the right to use the Work independently of the Production or advertising and promotion related thereto. The rights granted herein shall not confer in Licensor any rights of ownership in the Production, including, without limitation, the copyright thereto, all of which shall be and remain the exclusive property of Producer, except that Licensor shall retain copyright in the Work. Licensor understands and acknowledges that the Production may consist of several different formats of the same Production, each format compatible with a different delivery system of multi-media (by way of example only, a DOS format and a MacIntosh format).

2. DESCRIPTION OF WORK: _____(the "Work").

3. DESCRIPTION OF PRODUCTION:

4. CREDIT: In consideration of the rights granted to Producer herein, and provided the Work is used in the Production and the Production is actually released, Producer agrees to give Licensor credit either verbally or in writing in the Production in substantially the following form:

   Courtesy of: _____

   Any inadvertent failure to provide credit shall not be deemed a breach of this Agreement.

5. MONETARY CONSIDERATION: In further consideration of the rights granted to Producer herein, Producer shall pay to Licensor the sum of $_____ per each photographic

image scanned by Producer. Producer shall scan all images on Licensor's premises with Producer's own equipment.

5. REPRESENTATIONS AND WARRANTIES. Licensor represents and warrants to Producer that Licensor has the authority to grant to Producer the rights provided for herein.

6. ASSIGNMENT. Licensor acknowledges and agrees that Producer may assign its rights and obligations under this Agreement in whole or in part, subject to the advanced written approval of Licensor. Licensor consents herein to Producer assigning for publication and distribution the Production that the Work will be contained in.

7. REMEDIES. In the event of breach by Producer, remedies shall be limited solely to an action for damages at law.

8. ENTIRE UNDERSTANDING. The provisions herein constitute the entire understanding between the parties hereto with respect to the subject matter hereof. Any additions to or changes in the Agreement shall be valid only if set forth in writing and signed by the parties.

9. GENERAL. A waiver of any of the terms or conditions of this Agreement in any instance shall not be deemed or construed to be a waiver of such term or condition for the future.

10. HEADINGS. The headings at the beginning of each of the paragraphs hereof are for reference only and shall not affect the meaning or construction of this Agreement.

11. ARBITRATION. The parties agree that should a dispute arise between them, in any manner, concerning the attached Contract, and said dispute involves the sum of TWENTY FIVE THOUSAND DOLLARS ($25,000) or less in money damages, including interest, costs or attorneys' fees, the parties will submit the matter to Binding Arbitration in _____, _____ pursuant to the rules of the American Arbitration Association.

12. NON-DISCRIMINATION. The parties agree to be bound by applicable state and federal rules governing Equal Employment Opportunity and Non-Discrimination.

Accepted for Licensor: Accepted for Producer:

By: _____   By _____

Its: _____   Its: _____

13. Short Form Assignment to Developer

This agreement is used to record the transfer of a copyright to the developer in the Copyright Office. The developer must include either the registration number or title of the copyrightable work to have "constructive notice" of the transfer (see "Obtaining a License" Chapter 12). This short form assignment can also be used to record an assignment of less than all rights in the work (for example, an assignment of audio visual rights or motion picture rights). It can be modified to use for recording an exclusive license.

SHORT FORM ASSIGNMENT TO DEVELOPER

The author, _____, ("Author") for good and valuable consideration, the receipt of which is acknowledged, grants to Developer Company _____
("Devco"), its successors and assigns all right, title and interest in the copyrightable work named _____ ("Work") owned by Auhor. Author authorizes the recordation of this notice with the Copyright Office. The [registration number/name] of the Work is _____.

DEVCO: AUTHOR:

DEVELOPMENT COMPANY   _____
                                          Printed name

By: _____   By: _____

_____
Printed name

_____
Title

Address: Address:

_____   _____

_____   _____

_____   _____

14. Software Component License

This agreement is used when the developer is licensing software for use in a multimedia product. The agreement limits the use of the software to the developer's product or other products distributed by developer.

It includes the right to receive enhancements during the term of the agreement and a "most favored nation" clause (provision that gives the developer the right to receive the enhancements on the best terms offered by the licensor).

SOFTWARE COMPONENT LICENSE

THIS AGREEMENT ("Agreement") entered into as of_____, 19___, by and between Software Supplier Company ("SSC"), having its principal place of business at _____ and Development Company, a _____ corporation, having a place of business at _____ ("Devco").

NOW, THEREFORE, the parties agree as follows:

1. **Definitions.** The terms used in this Agreement shall have the following definitions:

    1.1 End User Documentation means the manuals and other documentation relating to the Program for the end user.

    1.2 Future Version means any modifications and updates, except Error Corrections, if any, to the Initial Release in object code form distributed by SSC.

    1.3 Error Corrections means bug fixes to the Initial Release and in the Enhancements.

    1.4 Devco's Products mean finished computer software or other products distributed by Devco. A Devco Product will consist of the original product and any new versions of such original product.

    1.5 Product Specifications mean (a), for the Initial Release, SSC's product specification sheet set forth on Exhibit A for the Program on the Effective Date; and (b), for Enhancements, SSC's product specification sheet, if any, for the Enhancements or if SSC has not published a product specification sheet for the Enhancements, the most recent version of SSC's product specification sheet for the Program.

    1.6 Program means the Initial Release, Error Corrections, and Enhancements.

    1.7 Source Code means the source code form of the Program.

2. **Term of Agreement.** The term of this Agreement will commence on the Effective Date and, unless earlier terminated as provided below, will continue for the term of the copyrights in the Program.

3. **Scope of Rights.**

    3.1 Software License.

    (a) SSC grants to Devco a perpetual, irrevocable, worldwide, nonexclusive, license, with right to sublicense, during the term of this Agreement, to do the following:

    (1)   Reproduce, modify, and distribute the Program for use as part of Devco's Products;

(2) Reproduce and use the Program for Devco's internal purposes.

(b) Devco shall be the sole and exclusive owner of all rights in the modifications of the Program and Source Code developed by Devco.

3.2 Error Correction. During the term of the Agreement, SSC will provide all of the Error Corrections and reasonable technical assistance to Devco without cost.

3.3 Enhancements. During the term of the Agreement, SSC shall give Devco the Enhancements as soon as they are distributed to other parties. SSC shall make Enhancements available to Devco on the most favorable terms which it offers to third parties. If SSC subsequently offers more favorable terms for an Enhancement to a third party, such terms shall retroactively apply to Devco.

3.4 Documentation. SSC grants to Devco a non-exclusive, worldwide, royalty-free license to use the End User Documentation for its own internal purposes and to reproduce, modify and distribute the End User Documentation to customers for the Devco's Products.

4. **Delivery and Acceptance.** SSC shall deliver to Devco one copy of the Initial Release (and Source Code) on magnetic media and one copy of the End User Documentation for the Program within ten days of the Effective Date. If Devco has the right to receive Enhancements, SSC shall deliver to Devco one copy of the Enhancement (and Source Code) on magnetic media and one copy of the End User Documentation for the Enhancement. Devco shall have thirty (30) days to review the Initial Release or Enhancement to ensure that it meets the Product Specifications. If the Initial Release or Enhancement fails to meet the Product Specifications, Devco may return such Initial Release or Enhancement and receive a refund of the royalty paid for it.

5. **Order and Payment.** Devco shall pay SSC the sum of for the first Devco Product which includes the Program ten days after the distribution of the Devco Product incorporating the Program. Devco shall pay SSC $ for each additional Devco Product that incorporates the Program ten days after the first distribution of such additional Devco Product. An additional Devco Product is a program that includes significantly different functions, not new versions of the original Devco Product.

6. **Warranty.** SSC warrants to Devco that the Initial Release and Enhancements (and the Source Code versions thereof) received during the Agreement will perform in accordance with the Program Specifications during the Agreement. SSC warrants that the End User Documentation shall be free of material errors during the warranty period of the Initial Release or Enhancement with which it is associated. Devco agrees to report in writing any failure to meet the warranties ("Error") to SSC. In the event Devco discovers and gives written notice of an Error within the relevant warranty period, SSC will, at its own expense, correct the Error within five (5) days of notice of the Error. If the Error cannot be corrected within such period, SSC will provide a workaround. Errors will be reported to SSC in a form and with supporting information reasonably requested by SSC to enable it to verify, diagnose and correct the Error. SSC DISCLAIMS ALL OTHER REPRESENTATIONS AND WARRANTIES, INCLUDING THE WARRANTIES OF MERCHANTABILITY AND FITNESS FOR A PARTICULAR PURPOSE.

7. **SSC's Warranty and Indemnification for Infringement of Proprietary Rights.** SSC represents and warrants that it is the sole and exclusive owner of all rights in the Program. Further, SSC represents and warrants that: (i) the Program is not subject to any restrictions or to any mortgages, liens, pledges, charges, security interests, encumbrances or encroachments, or to any rights of others of any kind or nature whatsoever which would prevent the grant of this license; (ii) the Program does not encroach or infringe any copyrights, trademarks, trade secrets or other proprietary rights of third parties; (iii) SSC has not received any notice of such encroachment or infringement; and (iv) SSC has not entered into any agreements or arrangements between SSC and any third party that have any effect upon SSC's rights to license the Program, as set forth in this Agreement. SSC agrees to indemnify and hold harmless Devco, its officers, directors, employees and agents against any claims, actions, or demands alleging that the modification, reproduction, or distribution of the Program (or Source Code) infringes any patents, copyrights, or trade secrets of any third parties.

8. **Termination.** This Agreement shall terminate upon the ninetieth (90th) day after either party gives the other notice of a material breach by the other of any term or condition of this Agreement, unless the breach is cured before that day.

9. **General Provisions.**

   9.1 **Assignment.** Devco may assign its rights under this Agreement to any person to whom it transfers all or substantially all of its proprietary rights in any of the Devco Product (it may assign its rights to different parties if it assigns rights in Devco Products to different parties). This Agreement will bind and inure to the benefit of the parties and their respective successors and permitted assigns. This Agreement will be governed by and construed in accordance with the laws of the United States and the State of California as applied to agreements entered into and to be performed entirely within California between California residents.

   9.2 **Notice.** Any notice provided for or permitted under this Agreement will be treated as having been given when (a) delivered personally, (b) sent by confirmed telex or telecopy, (c) sent by commercial overnight courier with written verification of receipt, or (d) mailed postage prepaid by certified or registered mail, return receipt requested, to the party to be notified, at the address set forth above, or at such other place of which the other party has been notified in accordance with the provisions of this Section.

   9.3 **Entire Agreement.** This Agreement, including all Exhibits to this Agreement, constitutes the entire agreement between the parties relating to this subject matter and supersedes all prior or simultaneous representations, discussions, negotiations and agreements, whether written or oral.

IN WITNESS WHEREOF, the parties have executed this Agreement as of the Effective Date.

"SSC":   "DEVCO":

SOFTWARE SUPPLIER COMPANY   DEVELOPMENT COMPANY

By: _____   By: _____

_____   _____
Printed name: Printed name:

_____   _____
Title: Title:

EXHIBIT A
Initial Release Description
Product Specifications for the Initial Release

15. Music License for CD-ROMs by Harry Fox

This agreement is the license used by the Harry Fox Agency to license synchronization rights in music for multimedia rights. (see "Option #2: Using Preexisting Music," Chapter 14). If the developer needs public performance rights, he or she will need a separate license.

The Harry Fox Agency, Inc.
205 East 42nd Street
New York, New York 10017

MULTI-MEDIA RIGHTS LICENSE (MMERL)

License No. _____

Date of Issuance _____

The following provisions shall apply as indicated in the body of this License:

(A) Licensee: _____

(B) Musical Composition: _____

(C) Licensor(s) and percentage of ownership: _____

(D) License Date: _____

(E) Term: _____

(F) Advance: _____

(G) Units: _____

(H) Royalty Per Unit: "Two times the so-called 'statutory royalty rate' (provided pursuant to Section 115 of the United States Copyright Act for the making and distribution of phono-records) [17 U. S. C. 115]. ", OR

(H) Royalty Per Unit: " cents" _____

(I) Territory: _____

(J) Software Serial Number: _____

Definitions

1. For the purposes hereof, the following terms shall have the following meanings:

    a) "MULTI-MEDIA" shall mean the medium in which a musical composition will be utilized in conjunction with, but not limited to, computer monitor visual displays.

    b) "MULTI-MEDIA DISK" which shall include, but not be limited to CD Rom or computer assisted laser disks, shall mean those Multimedia disks containing those musical recordings which is the subject of this license.

c) The term "MULTI-MEDIA DISK MARKET" shall refer to the sale, lease, license, use or other distribution of MULTI-MEDIA DISKS directly or indirectly to individuals for playback through, but not limited to, a personal computer, whether now in existence or hereafter developed.

d) "Copy" or "copies" shall mean all MULTI-MEDIA DISK copies manufactured and distributed by Licensee.

Now it is therefore agreed as follows:

1. Licensee is hereby applying to Licensor for a MULTI-MEDIA rights license to use the musical composition referred to in (B) (above) for the purposes of manufacturing, distributing and selling to the public throughout the territory [(I)], MULTI-MEDIA, embodying the musical composition.

2. Licensor hereby grants to the Licensee the following non-exclusive rights with respect to MULTI-MEDIA DISK, in all respects subject to the terms and conditions herein provided:
a) To record and re-record in digital, computer readable or other form consistent with the integral requirements of the MULTI-MEDIA, the musical composition for use in whole or in part in connection with and with respect to MULTI-MEDIA DISK;
b) To make and distribute copies of the MULTI-MEDIA DISK program throughout the territory only [(I)];
c) Licensee may make arrangements and orchestrations of the Composition for its recording purposes, however, this license does not include the right to alter the fundamental character of the Composition, to print sheet music or to make any other use of the Composition not expressly authorized hereunder, all rights to uses not expressly granted hereunder are hereby expressly reserved by the Licensor.

3. Licensee covenants that it shall place on the outside of all containers or, where possible, in every MULTI-MEDIA DISK copy a conspicuous notice to clearly read as follows:

c Title of Composition and Names of writers. Copyright © 19 (owner of composition). International Rights Secured. Not for broadcast transmission. All rights reserved. DO NOT DUPLICATE. NOT FOR SEPARATE RENTAL.

Warning: "It is a violation of Federal Copyright Law to synchronize this MULTI-MEDIA DISK with video tape or film, or to print this MULTI-MEDIA DISK in the form of standard music notation without the express written permission of the copyright owner. "

4. The musical composition recorded as a MULTI-MEDIA DISK shall not exceed _____ minutes and _____ seconds.

5. The use of the musical composition hereunder shall be:

_____

6. The term during which the rights licensed hereunder may be exercised shall be [the number referred to in (E)] years from the License date (D).

7. a) Licensee shall make the royalty payments hereunder, which shall be accompanied by a detailed accounting statement listing units distributed within 45 days after the end of each

calendar quarter during which the MULTI-MEDIA DISK copies are distributed, equal to [the amount referred to in (H)] per MULTI-MEDIA DISK copy of the work which is manufactured and distributed during each such respective calendar quarter. Within thirty (30) days after the execution of this license, Licensee shall make such payment and render such statement for all units distributed prior to the execution of this license.

b) In the event that Licensee fails to account and pay royalties as herein provided, Licensor shall have the right to give written notice to Licensee that unless the default is remedied within thirty (30) days from the date of the notice, this license shall be deemed terminated. Such failure to pay and cure default in such thirty (30) day period shall render either the making or the distribution, or both, of all MULTI-MEDIA DISK copies hereunder for which royalties have not been paid, actionable acts of infringement under, and fully subject to the remedies provided by the U. S. Copyright Act.

8. Upon ten business days prior written notice, Licensor, by the Harry Fox Agency ("HFA"), shall have the right during reasonable business hours at Licensee's place of business and at HFA's sole expense to examine, and make copies and extracts from the books and records of Licensee relating to its production, making and distribution of MULTI-MEDIA copies hereunder for the purpose of verifying the accuracy of statements and payments and the performance of Licensee's obligations hereunder. Licensee shall not be required to submit to such an examination more than once during any twelve (12) month period.

9. This license does not include the rights to:
    a) Rent separately the musical composition included in the MULTI-MEDIA copies or to permit purchasers or others to do so;
    b) Use the story of the musical composition or dramatically depict the musical composition;
    c) Parody the lyrics and/or music of the musical composition in any way;
    d) Publicly perform, broadcast/cablecast or transmit the work in any manner;
    e) Make, sell or distribute audio phonorecords of the musical composition;
    f) Utilize a sound recording and/or audiovisual master(s) not owned or separately licensed by Licensee.

10. All rights of every kind and nature with respect to the composition which are not expressly granted to Licensee hereunder are expressly reserved by Licensor.

11. Licensor warrants only that it has the right to grant this license, and this license is given and accepted without any other representation, warrant or recourse, express or implied, except for Licensor's agreement to repay the consideration paid for this license if the aforesaid warranty should be breached. In no event shall the total liability of the Licensor exceed the total amount of consideration received by it hereunder.

12. Upon the expiration of this license, all rights herein granted shall cease and terminate and the right to make or authorize any further use or distribution of any recordings made hereunder shall also cease and terminate subject to Licensee's right to sell off its inventory of MULTI-MEDIA DISK for an additional period of one year subject to the continuing obligation to pay royalties therefor. No right to make, sell, or distribute MULTI-MEDIA DISK programs or copies embodying the composition shall survive the termination of this license pursuant to Paragraph 7(a) hereof.

13. This license does not include a grant of performing rights. The public performance of the musical composition as part of the MULTI-MEDIA DISK which is the subject of this license, is expressly conditioned upon such performers or places of performance thereof, having valid performing rights licenses from the respective copyright owners or their designated performing rights societies.

14. This license supersedes and renders null and void any prior agreements otherwise in effect respecting the Composition and those rights which are the subject of this license.

15. This license is being entered into on an experimental and nonprejudicial basis, shall apply for the term set forth herein only, and shall not be binding upon or prejudicial to any position taken by Licensor or Licensee for any period subsequent to the period of this license.

16. This license sets forth the entire understanding of the parties hereto with respect to the subject matter thereof, may not be altered, amended or assigned without an express written instrument to such effect accepted by Licensor and shall be governed and construed by and under the laws of the State of New York applicable to contracts wholly to be performed therein.

By: _____

By: _____
(Licensee)

By: _____

THE HARRY FOX AGENCY, INC. on behalf of:

By: _____
(Licensor)

16. Music and Sound Recording License

This agreement is used to license a musical composition and the sound recording of the musical composition for use in a developer's multimedia product. It is most appropriate for music which is specially created for the developer. If the developer is using pre-existing music, the developer will probably have to use the license of the owner of such rights.

MUSIC AND SOUND RECORDING LICENSE

THIS AGREEMENT ("Agreement") entered into as of _____, 19___, by and between Development Company, a _____corporation with its principal place of business at _____ ("Devco"), and Composer Company, a _____corporation with its principal place of business at _____ ("Composer").

Recitals

WHEREAS, Composer owns the right to a certain musical composition and the master recording thereof;

WHEREAS, Devco wishes to license rights to that musical composition and the master recording thereof as provided under the terms of this Agreement.

Agreement

NOW, THEREFORE, the parties agree as follows:

1. **Definitions.** The terms used in this Agreement shall have the following definitions:

    Audiovisual Work means the Multimedia title developed by Devco.

    Master means the master recording of the Musical Composition embodying the performance of [Composer].

    Multimedia means the medium in connection which the Musical Composition and Master will be utilized, which includes, but is not limited to, a software program involving film, photographs, music, or text.

    Multimedia Disks means those Multimedia disks containing the Musical Composition and/or the Master, including but not limited to, CD-ROMs, laser disks, and floppy disks for any computing platforms.

    Musical Composition means the musical composition entitled written by .

2. **License Grant.** Composer hereby grants to Devco and Devco accepts, a worldwide, non-exclusive license, with the right to sublicense, during the term of this Agreement, to do the following:

    (a) reproduce and have reproduced, in digital, computer readable, or other form consistent with the integral requirements of the Multimedia, the Musical Composition for use in whole or in part in connection with the Multimedia Disk;

    (b) to synchronize the Master, or a portion thereof, in time-relation with the Audiovisual Work and in any promotions and advertisements of the Audiovisual Work;

(c) to reproduce and have reproduced, distribute copies of, and publicly perform the Multimedia Disks;

(d) to create derivative works of the Musical Composition and Master in order to make arrangements and orchestrations for reproducing the Musical Composition or to promote or advertise the Audiovisual Work; *provided, however,* Devco does not have the right to alter the fundamental character of the Musical Composition or Master, to print sheet music of the Musical Composition, or to make any other use of the Musical Composition or Master except as expressly authorized under this Agreement;

(e) to publicly perform the Musical Composition and the Master in connection with the Audiovisual Work;

(f) to use or refer to Composer in the credits, and in any promotions, advertisements and publicity in connection with the Audiovisual Work.

3. **Payment.** In consideration of the license and the rights granted herein, Devco shall pay to Composer the sum of_____ ($_____).

4. **Term.**
   (a) This license and grant of rights made herein shall subsist, at a minimum, for the remainder of the term of all copyrights in and to the Musical Composition and the Master, and any and all renewals or extensions thereof that Composer or its successors or assigns may now own or control or hereafter own or control without additional consideration therefor.

   (b) Upon the expiration of this license, all rights herein granted shall cease and terminate, and the right to make or authorize any further use or distribution of any recordings made hereunder shall also cease and terminate subject to Devco's right to sell off its inventory of Multimedia Disks for an additional period of two (2) years.

5. **No Obligation to Include Musical Composition or Master.** Nothing herein shall obligate or require Devco to include the Musical Composition or Master in the Audiovisual Work.

6. **Representation and Warranty; Indemnity.** Composer represents and warrants that it has the right to grant this license. Composer shall indemnify and hold harmless Devco, its officers, directors, employees, sublicensees, customers and agents against all claims, actions or demands, alleging that the reproduction, distribution, modification, or public performance of the Musical Composition or the Master libels, defames, infringes the copyright or trademarks, infringes the publicity or privacy rights of any individual, or violates other similar proprietary rights of third parties in any jurisdiction. Composer represents and warrants that Composer has paid any American Federation of Musicians or other union re-use fees to permit Devco to use the Musical Composition in Devco's Audiovisual Works.

7. **License Limitations.** This license does not include the right to:
   (a) rent separately the Musical Composition or Master included in the Multimedia Disks or to permit purchasers or others to do so;

   (b) use the story of the Musical Composition or dramatically depict the Musical Composition;

(c) parody the lyrics and/or music of the Musical Composition in any way;

(d) make, sell or distribute audio phonorecords of the Musical Composition or Master.

8. **Miscellaneous.** This Agreement sets forth the entire understanding of the parties hereto with respect to the subject matter hereof and supersedes all prior understandings, if any, whether oral or written pertaining thereto and may only be changed by mutual agreement of authorized representatives of the parties in writing. This Agreement shall bind and inure to the benefit of the parties and their successors and permitted assigns. This Agreement shall be governed in all respects by the laws of the State of California as applied to agreements entered into and performed entirely within California by California residents.

IN WITNESS WHEREOF, the parties have executed this Agreement as of the date indicated above.

DEVCO:

DEVELOPMENT COMPANY

By: _____

COMPOSER:

COMPOSER COMPANY

By: _____

17. Model Release

This model release is used to obtain the right to use a person's image in a photograph. The release is general and permits the use of the image in all media and any product. Some releases are more limited: for example, they may limit the use of an image to a particular product or prevent the modification of the image.

MODEL RELEASE

Job #: _____ Name: _____

Location: _____ Date: _____

Model Release / Development Company ("DEVCO")

For valuable consideration received, I hereby grant to Devco the absolute and irrevocable right and permission, in respect of the photographs that it has taken or has had taken of me or in which I may be included with others, to copyright the same, in its own name or otherwise (and assign my rights throughout the world in such photograph), to use, re-use, publish, and re-publish, and otherwise reproduce, modify and display the same, in whole or in part, individually or in conjunction with other photographs, and in conjunction with any copyrighted matter, in any and all media now or hereafter known, for illustration, promotion, art, advertising and trade, or any other purpose whatso-ever; and to use my name in connection therewith if it so chooses. I hereby release and discharge Devco from any and all claims and demands arising out of or in connection with the use of the photographs, including without limitation any and all claims for libel or invasion of privacy.

Devco may sell, assign, license or otherwise transfer all rights granted to it hereunder. This authori-zation and release shall also inure to the benefit of the heirs, legal representatives, licensees, and assigns of Devco, as well as the person(s) (if any) for whom it took the photographs.

I am of full age and have the right to contract in my own name. I have read the foregoing and fully understand the contents thereof. This release shall be binding upon me and my heirs, legal represen-tatives and assigns. I further release Devco from any responsibility for injury incurred during the photography session.

Signed: _____

_____
Address

_____
City, State, Zip

_____
Phone

_____
Soc.Sec #

18. Screen Actors Guild Interactive Media Agreement

Here are excerpts of key provisions from SAG's current collective bargaining agreement for multi-media developers. The agreement is discussed in Chapter 16.

10. PREFERENCE OF EMPLOYMENT

A. In recognition of the services performed by professional Performers, Producer agrees that in the hiring of Weekly Performers, Three-Day Performers, Day Performers, Singers, Dancers, Stunt Performers, Puppeteers, and Extra Performers employed for the day for work to be performed within the 300-mile, 75-mile or 50-mile zone as the case may be, referred to in Subsection C. of this Section 10 ("preference zone"), preference will be given to Qualified Professional Performers in each such preference zone who are reasonably and readily available in such zone.

B. The obligation of the Producer to give preference to Qualified Professional Performers shall require the employment of a Qualified Professional Performer in the hiring of a Performer employed as a Day Performer, Weekly and Three-Day Performers, unless no Qualified Professional Performer of the type required is reasonably and readily available to the Producer through the use of the present hiring practices generally and customarily followed by the Interactive Media industry. If a Qualified Professional Performer is reasonably and readily available to the Producer for employment in the locality where the Producer's production facility is based, he/she shall be deemed available regardless of the place within the 300-mile, 75-mile or 50-mile preference zone, as the case may be, at which the services are to be performed.

12. RIGHTS

A. In consideration of the initial compensation paid hereunder, Producer may exploit the results and proceeds of Principal Performers' services in the Interactive Programs for which the Performer was employed in all Interactive Media as defined in Subsection 4.C (I) including the right to adapt such Interactive Programs for any and all Platforms and, if Producer pays the additional compensation specified in Subsection 15.C, Producer's rights shall include Remote Delivery and/or Integration as defined in Subsection 4.C (ii) and 4.R, respectively, above. It is understood and agreed that Producer will have all of the foregoing rights, without payment of any additional compensation, with respect to the results and proceeds of the services of Performers who are not Principal Performers.

B. Producer also will have the right, without payment of any additional compensation except as provided in Section 14 below, to: (I) use Interactive Material for reference, file, private audition purposes, and for customary industry promotional purposes within the "trade" (i.e., at sales conventions and other events within the Interactive and entertainment industries); (ii) use and give publicity to the Performer's name and likeness, photographic or otherwise (including the use of stills and lifts in product packaging and in print) to advertise and promote the applicable Interactive Program including the use of excerpts of Interactive Programs at point-of-purchase to promote the sales of Interactive Programs.

13. **REUSE OF MATERIAL**

   A. Producer shall not re-use any part of the photography or soundtrack of an Interactive Program produced hereunder containing the results and proceeds of a Principal Performer's performance ("Reuse") without separately bargaining with the individual Principal Performer appearing therein and reaching an agreement therefor. The foregoing requirements shall be applicable to a Principal Performer only if the Principal Performer is recognizable and to stunts only if the stunt is identifiable. The foregoing requirements shall not be applicable to Extra Performers and shall not limit Producer's right to acquire Integration rights from Performers or to utilize Interactive Material in any manner otherwise authorized under the terms of this Agreement.

   B. The Day Performer rate for the field in which the Interactive Material is re-used (i.e., broadcast television, radio, etc.) shall be the minimum for purposes of the bargaining referred to above with respect to such Reuse of Interactive Material in accordance with the applicable Guild agreement unless compensation for such other use is provided for herein.

   SAG may, at its discretion, grant waivers of the requirements of this Section 13 with respect to the Reuse of Interactive Material containing a Performer's performance in public service, educational and like Linear Programs, and will follow a liberal policy in granting such waivers.

   C. If Producer fails to bargain separately with the Performer as provided herein, or if Producer and the Performer bargain but are unable to reach an agreement, consent for such Reuse shall not be deemed to have been given by the Performer. In the case of violation of the foregoing, the Performer shall be entitled to damages for such unauthorized Reuse of his/her performance equivalent to three (3) times the amount originally paid the Performer for the number of days of work covered by the Material actually re-used as well as the minimum fees, if any, applicable to the field in which the Material is exploited (i.e., broadcast television, radio, etc.). In lieu of accepting such damages, however, the Performer may elect to arbitrate the claim as provided hereunder.

   D. If Producer is unable to find a Performer within a reasonable time for the purpose of the bargaining pursuant to this Section 13, Producer shall notify the Guild within a reasonable period of time to allow the Guild the opportunity to locate such Performer. If the Guild thereafter is unable to notify Producer of a telephone number or an address at which the Performer may be contacted within a reasonable time to allow the Producer to comply with deadlines, Producer may re-use the Material without penalty.

15. **COMPENSATION**

   C. *Additional Compensation for Remote Delivery and Integration:*

   1. Producer shall pay Principal Performers the following for Remote Delivery and Integration rights in an Interactive Program:

      A. Remote Delivery:

         If acquired not later than one (1) year after initial release of the applicable Program in Interactive Media, one hundred percent (100%) of the Minimum

Applicable Compensation as specified below; otherwise, plus ten percent (10%) thereof.

B. *Integration:*

If acquired not later than one (1) year after initial release of the applicable Program in Interactive Media, one hundred percent (100%) of the Minimum Applicable Compensation as specified below; otherwise, plus ten percent (10%) thereof.

The "Minimum Applicable Compensation" shall be the Performer's actual salary for the total number of days or weeks employed, up to one hundred fifty percent (150%) of the minimum daily or weekly Scale, as detailed in Subsection A. or B., above, for the total employment period, excluding Overtime and Liquidated Damages, if any.

19. AFTRA Interactive Media Agreement

Here are excerpts from key provisions of AFTRA's current collective bargaining agreement for multimedia developers. The agreement is discussed in Chapter 16.

12. PREFERENCE OF EMPLOYMENT

  A. In recognition of the services performed by professional Performers, Producer agrees that in the hiring of Weekly Performers, Three-Day Performers, Day Players, Singers, dancers, stunt persons, puppeteers, and Extras employed for the day for work to be performed within the 300-mile, 75-mile or 50-mile zone as the case may be, referred to in Subsection C. of this Section 12 (*"Preference Zone"*), preference will be given to Qualified Professional Performers in each such Preference Zone who are reasonably and readily available in such zone.

  B. The obligation of the Producer to give preference to Qualified Professional Performers shall require the employment of a Qualified Professional Performer in the hiring of a Performer employed as a Day Player, Weekly and Three-Day Performers, unless no Qualified Professional Performer of the type required is reasonably and readily available to the Producer through the use of the present hiring practices generally and customarily followed by the Interactive Media industry. If a Qualified Professional Performer is reasonably and readily available to the Producer for employment in the locality where the Producer's production facility is based, he/she shall be deemed available regardless of the place within the 300-mile, 75-mile or 50-mile Preference Zone, as the case may be, at which the services are to be performed.

14. RIGHTS

  A. In consideration of the Total Applicable Base Compensation paid hereunder, Producer will have the right to exploit the results and proceeds of Principal Performers' services in the Program for which the Performer was employed in all Interactive Media as defined in Section 4.F(i) and, if Producer pays the additional compensation specified in Section 17.C, Producer's rights shall include Remote Delivery and/or Integration as defined in Section 4.F(ii) and 4.D, respectively, above. It is understood and agreed that Producer will have all of the foregoing rights, without payment of any additional compensation, with respect to the results and proceeds of the services of Performers who are not Principal Performers.

  B. Producer also will have right, without payment of any additional compensation, to: (i) use Interactive Material for reference, file, private audition purposes, and for customary industry promotional purposes (e.g., at sales conventions and other events within the Interactive and entertainment industries); (ii) use and give publicity to the Performer's name and likeness, photographic or otherwise (including the use of stills and lifts in product packaging and in print) to advertise and promote the applicable Interactive Program, including the use of excerpts of Interactive Programs at point-of-purchase to promote the sales of Interactive Programs.

15. REUSE OF MATERIAL

  1. Linear Programs

A. Producer shall not Reuse Interactive Material produced hereunder containing the results and proceeds of a Performer's performance in Linear Program(s) without separately bargaining with the individual Performer appearing therein and reaching an agreement therefor. The foregoing requirements shall be applicable to a Performer only if the Performer is recognizable and to stunts only if the stunt is identifiable, and shall not be applicable to Extras

B. The minimum payable to a Performer for the Reuse of any portion of an Interactive Program in a Linear Program shall be AFTRA Scale for the field in which the Interactive Material is Reused (broadcast television, cable, etc.) in accordance with the applicable AFTRA Code unless compensation for such other use is provided for herein.

AFTRA may, in its discretion, grant waivers of the requirements of this Section 15 with respect to the Reuse of video tape and sound track in public service, educational and like Programs, and will follow a liberal policy in granting such waivers.

C. If Producer fails to bargain separately with the Performer as provided herein, or if Producer and the Performer bargain but are unable to reach an agreement, consent for such Reuse shall not be deemed to have been given by the Performer. In the case of violation of the foregoing, the Performer shall be entitled to damages for such unauthorized Reuse of his/her performance equivalent to three (3) times the amount originally paid the Performer for the number of days of work covered by the Material actually Reused as well as the minimum fees, if any, applicable to the field in which the Material is exploited (i.e., broadcast television; radio, etc.). In lieu of accepting such damages, however, the Performer may elect to arbitrate the claim as provided hereunder.

D. If Producer is unable to find a Performer within a reasonable time for the purpose of the bargaining pursuant to this Section 15, Producer shall notify AFTRA within a reasonable period of time to allow AFTRA the opportunity to locate such Performer. If AFTRA thereafter is unable to notify Producer of a telephone number or an address at which the Performer may be contacted within a reasonable time to allow the Producer to comply with deadlines, Producer may Reuse the Material without a breach .

2. Interactive Programs

A. Producer shall not Reuse Interactive Material produced hereunder containing the results and proceeds of a Performer's performance in another Interactive Program (one for which he/she was not employed) except as set forth in Paragraph 3.D. *Integration*, without separately bargaining with the individual Performer seen or heard therein pursuant to this paragraph 1.A. above.

B. The minimum payable to a Performer for the Reuse of any portion of an Interactive Program in another Interactive Program not covered by Integration, shall be no less than the applicable minimum for such category of Performer.

20. Writers Guild Agreement

In this section, you'll find the Writers Guild's Interactive Program contract and the Writers Guild's policy on reuse of material in interactive programs.

INTERACTIVE PROGRAM CONTRACT

Letter Of Adherence • Single Production Only

Company: _____   Phone: (__) _____

Street Address: _____   City: _____

State: _____   Zip Code: _____

Financial Structure:

Corporation: [ ]   Partnership: [ ]   10% (or more) Ownership   [ ]

Joint Venture: [ ]   Sole Owner: [ ]   DBA: [ ]

If Corporation, State in which Corporation is registered: _____

If Corporation, names of officers and principal owners: _____

_____

_____

If a Partnership or Joint Venture, list names of Partners or Joint Venturers: _____

_____

_____

If a Limited Partnership, list names of General Partners and Limited Partners: _____

_____

_____

Title of Production: _____

Compensation (Writing and/or Designing Services): $ _____

_____ Length of Program: (in Minutes) _____

On behalf of the writer(s) employed on the above named Interactive Program, the undersigned Interactive Program Producer hereby agrees to make contributions to the Producer-Writers Guild of America Pension Plan ("Plan") and the Writers Guild-Industry Health Fund ("Fund") as set forth in Article 17 of the 1995 Writers Guild of America - AMPTP Theatrical and Television Basic Agreement ("the 1995 WGA-AMPTP MBA") and the 1995 Writers Guild of America Theatrical and Television Basic Agreement ("the 1995 WGA MBA"), by reference incorporated herein and available on request.* Producer agrees to be bound by the terms and conditions of the Plan Agreement and the Fund's Trust Agreement. No other terms of the 1995 WGA-AMPTP MBA and the 1995 WGA MBA shall apply to the employment of such writer(s).

As of September 1, 1989, the contribution rates set forth in Article 17 are six percent (6%) of gross compensation for writing services to the Plan and six and one half percent (6.5%) of gross compensation for writing services to the Fund.

Accepted and Agreed:

_____   _____
(Company)   (Print Name and Tide)

_____   _____
(Date)   (Signature)

Writers Guild of America, west, Inc.
on behalf of itself and its affiliate
Writers Guild of America, East, Inc.

By: _____   _____

_____   _____

Writer(s) Employed Under This Contract

Name:_____   SS# _____

Name:_____   SS# _____

— FOR OFFICE USE ONLY —

Accepted this _____ day of _____ , 19___.

Producer-Writers Guild of America Pension Plan and Writers Guild-Industry Health Fund

By: _____
   Title:

• Return completed form to: Department of Industry Alliances
WGAw, 8955 Beverly Blvd, W. Hollywood, CA 90048 •

Phone: (310) 205-2511   Fax: (310) 550-8185

REUSE OF MATERIAL IN INTERACTIVE PROGRAMS

[Background: The new provisions of the 1995 MBAs deal with payments to writers for the reuse in interactive programs-part of the "new technologies"of material already written under these and previous MBAs. The new provisions do not deal with the employment of writers to create original programming. In addition to existing MBA provisions applicable to that type of employment, the Guild already has a great/y simplified contract available to encourage the employment of WGA writers to create original programming for the new technologies.]

A. DEFINITION OF INTERACTIVE PROGRAMS

Both 1995 MBAs establish a broadly inclusive definition of "interactive programs." These will be defined as "non-linear"programs where a viewer/user manipulates program elements with a device. "Interactive programs" include those viewed on a television or computer screen via disc, cartridge, wireless or wire transmission, and arcade games.

B. PERCENTAGE OF GROSS PAYMENTS TO WRITERS FOR REUSE OF MATERIAL

The Agreements establish the amounts to be paid to writers for the reuse of literary material and/or motion picture footage (both theatrical and TV) in interactive programs.

Unlike some other percentage-based formulas in the MBA, percentages paid for these uses are based on gross. It is called "Applicable Gross" and defined as all monies or other consideration paid for the interactive program rights by the entity which exploits those rights. No distributor or middleman exclusions; the total amount paid by the licensing company.

The new provisions protect the gross from dilution by traditional "Hollywood Accounting Practices" in a number of ways. Generally, when there is expected to be any difficulty in determining the gross because of inter- or intra-company transactions, the gross will be determined by deciding what the "fair market value" of the interactive rights would have been in an independent, arms-length transaction.

C. PAYMENTS UNIQUE TO WRITERS FOR REUSE OF LITERARY MATERIAL

Unique to writers are provisions requiring payments to writers for the licensing of literary material for use in interactive programs. When the writer has separated rights, or has created a character, object or thing which is unique and upon which an interactive program is based, the payments are:

For Material Written for Television Motion Pictures:	3% of Applicable Gross. *
For Material Written for Theatrical Motion Pictures:	1.5 % of Applicable Gross.

D. PAYMENTS TO WRITERS FOR RE-USE OF ALL OR SUBSTANTIALLY ALL OF THE FOOTAGE FROM TELEVISION OR THEATRICAL MOTION PICTURES

When all or substantially all of the footage from a theatrical or TV motion picture is licensed for use in an interactive program, the payment is 1.2% of Applicable Gross.

* The differences in percentages between theatrical and television motion pictures are based upon the historically stronger separation of rights and similar provisions for writers in television.

E. REUSE OF EXCERPTS

When excerpts from one or more theatrical or TV motion pictures are licensed for use in an interactive program, the payment is a total of 2% of Applicable Gross.

F. COMBINATION PAYMENTS FOR LICENSING FOOTAGE AND LITERARY MATERIAL

When footage and literary material from the same motion picture are licensed together, a combined payment to the eligible writers will be made as follows:

> For Literary Material Written for, and Footage from, Television Motion Pictures:*
> 3% of Applicable Gross.

> For Literary Material Written for, and Footage from, Theatrical Motion Pictures:
> 2% of Applicable Gross.

G. NEWNESS OF AREA RECOGNIZED; COOPERATION IN INFORMATION SHARING; INTERACTIVE MEDIA COMMITTEE

A Guild-Company Interactive Media Committee will monitor the effectiveness of these new provisions and provide a forum to discuss any other issues related to interactive media that any party wishes to discuss.

H. INDUSTRY-WIDE NEW TECHNOLOGIES COOPERATIVE EDUCATION PROGRAM

The Guild and Companies will establish an industry-wide New Technologies Cooperative Education Program to support the education of writers in the creation of specialized material for the new media technologies. The Companies have agreed to contribute a total of $125,000 to be allocated by the Guild for use for this Program and the Campaign for Greater Appreciation of the Role of the Writer, the Guild to determine the allocation between the two programs. (Another $75,000 as agreed to for the Campaign. See Section 18, below.)

21. Budget Preparation Form

This form can be used to create the budget for a multimedia title. The budget categories and milestones used in the form are discussed in Chapter 9.

	Deal Memo or Contract	Script and Design Document	Functional Prototype	Alpha Due	Beta Due	GMC Due Master Delivered	Golden	TOTAL
	Title Begins	End of Month 2	End of Month 4	End of Month 7	End of Month 9	End of Month 10	End of Month 11	
Production								
Game Design								
Interface Design/Art								
Project Management								
Development Tools								
Subtotal								
Asset Creation								
Animation								
Movie								
Other Graphics								
Voice								
Music								
Subtotal								
Licensing								
Production								
Programming								
Platforms Defined								
Interactive Art/Sound								
Project Management								
Subtotal								
Post-Production								
In-house Testing								
Project Management								
Subtotal								
Travel								
Developer Overhead								
Subtotal								
TOTAL								

22. Development and Publishing Agreement

This agreement has been used by a multimedia publisher for external major development deals in which the publisher is paying virtually the entire cost of the development.

At the end of this agreement is a checklist that can be used for development agreements in general.

DEVELOPMENT AND PUBLISHING AGREEMENT

This Agreement is entered into on the _____ day of _____, 1994, by and between Publisher, a _____ Corporation with offices at _____ ("Publisher") and _____ , a _____ _____ corporation with a place of business at _____ ("Developer").

Recitals:

Developer has proposed development of the interactive multimedia product described in Appendix A with the working name "_____ ," which Developer is desirous of producing and distributing in interactive CD-ROM or other interactive form ("Title");

Publisher is in the business of developing, publishing and distributing CD-ROM-based and other electronic products;

Developer is desirous of having Publisher provide funding to develop the Title and to publish and distribute the Title on the terms and conditions set forth herein, and Publisher is willing to provide such funding on the terms and conditions set forth herein;

NOW, THEREFORE, in consideration of the premises, conditions, covenants and warranties herein contained, the parties agree as follows:

1. **Definitions**

    1.1   *"Add-On Products"* shall mean electronic software/multimedia products related to and intended to work with the Title;

    1.2   *"Advances"* shall mean all funds advanced by Publisher to Developer to create the Title (as defined below) or Add-On Products under this Agreement.

    1.3   *"Bundled Copies"* shall mean copies of the Title or Add-On Products distributed bundled with hardware, software or other products of Publisher or a third party.

    1.4   *"Confidential Information"* shall mean the information of either party which is disclosed to the other party pursuant to this Agreement, in written form marked "confidential", or if disclosed orally, confirmed in a writing summarizing such information within thirty (30) days of disclosure and marked "confidential." By way of example and without limiting the generality of the foregoing, Confidential Information shall include trade secrets, know-how, inventions, algorithms, structure and organization of software programs, source code, schematics, contracts, customer lists, financial information, sales and marketing plans, and business plans.

    1.5   *"Cost of Goods"* shall mean Publisher's actual cost of manufacturing and packaging copies of the Title or Add-On Products up to the time of shipment into the distribution channel, including the duplication costs for copies of the Title or Add-On Products on optical or magnetic media, packaging materials, manuals and other collateral materials and program components.

1.6 *"Deliverable Item"* shall mean each of the program components, materials or designs set forth in the relevant Delivery Schedule that Developer shall deliver to Publisher in accordance with the terms of this Agreement.

1.7 *"Delivery Schedule"* shall mean the schedule of Deliverable Items set forth in Exhibit B.

1.8 *"Effective Date"* shall mean the date first set forth above.

1.9 *"Net Revenue"* shall mean all revenues recognized in accordance with generally accepted accounting principles relating to the distribution or sale of the Title or Add-On Products or other products related thereto by Publisher or any of its affiliated, associated or subsidiary companies, less (a) units returned as defective, as a result of errors in billing or shipment, or otherwise returned in the ordinary course of business, (b) Cost of Goods, and (c) taxes collected by Publisher in connection with the Title or Add-On Products or other Title-related products for payment to any governmental authority. The foregoing deductions shall be consistent with the amounts paid in the industry for such items.

1.10 *"QA Testing"* shall mean quality assurance testing of an alpha or beta candidate or gold master for identification of bugs or errors.

1.11 *"Retail Copies"* shall mean all copies of the Title or Add-On Products distributed to third parties, except Bundled Copies, promotional copies and returns.

1.12 *"Specifications"* shall mean the functional specifications and description of features and content of the Title as set forth in Exhibit A.

1.13 *"Territory"* shall mean the entire world.

1.14 *"Title"* shall mean the interactive multimedia product described in Exhibit A known by the working name "Metal Research." The Title shall also include any product for which Publisher exercises its right of first refusal as further provided below.

2. Advances.

2.1 **Advances.** Publisher agrees to pay to Developer an advance against royalties of _____ United States dollars (US$_____), to be paid in installments upon approval of deliverables on the schedule set forth in Exhibit B. Developer agrees that this advance shall be sufficient to produce a complete game without live action video. The amount of this advance may be adjusted as follows:

2.2.1 Publisher and Developer agree to meet and confer regarding reducing the amount of this advance and modifying the Delivery Schedule in the event that, during the development of the Title, it appears that the Title can be developed in a shorter time frame or at a lower cost than presently anticipated.

2.2.2 Budgeted amounts included in the advance for salaries and overhead expenses such as office space shall be reduced pro rata and/or charged against other projects on which Developer is working concurrently with the Development of the Title under this Agreement.

2.2 **Advances for Video.** Publisher shall have the option, in its sole discretion, to add live action video to the present specifications and budget. It is presently anticipated that the additional cost of such video would be approximately US$_____ -US$ _____ . It is also agreed by the parties that the exercise of this option by Publisher shall not result in an extension of the delivery dates for the overall Title. To the extent that, at the time of exercise of the option, Developer believes that the schedule will slip as a result, Developer shall inform Publisher of this fact and the parties shall meet and confer regarding any adjustment to the Delivery Schedule. Developer shall investigate actual costs relating to such video, and shall rework the script to include such video, and shall submit a final cost estimate and script including such video at the time that game play is implemented and demonstrated on the target machine. Publisher shall make a decision within a reasonable time thereafter as to whether to include such video. If Publisher decides to do so, the parties shall mutually agree on a schedule of milestone deliverables and Advances relating to such video.

3. Proprietary Rights and Grant of License.

3.1 The Title and all revisions thereof, if any, and all original music composed for and utilized in the Title are written and commissioned at Publisher's request and direction, and shall be considered works-for-hire.

3.2 All rights to the Title, including but not limited to the copyright, shall be the property of Publisher or its assignee. Publisher shall have all rights in the Title, including the right to make or license derivative works, and the right to produce the Title and derivative works in all forms now known or hereafter developed. Developer shall not acquire any right, title or interest in or to the Title in any format through the exercise of any rights or performance of any obligations by Developer hereunder. Publisher shall have the right to revise the Title, and Developer shall not have any right to make revisions of the completed Title without Publisher's prior written consent.

3.3 Developer grants and assigns Publisher any and all rights Developer may now have or may be deemed to have in the future with respect to the Title, including but not limited to the copyright to the Title and any and all portions thereof. To the extent that any such rights do not automatically vest in Publisher as works for hire and are not presently assignable, Developer agrees to assign such rights to Publisher in the future, and Developer agrees to deliver to Publisher at Publisher's expense all documents reasonably necessary to effect the assignment of Developer's rights contemplated herein.

3.4 Publisher retains the exclusive right to distribute, market, sell, display, advertise, and promote the Title in perpetuity throughout the world. The timing and manner of exercise of these rights shall be solely within the discretion of Publisher.

3.5 Notwithstanding the foregoing, Publisher recognizes that the underlying computer software engine in the game will be developed based on certain existing and future-developed proprietary computer software developed by Developer. Publisher shall be the owner of all work performed on such engine specific to the Title, and shall be granted a non-exclusive, perpetual, royalty free, fully-paid up license to use the engine in every way and manner contemplated under this Agreement in order to exploit the Title and Publisher's rights in the Title.

3.6 Publisher grants Developer the exclusive worldwide license to exploit the non-interactive game uses of the Title subject to Publisher's prior written approval and payment of a royalty to Publisher as provided below.

3.7 **Developer's First Option.** Developer shall have a first option to develop any Add-On Products and/or derivative interactive works which Publisher desires to have developed by an outside developer. For purposes of this section, "first option" shall mean that Publisher will promptly notify Developer in writing of the nature of such proposed Add-On Product or derivative interactive work. Publisher shall give Developer the right to develop such Add-On Product and shall negotiate the terms and conditions of such development in good faith. If Publisher and Developer are unable to agree upon the terms and conditions within thirty (30) days of Publisher's written notice, then Publisher shall be free to approach any other developer or third party regarding development of such Add-On Product or derivative interactive work.

4. Royalties.

4.1 **Royalties on the Title.** The Advances shall be recouped by Publisher from royalties on revenues relating to the Title and Add-On Products. No royalties shall be paid to Developer relating to the Title or Add-On Products until all of the Advances paid to Developer has been recouped by Publisher. Publisher shall pay or credit royalties to Developer at the following rates:

4.1.1 _____% of Net Revenue on the Title up to _____ dollars (US$_____);

4.1.2 _____% of Net Revenue on the Title from_____ dollars up to _____ dollars (US$_____);

4.1.3 _____% of Net Revenue on the Title above _____ dollars (US$_____);

4.1.4 _____% of Net Revenue on Add-On Products if the Add-On Product is created by a developer other than Developer;

4.1.5 _____% of Net Revenue on Add-On Products if the Add-On Product is created by Developer.

4.2 **Royalties from Developer to Publisher.** Developer will pay Publisher a royalty based on all revenues generated from Developer's uses of the Title under the license granted by Publisher above. The amount of such royalty will be negotiated by the parties in good faith at the time Developer determines the nature of the ancillary product.

4.3 All royalty payments shall be made in U.S. dollars by a check drawn on a U.S. bank.

4.4 The above royalty rates shall include all royalties to be paid to third parties ("content royalties"). It will be Developer's responsibility to insure that all content and other third party royalties are paid when due.

4.5 Publisher shall render to Developer on a quarterly basis, within forty-five (45) days after the end of each calendar quarter during which the Title or Add-On Product is sold, a written statement of the royalties due to Developer with respect to such Title or Add-On Product. Such statement shall be accompanied by a remittance of the amount due, if any. Developer shall have the right, upon reasonable request, to review those records of Publisher necessary to verify the royalties paid no more than once per calendar year. Any such audit will be conducted at Developer's expense, by certified public accountants, and at such times and in such a manner as to not unreasonably interfere with Publisher's normal operations, and Developer and its auditor shall be required to treat information revealed during the audit as Confidential Information; provided, however, that if any such audit reveals an error of at least 5% in the payment of royalties, then Publisher shall pay the costs of the audit. If a deficiency is shown by such audit, Publisher shall immediately pay that deficiency. Non-payment of any deficiency within thirty (30) business days of the date on which Publisher receives notice of such deficiency shall constitute a material breach of this Agreement. Once royalties become due from Developer to Publisher pursuant to section 4.2, statements and remittance of royalties from Developer to Publisher shall also be made according to the terms of this paragraph.

5. Development and Approval Process.

    5.1   Developer agrees to develop the Title with Publisher in accordance with the terms of this Agreement and Exhibit A, and to deliver the Title and the Deliverable Items set forth in the Exhibit B to Publisher for approval, in Publisher's sole discretion, in the manner and on the dates specified in the Delivery Schedule. Developer and Publisher agree that no major additional enhancements to the Specifications set forth in Exhibit A will be required or made by Developer without the parties' prior mutual consent.

    5.2   Upon receipt of each Deliverable Item except the alpha, beta, or golden master of a Title, Publisher shall, within ten (10) business days, provide Developer with either:

    5.2.1. written approval of the Deliverable Item; or

    5.2.2. a written list of changes that must be made before Publisher will approve such Deliverable Item.

    Failure to approve or provide a written list of changes within ten (10) days shall constitute approval of the Deliverable Item.

    5.3   No Deliverable Item shall be considered to be approved by Publisher and no payment will be made for completion of such Deliverable Item until Developer has received written confirmation of such approval from Publisher, or a failure to approve or provide a written list of changes has occurred, and all preceding Deliverable Items have been approved by Publisher. If any Deliverable Item requires changes before it will be approved by Publisher, the steps set forth above shall be repeated until such Deliverable Item is accepted, or until Publisher exercises its termination or completion rights under section 5.7 below.

    5.4   The alpha, beta, and golden masters of a Title must be fully tested by Developer for conformity with the Specifications prior to delivery to Publisher, and must meet the following criteria:

    5.4.1 The initial alpha candidates must be delivered on or before the date set forth in Exhibit B, and must be fully feature and content complete, according to the description set forth in the Specifications.

    5.4.2. The initial beta candidates must be delivered on or before the date set forth in Exhibit B and shall be feature frozen and contain all agreed upon changes from alpha and implement all corrections of any bugs or errors identified during QA testing of alpha that cause system or program crashes, or otherwise significantly interfere with the user's ability to use and enjoy the Title (priority 1 bugs).

5.4.3. The golden masters shall be delivered promptly upon implementation of all remaining corrections of previously identified and agreed upon bugs or errors.

5.5 Upon receipt of the initial alpha, beta and golden master candidates, Publisher shall, within ten (10) business days, provide Developer with either:

5.5.1 written acceptance into QA testing of the alpha or beta candidates, which will trigger Publisher's payment obligations, if any, as set forth in Exhibit B; or

5.5.2. written acceptance of the golden master; or

5.5.3. a written list of changes that must be made before Publisher will accept the alpha or beta candidates into testing, or the golden master.

Publisher's failure to approve or reject the candidate or golden master in writing within ten (10) business days of receipt shall constitute approval.

5.6 If changes are required by Publisher before Publisher will accept the alpha or beta candidate into testing, or accept the golden master, then the steps set forth above shall be repeated until the alpha or beta is accepted into QA testing, or the golden master is accepted, or until Publisher terminates the agreement or exercises its completion rights, as described in section 5.7 below.

5.7 If Developer has not provided an acceptable Deliverable Item or alpha, beta, or golden master candidate within four (4) weeks of the date the Deliverable Item or candidate was originally due to be delivered, or if Publisher reasonably believes that the development of the Title is or will be at any time more than five percent (5%) over budget, Publisher shall be entitled to terminate this Agreement or exercise its completion rights as follows: If Publisher chooses to complete the Title, then Developer shall deliver to Publisher within five (5) business days of receipt of notice from Publisher the most current version of the source code for the Title, together with all related development and production materials, including video and audio master tapes, scripts, documentation, notes, hint sheets, and bug reports, and Developer shall cooperate fully with Publisher's efforts to complete the Title. Any amount spent by Publisher to complete the Title shall be considered an additional Advance, to be recouped from the royalties that would otherwise be paid to Developer relating to the Title. Such additional advance shall be recouped at the relevant rate for the Title from Net Revenues until fully recouped. In addition, if Publisher completes the Title under the terms of this section, the royalty to be paid to Developer relating to the Title shall be reduced by five percent (5%). Publisher shall have sole discretion as to whether it chooses to complete the title, if Publisher terminates under this section.

5.8 Upon acceptance of an alpha candidate, Publisher shall commence QA Testing. During this period, Publisher shall provide Developer with notice of any bugs or errors identified by QA Testing, and Developer shall work expeditiously to correct any bugs or errors so notified. When Publisher determines, in its sole discretion, that all agreed upon changes from alpha and all corrections of any bugs and errors identified during QA Testing of alpha that cause system or program crashes or otherwise significantly interfere with program operation have been made, Publisher will notify Developer that Publisher is ready to receive the initial beta candidates as set forth above. Upon such notification, Developer shall promptly prepare and deliver beta candidates to Publisher as set forth above, and such candidates shall be delivered in any event prior to the date set forth in Exhibit B. A QA Testing period shall then commence on the date that Publisher accepts the beta candidates into QA Testing. During this period, Publisher shall provide Developer with notice of any bugs or errors identified by QA Testing, and Developer shall work expeditiously to correct any errors so notified. When Publisher determines, in its sole discretion, that all bugs or errors identified during QA Testing have been corrected, Publisher will notify Developer that Publisher is ready to receive golden masters as set forth above.

5.9 Publisher shall have the right, at Publisher's expense, to send Publisher personnel to Developer's place of business upon reasonable notice during normal business hours for consultation with respect to the Title's development.

5.10 Developer shall be responsible for all development costs associated with the Title, including, but not limited to, the costs of any fees payable for software or other licensing rights or acquiring services or materials in connection with the Title. If any Deliverable Item contains any non-original material, including music, Developer shall identify the material and the owner or copyright holder thereof at the time of delivery of such Deliverable Item, and Developer shall obtain, at Developer's expense, all authorizations necessary to secure from the owner or copyright holder of such material the rights for Publisher granted in section 3 above in connection with such material without additional costs to Publisher and without restriction. In addition, Developer shall deliver to Publisher along with the Deliverable Item containing such material, all documentation establishing Developer's and Publisher's right to use such material.

5.11 **Incentives/Over budget.**

5.11.1 If the development of the Title is over budget, Developer shall have the obligation to pay for the overage. If Developer fails to do so, Publisher may in its sole discretion cover the overage, but if Publisher chooses to do so, the salaries of Developer's Executive Producer and Producer will be cut 50% beginning immediately upon Publisher first obtaining information which would lead a reasonable person to believe that a budget overage will occur, and the amount not paid as salary shall be used to reduce such overage until such overage (or the grounds for belief that such overage will occur) is eliminated. If Publisher covers the overage and the project remains over budget at the time the golden master is accepted by Publisher, the royalties to be paid to Developer will be reduced one percent (1%) for every $25,000 or portion thereof that the Title is over budget. Any amount paid by Publisher to reduce a budget overage (or in any event in addition to the Advances set forth above) shall be fully recoupable from royalties which would otherwise be paid to Developer.

5.11.2 In the event that the Title is delivered before the time it is due and on or under budget as of the delivery date of the relevant deliverable item and for the Title as a whole, incentive payment(s) may be awarded to Developer in Publisher's sole discretion. This incentive payment or payments shall be limited at a maximum to the following: (a) If the Title is finished in acceptable form, under budget and early, Publisher may pay Developer the remaining amounts in the budget for Developer salaries, which amount shall count as an Advance to be recouped hereunder; (b) If the alpha, beta, golden master, and demo deliverables are delivered on or before the dates that they are due and on or under budget, Publisher may pay to Developer a bonus of up to $2,000 for each of these deliverables (to a maximum of $8,000), which amounts shall count as an additional Advance to be recouped hereunder; and (c) For each top rating that the Title receives from reviews in reputable industry-recognized publications, Publisher may pay Developer an incentive bonus of up to $2,000 which shall not count as an Advance, provided, however, that the maximum amount payable to Developer under this subsection shall be $10,000, and such bonuses shall be paid only if all of the relevant deliverables are completed on or before the date that they are due and on or under budget.

5.12 Reports. Developer shall provide Publisher with monthly status reports, including updates of budget versus actual expenditures, and progress against the Delivery Schedule, on the first of each month within the term of the development of the Title. In addition, Developer shall inform Publisher promptly as soon as Developer becomes aware that there is a risk as to: (a) exceeding the budget, (b) failing to meet the schedule, (c) inability of the Title to perform up to the technical requirements contemplated in the Specifications or any other design materials or documents, or (d) inability to provide the feature functionality contemplated in the Specifications or any other related design materials or documents.

5.13 Equipment. Equipment purchased by Developer using funds from the Advances shall be owned by Publisher until such time as all Advances are recouped. The equipment presently owned by Developer is listed in Exhibit D. It shall be presumed that any equipment purchased by Developer from the effective date of this Agreement until the date development of the Title is completed is owned by Publisher pursuant to the terms of this section.

6. Product Name, Marketing and Promotion, and Credits.

6.1 The parties agree to work together to choose the name under which the Title is distributed. Publisher understands that the choice of a name is important to Developer, and will use reasonable efforts to accommodate Developer's concerns. Notwithstanding the foregoing, the final decision as to the name of the Title shall be Publisher's. Publisher shall own the name of the Title as Publisher's trademark, but shall allow Developer to use such name in connection with any approved ancillary product.

6.2 Developer will provide Publisher with all commercially reasonable cooperation and support of Publisher's efforts to market and promote each Title. In particular, but without limiting the generality of the foregoing, Developer agrees at its own expense:

6.2.1 to permit the use of the images, voices, names, likenesses and biographies of the persons involved in the creation of each Title and the persons involved in creating or appearing in the content incorporated in the Titles in connection with the advertising, marketing, publicity, and promotion of the Titles; and

6.2.2. to provide Publisher with demonstration videos, interactive and non-interactive demonstration discs or diskettes, photos or screen shots and abstracts of story lines of each Title, as reasonably requested by Publisher.

6.3 Publisher will consult with Developer regarding the packaging and marketing of each Title. Publisher will use reasonable efforts to accommodate Developer's packaging and marketing suggestions. Notwithstanding the foregoing, Publisher shall have the final decision on all packaging and marketing matters, and shall pay all costs related thereto. Developer shall not engage in any independent marketing or promotional activities without consulting with the appropriate Publisher personnel and receiving Publisher's prior consent.

6.4 Developer shall include Publisher's title animation on the first screen to be viewed by end-users of the Title.

6.5 Developer shall be given credits in the Titles consistent with industry standards, subject to Publisher's approval in Publisher's sole discretion. In particular, Developer shall be given at least the credits listed in Exhibit C, provided that Developer and any individuals named thereon carry out their responsibilities throughout the development of the Title.

6.6 Publisher shall include Developer's logo (as provided by Developer in suitable electronic format) on the packaging for the product. The size and placement of Developer's logo shall be within Publisher's sole discretion.

6.7 Publisher shall be responsible for all costs of focus group testing of the Title and Add-On Products.

7. Developer Copies.

7.1 Developer shall be given a total of twenty five (25) copies of the Title for each platform free of charge at the time the Title is first shipped for a platform in commercial quantities in the retail channel.

7.2 Developer shall be entitled to purchase a reasonable number of additional copies of the Title for each platform at Publisher's cost in any calendar quarter beginning with the calendar quarter after the Title first ships in commercial quantities in the retail channel. Such copies shall be supplied from stock on hand and shall not be resold by Developer, but shall be used for promotional purposes only, after consultation with the appropriate Publisher personnel. In the event Publisher does not have sufficient copies of the Title to satisfy Developer's request, Publisher shall deliver enough copies of the Title to satisfy the request from the next pressing of the Title.

8. Maintenance. Developer agrees to perform maintenance on the Title and Add-Ons created by Developer for as long as the Title is being offered for sale. Such maintenance shall include, but not be limited to, fixing any bugs or errors in the Titles within thirty (30) days of being notified of such a bug or error, and providing updated versions of the Title and source code containing such corrections. Such maintenance shall be provided at Developer's expense in the first ninety (90) days after commercial release of the Title for the initial platforms, and thereafter at Developer's reasonable and customary work for hire rates.

9. **Source Code.** Developer shall send to Publisher the most recent version of the source code for the Title at the end of each calendar month on a medium and in a format to be mutually agreed upon by the parties, until the Titles which have been finished and finally accepted by Publisher, and a final version of the source code has been provided to Publisher.

10. **Customer Service and Information.**

   10.1 Publisher will be responsible for providing reasonable and customary customer service for the Title. Developer agrees to provide such technical assistance and information to Publisher as shall be reasonably necessary for Publisher to provide such customer service.

   10.2 Publisher agrees to provide to Developer upon request, but not more than once per quarter, a list of all registered users of the Titles, containing names, addresses, phone numbers, and other relevant marketing data, if known to Publisher. Such information shall be treated as Confidential Information under this Agreement.

11. **Documentation.** In addition to any documentation called for in the Delivery Schedule for any Title, Developer shall provide user documentation for the Title at Developer's expense.

12. **Warranties, Indemnification, and Remedies.**

   12.1 Developer warrants that it will proceed expeditiously to complete the Title, and that upon completion of the Title, it shall conform in all material respects to the Specifications and other descriptions prepared by Developer and contained in any accompanying written materials, and shall contain no viruses.

   12.2 Developer represents, warrants and covenants that it has full right, power and authority to enter into this Agreement and to grant the rights granted herein without violating any other agreement or commitment of any sort; that it has no outstanding agreements or understandings, written or oral, concerning the Title; that Developer has not previously sold, licensed, encumbered or pledged the Title or any portion thereof as security to any third party; that the Deliverable Items provided hereunder shall be original; and that the Title does not and will not infringe or constitute a misappropriation of any trademark, patent, copyright, trade secret or other proprietary, publicity, or privacy right of any third party and Publisher's use, reproduction, sale, licensing and/or distribution of each Title as provided in this Agreement shall not violate any rights of any kind or nature of any third party.

   12.3 Developer shall defend, indemnify and hold harmless Publisher, its successors, assigns, parents, subsidiaries, affiliates, licensees and sublicensees, and their respective officers, directors, agents and employees, from and against any action, suit, claim, damages, liability, costs and expenses (including reasonable attorneys' fees), arising out of or in any way connected with any breach of any representation or warranty made by Developer herein or any claim that the Title infringes any intellectual property rights or other rights of any third party. Publisher shall give Developer prompt notice of any such claim or of any threatened claim, and reasonably cooperate with Developer in the defense thereof.

   12.4 If Publisher receives notice of any claim, demand or suit, or of any facts which would lead a reasonable person to believe that there has been a breach of Developer's warranties as set forth herein, Publisher shall have the right to withhold from any payments due to Developer under this Agreement, and deposit in an interest-bearing escrow account with a commercial bank, reasonable amounts as security for Developer's obligations hereunder, unless Developer posts other security reasonably acceptable to Publisher. Upon resolution of the claim, the amount in escrow including accrued interest thereon shall be distributed to Developer after deductions of any amounts required to be paid to Publisher or third parties under this indemnity.

12.5 Publisher hereby represents, warrants and covenants that it has the full right, power and authority to enter into this Agreement. Publisher shall defend, indemnify and hold harmless Developer, its successors, assigns, parents, subsidiaries, affiliates, licensees and sublicensees, and their respective officers, directors, agents and employees, from and against any action, suit, claim, damages, liability, costs and expenses (including reasonable attorneys' fees), arising out of or in any way connected with any breach of any representation or warranty made by Publisher herein. Developer shall give Publisher prompt notice of any such claim or of any threatened claim, and shall reasonably cooperate in the defense thereof.

12.6 Neither Developer nor Publisher shall agree to the settlement of any such claim, demand or suit prior to final judgment thereon without the consent of the other party, whose consent shall not unreasonably be withheld.

12.7 The parties' indemnification obligations set forth in the foregoing paragraphs shall survive termination of this Agreement.

13. Termination.

13.1 This Agreement will terminate on the thirtieth (30th) day after one party gives the other notice of a material breach by the other of any term of this Agreement, unless the breach is cured before that day; provided, however, that if the material breach relates only to a particular Add-On Product, then only the rights with respect to that Add-On Product shall be terminated. Publisher shall have the right to suspend payment for milestones or royalties from the time Publisher notifies Developer of a breach until the time such breach is cured by Developer.

13.2 This Agreement may be terminated by either party without prior notice if: (a) the other party files a petition for bankruptcy or is adjudicated a bankrupt, (b) a petition in bankruptcy is filed against the other party, (c) the other party becomes insolvent or makes an assignment for the benefit of its creditors or an arrangement for its creditors pursuant to any bankruptcy law, (d) the other party discontinues its business, or (e) a receiver is appointed for the other party or its business.

13.3 This Agreement also may be terminated by Publisher immediately upon notice pursuant to the terms of section 5.7 above.

13.4 In the event of any termination of this Agreement, Developer shall within five (5) days turn over to Publisher all copies of the source code, artwork, text files, graphics, design documents, bug reports and databases, and all other materials related in any way to development of the Title.

13.5 Notwithstanding any termination of this Agreement, Publisher shall retain the rights granted herein for the Title.

13.6 Termination of this Agreement shall not extinguish any of Publisher's or Developer's rights or obligations under this Agreement which by their terms continue after the date of termination. Termination of this Agreement shall be without prejudice to any other rights that either party may have at law or in equity, and shall not effect the rights of end-users to continue to use all distributed copies of the Titles.

14. Confidential Information.

14.1 Neither party shall disclose any of the Confidential Information of the other party during or after the time this Agreement is in effect. Information shall not be deemed confidential if it:

14.1.1 is now or hereafter becomes, through no act or omission on the part of the receiving party, generally known or available within the industry, or is now or later enters the public domain through no act or omission on the part of the receiving party;

14.1.2 was acquired by the receiving party before receiving such information from the disclosing party and without restriction as to use or disclosure;

14.1.3 is hereafter rightfully furnished to the receiving party by a third party, without restriction as to use or disclosure;

14.1.4 is required to be disclosed pursuant to law, provided the receiving party uses reasonable efforts to give the disclosing party reasonable notice of such required disclosure, and cooperates in any attempts by the disclosing party to obtain a protective order or other similar protection against disclosure of the Confidential Information;

14.1.5 is disclosed with the prior written consent of the disclosing party.

14.2 Developer will not disclose or prerelease any Title or any Deliverable Item or component thereof to any person or entity without the prior written consent of Publisher.

15. Freedom to Compete. Subject to the terms of this Agreement, each party agrees that nothing in this Agreement will be construed as restricting or prohibiting either party from lawfully competing with the other party in any other aspect of its business, including, but not limited to, the development or distribution of other products or services, or the publishing of products competitive with those contemplated under this Agreement, and each party agrees to continue to compete vigorously in all other such aspects of its business.

16. Export Controls. Each party assures the other that it will comply with all export laws and restrictions and regulations of the Department of Commerce or other United States or foreign agency or authority, and not export, or allow the export or reexport of any Title in violation of any such restrictions, laws or regulations.

17. Assignment. This Agreement may not be assigned by Developer without the prior written consent of Publisher, except that Developer shall be entitled to assign this Agreement to the corporate entity to be created by Developer provided that such corporate entity assumes all rights and obligations of Developer hereunder, and provided that the same personnel are devoted to the Title by the corporate entity. An assignment by Developer in accordance with the foregoing requirements shall operate to relieve Developer of any personal obligations regarding this Agreements, except as such obligations may arise from Developer's affiliation as an officer, director, or employee of the assignee corporate entity. Publisher may assign this

Agreement freely. Subject to the foregoing, this Agreement will bind and inure to the benefit of the parties and their respective successors and permitted assigns.

18. **Integration.** This Agreement sets forth the entire agreement between the parties with respect to the subject matter hereof, and may not be modified or amended except by written agreement executed by the parties hereto.

19. **Severability.** If any provision of this Agreement is declared by a court of competent jurisdiction to be invalid, void or unenforceable, the remaining provisions of this Agreement shall continue in full force and effect, and the invalid provision shall be replaced by the legal provision which most closely achieves the intent of the invalid provision.

20. **Governing Law.** This Agreement shall be governed by the laws of the State of California applicable to agreements made and to be wholly performed therein (without reference to conflict of laws). In any action to enforce the terms of this Agreement, the prevailing party shall be entitled to recover its reasonable attorneys' fees and expenses.

21. **Force Majeure.** If the performance of this Agreement or any obligation under it (except payment of monies due) is prevented, restricted or interfered with by reason of acts of God, acts of government, or any other cause not within the control of either party, the party so affected shall be excused from such performance, but only for so long as and to the extent that such a force prevents, restricts or interferes with that party's performance. Notwithstanding the foregoing, the non-affected party may terminate this Agreement immediately upon written notice if the force majeure circumstances continue for more than sixty (60) days.

22. **Independent Contractor.** Developer shall be deemed to have the status of an independent contractor, and nothing in this Agreement shall be deemed to place the parties in the relationship of employer-employee, principal-agent, partners or joint venturers. Developer shall be responsible for any withholding taxes, payroll taxes, disability insurance payments, unemployment taxes and other similar taxes or charges on the payments received by Developer hereunder.

23. **Notices.** The address of each party hereto as set forth above shall be the appropriate address for the mailing of notices, checks and statements, if any, hereunder. Notices sent to Publisher shall be sent to the attention of _____. Notices sent to Developer shall be sent to the attention of _____. All notices which either party is required or may desire to serve upon the other party may be served personally or by certified or registered mail (postage prepaid), reputable commercial courier, or by facsimile transmission, and shall be effective upon receipt. Either party may change its address by written notice to the other.

24. **No Brokers.** All negotiations relative to this Agreement have been carried on by the parties directly, without the intervention of any person as a result of any act of either party (and, so far as known to either party, without the intervention of any such person) in such manner as to give rise to any valid claim against the parties hereto for brokerage commissions, finder's fees or other like payment.

25. **Waiver.** No waiver by either party, whether express or implied, of any provision of this Agreement shall constitute a continuing waiver of such provision or a waiver of any other provision of this Agreement. No waiver by either party, whether express or implied, of any breach or

default by the other party, shall constitute a waiver of any other breach or default of the same or any other provision of this Agreement.

26. **Paragraph Headings.** Paragraph headings contained herein are for the convenience of the parties only. They shall not be used in any way to govern, limit, modify, or construe this Agreement and shall not be given any legal effect.

27. **Counterparts.** This Agreement may be executed in two or more counterparts and all counterparts so executed shall for all purposes constitute one agreement, binding on all parties hereto.

IN WITNESS WHEREOF, the parties have caused this Development Agreement to be executed on the date set forth above by their duly authorized representatives.

Developer   Publisher

_____   _____
Signature: Signature:

_____   _____
Title: Title:

_____   _____
Date: Date

Exhibit A: SPECIFICATIONS (including Budget)

Budgeted amounts for salaries and overhead expenses such as office space shall be reduced pro rata and/or charged against other projects on which Developer is working concurrently with the Development of the Title under this Agreement.

Exhibit B: DELIVERABLE ITEMS AND DELIVERY SCHEDULE

Date	Delivered Item	Amount To Be Paid Upon Acceptance Of Deliverable Item
_____	_____	_____

C: Credits

Exhibit D: Developer Equipment

CHECKLIST FOR DEVELOPMENT AGREEMENTS

This checklist covers all types of development agreements. However, a particular development agreement may not include each provision. Some of the provisions are alternatives and cannot all be included in a particular agreement. We have included cross-references to the accompanying development agreement. This agreement is also a publishing agreement so it includes additional provisions which relate to distribution issues.

   I. Define what is being developed. This definition should be as specific as possible and may be included in an exhibit.
     A. Definition of product (See Section 1.14)
       1. Material included
       2. Appearance of graphic user interface
       3. Run time version of software
       4. Performance specifications
       5. Hardware or operating software platforms
     B. Definition of additional materials (Section 11/Exhibit A)
       1. Customer documentation
       2 Internal documentation (technical documentation for maintenance)
       3. Advertising "trailers" and/or package design

  II. Responsibilities of Developer
     A. Scope of work (Section 5.1)
       1. Define design specifications
       2. Define milestones
       3. Define performance specifications
       4. Develop the product
       5. Test the product on various configurations
     B. Define deliverables or milestones (Exhibit A)

 III. Nature of rights transferred.
     A. Ownership (see assignment); the agreement may provide for assignment of rights to the new material, but a license to a software engine or other "basic" technology of the developer (Section 3.1/3.2)
     B. Joint ownership
     C. License (Section 3.5)
       1. Exclusive/non-exclusive
       2. Term
       3. Minimum royalties or payments
       4. Territory
       5. Hardware (IBM-compatible, Mac, Sun)
       6. Operating system (be careful of computers which run multiple operating systems or which have "emulation" programs to permit them to run programs for other operating systems)
       7. Distribution channel
       8. Media (such as CD-ROM, CD-I, diskette)
       9. Broadcast (such as satellite, online, TV)

    10. Language

    11. Field of Use

    12. Reservation of rights not licensed

  D. Advertising (Section 3.4/6.1/6.5/6.6)

    1. Right to use developer name, image, likeness and biography

    2. Use of developer trademark (mandatory or voluntary)

III. Payment

  A. Lump Sum

  B. Time and materials

  C. Royalty (Section 4.1)

    1. Fixed royalty per unit

    2. Gross receipts (occasionally includes some deductions of "costs" such as taxes, shipping and returns)

    3. Net receipts

    4. Royalty due

      a. Upon shipment

      b. Upon receipt of payment

      c. Frequency

    5. Advances

      a. Refundable/non-refundable

      b. Recoupable against future royalties and rate of crediting (i.e. 100% which is "dollar for dollar")

      c. Cross-recoupment (recoupment against more than one product)

      d. Minimums

    6. Reserves for returns

    7. Other Provisions

      a. Reports with payment

      b. Record keeping

        1. What records

        2. How long need they be retained

      c. Audit rights

        1. Who can audit the records

        2. How often can the audits be performed

    3. Who pays if an underpayment is found

  C. Liability for sales or use taxes (Section 1.9)

IV. Scope of Obligations

  A. Identify the "tangible" materials which will be delivered and the format (Section 5.2/ Exhibit A)

    1. Design specifications

    2. Milestone schedule

    3. Performance specifications

    4. Milestones

      a. Alpha

      b. Beta

        c. Final or "Golden Master"

        d. Customer documentation

        e. Internal documentation

        f. Advertising material

  B. Time of delivery (Exhibit A)

  C. Acceptance (Section 5.4/5.5/5.6/5.8)

    1. Standard for acceptance

        a. Conformance with specifications

        b. Completion of certain tests

        c. Reasonable satisfaction (sometimes limited to "commercial viability")

    2. Period to review

    3. Person or entity which decides

    4. Form of Notice

        a. Written notice

        b. "Default" (i.e. failure to give noticeafter certain period is deemed approval)

  D. Remedy for late delivery or failure to meet specifications (Section 5.7)

  E. Future rights and obligations (Section 3.7/5.5/8)

    1. Right of first refusal/negotiation for porting to other languages or platforms

    2. Right of first refusal/negotiation for sequels

    3. Error correction

    4. Maintenance of underlying software

  F. Confidentiality (Section 14)

    1. Define "confidential information"

        a. Marked information

        b. Know or reason to know

        c. Specified information, such as business plans or product design

    2. Disclosure by both parties or only one

    3. Limits on use to purposes of agreement

    4. Period during which information must be maintained in confidence

    5. Limits

        a. Enters public domain

        b. Written permission from disclosing party

        c. Court or administrative proceedings

V. Warranties

  A. No warranties (sometimes called "AS-IS" or quitclaim; it is rather rare)

  B. Ownership (Section 12.2)

  C. No conflicting transfers (Section 12.2)

  D. No liens or other encumbrances (Section 12.2)

  E. No infringement of third party rights (including patent, copyright, trade secret, trademark, publicity and privacy) (Section 12.2)

  F. Performance (Section 12.1)

    1. Specifications

    2. Free of defects in materials and workmanship

    3. Development work by professionals

4. No viruses, time-bombs or other similar devices

5. Disclaimer of "implied warranties"

G. Licensed all pre-existing works or obtained appropriate waiver (rights of publicity) (Section 5.10/12.2)

H. Special copyright issues (Section 12.2)

    1. Not in public domain

    2. Original work

I. Special trademark issues (Section 6.2)

    1. Who owns: publisher or developer

    2. Who registers

J. Term of performance warranties (Section 12.2)

K. Limitation of remedies

    1. Repair

    2. Replace

    3. Terminate

V. Indemnity

  A. Scope (Section 12.3)

    1. Defend-pay for the defense

    2. Indemnify-pay damages

    3. Hold harmless-pay for other expenses

  B. Terms (Section 12.4/12.6)

    1. Notice

    2. Co-operation

    3. Payment of expenses

  C. Limits (Section 12.5)

    1. Territory

    2. Combinations with other materials

    3. No settlement without permission

    4. Remedies

      a. Replace

      b. License

      c. Terminate

    5. Amount

VI. Limitations

  A. Limit on amount for specific liabilities (for example, performance or indemnity for i n - tellectual property infringement)

  B. Disclaimer of consequential damages

VII. Remedies

  A. Failure of performance (Section 5.7/12.4)

    1. Suspend payment/withhold royalty

    2. Suspend performance

    3. Terminate agreement

    4. Sue for monetary damages only

    5. Injunctive relief (order by a court to do or cease doing something)

B. Procedure (Section 13.3)

  1. Notice

  2. Right to cure

C. Termination for convenience

D. Effect of Termination (Section 13.4/13.5)

  1. Right to complete

  2. Discontinue work

  3. Reduce royalty

  4. Delete credit for developer

  5. Who owns materials developed prior to termination?

  6. Special issues due to termination for convenience

D. Survival of Obligations after Termination (Section 13.6)

  1. Warranties

  2. Indemnity

  3. Confidentiality

  4. Payments

VIII. Other Issues

A. Governing law (Section 20)

  1. Substantive

  2. Procedural

B. Dispute Resolution

  1. Mediation

  2. Court litigation

  3. Arbitration

    a. Rules

    b. Governing authority (American Arbitration Association, International Chamber of Commerce)

    c. Number of arbitrators

    d. Limitation on authority to grant certain damages

C. Assignment (Section 17)

  1. No assignment

  2. Prohibited assignees

  3. Permitted assignees (merger, sale of assets)

C Rights Clearance Agencies, Search Firms, and Licensing Agents

This appendix lists rights clearance agencies, search firms, and licensing agents that can help you clear rights to use third-party content. (Clearing rights is covered in Chapter 12.)

Rights clearance agencies will clear rights and obtain licenses for you. They are described in "Rights Clearance Agencies," Chapter 12.

Search firms help you find out who owns copyrights and other intellectual property rights in third-party works. They will not assist you in obtaining the rights to use third-party works in your project. Search firms should be used when you are performing the "clearance" work yourself. (See "Determining Who Owns the Copyright," Chapter 12.)

Licensing agents have authority to grant licenses on behalf of content owners. The professional organizations ASCAP, BMI, and SESAC handle public performance right licenses for musical compositions. They are discussed in Chapter 14.

This list of agencies, firms, and individuals has been compiled from a variety of sources. None of these businesses paid to be listed in this book, and we don't endorse any of them. If you use them, make sure they have experience relevant to your particular project.

Rights Clearance Agencies

Jill Alofs
Total Clearance
P.O. Box 836
Mill Valley, CA 94942
Telephone: (415) 389-1531

Cherchez L'Image
6107 Avenue Durocher
Outremont, Quebec
CANADA H2V 3Y7
Telephone: (514) 277-5144
Fax: (514) 277-2538

The Content Company
C/O Richard Curtis Associates, Inc.
171 East 74th St., 2nd Floor
New York, NY 10021
Telephone: (212) 772-7363
Fax: (212) 772-7393

deForest Research
8899 Beverly Blvd., Suite 500
Los Angeles, CA 90048
Telephone: (310) 273-2900
Fax: (310) 888-3270

The Permissions Group
1247 Milwaukee Ave., Suite 303
Glenview, Il 60025
Telephone: (847) 635-6550
Fax: (847) 635-6968
Email: PermGroup @aol.com

Betsy Strode
1109 Southdown Road
Hillsborough, CA 94010
Telephone: (415) 340-1370
Fax: (415) 340-1370

Barbara Zimmerman
BZ/Rights & Permissions, Inc.
125 West 72nd St.
New York, NY 10023
Telephone: (212) 580-0615
Fax: (212) 769-9224

Copyright Search Firms

Government Liaison Services
3030 Clarendon Blvd., Suite 209
Arlington, Va. 22201
Telephone: (800) 642-6564
Fax: (703) 525-8451

Robert Roomian
P.O. Box 7111
Alexandria, VA 22307
Telephone: (703) 690-6451
Fax: (703) 690-0074

Thomson & Thomson Copyright Research Group
1750 K St., NW, Suite 200
Washington, D.C. 20006
Telephone: (800) 356-8630
Fax: (800) 822-8823

XL Corporate Services
ATTN: Mark Moel, Esq.
62 White St.
New York, NY 10013
Telephone: (800) 221-2972
Fax: (212) 431-1441
(Handles copyright filings and trademark searches as well)

Trademark Search Firms

Coresearch
16 West 22nd St., 8th Floor
New York, NY 10010
Telephone: (800) 732-7241
Fax: (800) 233-2986

Thomson & Thomson
500 Victory Road
N. Quincy, MA 02171
Telephone: (800) 692-8833
Fax: (617) 786-8273

Licensing Agents

Copyright Clearance Center, Inc.
222 Rosewood Dr.
Danvers, Massachusetts 01923
Telephone: (508) 750-8400

Music Reports, Inc.
405 Riverside Dr.
Burbank, Ca. 91506
Telephone: (818) 558-1400
Fax: (818) 558-3484

American Society of Composers, Authors & Publishers (ASCAP)
Chicago office:
Telephone: (312) 481-1194
Fax: (312) 481-1195
Los Angeles office:
Telephone: (213) 883-1000
Fax: (213) 883-1049
Nashville office:
Telephone: (615) 742-5000
Fax: (615) 742-5020
New York office:
1 Lincoln Plaza
New York, NY 10023
Telephone: (212) 595-3050
Fax: (212) 724-9024

Broadcast Music, Inc. (BMI)
Hollywood office (song indexing):
Telephone: (213) 659-9109
New York office (headquarters and eastern U.S. licensing):
320 W. 57th St.
New York, NY 10019
Telephone: (800) 326-4264
Nashville office:
10 Music Square East
Nashville, TN 37203
Telephone: (800) 326-4264

Society of European Stage Authors & Composers (SESAC)
Nashville office:
Telephone: (615) 320-0055
New York office:
421 West 54th St.
New York, NY 10019
Telephone: (212) 586-3450
Fax: (212) 489-5699

The Harry Fox Agency
711 Third Ave., 8th Floor
New York, NY 10017
Telephone: (212) 370-5330
Fax: (212) 953-2384

D Stock Houses and Other Content Sources

Stock houses and music and sound libraries are described in "Stock Houses and Libraries," Chapter 12. This list was obtained from a variety of sources, including trade shows, advertisements, and recommendations. We have chosen to provide you a large set of choices, rather than screening the entries. Consequently, you have the responsibility to ensure that they can provide you with the materials which you need for your project. None of these firms paid to be listed here, and we don't endorse any of them.

The standards for licensing these stock materials are still being established. If you license content from one of these sources, make sure your license covers all the rights you need for your intended use (see "Determining What Rights You Need," Chapter 12, and "Option #2: Using Preexisting Music," Chapter 14).

Music and Sound Libraries

Associated Production Music
6255 Sunset Blvd.
Suite 820
Hollywood, CA 90028-9804
Telephone: (213) 461-3211
(800) 543-4276
Fax: (213) 461-9102

OGM Production Music
6922 Hollywood Blvd. #718
Hollywood, CA 90028
Telephone: (800) 421-4163
Fax: (213) 461-1543

Creative Support Services
1950 Riverside Dr.
Los Angeles, CA 90039
Telephone: (213) 666-7968
(800) 468-6874

FirstCom/Music House
13747 Montfort, Suite 220
Dallas, TX 75240
Telephone: (800) 858-8880
Fax: (214) 404-9656

Killer Tracks, the Production Music Library
6534 Sunset Blvd.
Hollywood, CA 90028
Telephone: (800) 877-0078
Fax: (213) 957-4470

More Media
853 Broadway
Suite 1516
New York, NY 10003
Telephone: (212) 677-8815

MPI Multimedia
16101 S. 108th Ave.
Orland Park, IL 60462
Telephone: (800) 777-2223
Fax: (708) 460-0175

Outlaw Sound
1140 N. LaBrea Ave.
Los Angeles, CA 90038
Telephone: (213) 462-1873
Fax: (213) 856-4311

Pro Music
941-A Clint Moore Rd.
Boca Raton, FL 33481
Telephone: (800) 322-7879
Fax: (407) 995-8434

**Selected Sound Recorded Music Library/
Southern Library of Recorded Music**
4621 Coalinga Blvd.
Toluca Lake, Ca. 91602
Telephone: (818) 752-1530
Fax: (213) 656-3298

SoperSound Music Library
P.O. Box 498
Palo Alto, CA 94301
Telephone: (415) 321-4022
(800) 227-9980
Fax: (415) 321-9261

The Blue Ribbon Soundworks, Ltd.
Venture Center
1605 Chantilly Dr.
Suite 200
Atlanta, GA 30324
Telephone: (404) 315-0212
Fax: (404) 315-0213

Valentino, Inc.
P.O. Box 534
Elmsdorf, NY 10523
Telephone: (800) 223-6278
Fax: (919) 347-4764

Voyetra Technologies
50 Dell Plaza
Yonkers, NY 10701
Telephone: (800) 233-9377
Fax: (914) 966-1102

Video Clips/Film

Archive Films Stock Footage Library
530 West 25th St.
New York, NY 10001
Telephone: (800) 886-3980
Fax: (212) 645-2137

Budget Films
4590 Santa Monica Blvd.
Los Angeles, CA 90029
Telephone: (213) 660-0187
Fax: (213) 660-5571

CBS News Archives
524 West 57th St.
New York, NY 10019
Telephone: (212) 975-4321
Fax: (212) 975-5442

Cinema Network (CINENET)
2235 First St. #111
Simi Valley, CA 93065
Telephone: (805) 527-0093
Fax: (805) 527-0305

Classic Images
1041 N. Formosa Ave.
West Hollywood, CA 90046
Telephone: (213) 850-2980
Fax: (213) 850-2981

Creative Digital, Inc.
1465 Northside Dr.
Suite 110
Atlanta, GA 30318
Telephone: (404) 355-5800
Fax: (404) 350-9825

Dick Clark Media Archives
3003 W. Olive Ave.
Burbank, CA 91510
Telephone: (818) 841-3003
Fax: (818) 954-8609

Educorp
7434 Trade St.
San Diego, CA 92121
Telephone: (800) 843-9497
Fax: (619) 536-2345

Energy Productions
12700 Ventura Blvd.
Studio City, CA 91604
Telephone: (818) 508-1444
Fax: (818) 508-1923

Filmbank
425 South Victory Blvd.
Burbank, CA 91502
Telephone: (818) 841-9176
Fax: (818) 567-4235

Form and Function
1595 17th St.
San Francisco, CA 94122
Telephone: (415) 664-4010
Order: (800) 779-5471

Imageways
412 West 48th St.
New York, NY 10036
Telephone: (800) 862-1118
Fax: (212) 586-0339

Macromedia
600 Townsend St.
Suite 310W
San Francisco, CA 94103
Telephone: (415) 252-2000
Fax: (415) 624-0554

Mediacom
P.O. Box 36173
Richmond, VA 23235
Telephone: (804) 794-0700
Fax: (804) 794-0799

MPI Multimedia (WPA Film Library)
See listing under Music and Sound Libraries

NBC News Video Archive
30 Rockefeller Plaza
New York, NY 10112
Telephone: (212) 664-3797
Fax: (212) 957-8917

Prelinger Archives
430 West 14th St.
Suite 403
New York, NY 10014
Telephone: (212) 633-2020
Fax: (212) 255-5139

The Image Bank Films
4526 Wilshire Blvd.
Los Angeles, CA 90010
Telephone: (213) 930-0797
Fax: (213) 930-1089

Video Tape Library, Ltd.
1509 N. Crescent Heights Blvd.
Suite 2
Los Angeles, CA 90046
Telephone: (213) 656-4330
Fax: (213) 656-8746

Photo Stock Houses

Archive Photos
530 W. 25th St.
New York, NY 10001
Telephone: (800) 688-5656
Fax: (212) 675-0379

Bettman Archives
902 Broadway
Fifth Floor
New York, NY 10010
Telephone: (212) 777-6200
Fax: (212) 533-4034

FPG International
32 Union Square East
New York, NY 10003
Telephone: (212) 777-4210
Fax: (212) 995-9652

Harris Design/The Digital Directory
301 Cathedral Parkway
Suite 2N
New York, NY 10026
Telephone/Fax: (212) 864-8872

Index Stock Photography, Inc.
126 Fifth Ave.
7th Floor
New York, NY 10011
Telephone: (800) 729-7466
(212) 929-4644
Fax: (212) 633-1914

Liaison International, Inc.
11 East 26th St.
17th Floor
New York, NY 10010
Telephone: (800) 488-0484
Fax: (212) 779-6383

Natural Selection Stock Photography, Inc.
183 St. Paul St.
Rochester, NY 14604
Telephone: (716) 232-1502
Fax: (716) 232-6325

Photo Researchers, Inc.
60 East 56th St.
New York, NY 10022
Telephone: (800) 833-9033
(212) 758-3420
Fax: (212) 355-0731

Picture Research
6107 Roseland Drive
Rockville, MD 20852-3642
Telephone: (301) 230-0043

Sharpshooters, Inc.
4950 Southwest 72nd Ave.
Suite 114
Miami, FL 33155
Telephone: (800) 666-1266
(305) 666-1266
Fax: (305) 666-5485

Stock Boston, Inc.
36 Gloucester St.
Boston, MA 02115
Telephone: (617) 266-2300
Fax: (617) 353-1262

Swanstock Agency
P.O. Box 2350
Tucson, AZ 85702
Telephone: (520) 622-7133
Fax: (520) 622-7180

The Image Bank
Los Angeles office:
4526 Wilshire Blvd.
Los Angeles, CA 90010
Telephone: (213) 930-0797
Fax: (213) 930-1089
New York office:
111 Fifth Ave.
New York, NY 10003
Telephone: (212) 529-6700
Fax: (212) 529-8889
Texas Office:
5221 North O'Conner Blvd.
Suite 700
Irving, TX 75039
Telephone: (214) 432-3900
Fax: (214) 432-3960

The Stock Market Photo Agency
360 Park Ave. South
New York, NY 10010
Telephone: (212) 684-7878
Fax: (212) 532-6750

Time and Life Syndication
1271 Ave. of the Americas
New York, NY 10020
Telephone: (212) 522-3866
Fax: (212) 522-0150

Tony Stone Images
Chicago office:
500 N. Michigan
Suite 1700
Chicago, IL 60611
Telephone: (800) 234-7880
Fax: (312) 644-8851
Los Angeles office:
6100 Wilshire Blvd. #1250
Los Angeles, CA 90048
Telephone: (800) 234-7880
Fax: (213) 938-0731
Seattle office:
222 Dexter Ave. North
Seattle, WA 98109
Telephone: (206) 622-6262
Fax: (206) 622-6662

Westlight
2223 So. Carmelina Ave.
Los Angeles, CA 90064
Telephone: (800) 872-7872
(310) 820-7077
Fax: (310) 820-2687

Woodfin Camp & Associates, Inc.
116 E. 27th St.
New York, NY 10016
Telephone: (212) 481-6900
Fax: (212) 481-6909

Text

Corporation for National Research Initiatives/The Digital Library Project
1895 Preston White Dr.
Suite 100
Reston, VA 22091
Telephone: (703) 620-8990
Fax: (703) 620-0913

E Multimedia Organizations

Organizations

Interactive Digital Software Association
(Entertainment Software Rating Board)
845 Third Ave.
14th Floor
New York, NY 10022
Telephone: (212) 223-8936
Fax: (212) 223-8970

Interactive Multimedia Association
48 Maryland Ave.
Annapolis, MD 21401-8011
Telephone: (410) 626-1380
Fax: (410) 263-6590

International Communications Industries Association
3150 Spring St.
Fairfax, VA 22301
Telephone: (703) 273-7200
Fax: (703) 278-8082

International Interactive Communications Society (IICS)
14657 SW Teal Blvd., Suite 119
Beaverton, OR 97007
Telephone: (503) 579-4427
Fax: (503) 579-6272

Multimedia Development Group
2601 Mariposa St.
San Franciso CA 94110
Telephone: (415) 553-2300
Fax: (415) 553-2403

Software Publishers Association
1730 M Street, N.W. #700
Washington, D.C. 20036
Telephone: (202) 452-1600
Fax: (202) 223-8756

F Unions, Guilds, and Trade Associations

This appendix provides contact information for union and guild representatives with responsibilty for interactive media production, if reponsibility for that area has been delegated to one individual or office. Otherwise, general contact information is given.

American Federation of Musicians (AFM):
Telephone: (800) 237-0988
(Sue Collins, agreements for interactive multimedia recording; Colleen Howell, permission for "phono new use")

American Federation of Television and Radio Artists (AFTRA):
Robert Brown, Director of New
  Technologies
Telephone: (213) 461-8111, ext. 219

Authors Guild
Telephone: (212) 563-5904

Directors Guild of America (DGA)
Bryan Unger
Telephone: (310) 209-5330

Graphic Artists Guild
11 West 20th St.
8th Floor
New York, NY 10011-3704
Telephone: (212) 463-7730
Fax: (212) 463-8799

Music Publishers' Association of the United States
205 East 42nd St.
New York, NY 10017
Telephone: (212) 370-5330

National Writers Union
(212) 254-0279

Screen Actors Guild (SAG)
Michael A. Prohaska
Telephone: (213) 549-6847
Fax: (213) 549-6801

Screen Cartoonists Union
(Local 839 of the IATSE)
Telephone: (818) 766-7151

Songwriters Guild of America (SGA)
Hollywood office:
6430 Sunset Blvd. #102
Hollywood, CA 90028
Telephone: (213) 462-1108
Fax: (213) 462-5430
Nashville office:
1222 Sixteenth Ave. S. #75
Nashville, TN 37212
Telephone: (615) 329-1782
Fax: (615) 329-2623

Writers Guild of America (WGA)
Los Angeles office:
Industry Alliances
7000 West 3d St.
Los Angeles, Ca. 90048-4329
Telephone: (213) 782-4511
Fax: (213) 782-4807
Northern California Representative:
Susan Gerakaris
Telephone: (408) 323-1898
Fax: (408) 323-1897
Reuse: Pam Ewing
Telephone: (213) 782-4628

Other Agencies

Multimedia PC Marketing Council
1730 M St., N.W.
Suite 707
Washington D.C. 20036
Telephone: (202) 331-0494
Fax: (202) 785-3197

Photo-CD
Rita S. Ignizio
License Administration
Eastman Kodak Company
1700 Dewey Ave.
Rochester, NY 14650-1924
Telephone: (716) 588-4155
Fax: (716) 722-9230

G Copyright Forms

Forms

1. Search Request Form
2. Cover Sheet for Recording Documents
3. Form PA: Registration Application and Instructions

Form 1. Search Request Form

search request form

Copyright Office
Library of Congress
Washington, D.C. 20559

Reference & Bibliograpy
Section
(202) 707-6850
8:30 a.m.-5 p.m. Monday-Friday
(Eastern time)

Type of work:

☐ Book ☐ Music ☐ Motion Picture ☐ Drama ☐ Sound Recording
☐ Photograph/Artwork ☐ Map ☐ Periodical ☐ Contribution ☐ Architectural Work

Search information you require:

☐ Registration ☐ Renewal ☐ Assignment ☐ Address

Specifics of work to be searched:

TITLE: _____

_____

AUTHOR: _____

_____

COPYRIGHT CLAIMANT (if known): _____
(name in © notice)

APPROXIMATE YEAR DATE OF PUBLICATION/CREATION: _____

REGISTRATION NUMBER (if known): _____

OTHER IDENTIFYING INFORMATION: _____

_____

_____

If you need more space please attach additional pages.

Estimates are based on the Copyright Office fee of $20.00 an hour or fraction of an hour consumed. The more information you furnish as a basis for the search the better service we can provide.

Names, titles, and short phrases are not copyrightable.

Please read Circular 22 for more information on copyright searches.

YOUR NAME: _____ DATE: _____

ADDRESS: _____

_____

_____

DAYTIME TELEPHONE NO. (_____) _____

Convey results of estimate/search by telephone   Fee enclosed? ☐ yes   Amount $ _____
☐ yes   ☐ no   ☐ no

Form 2. Cover Sheet for Recording Documents

DOCUMENT COVER SHEET
For Recordation of Documents
UNITED STATES COPYRIGHT OFFICE

DATE OF RECORDATION
(Assigned by Copyright Office)

Month	Day	Year

Volume _____ Page _____

Volume _____ Page _____

DO NOT WRITE ABOVE THIS LINE.

REMITTANCE _____

To the Register of Copyrights:
Please record the accompanying original document or copy thereof. FUNDS RECEIVED _____

1 NAME OF THE PARTY OR PARTIES TO THE DOCUMENT, AS THEY APPEAR IN THE DOCUMENT.

Party 1: _____
(assignor, grantor, etc.)

_____
(address)

Party 2: _____
(assignee, grantee, etc.)

_____
(address)

2 DESCRIPTION OF THE DOCUMENT:
☐ Transfer of Copyright   ☐ Termination of Transfer(s) [Section 304]   ☐ Transfer of Mask Works
☐ Security Interest   ☐ Shareware   ☐ Other _____
☐ Change of Name of Owner   ☐ Life, Identity, Death Statement [Section 302]

3 TITLE(S) OF WORK(S), REGISTRATION NUMBER(S), AUTHOR(S), AND OTHER INFORMATION TO IDENTIFY WORK.
Title   Registration Number   Author

_____   _____   _____   Additional sheet(s) attached?
_____   _____   _____   ☐ yes
_____   _____   _____   ☐ no
                                                          If so, how many? _____

4 ☐ Document is complete by its own terms.
☐ Document is not complete. Record "as is."

5 Number of titles in Document: _____

6 Amount of fee enclosed or authorized to be charged to a
Deposit Account _____ .

7 Account number _____
Account name _____

8 Date of execution and/or effective date of accompanying
document _____
(month)   (day)   (year)

9 AFFIRMATION:* I hereby affirm to the Copyright Office that the information given on this form is a true and correct representation of the accompanying document. This affirmation will not suffice as a certification of a photocopy signature on the document.

10 CERTIFICATION: * Complete this certification if a photocopy of the original signed document is submitted in lieu of a document bearing the actual signature.
I certify under penalty of perjury under the laws of the United States of America that the accompanying document is a true copy of the original document.

_____
Signature

_____
Date

_____
Signature

_____
Duly Authorized Agent of:

_____
Date

MAIL RECORDA-TION TO:

Name▼ _____

Number/Street/Apartment Number▼ _____

City/State/ZIP▼ _____

YOU MUST
· Complete all necessary spaces
· Sign your cover sheet in space 9
SEND ALL 3 ELEMENTS IN THE SAME PACKAGE:
1. Two copies of the Document Cover Sheet
2. Fee in check or money order payable to *Register of Copyrights*
3. Document
MAIL TO:
Documents Unit, Cataloging Division, Copyright Office, Library of Congress Washington, D.C. 20559

The Copyright Office has the authority to adjust fees at 5-year intervals, based on changes in the Consumer Price Index. The next adjustment is due in 1996. Please contact the Copyright Office after July 1995 to determine the actual fee schedule.

*Knowingly and wilfully falsifying material facts on this form may result in criminal liability. 18 U.S.C.§1001.

January 1993—50,000

☆ U.S. GOVERNMENT PRINTING OFFICE: 1993-342-582/60.033

3. Form PA: Registration Application and Instructions

◐ Filling Out Application Form PA

Detach and read these instructions before completing this form.
Make sure all applicable spaces have been filled in before you return this form.

BASIC INFORMATION

When to Use This Form: Use Form PA for registration of published or un-published works of the performing arts. This class includes works prepared for the purpose of being "performed" directly before an audience or indirectly "by means of any device or process." Works of the performing arts include: (1) musical works, including any accompanying words; (2) dramatic works, including any accompanying music; (3) pantomimes and choreographic works; and (4) motion pictures and other audiovisual works.

Deposit to Accompany Application: An application for copyright registration must be accompanied by a deposit consisting of copies or phonorecords representing the entire work for which registration is made. The following are the general deposit requirements as set forth in the statute:

Unpublished Work: Deposit one complete copy (or phonorecord).

Published Work: Deposit two complete copies (or one phonorecord) of the best edition.

Work First Published Outside the United States: Deposit one complete copy (or phonorecord) of the first foreign edition.

Contribution to a Collective Work: Deposit one complete copy (or phonorecord) of the best edition of the collective work.

Motion Pictures: Deposit *both* of the following: (1) a separate written description of the contents of the motion picture; and (2) for a published work, one complete copy of the best edition of the motion picture; or, for an unpublished work, one complete copy of the motion picture or identifying material. Identifying material may be either an audiorecording of the entire soundtrack or one frame enlargement or similar visual print from each 10-minute segment.

The Copyright Notice: For works first published on or after March 1, 1989, the law provides that a copyright notice in a specified form "may be placed on all publicly distributed copies from which the work can be visually perceived." Use of the copyright notice is the responsibility of the copyright owner and does not require advance permission from the Copyright Office. The required form of the notice for copies generally consists of three elements: (1) the symbol "©", or the word "Copyright," or the abbreviation "Copr."; (2) the year of first publication; and (3) the name of the owner of copyright. For example: "© 1993 Jane Cole." The notice is to be affixed to the copies "in such manner and location as to give reasonable notice of the claim of copyright." Works first published prior to March 1, 1989, **must** carry the notice or risk loss of copyright protection.

For information about requirements for works published before March 1, 1989, or other copyright information, write: Information Section, LM-401, Copyright Office, Library of Congress, Washington, D.C. 20559.

LINE-BY-LINE INSTRUCTIONS

Please type or print using black ink.

1 SPACE 1: Title

Title of This Work: Every work submitted for copyright registration must be given a title to identify that particular work. If the copies or phonorecords of the work bear a title (or an identifying phrase that could serve as a title), transcribe that wording *completely* and *exactly* on the application. Indexing of the registration and future identification of the work will depend on the information you give here. If the work you are registering is an entire "collective work" (such as a collection of plays or songs), give the overall title of the collection. If you are registering one or more individual contributions to a collective work, give the title of each contribution, followed by the title of the collection. Example: " 'A Song for Elinda' in *Old and New Ballads for Old and New People*."

Previous or Alternative Titles: Complete this space if there are any additional titles for the work under which someone searching for the registration might be likely to look, or under which a document pertaining to the work might be recorded.

Nature of This Work: Briefly describe the general nature or character of the work being registered for copyright. Examples: "Music"; "Song Lyrics"; "Words and Music"; "Drama"; "Musical Play"; "Choreography"; "Pantomime"; "Motion Picture"; "Audiovisual Work."

2 SPACE 2: Author(s)

General Instructions: After reading these instructions, decide who are the "authors" of this work for copyright purposes. Then, unless the work is a "collective work," give the requested information about every "author" who contributed any appreciable amount of copyrightable matter to this version of the work. If you need further space, request additional Continuation Sheets. In the case of a collective work, such as a songbook or a collection of plays, give the information about the author of the collective work as a whole.

Name of Author: The fullest form of the author's name should be given. Unless the work was "made for hire," the individual who actually created the work is its "author." In the case of a work made for hire, the statute provides that "the employer or other person for whom the work was prepared is considered the author."

What is a "Work Made for Hire"? A "work made for hire" is defined as: (1) "a work prepared by an employee within the scope of his or her employment"; or (2) "a work specially ordered or commissioned for use as a contribution to a collective work, as a part of a motion picture or other audiovisual work, as a translation, as a supplementary work, as a compilation, as an instructional text, as a test, as answer material for a test, or as an atlas, if the parties expressly agree in a written instrument signed by them that the work shall be considered a work made for hire." If you have checked "Yes" to indicate that the work was "made for hire," you must give the full legal name of the employer (or other person for whom the work was prepared). You may also include the name of the employee along with the name of the employer (for example: "Elster Music Co., employer for hire of John Ferguson").

"Anonymous" or "Pseudonymous" Work: An author's contribution to a work is "anonymous" if that author is not identified on the copies or phonorecords of the work. An author's contribution to a work is "pseudonymous" if that author is identified on the copies or phonorecords under a fictitious name. If the work is "anonymous" you may: (1) leave the line blank; or (2) state "anonymous" on the line; or (3) reveal the author's identity. If the work is "pseudonymous" you may: (1) leave the line blank; or (2) give the pseudonym and identify it as such (example: "Huntley Haverstock, pseudonym"); or (3) reveal the author's name, making clear which is the real name and which is the pseudonym (for example: "Judith Barton, whose pseudonym is Madeline Elster"). However, the citizenship or domicile of the author **must** be given in all cases.

Dates of Birth and Death: If the author is dead, the statute requires that the year of death be included in the application unless the work is anonymous or pseudonymous. The author's birth date is optional, but is useful as a form of identification. Leave this space blank if the author's contribution was a "work made for hire."

Author's Nationality or Domicile: Give the country of which the author is a citizen, or the country in which the author is domiciled. Nationality or domicile **must** be given in all cases.

Nature of Authorship: Give a brief general statement of the nature of this particular author's contribution to the work. Examples: "Words"; "Co-Author of Music"; "Words and Music"; "Arrangement"; "Co-Author of Book and Lyrics"; "Dramatization"; "Screen Play"; "Compilation and English Translation"; "Editorial Revisions."

3 SPACE 3: Creation and Publication

General Instructions: Do not confuse "creation" with "publication." Every application for copyright registration must state "the year in which creation of the work was completed." Give the date and nation of first publication only if the work has been published.

Creation: Under the statute, a work is "created" when it is fixed in a copy or phonorecord for the first time. Where a work has been prepared over a period of time, the part of the work existing in fixed form on a particular date constitutes the created work on that date. The date you give here should be the year in which the author completed the particular version for which registration is now being sought, even if other versions exist or if further changes or additions are planned.

Publication: The statute defines "publication" as "the distribution of copies or phonorecords of a work to the public by sale or other transfer of ownership, or by rental, lease, or lending"; a work is also "published" if there has been an "offering to distribute copies or phonorecords to a group of persons for purposes of further distribution, public performance, or public display." Give the full date (month, day, year) when, and the country where, publication first occurred. If first publication took place simultaneously in the United States and other countries, it is sufficient to state "U.S.A."

4 SPACE 4: Claimant(s)

Name(s) and Address(es) of Copyright Claimant(s): Give the name(s) and address(es) of the copyright claimant(s) in this work even if the claimant is the same as the author. Copyright in a work belongs initially to the author of the work (including, in the case of a work made for hire, the employer or other person for whom the work was prepared). The copyright claimant is either the author of the work or a person or organization to whom the copyright initially belonging to the author has been transferred.

Transfer: The statute provides that, if the copyright claimant is not the author, the application for registration must contain "a brief statement of how the claimant obtained ownership of the copyright." If any copyright claimant named in space 4 is not an author named in space 2, give a brief statement explaining how the claimant(s) obtained ownership of the copyright. Examples: "By written contract"; "Transfer of all rights by author"; "Assignment"; "By will." Do not attach transfer documents or other attachments or riders.

5 SPACE 5: Previous Registration

General Instructions: The questions in space 5 are intended to show whether an earlier registration has been made for this work and, if so, whether there is any basis for a new registration. As a general rule, only one basic copyright registration can be made for the same version of a particular work.

Same Version: If this version is substantially the same as the work covered by a previous registration, a second registration is not generally possible unless: (1) the work has been registered in unpublished form and a second registration is now being sought to cover its first published edition; or (2) someone other than the author is identified as copyright claimant in the earlier registration, and the author is now seeking registration in his or her own name. If either of these two exceptions apply, check the appropriate box and give the earlier registration number and date. Otherwise, do not submit Form PA; instead, write the Copyright Office for information about supplementary registration or recordation of transfers of copyright ownership.

Changed Version: If the work has been changed, and you are now seeking registration to cover the additions or revisions, check the last box in space 5, give the earlier registration number and date, and complete both parts of space 6 in accordance with the instructions below.

Previous Registration Number and Date: If more than one previous registration has been made for the work, give the number and date of the latest registration.

6 SPACE 6: Derivative Work or Compilation

General Instructions: Complete space 6 if this work is a "changed version," "compilation," or "derivative work," and if it incorporates one or more earlier works that have already been published or registered for copyright or that have fallen into the public domain. A "compilation" is defined as "a work formed by the collection and assembling of preexisting materials or of data that are selected, coordinated, or arranged in such a way that the resulting work as a whole constitutes an original work of authorship." A "derivative work" is "a work based on one or more preexisting works." Examples of derivative works include musical arrangements, dramatizations, translations, abridgments, condensations, motion picture versions, or "any other form in which a work may be recast, transformed, or adapted." Derivative works also include works "consisting of editorial revisions, annotations, or other modifications" if these changes, as a whole, represent an original work of authorship.

Preexisting Material (space 6a): Complete this space **and** space 6b for derivative works. In this space identify the preexisting work that has been recast, transformed, or adapted. For example, the preexisting material might be: "French version of Hugo's 'Le Roi s'amuse'." Do not complete this space for compilations.

Material Added to This Work (space 6b): Give a brief, general statement of the **additional** new material covered by the copyright claim for which registration is sought. In the case of a derivative work, identify this new material. Examples: "Arrangement for piano and orchestra"; "Dramatization for television"; "New film version"; "Revisions throughout; Act III completely new." If the work is a compilation, give a brief, general statement describing both the material that has been compiled **and** the compilation itself. Example: "Compilation of 19th Century Military Songs."

7,8,9 SPACE 7, 8, 9: Fee, Correspondence, Certification, Return Address

Fee: The Copyright Office has the authority to adjust fees at 5-year intervals, based on changes in the Consumer Price Index. The next adjustment is due in 1996. Please contact the Copyright Office after July 1995 to determine the actual fee schedule.

Deposit Account: If you maintain a Deposit Account in the Copyright Office, identify it in space 7. Otherwise leave the space blank and send the fee of $20 with your application and deposit.

Correspondence (space 7): This space should contain the name, address, area code, and telephone number of the person to be consulted if correspondence about this application becomes necessary.

Certification (space 8): The application cannot be accepted unless it bears the date and the **handwritten signature** of the author or other copyright claimant, or of the owner of exclusive right(s), or of the duly authorized agent of the author, claimant, or owner of exclusive right(s).

Address for Return of Certificate (space 9): The address box must be completed legibly since the certificate will be returned in a window envelope.

MORE INFORMATION

How to Register a Recorded Work: If the musical or dramatic work that you are registering has been recorded (as a tape, disk, or cassette), you may choose either copyright application Form PA (Performing Arts) or Form SR (Sound Recordings), depending on the purpose of the registration.

Form PA should be used to register the underlying musical composition or dramatic work. Form SR has been developed specifically to register a "sound recording" as defined by the Copyright Act—a work resulting from the "fixation of a series of sounds," separate and distinct from the underlying musical or dramatic work. Form SR should be used when the copyright claim is limited to the sound recording itself. (In one instance, Form SR may also be used to file for a copyright registration for both kinds of works—see (4) below.) Therefore:

(1) **File Form PA** if you are seeking to register the musical or dramatic work, not the "sound recording," even though what you deposit for copyright purposes may be in the form of a phonorecord.

(2) **File Form PA** if you are seeking to register the audio portion of an audiovisual work, such as a motion picture soundtrack; these are considered integral parts of the audiovisual work.

(3) **File Form SR** if you are seeking to register the "sound recording" itself, that is, the work that results from the fixation of a series of musical, spoken, or other sounds, but not the underlying musical or dramatic work.

(4) **File Form SR** if you are the copyright claimant for both the underlying musical or dramatic work and the sound recording, *and* you prefer to register both on the same form.

(5) **File both forms PA and SR** if the copyright claimant for the underlying work and sound recording differ, or you prefer to have separate registration for them.

"Copies" and "Phonorecords": To register for copyright, you are required to deposit "copies" or "phonorecords." These are defined as follows:

Musical compositions may be embodied (fixed) in "copies," objects from which a work can be read or visually perceived, directly or with the aid of a machine or device, such as manuscripts, books, sheet music, film, and videotape. They may also be fixed in "phonorecords," objects embodying fixations of sounds, such as tapes and phonograph disks, commonly known as phonograph records. For example, a song (the work to be registered) can be reproduced in sheet music ("copies") or phonograph records ("phonorecords"), or both.

FORM PA
For a Work of the Performing Arts
UNITED STATES COPYRIGHT OFFICE

REGISTRATION NUMBER

_____

PA   PAU

EFFECTIVE DATE OF REGISTRATION

_____

Month   Day   Year

DO NOT WRITE ABOVE THIS LINE. IF YOU NEED MORE SPACE, USE A SEPARATE CONTINUATION SHEET.

1

TITLE OF THIS WORK ▼

PREVIOUS OR ALTERNATIVE TITLES ▼

NATURE OF THIS WORK ▼ See instructions

2

a

NAME OF AUTHOR ▼

DATES OF BIRTH AND DEATH
Year Born ▼   Year Died ▼

Was this contribution to the work a "work made for hire"?
☐ Yes
☐ No

AUTHOR'S NATIONALITY OR DOMICILE
Name of Country
OR { Citizen of ▶ _____
Domiciled in▶ _____

WAS THIS AUTHOR'S CONTRIBUTION TO THE WORK
Anonymous? ☐ Yes ☐ No
Pseudonymous? ☐ Yes ☐ No
If the answer to either of these questions is "Yes," see detailed instructions.

NATURE OF AUTHORSHIP Briefly describe nature of material created by this author in which copyright is claimed. ▼

NOTE
Under the law, the "author" of a "work made for hire" is generally the employer, not the employee (see instructions). For any part of this work that was "made for hire" check "Yes" in the space provided, give the employer (or other person for whom the work was prepared) as "Author" of that part, and leave the space for dates of birth and death blank.

b

NAME OF AUTHOR ▼

DATES OF BIRTH AND DEATH
Year Born ▼   Year Died ▼

Was this contribution to the work a "work made for hire"?
☐ Yes
☐ No

AUTHOR'S NATIONALITY OR DOMICILE
Name of Country
OR { Citizen of ▶ _____
Domiciled in▶ _____

WAS THIS AUTHOR'S CONTRIBUTION TO THE WORK
Anonymous? ☐ Yes ☐ No
Pseudonymous? ☐ Yes ☐ No
If the answer to either of these questions is "Yes," see detailed instructions.

NATURE OF AUTHORSHIP Briefly describe nature of material created by this author in which copyright is claimed. ▼

c

NAME OF AUTHOR ▼

DATES OF BIRTH AND DEATH
Year Born ▼   Year Died ▼

Was this contribution to the work a "work made for hire"?
☐ Yes
☐ No

AUTHOR'S NATIONALITY OR DOMICILE
Name of Country
OR { Citizen of ▶ _____
Domiciled in▶ _____

WAS THIS AUTHOR'S CONTRIBUTION TO THE WORK
Anonymous? ☐ Yes ☐ No
Pseudonymous? ☐ Yes ☐ No
If the answer to either of these questions is "Yes," see detailed instructions.

NATURE OF AUTHORSHIP Briefly describe nature of material created by this author in which copyright is claimed. ▼

3

a

YEAR IN WHICH CREATION OF THIS WORK WAS COMPLETED This information must be given ◀ Year in all cases.

b DATE AND NATION OF FIRST PUBLICATION OF THIS PARTICULAR WORK
Complete this information ONLY if this work has been published.
Month ▶ _____ Day ▶ _____ Year ▶ _____ ◀ Nation

4

See instructions before completing this space.

COPYRIGHT CLAIMANT(S) Name and address must be given even if the claimant is the same as the author given in space 2. ▼

TRANSFER If the claimant(s) named here in space 4 is (are) different from the author(s) named in space 2, give a brief statement of how the claimant(s) obtained ownership of the copyright. ▼

APPLICATION RECEIVED

ONE DEPOSIT RECEIVED

TWO DEPOSITS RECEIVED

FUNDS RECEIVED

DO NOT WRITE HERE OFFICE USE ONLY

MORE ON BACK ▶ • Complete all applicable spaces (numbers 5-9) on the reverse side of this page.
• See detailed instructions. • Sign the form at line 8.

DO NOT WRITE HERE
Page 1 of _____ pages

EXAMINED BY	FORM PA
CHECKED BY	
☐ CORRESPONDENCE Yes	FOR COPYRIGHT OFFICE USE ONLY

DO NOT WRITE ABOVE THIS LINE. IF YOU NEED MORE SPACE, USE A SEPARATE CONTINUATION SHEET.

PREVIOUS REGISTRATION Has registration for this work, or for an earlier version of this work, already been made in the Copyright Office?

☐ Yes ☐ No If your answer is "Yes," why is another registration being sought? (Check appropriate box) ▼

a. ☐ This is the first published edition of a work previously registered in unpublished form.

b. ☐ This is the first application submitted by this author as copyright claimant.

c. ☐ This is a changed version of the work, as shown by space 6 on this application.

If your answer is "Yes," give: **Previous Registration Number ▼**   **Year of Registration ▼**

5

DERIVATIVE WORK OR COMPILATION Complete both space 6a and 6b for a derivative work; complete only 6b for a compilation.

a. **Preexisting Material** Identify any preexisting work or works that this work is based on or incorporates. ▼

b. **Material Added to This Work** Give a brief, general statement of the material that has been added to this work and in which copyright is claimed. ▼

6

See instructions before completing this space.

DEPOSIT ACCOUNT If the registration fee is to be charged to a Deposit Account established in the Copyright Office, give name and number of Account.

Name ▼   **Account Number ▼**

7

CORRESPONDENCE Give name and address to which correspondence about this application should be sent.   Name/Address/Apt/City/State/ZIP ▼

Area Code and Telephone Number ▶

Be sure to give your daytime phone ◄ number

CERTIFICATION* I, the undersigned, hereby certify that I am the

Check only one ▼

☐ author

☐ other copyright claimant

☐ owner of exclusive right(s)

☐ authorized agent of _____

Name of author or other copyright claimant, or owner of exclusive right(s) ▲

8

of the work identified in this application and that the statements made by me in this application are correct to the best of my knowledge.

Typed or printed name and date ▼ If this application gives a date of publication in space 3, do not sign and submit it before that date.

date ▶

Handwritten signature (X) ▼

MAIL CERTIFI-CATE TO	Name ▼
Certificate will be mailed in window envelope	Number/Street/Apartment Number ▼
	City/State/ZIP ▼

YOU MUST
• Complete all necessary spaces
• Sign your application in space 8
SEND ALL 3 ELEMENTS IN THE SAME PACKAGE
1. Application form
2. Nonrefundable $20 filing fee in check or money order payable to *Register of Copyrights*
3. Deposit material
MAIL TO
Register of Copyrights
Library of Congress
Washington, D.C. 20559-6000

9

The Copyright Office has the authority to adjust fees at 5-year intervals, based on changes in the Consumer Price Index. The next adjustment is due in 1996. Please contact the Copyright Office after July 1995 to determine the actual fee schedule.

*17 U.S.C. § 506(e): Any person who knowingly makes a false representation of a material fact in the application for copyright registration provided for by section 409, or in any written statement filed in connection with the application, shall be fined not more than $2,500.

July 1993—300,000   ♲ PRINTED ON RECYCLED PAPER   ☼U.S. GOVERNMENT PRINTING OFFICE: 1993-342-582/80.017

Glossary

For definitions of terms used in the Copyright Act, see the excerpt from Section 101 of the Copyright Act in Appendix A.

Some of the definitions used here came from the newsletter *Multimedia Monitor,* telephone (703) 241-1799. They are used with permission.

Acceptance: In contract law, the offeree's assent to the terms of an offer.

Advance: Initial payment that a developer receives from a publisher before distribution of the developer's product.

Answer: In a civil lawsuit, the defendant's document responding to the charges made in the plaintiff's complaint.

Arbitration: Resolution of a dispute by a neutral third-party rather than by a judge or jury.

Assignee: Individual or company to whom ownership of intellectual property is transferred.

Assignment: A transfer of ownership of a copyright, patent, trademark, or trade secret.

Authoring system/authoring tools: Software for designing interactive multimedia products.

BBS: Bulletin Board Service (which allows subscribers to upload and download data and post messages).

Beta version: The version of a multimedia product or software that is made available to testers, prior to commercial release, to find design flaws and bugs.

Breach of contract: Failure to meet contractual obligations.

CD-I: A product developed as a consumer device by Phillips capable of playing audio and video when connected to a television.

CD-ROM: Compact Disc Read Only Memory. This looks like a typical CD used for music, but has computer data stored on it.

Civil case: A lawsuit brought by one party against another party to resolve a legal dispute involving rights based on statutory law or common law.

Collective bargaining agreement: Agreement between a union and employers that defines the obligations of employers concerning matters such as hiring, work conditions, and pay.

Common law: Law that is not based on statutes.

Complaint: In a civil lawsuit, the documents containing the plaintiff's charges that the defendant has wronged the plaintiff.

Computer graphics: Visual images created using a computer.

Consideration: In contracts law, the parties' mutual promises, which define the rights and obligations of each party to the contract; what one party to a contract gets for performing its obligations.

Content provider: A company, organization, or person that has/owns content and provides it to users, typically packaged in an application or service.

Contract: A legally enforceable agreement between two or more parties.

Copyright: The exclusive right granted to the author of original, fixed works to reproduce, modify, distribute, publicly perform, and publicly display the author's works.

Counterclaim: In a civil lawsuit, the defendant's allegations that the plaintiff has wronged the defendant.

Counteroffer: An offer made by the offeree to the offeror on the same subject as the original offer, but proposing different terms.

Criminal case: A lawsuit brought by the federal or state government to prosecute violations of criminal law.

Cross-recoupment: Recoupment of advances paid by the publisher on one multimedia product out of the royalties due the developer on another product.

Damages: A remedy, usually money, awarded a victorious plaintiff in a civil lawsuit.

Database: A compilation of information stored in digital form.

Defamation: A false statement about a person, communicated to at least one other person, that injures the libeled person's reputation or subjects the person to hatred, contempt, or ridicule. Also known as libel.

Defendant: The party being sued in a criminal or civil lawsuit.

Demo: Sample art, sound, and interface design for multimedia title.

Derivative work: In copyright law, a work that is created based on a preexisting work.

Digital media: Refers to video and audio which has been digitized into 1s and 0s.

Digital sampling: Extracting portions of an existing recording of music or other sounds for use in a new recording using a device that can store the copied material in a computer's memory.

Digitization: Converting analog video, images, or audio into digital format (i.e., 1s and 0s).

Distance learning: Exchange of information for instructional purposes accessible from remote sites (one way or two way). A new form of learning whereby a student can learn from distant sources via a computer or television.

Distributor: A company that warehouses a multimedia product, ships it, and sells it to retailers.

Download: To transfer information from the Internet or a Bulletin Board Service to one's own computer.

Edutainment: Educational material that includes content designed to entertain the user.

Email (electronic mail): Text and images that are created and distributed electronically.

Fair use: In copyright law, a doctrine permitting copyrighted material to be used without the permission of the copyright owner for limited purposes.

File server (server): A dedicated computer which serves as a central repository for shared data files that are accessed electronically.

Fixed: In copyright law, made sufficiently permanent or stable to permit the material to be perceived, reproduced, or otherwise communicated for a period of more than transitory duration.

GATT: The international treaty General Agreement on Tariffs and Trade.

Gold disk: Final CD-ROM version of a multimedia product.

Home Page: An electronic location on the World Wide Web that contains basic information about its owner and creator.

Intellectual property: Material protected under copyright law, patent law, trademark law, and trade secret law.

Interactive Multimedia Association (IMA): A not-for-profit trade association of more than 350 companies focusing on interpretability and compatibility issues surrounding multimedia for CD-ROMs, PCs, Macintoshes, Internet, on-line services, and Broadband Interactive Television.

Interactivity: Refers to computer programs, on-line services, and "interactive TV" whereby the user can make inputs which direct subsequent delivery of services.

Channel surfing is a crude form of interactivity. Internet and on-line services provide simple forms of interactivity, i.e., point-and-click.

Internet: Originally a network funded by the US Defense Department (DARPA) to provide a network of interconnected computers with multiple paths to each so that if any single computer or network link was destroyed in a war, information could still be transmitted and received by alternative computers and network paths. Today Internet has become the Global Information Highway connecting almost every country in the world. Anybody with a computer, a modem, and some money can connect. Most on-line services also are providing Internet connectivity in order to survive. Internet is not a broadband network. It is a network of networks operating wide area computer networks topologies.

Infringement: A violation of the exclusive rights of an intellectual property owner.

Infringer: One who violates the exclusive rights of an intellectual property owner.

Injunction: An order issued by a court.

Joint work: In copyright law, a work prepared by two or more authors with the intention that their contributions be merged into a whole.

Lanham Act: The federal trademark statute.

Libel: A false statement about a person, communicated to at least one other person, that injures the libeled person's reputation or subjects the person to hatred, contempt, or ridicule. Also known as defamation.

License: A grant of permission to use material protected by copyright, patent, trademark, or trade secret law in a way that would otherwise infringe the intellectual property owner's exclusive rights. The party granting permission is known as the licensor, and the party receiving permission is known as the licensee.

Master recording license: A license granting permission to copy a sound recording. Also known as a master license.

Mechanical license: A license to copy and distribute a musical composition in the form of records, tapes, or compact discs.

Merchandise license: A license authorizing the licensee to use the licensed character or title in connection with the manufacture, sale, and distribution of specified products.

Merger clause: In a contract, a statement that the written document contains the entire understanding of the parties.

Modem: A device that modulates/demodulates. A modem is typically used to connect a computer to a telephone line.

Modification right: In copyright law, the right to modify the protected work to create a new work.

Moral rights: A right of the author of a work, recognized in many European countries, to control changes to the work and the use of the author's name in connection with the work

NAFTA: North American Free Trade Agreement, a treaty to which the United States, Mexico, and Canada are parties.

National Information Infrastructure: Refers to the concept of a high bandwidth network that links everyone and can transport all media types. The Information Superhighway links the concepts of on-line services, Internet, and Interactive TV together.

Nontrade books: Reference and educational books.

Offer: In contract law, a proposal to form a contract.

On-line service provider: Refers to services such as America Online, CompuServe, and Prodigy that enable a user with a computer and a modem to access content and services over phone lines and increasingly over Cable TV networks.

Original: In copyright law, originating with the party claiming authorship.

Patent: A grant of exclusive rights issued by the U.S. Patent and Trademark Office to an inventor.

Plaintiff: One who files a civil lawsuit against another party (the defendant).

Privacy (right of): The basis for an individual's legal claim against one who intrudes on that individual's solitude or seclusion or publicly discloses private facts.

Prototype: A technologically functional embodiment of a multimedia title which proves that the title will work and play as the developer envisions.

Public display right: In copyright law, the right to show a copy of the work directly or by means of a film, slide, or television image at a public place or to transmit it to the public.

Public domain work: In copyright law, a work which is not protected by copyright.

Public performance right: In copyright law, the right to recite, play, dance, act, or show the work at a public place or to transmit the work to the public.

Publicity (right of): The basis for an individual's legal claim against one who uses the individual's name, face, image, or voice for commercial benefit without obtaining permission.

Publisher: A company that makes a multimedia product ready for market, packages the product, determines the price, reproduces the product, and chooses distribution channels for the product.

Recoupment: Repayment to the publisher, out of royalties due the developer, of the advance previously paid to the developer.

Reproduction right: In copyright law, the right to copy the protected work.

Reuse fee: An additional payment owed to the creator of a work when the work is used in a product other than the one for which it was created or released in a market other than the one for which it was created.

Service mark: A word, name, symbol, or device used by a provider of services to identify those services and distinguish them from services provided by others.

Sound recordings: Works that result from the fixation of a series of musical, spoken, or other sounds.

Statute: A law adopted by a legislative body such as Congress or a state legislature.

Synchronization license: License granting permission to use music in synchronization with an audiovisual work.

Termination clause: In a contract, a statement of circumstances under which one of the parties has a right to end the contractual relationship.

Trade books: Books of general interest (fiction, nonfiction, and poetry).

Trade secret: Information of a sort that is valuable to its owner, not generally known, and has been kept secret by the owner.

Trademark: A word, name, symbol, or device used by a manufacturer of goods to identify those goods and distinguish them from goods manufactured by others.

Upload: Transfer information from one's own computer to an Internet or Bulletin Board Service site.

Warranty: A legally enforceable promise that certain facts are true.

Work made for hire rule: In copyright law, rule stating that the employer or hiring party owns the copyright in a work created by the hired party (unless the parties have agreed otherwise in a signed written document).

Works made for hire: In copyright law, works created by employees for the employer; also, certain types of specially commissioned works which the hiring party and hired party have agreed, in writing, to treat as works made for hire.

World Wide Web: Part of the Internet, an interlinked collection of hypertext documents (called Web pages) on Web servers and other documents available via uniform resource locators (URLs). Also known as the Web and the WWW.

Index

A

Acceptance clause
  in contracts 54
Advances 83, 98, 243–44, 258
AFTRA Interactive Media Agreement 189
Agent fees 90
American Federation of Musicians 185
  contract 190–91
American Federation of Television and Radio Artists 185
  collective bargaining agreements 186–89
American Geophysical Union v. Texaco 312
Amsinck v. Columbia Pictures Industries, Inc. 183
Ancillary rights 241, 256
Anti-copying technology 276
Appeals 6–7
  to the Supreme Court 7
Arbitration 10
  clause 45
ASCAP Hit Songs 173
Assignment 47
  advantages for publisher 253
  copyright 137
  later 125
  limited 238
  multiple 125
  of copyright 34–35
    by independent contractor 73–74, 76
  of developer's rights 235–36
  of trademarks, patents, and trade secrets 37
  recording 34
  search 122–23
  secret 124
  termination of 35–36
  via Employment Agreement 66, 68

B

Bankruptcy
  effect on agreements and licenses 259–61
Basic Books, Inc. v. Kinko's Graphics Corp. 313
Baxter v. MCA 163
Berne Convention for the Protection of Literary and Artistic Works 17, 139, 216
Bonuses 99–100
Books
  all rights assignment 145
  licensing 144–47
  nontrade 145
Bourne Co. v. Walt Disney Co. 130
Breach of contract 230, 251–52
Budgeting
  multimedia projects 86–90
Bundling 247, 259
  and royalties 99

C

California Labor Code 76
Campbell v. Acuff-Rose Music, Inc. 114
Carson v. Here's Johnny Portable Toilets, Inc. 178
Carter v. Helmsley-Spear, Inc. 66
Case law 9
Catalog of Copyright Entries 122

CD-ROM 263–69
  bundling titles 265
  children's titles
    design flaw in 265
  marketing calendar 266–69
  marketing plans 267–68
  packaging 266–68
  pricing 263–64
  replication 267
  series approach 264–66
Certiorari 7
Chain of title
  tracing 122–24
Characters
  fictional 144
  licensing 155
  protected 111
  stock 114
  use in photographs 148
  use on Web site 284
Chat functions 287
Childress v. Taylor 32
Choreography
  licensing 153
Citations 9
Civil lawsuits 5
  appealing 6–7
  stages of 6–7
Clip art
  licensing 150
Collateral use 144
Collective bargaining agreements 185–86
  with AFTRA 186–89
  with SAG 186–89
Comment period 96
Commerce clause 3
Common law 4
  rights in trademarks 25
Community for Creative Non-Violence v. Reid 31–32
Community property
  effects on contracts with independent contractors 74
  effects on copyright ownership 33
Compensation
  factors in setting 84
  for developers 82–84
  for writers 97–100
  in AFTRA IMA 189
  in DGA contracts 190
  in SAG IMA 188
  in WGA contracts 189
  non-royalty 84
Concept 94
Confidentiality 68, 102
Consent requirements 192–93

Consequential damages 230
Consideration 44
Constitutionality cases 4
Content
  ownership
    factor in compensation 84
Contingency fees 90
Contracts
  according to Article Two 224–26
  arbitration clause in 45
  definition of 39
  for creating original music 162
  general guidelines 46–47
  merger clause in 45, 59
  mirror image rule 224
  offer and acceptance in 42–43
  one production only 186
  provision for duties and obligations 44–45
  remedy clause in 45
  termination clause in 45, 59
  to create multimedia work for client 52–60
  who can enter into 41–42
  with independent contractor 77–78
  Writers Guild of America 189
  written vs. oral 40–41, 46
Contracts law 39–47
Copying
  by commercial copy center 310
  by teachers 307–11
  copyrighted work 108
  facts 113
  for educational use 109, 111, 300–307
  for library's reserve shelf 310–11
  ideas 113–14
  material from the Internet 274–75, 279
  music 163–65
Copyright
  assignment of 34–35, 101, 137
  deposit requirements 214–15
  determining who owns it 122–29, 143
  film and television clips 151
  finding owner's address 126
  fine art 150
  in foreign works 116–18
  infringement 4, 15, 108, 110
    criminal violation 277
    on-line 291–93
  joint ownership 61, 126
    by teachers 315
    in work made for hire 70
  licenses 35
  music 159–61
  notice 14, 110, 115, 122, 215–16, 274
    sound recording 161
  of components 126–27

of graphics and illustrations 150
ownership 29–37, 249–50
 and community property 33
 and joint authorship 32–33
 by teachers and faculty 313–16
 client 55–56
 developer 56
 factor in compensation 84
 in photographs 149
 of preexisting work 118–19
 of work made for hire 30–32
 transferring to employee 70
protection 13–14, 110
 for Web site 288
 international 17, 216
owner's rights 209
registration 14, 210–12
 components separately 215
registration search 122–23
renewal 115
 search 123
sound recordings 160–61
split 127–29
term 16, 115
unregistered 124
Copyright Act 3, 4, 6, 11
adequate for new technology 276
default rule 29
of 1909 31
on ownership 29–30
Section 108 300–301
 and new copying technologies 303–304
 recommended changes 304–305
Section 110 301, 305–307
Copyright law 11–17
application to the Internet 281
no exceptions for nonprofit organizations 300
proposed changes for on-line 276–77
state 11
uncopyrightable works 14
using material on Web site 284
work protected by 12
Corporate law 41
Correspondence courses 316–17
Counteroffer 43
Courts
appellate 5, 7
role of 4–8
trial 5
types of 5
Credits 100, 110, 251
Criminal case 5
Cross-recoupment 244
Cubby v. CompuServe 294

D

Deadlines
for writing 94
including in contracts 54
Defamation. *See* Libel
Deliverables 53, 94
Derivative works 117–18, 127, 151
Design document 88, 95
Developers
compensation 82–84
of multimedia 233
Development technology 88
Digital sampling 163
Dilution 206
Directors
and work made for hire 152
consent of 193
in multimedia 190
Directors Guild of America 185
contract 190
Distance learning 316–321
Distribution agreements 233–53
for educational materials 321–22
geographic scope of 240
warranties 248–51
Distribution right 15, 131
film and television clips 153
photographs 147
proposed amendment 276
text 143
Distributors
of multimedia 234
Domain names 288–90
abuses 289
as trademarks 290
choosing 289
conflicts 290
registering 289
warehousing 290
Due diligence 249, 256–58

E

Educational use
and fair use 311–12
copying exceptions 300–307
in face-to-face teaching 305–306
in instructional broadcasts 306–307
Effects Associates, Inc. v. Cohen 8
Employee
factors defining 64–65, 71–72
Employment Agreement 65–69
Employment law 78

Exclusive rights
    in copyrighted work 14–17
    of patent owners 21–22
    of trade secret owners 27
    of trademark owners 24–25
Extras 189
    in multimedia 188

F

Facts
    copying 113, 146
    copyright protection of 13, 16
Fair use 16, 109, 111–12
    and educational use 300, 311–12
    in newspapers and magazines 178–79
    of on-line material 277–79
Film and television clips
    copyright ownership 151
    licensing 150–54
    releases 180
Fine art
    copyright ownership 150
First sale doctrine 36
Flat fee 98
Fogerty v. Fantasy, Inc. 211
Foreign laws
    complying on the Internet 295–96
Foreign rights 75, 111, 143, 295
Form PA
    filling out 212–15
Fund-raisers
    use of copyrighted materials in 322

G

General Agreement on Tariffs and Trade (GATT) 116
General partnership 61
Gill v. Hearst Publishing Co. 178
Grand Upright Music Ltd. v. Warner Bros. Records, Inc. 164
Graphics and illustrations
    copyright ownership 150–51
Gratuitous promise 44
Gross revenues 245
    common deductions 246
Guidelines for Classroom Copying 307

H

Harcourt Brace Jovanovich, Inc. v. Goldwater 259
Harper & Row Publishers, Inc. v. Nation Enterprises 108
Harry Fox Agency 165
Home videotaping 113
Hormel Foods Corp. v. Jim Henson Productions, Inc. 203
Hourly rates 98

I

Ideas
    copying 113–14
Incidental damages 230
Indemnity 57, 133, 144, 148
    for independent contractor 77
Independent contractors 67, 69, 71–72
    as copyright owner 72–76
    contracts with 77–78
    photographs created by 149
    teachers as 314–15
Instructional television 319
Instructional videos
    use of copyrighted materials in 317
Insurance 89
Integration rights 188
Intent to use application 203
Interactive multimedia product 317–18
Interactive Network Inc. v. NTN Communications 114
Interactive Program Contract 189
Interface design 88
Internet
    copying material from 274–75, 279–84
    distribution of products over 295–97
    operator liability 290–95
    posting material on 275, 278–79
    use of licensed material 284–85
    use of public domain work 285

J

Joint authorship
    copyrights in 32–33, 61
    granting license by joint owner 61
Joint development agreement 61
Journals
    licensing 146
Judicial circuits 5
Jurisdiction 5
    diversity 5

K

Kill fees 90, 99

L

Lanham Act 6, 23
Lawyers Edition 9
Legal research 9
Legal system 3–10
Lexis 9
Libel 177, 181–82
    how to avoid 181–82
    liability in cyberspace 293–94

Libraries
  and subscription sharing 304
  and systematic reproduction 302
  photocopying exceptions 276, 299, 301–305
    using new technologies 303–304
Licenses 109, 111, 119
  and title defect 134–35
  clip art 150
  compulsory 160, 319
  copyright 35
  determining who owns the copyright 122–29
  determining what rights you need in 129–32
  exclusive 125–26, 133–34, 236–38, 249
  fees 142
  from independent contractor 76
  granted by joint owner 61, 126
  granting rights to trademarks, patents, and trade
    secrets 37, 144
  implied 76–77
    in cyberspace 280
  master recording 170–71
  mechanical 168
  merchandise 155
  nonexclusive 125–26, 134, 236–38
  obtaining 121–39, 132–35
  public performance 171–72
  synchronization 168
  termination of 35–36, 134
  to use public domain work 115
  warranties 133
  when you need one 107
License back 236, 238
Licensing 87
  books 144–47
  characters 155
  choreography 153
  content for multimedia projects 141–57
  film and television clips 150–54
  journals 146
  logos 155
  magazines 146
  music 153, 161, 163–72
    fees 169
  newspapers 146
  noncore product rights 254–56
  of developer's rights 236–38
  photographs and still images 147–50
  software 155
  sound recordings 180
  text 142–47
  video 154–55
Limited permission grants 281–82
Logos
  licensing 155
*LucasArts Entertainment Co. v. Humongous
    Entertainment Co.* 234

M

Magazines
  licensing 146
Magnuson-Moss Warranty Act 227
Marcus v. Rowley 301
*Mead Data Central, Inc. v. Toyota Motor Sales, U.S.A.
    Inc.* 206
Media
  rights granted in distribution agreements 239–40
Media libraries 136, 154
Merchandising rights 193, 256
Merger clause 227
  in contracts 45
  in development contracts 59
Midler v. Ford Motor Co. 171
Milestones 85, 87, 94
Mirroring 287
Modification right 15, 36, 110, 130, 254
  film and television clips 153
  text 143
Moral rights 139, 144, 153
Motschenbacher v. R.J. Reynolds Tobacco Co. 179
Multimedia products
  localizing in foreign languages 242, 254–55
  porting to other platforms 238–39, 242, 254–55
Music
  contract for arranging and composing 162
  copying 163–65
  copyright 159–61
  creating original work 161–63
  licensing 153, 161, 163–72
  public domain 172–74
  recording your own version 171
  sound-alike recordings 171
  use on Web site 284
Music libraries 174
Musicians
  consent of 193

N

National Commission on New Technological Uses
    of Copyright Works 302
National Information Infrastructure 276
Net revenues 245–46
Network Solutions, Inc. 289
New use fees. *See* Reuse fees
Newspapers
  licensing 146
Nichols v. Universal Pictures Corp. 114
Nondisclosure agreement 59–60, 102
  with independent contractor 78
Nonprofit organizations
  no exception from copyright law 300
North American Free Trade Agreement
    (NAFTA) 116

O

On-line
  instruction 319–20
  legal issues 273–97
Option agreement 101
Overhead
  on multimedia projects 89
Owning a copy of a work
  rights according to copyright law 36, 108, 149

P

Page count 95
Parallel rights 250
Parody 114
  authorization 168
Patents
  application to work made for hire 67
  assignment of 37
  design 19–21
  infringement 21–22
  licenses 37
  pending 21
  protection 21, 216
    international 28
  terms 22
  utility 19–21
  validity 22
  warranties 58
Patent Act 19, 36
Patent law 11, 19–22
  in cyberspace 286
  no work made for hire rule 36
  work protected by 19–20
Payment
  in distribution agreements 243–48
  mechanics of 246–47
  publisher's perspective 258–61
Pension and health plans 188
Performance right
  proposed change 277
Performers
  consent of 192
  in multimedia 187
  work made for hire 152
Permits
  for filming or shooting photographs 182
  for teacher photocopying 309–10
  for using copyrighted items in multimedia 182
  to use material found on the Internet 281–84
  to use trademarked items 208
Photographs and still images
  by independent contractors 149
  licensing 147–48
  made by employees 148
  releases 179–80

  use of trademarks in 148
Platforms 86
  identifying in distribution agreements 238–39
  porting multimedia products 238–39, 242, 254–55
Playboy Enterprises, Inc. v. Dumas 72, 76
Playboy Enterprises v. Frena 292–93
Pointing 287
Posting
  material on the Internet 275, 278–79
Power of attorney 68
Precedent 7–8
Products
  distributing over the Internet 295–97
Programming 89
Project design 88
Project management 88
Proposals 51–52
  protected by copyright 52
  written vs. oral 52
Prototype 85
Provisional patent application 21
Public display right 15, 131, 305
  photographs 147
  text 143
Public domain works 14, 115–18, 142
  finding 117
  music 172–74
  on the Internet 274, 285
Public performance right 15, 36, 56, 109,
    131, 171, 305
  exceptions to 131–32
  on film and television 153
Publication right 192
Publicity and privacy rights 177–83
  "media use" exceptions 179
  of deceased individuals 180–81
  on the Internet 286
Publishers
  choosing titles 81–82
  concerns 253–62
  of multimedia 234

R

Recording artists
  consent of 193
Recoupment 83–84, 258
Releases 78, 148, 152, 177, 179, 317
  to use film and television clips 180
  to use photographs 179–80
*Religious Technology Center v. Netcom On-Line
    Communication Services, Inc.* 276, 291–92
Remedies
  for breach of contract 230, 251–52
Remedy clause
  in contracts 45

Remote delivery rights 188
Reporters 9
Reproduction right 15, 36, 130
   film and television clips 153
   photographs 147
   text 143
Reuse 188, 235
   fees 152, 191–92
   provisions 191–93
Reverse engineering
   of software 112
Revisions 96–97
Rey v. Lafferty 129
Right of first refusal 254
Right of last look 255
Right to complete 256
Right to sue for infringement 261–62
Rights clearance agency 136, 165–66
Robinson v. Random House, Inc. 113
Roe v. Wade 4
Rogers v. Grimaldi 179
Rossner v. CBS, Inc. 216
Royalties 82, 99–100, 245–48, 258–59
   annual minimum 248
   based on 245–46
   for derivative works 259
   minimum unit 247–49

S

Sales law 221–31
Scheduling
   multimedia projects 85
Schiller & Schmidt, Inc. v. NordiscoCorp. 76
Screen Actor's Guild 185
   collective bargaining agreements 186–89
Screen Actors Guild-Producer Interactive Media
      Agreement 187
Sega Enterprises, Ltd. v Accolade, Inc. 112
Sega Enterprises Ltd. v. MAPPHIA 292–93
Separation of rights provision 192
Sequel rights 192, 241–42, 255–56
Service marks 22–24, 197
Shared jurisdiction 187
Shreve v. World Championship Wrestling, Inc. 180
Shrink-wrap agreements 296–97
Software
   licensing 155
Sony Corp. v. Universal City Studios, Inc. 113
Sound recordings
   copyright 160–61
   copyright notice 161
   licensing 180
Split rights 145
Spoken-word rights 143
Stare decisis 8

Statutes
   federal 3–4
   state 4
Stewart v. Abend 135
Stock houses 136
Stratton Oakmont, Inc. v. Prodigy Services Co. 294
Sublicensing rights 143
Subsidiary rights 143
Supplemental market fees. *See* Reuse fees
Supreme Court Reporter 9
Synopsis 95

T

Teacher photocopying 307–11
Technology
   ownership
      factor in compensation 84
Termination clause
   in contracts 45
   in development contracts 59
Testing 86, 89
Tin Pan Apple v. Miller Brewing Co. 163
Titles
   book 202
      protection of 144
   film 202
Tom Doherty Associates Inc. v. Saban Entertainment
      241
Trade secrets
   application to work made for hire 67
   assignment of 37
   definition of 26–27
   licenses 37
   ownership of 37
   protection 27, 218
      international 28
Trade secret law 11, 26–28
   in cyberspace 286
   work protected by 26
Trademarks 22–26, 197–208, 243
   and dilution 206
   application to work made for hire 67
   arbitrary and fanciful 200, 203
   assignment of 37
   choosing 197–200
   clearing 200–202
   descriptive 198–99, 203
   determining confusing similarity in 203
   federal registrations search 201
   generic 198
   identical 204
   in computer industry 204
   licenses 37, 144
   ownership of 37
   protection 23–24, 217–18
      international 28, 207

registering domain names as 290
registration 24–25
state and common law search 202
suggestive 200, 203
term of registration 25
unregistered 24
use in photographs 148
using third-party 207–208
Trademark law 4, 11, 22–26
in cyberspace 286
scope of 202–206
state 23
work protected by 23
Treatment 95
Twin Books Corp. v. Walt Disney Co. 117

U

U.S. Copyright Office 10
U.S. Patent and Trademark Office 10, 21, 24, 204
U.S. Supreme Court
binding decisions 8
criteria for reviewing cases 7–8
Uniform Commercial Code 221–22, 296
Article Two 221–31
Uniform Trade Secrets Act 26
Unions 185–93
and hiring nonunion workers 186
United Nations Convention on the International Sale
of Goods 221
United States Code 9
United States Code Annotated 9
United States Reports 9
United States v. LaMacchia 277
Universal Copyright Convention 17, 216

V

Video
licensing 154–55
Videoconferencing 318–19
Videotaping
educational broadcasts for use in the classroom
312
Visual art
definition of 138
Visual Artists Rights Act 110, 119, 137–39
duration of right according to 138
rights under 137–38
waiver of rights under 139
Voice-over 143

W

Warranties 133
absolute 57, 249
actual knowledge 57, 249

and representations 144, 148
express 227–28
for independent contractor 77–78
implied 60
fitness 228–29
merchantability 228
title and noninfringement 229
in contracts 45
in development agreements 57–58
in distribution agreements 248–51
know or should know 57, 249
music 162
of noninfringement of third-party rights 250
patent 58
performance 250–51
provided for by Article Two 227–29
term 58
Web site
copying existing Web pages 286
copyright protection for 288
developing 284–88
Web-wrap agreements 296–97
Westlaw 9
White Paper 275–77, 291
White v. Samsung Electronics America, Inc. 178
Word count rates 98
Work made for hire 134
application to patents, trademarks, and trade secrets
36, 67
by director 152
by employees 30, 146
by independent contractors 73–77
by performers 152
copyright owner of 30–32, 63–64
international copyright ownership of 32, 66
limitations to 66–67, 74
not considered visual art 138
outside scope of employment 66
specially commissioned 31–32, 146
use in existing work 75
use in unsolicited work 75
Writers
rights 192–93
Writers Guild of America 185, 251
contract 189–90
Writing
and editing 88
compensation for 97–100
copyright ownership issues 101, 152
for multimedia 93–103

About the Authors

J. Dianne Brinson teaches "Law for Internet Users" at the Internet Education Institute at San Jose State University's Professional Development Center. The author of a number of articles in the intellectual property field, Brinson has practiced law at firms in Los Angeles and Atlanta. She is an arbitrator and mediator for the U.S. District Court, Northern District of California. Brinson received her law degree from Yale Law School in 1976 and a Bachelor of Arts in Political Science and Russian, summa cum laude, from Duke University. She is a former tenured law professor at Georgia State University and has taught at Golden Gate Law School and Santa Clara University Law School.

Mark F. Radcliffe is a partner in the law firm of Gray Cary Ware & Freidenrich in Palo Alto, California (formerly Ware & Freidenrich). He has been practicing intellectual property law, with a special emphasis on computer law, for more than 10 years, and represents many multimedia clients, both publishers and developers. Considered an expert in multimedia law, Radcliffe has been quoted on the subject in *The New York Times, The Wall Street Journal,* and the *San Jose Mercury News.* He also has spoken on legal issues in multimedia at the National Association of Broadcasters' Annual Convention, the Magazine Publishers' Association Annual Meeting, Multimedia Now, Seybold–San Francisco, Game Developers' Workshop, IEEE, and the Electronic Book Fair. Radcliffe has a Bachelor of Science in Chemistry, magna cum laude, from the University of Michigan, and a law degree from Harvard Law School. He is the author of the chapter on legal issues in the National Association of Broadcasters' book, *Multimedia 2000.*

Additional Sample Contracts!

MULTIMEDIA CONTRACTS 1996

Actual Contracts from the Multimedia Industry

Over 600 pages—56 full agreements (also available on disk)

If you are interested in a deeper look at the types of agreements that are being used in the multimedia industry, Ladera Press also publishes *Multimedia Contracts 1996*, a new 600-page book with 56 contracts that actually have been used in the multimedia industry. The first book of its kind, it includes all types of multimedia contracts from personal releases to development agreements to publishing agreements. These contracts are not available elsewhere. The contracts in *Multimedia Contracts 1996* have been submitted by well-known lawyers and companies in the multimedia industry. The book includes agreements submitted by Jeremy Salesin, General Counsel of Sanctuary Woods, and by Ian Rose, General Counsel of Mindscape, Inc. The book has been endorsed by the Interactive Multimedia Association, the largest and oldest multimedia trade association.

The multimedia industry is still developing and has not yet established the "standard" type of contract found in more mature industries such as film and book publishing. *Multimedia Contracts 1996* gives you the opportunity to see how companies in the multimedia industry are solving their problems. The book is divided into seven sections: Releases and Licenses, Copyright Assignments, Production Contracts, Development Contracts, Publishing Agreements, Source Code Escrow Agreements, and Union Contracts. It includes licenses for still photos, video, and music as well as eight development agreements and nine publishing agreements. The book also includes a brief overview of legal issues in the multimedia industry. *Multimedia Contracts 1996* is an essential reference for lawyers, publishers, corporate trainers, and independent developers.

Additional details on the next page

What you'll find in Multimedia Contracts 1996:

➤ Releases for individuals and locations

➤ Music licenses such as a recording artist license and the Warner/Chappell Synch license

➤ Production agreements including an actor's agreement, director's agreement, and writer's agreement

➤ Content and software licenses

➤ Eleven publishing agreements, including two used by Philips Interactive Media

➤ Eight development contracts

➤ On-line services agreement from a major on-line information service

➤ Eight software escrow agreements

➤ Interactive agreements from SAG, AFTRA, and Writers Guild

➤ Copyright assignments, including some specifically designed for screenplays

➤ Three different forms of nondisclosure agreements

➤ Work for hire and independent contractor agreements

The price of the *Multimedia Contracts* book is $89.95 (plus $7 shipping).

The actual contracts also are available on diskette
(IBM or MAC) for $99.95 (shipping included).

Mailing List and Comments

If you would like to receive information on future publications from Ladera Press, fill out this form and fax or mail it to:

Ladera Press
3130 Alpine Road, Suite 200-9002
Menlo Park, CA 94025
Fax: 650-854-0642

Name _____

Title_____ Email address: _____

Company _____

Address _____

City _____State _____ Zip _____

Telephone _____ Fax _____

We are interested in your comments and suggestions on how to improve this book. Please send them to us by mail at the address above, or by email at laderapres@aol.com.

Web Site

For sample chapters from our books and announcements of new books, check out our Web Site at www.laderapress.com.

Need Additional Copies?

Additional copies of the *Multimedia Law and Business Handbook* and copies of *Mulitmedia Contracts 1996* and *Internet Legal Forms for Business* are available by phone, mail, or fax. Use the product and shipping information below and the order form on the following page to complete your order. Or order from our Web Site at www.laderapress.com.

TO ORDER BY MAIL: Send order information to:
Ladera Press
c/o Port City Fulfillment
408 Grand River
Port Huron, MI 48060

TO ORDER BY FAX: Fax order to (810) 987-3562

TO ORDER BY PHONE: Have your credit card handy and call (800) 523-3721.

Ladera Press Products

Multimedia Law and Business Handbook	$44.95
Handbook disk (PC or Macintosh)	$12.00
Multimedia Contracts 1996	$89.95
Multimedia Contracts on Diskette (PC or Macintosh)	$99.95
Internet Legal Forms for Business (book)	$24.95
Internet Legal Forms for Business (disk PC only)	$12.00

Prices subject to change without notice.

Shipping

Please allow 2–3 weeks for delivery.

WITHIN THE UNITED STATES:
$7.00 for first book and $4.00 for each additional book

TO CANADA OR MEXICO:
$9 per book

TO OTHER FOREIGN COUNTRIES (U.S. MAIL, AIR MAIL BOOK RATE)
$25 per book

No charge for shipping disk orders to U.S. addresses.
For diskettes toCanada or Mexico, add $2.00
For diskettes to other countries, add $10.00

In a Rush?

UPS 2ND DAY DELIVERY IS AVAILABLE: For delivery in the continental United States, add $10 to the regular shipping fee. For delivery to Alaska or Hawaii, add $15 to the regular shipping fee.

Ladera Press Order form

Use this form to order additional Ladera Press products.

TO ORDER BY MAIL: Complete the form and mail to:
Ladera Press
c/o Port City Fulfillment
408 Grand River
Port Huron, MI 48060

TO ORDER BY FAX: Complete the form and fax to (810) 987-3562.

TO ORDER BY PHONE: Have your credit card handy and call (800) 523-3721.

Name _____

Title _____ Email address: _____

Company _____

Address _____

City _____ State _____ Zip _____

Telephone _____ Fax _____

Method of payment: ❏ Check enclosed   ❏ Visa   ❏ Mastercard

Type of diskette needed: ❏ PC   ❏ Macintosh

Credit Card Account Number: _____

Expiration Date: _____

Signature _____

Quantity	Item	Price	Total
	Subtotal		
	8.25% Sales Tax (CA Residents)		
	Shipping		
	UPS 2nd Day		
	TOTAL		

Please allow 2–3 weeks for delivery.

Internet Legal Forms for Business

Our latest book, Internet Legal Forms for Business, is a practical guide to the legal issues in doing business on the Internet. This book includes the basic form contracts you'll need to do business on the Internet and an overview of Internet legal issues. This book can save you thousands of dollars in legal fees you might otherwise spend to create these contracts and avoid legal disputes. There are twelve form contracts in the book. The forms are also available on diskette.

WHAT PEOPLE SAY ABOUT THE BOOK

John Place, General Counsel and Secretary of Yahoo, Inc. says: **"Internet Legal Forms for Business takes a practical and comprehensive, yet concise approach. I'm sure that it will be of great value to anyone faced with negotiating agreements in the emerging, shifting environment of cyberlaw."**

Communication Arts says: **"In a concise 140 pages, written in clear, jargon-free language, the authors provide twelve useful forms that can be copied, adapted and used by the purchaser. . . . Even better, they explain the fundamental legal issues at stake that require the use of the form in the first place. "**

What you'll find in the book:

An introduction to the basic legal principles in doing business on the Internet

The following form contracts:

> Development and Transfer Agreement (for Copyrighted Material)
> Content License (Text) - Content License (Photos and Video)
> Web Site Terms and Conditions of Use - Web Site Development Agreement
> Internet Advertising Contract - Chat Room Agreement
> Internet Use Policy - Clickwrap Agreement
> Linking Agreement - Domain Name Transfer Agreement

Each contract is described in its own chapter, which includes an overview of the agreement and when it is to be used, a checklist of contractual issues, and negotiating tips. The chapter on Domain Name Transfer Agreements includes a description of the domain name system and how to apply for one. (The diskette does not include the additional material, just the forms themselves).

The price of Internet Legal Forms for Business is $24.95 (plus shipping). The diskette is $12.